Conspicuous Production

Automobiles and Elites in Detroit, 1899–1933

Technology and Urban Growth
A series edited by
Blaine Brownell
Donald T. Critchlow
Mark S. Foster
Mark Rose
Joel A. Tarr

Donald
Finlay
Davis

Conspicuous Production

Automobiles and Elites in Detroit, 1899–1933

 Temple University Press
Philadelphia

Temple University Press, Philadelphia 19122
Copyright © 1988 by Temple University. All rights reserved
Published 1988
Printed in the United States of America

The paper used in this publication meets the minimum
requirements of American National Standard for Information
Sciences—Permanence of Paper for Printed Library Materials,
ANSI Z39.48-1984

Library of Congress Cataloging-in-Publication Data

Davis, Donald Finlay, 1947–
Conspicuous production: automobiles and elites in Detroit,
    1899–1933 / Donald Finlay Davis.
    p.   cm. — (Technology and urban growth)
    Bibliography: p.
    Includes index.
    ISBN 0-87722-549-4 (alk. paper)
1. Automobile industry and trade—Michigan—Detroit—History.
2. Automobile industry and trade—United States—History.
3. Automobiles—Social aspects—United States—History. 4. Elite
(Social sciences)—Michigan—Detroit—History—20th century.
5. Detroit (Mich.)—Economic conditions. 6. Detroit (Mich.)—Social
conditions. I. Title. II. Series.
HD9710.U53D473   1988
338.4'76292'0977434—dc19   87-26745
                                                        CIP

Contents

Tables   vii

Preface   ix

Introduction   1

Chapter One
The Automotive Paradigm   14

Chapter Two
Detroit's Upper Class Creates an Industry   40

Chapter Three
The Upper Class Exits the Industry   67

Chapter Four
Middle-Class Entrepreneurs and Their Firms   84

Chapter Five
An Isolated Survivor in the Lower Class   117

Chapter Six
The Absentee-Owned Firms   144

Chapter Seven
The Auto Community and Mass Transit   159

Chapter Eight
The Price Paid for Conspicuous Production   177

Conclusion   206

Notes   215

Index   269

Tables

1. Auto Leaders, 1890–1930: Position   26
2. Auto Leaders and Executives, 1890–1930: Age (1914)   27
3. Auto Leaders and Executives, 1890–1930: Place of Birth   28
4. Auto Leaders and Executives, 1890–1930: Education   29
5. Auto Leaders and Executives, 1890–1930: Prior Occupation   30
6. Auto Leaders and Executives, 1890–1930: Father's Occupation   31
7. Auto Leaders and Executives, 1890–1930: Father's Occupation and Son's Entry into the Industry   32
8. Makes and Price-Classes   33
9. Auto Leaders, 1890–1930: Type of Company   34
10. Auto Leaders, 1890–1930: Place of Birth and Type of Company   35
11. Auto Leaders, 1890–1930: Father's Occupation and Type of Company   36
12. Auto Leaders, 1890–1930: Career Background and Type of Company   37
13. Auto Leaders, 1890–1930: Education and Type of Company   38
14. Auto Leaders, 1890–1930: Arrival in Detroit and Type of Company   39
15. Automobile Production by State, 1904   42
16. Financial Elite, 1899–1902: Business Interests   46
17. Mechanical and Manufacturing Industries in Detroit, 1900   52
18. Output of Companies Owned by Pre-Automotive Elite   77
19. Relative Output of Companies Owned by Pre-Automotive Elite   78
20. Detroit Automobile Industry: Entries and Exits   86
21. Major Detroit Motor Vehicle Companies before 1925   87
22. Political Affiliation of Auto Elite, 1896–1930   112
23. Top Contributors, Associated Charities of Detroit, 1909–1911   113
24. Top Contributors, Associated Charities of Detroit, 1914–1915   114
25. Top Contributors, Detroit Community (Patriotic) Fund, 1918–1920   115
26. Elite Membership in Social Clubs, 1914   116
27. Principal Stockholders in Detroit Bankers Company, February 1933   187
28. Trustees of Detroit Bankers Company, 1930   189

Preface

Between 1900 and 1930 Detroit grew as rapidly as any major American city ever has. Its metropolitan population increased sixfold—from 305,000 to 1,837,000. That was an almost unparalleled achievement: although many American cities, including Detroit itself between 1820 and 1850, witnessed comparable growth during their frontier stage of development, only two others—Los Angeles and Chicago—have been able to match Detroit's accomplishment *after* reaching a population over 100,000. There was, of course, no secret formula to Detroit's burgeoning population in this era. It owed to the city's dominant position in the nation's fastest-growing and, by 1929, biggest industry: motor vehicle manufacturing.[1]

It was this hypergrowth after 1900 that first interested me in Detroit's history. I wanted to learn more about the entrepreneurs who presided over it. Who were the "gasoline aristocracy," as C. B. Glasscock labeled them in 1937? Were they, as he intimated, social parvenus, relative nobodies until they rode the industry to fame and fortune? Or were they, as one might infer from the research of sociologists T. D. Schuby and Lynda Ann Ewen and historian Olivier Zunz, the scions of old Detroit families? The answers to these questions would enable us, I thought, to determine just how "revolutionary" Detroit's automotive revolution had been.[2]

It would also help us to understand the subsequent evolution of Detroit itself, for the automobile turned the city into a one-industry metropolis. The question of ownership and control of the automotive industry has been of supreme importance to Detroit since World War I. The industry came to dominate the local economy with stunning rapidity: as early as 1909, a mere decade after the Olds Motor Works founded the local auto industry, motor vehicles, bodies, and parts contributed almost one-quarter of the value of the city's manufactures. By 1919 that share had risen to four-ninths. In 1927, a year

ix

that saw Ford close down production for six months to retool for the (second) Model A, the auto industry's share stood at 57 percent—an extraordinary degree of specialization for a city of Detroit's size. By way of comparison, the leading product of Pittsburgh, Chicago, Cleveland, New York, and Philadelphia, respectively, contributed less than 27 percent of the industrial output by value in each of these cities in 1927.[3]

Detroit was also unusually dependent on manufacturing for its living. Its commercial and financial sectors had always been relatively weak. In 1914 it was such a minor banking center that, as historian Norman S. B. Gras remarked, "it did not even put in a claim for a Federal Reserve Bank, though thirty-seven other cities did." Gras concluded in 1922 that Detroit was "relatively insignificant as [a] marketing [center] for the adjoining district." And the 1929 census of business revealed that it still did not rank among the top forty cities in per capita sales by merchant wholesalers even though it then ranked fourth in population and third in industrial output.[4]

Until the rise of industrial unionism in the 1930s, there were few countervailing powers to the gasoline aristocracy. Its members thus had the rare opportunity to oversee the construction not just of a new industry but also of a new community, the Motor City. It is important, then, to know more about these entrepreneurs. But how should they be approached? I decided on two basic strategies, both of which inform this book.

First came the decision to study the automotive elite within an institutional context. Typically, an institutional approach has led historians of elites to examine the ways in which the education, marriages, clubs, and neighborhoods have structured the lives of the rich and powerful. In general, research has focused on quantifiable sources, with heavy use of city and club directories as well as the *Social Register*. Historians have, as a result, tended to overlook the one institution that has most clearly defined and shaped the economic elite in this century: the business corporation. The corporation has been the most important social milieu in which American businessmen have functioned since the rise of big business. It has not only absorbed much of their time and attention but also structured their social networks and, as authors on corporate culture have remarked, given them a stock of common values. The corporation is, accordingly, the social unit around which this study is organized.

Yet this book is not a standard business history, for it both assumes and demonstrates the necessity of studying the history of a firm and of its host community conjointly. In other words, this book attempts to bridge the gap that normally divides the two academic realms of urban and business history. Its image of entrepreneurship—within both the firm and the urban community—is that of a feedback loop in which the decisions and output of one sphere are amplified by the decisions and output of the other. The social and business domains are not separate but are in constant, iterative interaction, which means that the culture of the corporation extends and modifies the culture of the larger community, and vice versa. In short, community values not only shape business decision-making (for example, the choice of market) but are themselves transformed by the choices of the firm.

One half of this feedback loop was well known when I started this research. Thanks to the pioneering efforts of Samuel P. Hays and James Weinstein, urban historians have long recognized that businessmen derived their models for urban reform from their corporate experience.[5] It was thus fairly predictable that the gasoline aristocrats would deem their corporate organizations a worthy prototype for municipal administration. As a result, the book does not devote very many pages to the urban initiatives of Detroit's automotive elite, for these were quite conventional.

Because the other half of the feedback loop is not as well known, more space has been given to it. Indeed, the very title *Conspicuous Production* testifies to the importance I now attach to this half of the community-corporation connection. For me, the most surprising discovery has been the extent to which the gasoline aristocracy's corporations reproduced and amplified the social patterns of the larger community. To be sure, my research strategy led me to be on the lookout for mimesis, but I did not anticipate that the community's prestige hierarchy would offer a prototype for the industry's own price-class hierarchy. I could not have predicted that the auto entrepreneurs' quest for social prestige would have had such a profound impact on their marketing dicisions. That is perhaps why I have devoted so many chapters to demonstrating that the search for social status made people want to build as well as to buy ever more costly automobiles.

Once I had identified conspicuous production as an element in industry decision-making, I realized that it must have had—via the feedback loop—an impact on the development and organization of the community itself. In my search for the social effects of conspicuous production, the evidence led ineluctably to the 1933 bank crash, the climactic moment in the history of modern Detroit. The crash thus forms the climax of this book as well. It is not an ending that Detroiters would have predicted during the heady days of the automotive boom, nor is it one that I projected when I started the research. After all, I was studying some of the most successful entrepreneurs in history. Whence, then, did this book's tragic sensibility come? Why does it end with a community setback rather than with a record automotive sales year? I am not quite sure why. The tragic sense may be something I brought with me to the topic or something that emerged from the research. Or perhaps it simply came upon me as I walked at night through the deserted streets of Detroit's inner city, gazing upon empty lots, shuttered shops, and boarded-up homes. I did much of my thinking about Detroit's automotive revolution during those walks, and this is the book that resulted.

As solitary as writing sometimes seems, every book is a joint endeavor. An author can get by only with a little help from his friends. Needless to say I have many people to thank, starting with Professor Oscar Handlin, who first suggested this topic and oversaw the ensuing doctoral dissertation. The Canada Council financed the original research; additional funds came from the University of Ottawa. The latter provided me, for example, with a research assistant, Carol Karamessines, who put in countless hours on my behalf at the Library of Congress and the National Archives.

I wish to thank the staff of the various libraries where I did my research, most notably the Detroit Public Library, the Bentley Library and its Michigan Historical Collection, the General Motors Institute, the Ford Archives, the Chrysler Corporation, American Motors, the Library of Congress, the National Archives, the Oral History Collection at Columbia University, the George Arents Library of Syracuse University (then the home of the Studebaker-Packard papers), and the libraries and archival collections of Wayne State University, Michigan State University, the University of Michigan, and Harvard University. Everyone was helpful but none more so than Richard Scharchburg of the General Motors Institute and the late James Bradley of the National Automotive History Collection in the Detroit Public Library. Both allowed me to see work in progress as well as notes from their own research. As automotive historians know, Jim Bradley did more than anyone to make the study of automotive history possible; he is sorely missed.

The people who deserve the most credit, however, are the ones who pushed me to complete this project. Like many of my age group I was an academic gypsy during my first three years of teaching, and this project correspondingly suffered; I was even tempted to put it aside. Yet many people believed in this book and persuaded me to finish it. It would not have been written without the encouragement of Gerald Bloomfield, Roy Church, Mark Foster, Patrick Fridenson, Frank Friedel, John Ingham, Toby Jackman, James Laux, Harold Livesay, Zane Miller, Mark Rose, Michael Sibalis, Susan Mann Trofimenkoff, and Olivier Zunz, and others as well whom I wish I had the room to name. None of these individuals is responsible for any errors that may have crept into either the argument or the evidence.

The illustrations were obtained with the invaluable assistance of Ron Grantz and John Gibson of the National Automotive History Collection, Detroit Public Library, of William Bailey, Royal Oak, Michigan, and especially of Kevin Solomon, Windsor, Ontario. I also thank Temple University Press's ever-patient editor-in-chief, Mike Ames, and production editor, Mary Capouya, who have offered me not only professional expertise but also warmth and understanding. Copyeditor Patricia Sterling has both improved my style and rescued me from self-contradiction. Finally, I thank David Drummond. He has always been there when I have needed help and encouragement, and the book is dedicated to him.

Conspicuous Production

Automobiles and Elites in Detroit, 1899–1933

Introduction

■   Automobiles evoke passion. For a minority they symbolize the misplaced priorities of technological society. For the vast majority, however, the automobile has traditionally been the most luxurious, the most conspicuous, and the most technologically sophisticated product they will ever have the fortune to buy. Countless millions have experienced the rapture Walter P. Chrysler felt when he chanced upon the car of his dreams, a Locomobile touring car, at the 1908 Chicago automobile show. "Creamy white, with red upholstery and a khaki top," it held a "fascination" for Chrysler "that must have seemed to others the equivalent of madness," he later recalled. He spent four days "hanging around the show, held by that automobile as by a siren's song," and bought the machine by borrowing $4,300, an enormous sum for a railway mechanic then making $350 a year.[1]

Yet he was not atypical in expending his life savings and going heavily into debt to purchase one of what Chrysler called "the most astonishing machines that had ever been offered to men." In the 1920s Robert and Helen Lynd found, for example, that the average family in Muncie, Indiana, owed more money on its car than on its home. What did make Chrysler highly unusual was his decision to disassemble the Locomobile rather than to drive it. For three months the parts lay strewn about a back shed while he became acquainted with its workings. Only when he felt he "understood" the Locomobile did he actually take it for a drive. He was soon hooked: four years later he accepted a 50 percent cut in pay in order to join the automobile industry as a plant manager for Buick. The move ultimately made him a multimillionaire, but it was as much his obsession with automobiles as his business acumen that brought him into the fledgling industry.[2]

His behavior was typical of the early automotive entrepreneurs.

1

They had "one thing in common," writes John B. Rae, dean of American automotive historians. "They became utterly dedicated to the manufacture of motor vehicles, to the point where they seem to have preferred to go broke manufacturing automobiles than to get rich doing something else." So daunting were the odds against survival—the failure rate before 1910 was 74 percent—that one had to be slightly crazed, according to industry pioneer Benjamin Briscoe, to undertake auto manufacturing. "In those days," he recalled in 1921, "when a man became infected with the automobile germ," it was as though he had a disease: "No man . . . in the early stages of the industry would have gone into the automobile business if he had been a hard-boiled conservative business man." Designing and making automobiles, the press frequently remarked before World War I, could become a mania. As a result, American automotive pioneers were not always objective about their product and their industry.[3]

Indeed, their behavior as entrepreneurs was, as the following pages argue, less rational in a business sense than both the critics and the apologists of American capitalism have generally admitted. The founders of the American automotive industry were not one-dimensional men, interested only in maximizing return on their investments. Their motivation, like that of all entrepreneurs, was exceedingly complex. As Joseph Schumpeter explained, entrepreneurs may be driven by the "will to conquer: the impulse to fight, to prove oneself superior to others, to succeed for the sake . . . of success itself." Schumpeter also pointed to the "joy of creating, of getting things done, or simply of exercising one's energy and ingenuity." Finally, one must recognize, he wrote, that economic action is "akin to sport" where the "financial result is a secondary consideration . . . mainly valued as an index of success and as a symptom of victory."[4] It took all these passions and more to impel the automotive pioneers to work the killing hours and to take the desperate financial gambles necessary for survival in a fiercely competitive infant industry. Money alone was not sufficient incentive.

Indeed, it may not even have been the primary consideration. Henry Ford, for one, professed to be more interested in boosting his company's output than in its profits. That may seem a self-serving statement for a billionaire to make; nonetheless his stockholders did successfully sue him in 1916–1917 for failing to run the Ford Motor Company as a profit-seeking enterprise. Others were perfectionists who allowed their "technological obsessions" to distract them from the pursuit of commercial viability. They sought the esteem of their peers in the engineering profession rather than the approval of consumers.[5]

And finally, virtually every automotive entrepreneur was intent on social advancement. Since entrepreneurs self-evidently belong to communities as well as to firms, it is reasonable to expect them to seek promotion in the hierarchies of both; accordingly, they tailor their business policies to conform to their social ambitions. There is nothing particularly unusual in such behavior. As Thomas Cochran has observed, "Most men will not persist in a policy that meets social disapproval and resulting penalties, and they will be led to assume roles that carry social praise and added prestige." As a result, the pattern of sanctions within each community constricts the room its entrepreneurs have for maneuver. Or, as Robert Lamb put it: "Economic decisions . . . are most meaningful, and often only meaningful, within their social context." The converse also holds, for as Lamb reminds us, communities are transformed by the economic decisions made by their business leaders. Consequently, the relationship between a community and its business people is reciprocal in nature and cumulative in effect. They grow together, the development of one intelligible only in terms of the other. Hence we should assume that the social ambitions of the Detroit auto entrepreneurs, the "gasoline aristocracy," were not peripheral but central to their careers.[6]

Under normal circumstances they would have had no difficulty reconciling their quest for social prestige with their pursuit of profit. Indeed, nothing quite so facilitates social climbing in the United States as the attainment of riches, for it is a capitalist society that honors material accumulation. As C. Wright Mills observed, "Money—sheer, naked, vulgar money—has with few exceptions won its possessors entrance anywhere and everywhere into American society."[7] It has always been possible to buy admission into the American upper class, provided one has the necessary cash; hence, the desire for social respectability has usually provided an incentive to entrepreneurship and to profit maximization. Exceptions to this rule have been infrequent (outside of the Old South, at least) and almost unheard of in the nation's boomtowns, which tend to worship economic growth and to canonize the individuals deemed responsible for its achievement.

The social ambitions of Detroit's auto leaders, then, should have honed their entrepreneurial skills to perfection. Certainly that would have been the case had the automobile not held, since its debut in Newport high society in the 1890s, a unique position in the American status system: it became, simply, *the* most important status symbol. Its manufacturers apparently felt—at least in the formative years of the industry—that as such, they had to treat it deferentially. For them it was not just another manufactured good. Those bent on social advancement—and they were the vast majority—appeared to believe that they could jeopardize as well as enhance their social prestige if they became too single-minded in their quest for profits from automotive production. In other words, they behaved as though for them the rules had changed: that the manufacturer of a product as exceptionally status-laden as the automobile could not be certain that his moneymaking activities would suffice to buy him the esteem he coveted. Indeed, they seemed to have been as leery of building or selling a car of low prestige value (such as the Model T Ford) as of buying one. That is, the typical Detroit auto leader apparently imposed the same social constraints on his role as producer as on his role as consumer. And while snobbery should not be seen as the sole or even prime cause of failure in the early auto industry (financial and technical considerations mattered more), the record of the leading Detroit firms suggests that virtually all of them did allow social considerations to influence their model policy and thus their prospects for survival. In brief, they designed cars more reflective of their status yearnings than of a calm appraisal of the market. Most of them would have fared better in business had they been able to overlook the status connotations of the product—but for them that was impossible.

This is not to say that "technology" in any way dictated their behavior. Indeed, what may at first appear an instance of technological determinism is in fact further evidence that people react to machines in socially prescribed ways. It was perhaps inevitable that the automakers would be unable to deal with the automobile objectively, but only because of its centrality to the American system of social prestige. In the United States, as Thorstein Veblen recognized in 1899—the very year that automotive manufacturing commenced in Detroit—social prestige is attached to the conspicuous consumption and display of prized commodities. In *The Theory of the Leisure Class*, Veblen asserted that "the basis on which good repute in any highly organized industrial community ultimately rests is pecuniary strength; and the means of showing pecuniary strength and so of gaining or retaining a good name, are leisure and a conspicuous consumption of goods."[8] Only in this way can the full extent of a newly gained or refurbished fortune be made manifest and the relevant social arbiters suitably impressed.

It is not sufficient merely to be rich or even to spend lavishly, however; to win admission to the American upper class, one must also adopt its consumption *style*. Veblen contended that the status seeker must "differentiate with some nicety between the noble and the ignoble in consumable goods." There are wide variations in the prestige imputed to material objects, and in choosing among them the status seeker delimits his place in society, for an individual's "consumption class" affects the social status he is accorded by others. In other words, the hierarchy of prestige in American society is built on a "hierarchy of differential consumption."[9]

Much of modern property is inconspicuous and therefore of little value in defining the status of individuals and of their families. The automobile, by contrast, is exceptionally visible and mobile; potentially, it can bear witness to its owner's wealth and patrician sensibilities in every country club district in the United States. As a result, the automobile has since 1899 been the "most Veblenian of all American artifacts," the "symbol most favored by Americans for staking their status claims," Vance Packard concluded in *The Status Seekers*. At first, the mere ownership of a motorcar brought prestige, and the American upper class expected to monopolize motoring as it had yachting. Not only did several New York patricians form the socially exclusive Automobile Club of America in a bid to control the new pastime, but socially elite businessmen also sought to prevent the democratization of the automobile by manipulating the patent pool they controlled, the Association of Licensed Automobile Manufacturers, to restrict entry into the industry and to inflate motor vehicle prices. Not until a group of industry renegades led by Henry Ford defeated them did the automobile become the mass-produced item that the national ideology demanded and the country's prosperity permitted.[10]

As automobiles proliferated, distinctions between makes became ever more invidious and precise; it then became incumbent on the status seeker to own a motorcar of the right pedigree and vintage. In the mid-1920s General Motors formalized the automotive pecking order by adopting the annual model change. "The annual model," according to Daniel Boorstin, "provided a visible and easily understood symbol of personal progress, and so produced . . . a 'ladder of consumption'" for social climbers. Moreover, since each of the General Motors car divisions occupied a separate and distinct price-class, the upwardly mobile individual could signal each stage of his journey by trading in his Chevrolet for a Pontiac, his Buick for a Cadillac.[11]

General Motors was not alone in deliberately promoting the automobile as an honorific object. Industry advertisements, Vance Packard remarked in 1959, implied that "the primary function of the motorcar in America was to carry its owner . . . into a higher social stratum." And while automotive companies were probably most successful in preying upon the status anxieties of their customers in the 1950s, the practice was as old as their trade. In 1910, for example, an advertising executive told a sales meeting at the Hudson Motor Car Company that "a good advertising point is this . . . a business man cannot afford to drive a car such as the Hupp, Brush, or any car of the small runabout type, owing to the fact that it is liable to detract from his personality and success, in the eyes of the public." Automobile companies hammered this message home with massive advertising budgets. No product was more publicized: as early as 1902, firms like Olds were spending $100,000 a year on advertising; by 1911 the industry took an estimated one-eighth of all advertising space in nationally circulated magazines; in 1917, with expenditures of $10.3 million, it absorbed one-fourth. The industry also benefited from reams of free publicity: virtually every newspaper quickly added an automotive section—often filled with stories and photographs supplied by the manufacturers themselves.[12]

Thus, it was partially through the industry's own prodigious efforts that the automobile became "the most important status symbol in American society." Yet the contribution of the automobile entrepreneurs to this outcome should not be over-emphasized; they did, after all, have the incomparable advantage of selling a product ideally suited to conspicuous display. And while corporate advertisers, as some have charged, may have urged Americans to vent their social insecurities and frustrations in consumerism, the tendency to conspicuous consumption is, as Veblen pointed out, not an invention of corporate capitalism but rather a behavior found in many cultures, including some of the most primitive. The auto industry, in other words, stands unfairly accused of brainwashing Americans into regarding their product as a status object. Americans needed little persuasion: it was plain to see that the boss typically drove a more impressive car than his employees and that limousines were more frequently parked in front of mansions than in slum alleys.[13]

Yet even if the Detroit automakers did not *create* the social attitudes that bound their entrepreneurship, their advertising policies did reinforce the pressures on them to build a motorcar worthy of their family names. Not only did they constantly remind Americans of the prestige value of their product, but "it was also common," according to a historian of Ford's public relations, "for the presidents of auto companies to be featured in advertisements. Indeed, many of them . . . wrote and/or signed advertising copy themselves." The producer thereby personalized his product and, by linking his own reputation (or that of a celebrated engineer) to it, sought to reassure potential customers of its essential integrity. In fact, Americans at first preferred to have cars named after some individual of note, whose virtues they apparently hoped it would share. As of 1950, the year Rudolph Anderson sat down to count them, virtually all the surviving makes bore a family name.[14]

Since then, the auto companies have offered us a menagerie of models, and it has become difficult to understand why the industry's first customers were so insistent that their cars carry some familiar surname. The reason is fairly straightforward. During the first two decades of experimentation, buyers had minimal protection against unscrupulous, fly-by-night operators. There were literally thousands of automobile companies vying for the consumer's attention. Some of them existed only on paper; others lacked the financial resources to survive a single season, and such failures left their customers with the unenviable task of finding spare parts for an "orphan car." It made sense, then, to buy from a company known for its engineering talent or for its financial probity. For the vast majority, who did not read the trade papers, that meant looking for a make with a respected name behind it. Sometimes the reputation came ready-made: the Hudson Motor Car Company, for example, basked in the reflected glory of its president, J. L. Hudson— Detroit's leading retail merchant and probably its most honored citizen in 1909—even though he did little more for the firm than to sell it the right to use his name. But that sufficed for the customers of Hudson's department store; they were sure that he would not jeopardize his hard-earned prestige by knowingly selling inferior merchandise.[15]

Most auto entrepreneurs lacked Hudson's name recognition, even in their home market, and found it necessary to publicize themselves, their strengths, and their virtues in order to create product personality and public confidence in their firms. Their advertisements accordingly boasted of their personal integrity and accomplishments. Willys-Overland, for example, described its president, John N. Willys, as a "man of wonderful breadth and attainment" and asserted that "it is absolutely essential that the reader understand this personality to realize fully the character and standard of the product which he controls." Advertisements often employed the first person singular to emphasize the degree to which the company's president or engineering chief was putting his personal reputation on the line. A 1905 advertisement typified this genre: "It has always been my ambition to build one of the world's best cars," E. R. Thomas proclaimed, "and I have done it." By 1911 such claims were so ubiquitous that the Herreshoff Motor Company of Detroit complained, "We also have a personality—a mechanical genius behind the Herreshoff car, but we are not advertising him—because he is not for sale."[16]

Yet Herreshoff was the exception: its competitors were all too eager to sell the reputations and personalities of their key entrepreneurs to the public. In effect, they advised society that the machine was the embodiment of the man. The prestige of one they linked to the other. They consequently intensified the pressure—already severe, thanks to their own advertising message and the automobile's inherent attractiveness as a status object—to use their business to make a social statement. If machine and man were one, then it was crucial that the machine be not only socially respectable but also upward bound in price and prestige, along with the man himself. In other words, each automotive entrepreneur built cars appropriate to his social background and present station in life. As he moved upward in the social hierarchy, his product climbed correspondingly in the industry's price-class hierarchy. "As prosperity came their way," C. C. Parlin and Henry S. Younker observed in 1914, manufacturers "thought that the whole world grew more prosperous with them. . . . They built cars for themselves instead of for the public."[17]

The founders of Detroit's automotive industry were guilty, then, of *conspicuous production*. It may be difficult for many readers to credit such collective folly, and admittedly, what is here characterized as prestige behavior has been dismissed by European automotive historians as merely technological perfectionism. Moreover, sociological theory does not seem to allow for conspicuous production as a social strategy. Veblen, for instance, so insisted on the wastefulness of competitive display that he appears never to have contemplated the possibility that it might be linked to the production of a useful commodity. And Max Weber maintained that "'classes' are formed in accordance with *relations of production* and the acquisition of wealth, while 'status groups' are formed according to the principles governing the *consumption of goods* in the context of specific 'life-styles.'" But there is no need to quarrel with Weber. While it may be objectively true, as he argues, that "it is life-style which determines social status," Detroit's auto entrepreneurs appear to have *believed* that the role of producer also impinged on their social prestige, at least when it came to manufacturing automobiles.[18]

This book argues that the quest for reputability through display extended to the production as well as to the consumption of automobiles, at least in the three decades before the Great Depression. It shows that prestige-related behavior helped determine the outcome of the struggle for supremacy in the early auto industry. Automotive entrepreneurs behaved like snobs.[19] Most of them decided to build ever more expensive machines and, in doing so, priced themselves out of the mass market, where the bulk of the industry's profits lay. The attitude of John Wendell Anderson was typical: a silent partner who made millions from a $5,000 investment in Ford, he boasted in court that he had never driven a Ford automobile in his life; he owned a car more worthy of his station in life.[20]

Such attitudes, when carried from the sphere of consumption into the realm of production, could prove disastrous. The fate of Hugh Chalmers, president of the Chalmers Motor Company and a civic leader in Detroit, has often been reprised: "Ambitious Hugh," an automotive historian relates, "wanted to build the type of car—the big car—that he himself would have liked to ride in, so he kept going up in price brackets until he got into a field where there was real competition," and in 1917 he lost control of his company.[21]

By arguing that status considerations distorted entrepreneurship in the American auto industry, this book departs significantly from the theoretical model or paradigm that has guided research in automotive history since the 1920s. Accordingly, the first task of this book, in Chapter One, is to delineate the paradigm that dominates the field. We shall see that current theory has no place for prestige behavior: assuming an essentially classless society with minimal barriers to social mobility, it depicts the early auto industry as a world of equal opportunity where success went to the talented; as a result the "founders" were, to quote John B. Rae, "as complete a cross section of their contemporary society as could have been devised." (Were this true, however, the American auto industry would be unique in the annals of American business, since every collective biography yet compiled has found a disproportionate number of wealthy heirs among national and local business elites.)[22] The paradigm, built on impressionistic evidence, becomes untenable once data on the actual backgrounds of automotive entrepreneurs have been collected and categorized. Contrary to legend, it did help to be wealthy; and not all would-be automobile manufacturers had the same chance to succeed. Once the myth of equal opportunity has been dispelled, it becomes possible to examine in some detail the dynamics of social class at work within the automotive sector.

Following a discussion of the social origins of Detroit's automotive leaders, then, the largest portion of the text is devoted to demonstrating the extent to which prestige-related behavior shaped the early auto industry. The goal is to provide a sufficient number of counter-instances to constitute a plausible alternative to the existing interpretation of automotive history. Because the battles with wealthy backers fought by Henry Ford or Ransom Olds or Robert Hupp have each been explained as an instance of warring egos or an honest difference of opinion over the future course of the industry, it is necessary to show that there is a common pattern to incidents hitherto regarded as isolated phenomena. In other words, the proof of conspicuous production lies not in the actual pronouncements of the industry's leaders nor in the minute books of the companies they commanded—though I have utilized both where available—but rather in the repetition of behavior. The case studies taken as a whole suggest that any attempt to explain the outcome of the struggle for control of the American automobile industry must take into consideration the status yearnings of producers as well as of consumers.

This book argues that the old families spurned the mass market when they entered the automobile industry. The Packard was more their style—"a gentlemen's car built by gentlemen." Through investments in such luxury manufacturers as Packard, Lincoln, Wayne, and Northern, the pre-automotive elite prospered. Yet none of these companies developed the kind of volume business needed to control either the auto industry or the local economy, both of which were by the late 1920s dominated by the Big Three: General Motors, Ford, and Chrysler. In these companies the old elite had scarcely a stake: General Motors and Chrysler were controlled by outside capital; Ford was by then a sole proprietorship.

Thus, the main thing we are going to discover about the impact of conspicuous production on Detroit between 1899 and 1933 is that it confounded the efforts of Detroit's pre-automotive elite to maintain their economic and social position in the city's affairs. Even though they originated the local auto industry, by 1910 they had allowed their social prejudices to cost them control over it. The automobile and the status anxieties it encapsulated helped to undermine the rule of Detroit's old families, thereby accelerating the circulation or replacement of elites within the Motor City.

Indeed, the automotive investments of the pre-automotive elite demonstrated that "fatal conservatism" which Suzanne Keller identified in *Beyond the Ruling Class* as the source of elite declension, the conservatism she attributed to "excessive social distance" and "estrangement from the world of reality."[23] Keller was not specifically discussing Detroit's pre-automotive elite, but her comments seem remarkably pertinent to the fate of the members of a local upper class that failed to recognize the opportunities afforded by the growing purchasing power of the American middle and lower classes. The class's myopia led not only to growing irrelevance within the automotive industry but also to a succession of social, political, and economic setbacks within the community itself. It was undone, in other words, by its earlier success in establishing itself as a social elite with values and priorities distinct from those of the average Detroiter.

Contributing to its distress was its failure to complete the task, which it evidently set for itself, of co-opting the businessmen most enriched by the automotive revolution. Once again, the elite was foiled by the dynamic of conspicuous production: the automotive entrepreneurs most eager to win acceptance from Detroit's social arbiters were precisely those most susceptible to the "big-car bug." That is, they were prone to combine their climb up the city's status ladder with their products' ascent in the automotive price-class hierarchy. As a result, they tended to back themselves into a small corner of the automobile market and therefore added little to the economic clout of Detroit's upper class. The book charts the passage of the industry's new men into the upper echelons of Detroit's status system, showing that the old families and the industry's new men were largely operating as a single group in Detroit's public affairs in the 1910s and 1920s. Henry Ford and his erstwhile business partner, James Couzens, remained social outsiders even after they had gained the ability to buy and sell most of Detroit's establishment. Mastery over the low-priced automobile market, in the years before Ford had proved its immense profitability, was bound to go to individuals estranged from the existing social order. In part, this was due to the tendency for key innovators like Ford to come from a group that was, as E. E. Hagan has said, "derogated in its own society—looked down upon unjustly and unreasonably in its own eyes—by the social leaders of the society." The kind of creative entrepreneurship that we associate with Ford's decision to mass-produce the Model T was, many theorists argue, most likely to come from a social outsider.[24]

However, the dynamic of conspicuous production also explains Ford's commitment to mass production of a cheap utility car. Of all Detroit's automotive leaders, he appears to have been the one to identify most with the lower classes. They were his peer group, and he accordingly targeted them for his sales. His associate William Stout observed that Ford was "the only one who did *not* have the idea that he was in the luxury business."[25] Even so, why did the cars built by Ford not rise in price as he grew more prosperous? Why did he not succumb to the big-car bug?

The answer is found in the chapters chronicling the business and civic activities of Ford and Couzens, who until 1915 was second-in-command at the Ford Motor Company. These chapters show that the industrial policy adopted by the two men developed dialectically in opposition to their community experiences: that is, their confrontations with the local establishment strengthened and prolonged their commitment to the lowest price-class by reducing whatever allure the country club set might once have had for them. It was not likely, for example, that Detroit's upper class could add Ford to its ranks after publicly accusing his son Edsel in 1918 of cowardice in dodging wartime service. Ford instead increased his identification with the low- and middle-income groups who bought the Model T and, in doing so, made it all the more inevitable that he would retain the sorts of attitudes—for example, an animosity toward bankers—that led ineluctably to conflict with the local establishment. For him and for Couzens the car wars and the social wars were mutually reinforcing aspects of a single, grand campaign. Instead of being co-opted by Detroit's upper class, they became increasingly suspicious of it.

Ford's alienation by 1933 verged on paranoia, yet historians have missed the mark in seeking the sources of his discontent in a childhood trauma or the wayward chemistry of his mind. Ford was less the victim of a personality disorder than of the incongruence between the social attitudes necessary for victory in the low-price automobile market and those requisite for fitting into Detroit's social elite. Ford was a rarity: someone who gained great wealth without adopting the values of the wealthy. Thanks to the peculiar dynamic of conspicuous production, it was predictable that control over the most lucrative sector of the auto industry—the mass market—would go to the entrepreneur and company most at odds with the Detroit establishment. The latter's fate came to depend in no small measure on the goodwill of an individual who despised it.

By the late 1920s General Motors had overtaken Ford, and Chrysler had evolved into a powerful competitor; had Detroit's pre-automotive elite controlled either of these two corporations, they might have been able to deflect and to contain Ford's antagonism. But these companies had come to be owned by outside capital; as a result, they tended to avoid taking sides in the community battles waged between Ford and Couzens and their upmarket rivals. The two absentee-owned automobile corporations stood aloof while Ford chipped away at the power of the old families and their newfound allies among the upwardly mobile automotive entrepreneurs; during the nationwide credit crisis in February and March 1933, they did virtually nothing to prevent the collapse of the last bastion of old-line economic power in Detroit: two banking groups that together controlled 93 percent of the city's bank deposits. Instead, they joined Ford in picking the bones: by August 1933, Ford and General Motors controlled the remnants oi the banking empire fashioned by Detroit's pre-automotive elite, and by then the latter's eclipse was virtually complete.

In summary, this book endeavors to establish the price paid, first by Detroit's pre-automotive elite and then by the people of Detroit, for the high incidence of conspicuous production in the early automobile industry. It follows the skein of two interwoven tales. The first tells how the founders of Detroit's auto industry, the city's old families, lost the control of it to the Big Three; the explanation is to be found in the price-class prejudices of the various actors in the community drama. The second story chronicles the attempt by Detroit's pre-automotive elite to maintain its preeminence even as control over the city's dominant industry passed into the hands of outsiders: literal outsiders in the instance of the absentee-owned corporations; figurative in the case of Ford, a social renegade. By 1933 their efforts to ride out the automotive revolution in the city's economy had ended in failure.

Taken together, the two tales relate not only the decline of an old elite or the rise of a new industry but also the process by which Detroiters lost control over their economic destiny. By 1933 the city had seen its local elite crippled and the ownership of its key industry forfeited. The entire community thus suffered because of the atavistic behavior of the early automotive leaders. It is a complex story but one that almost tells itself once the most powerful belief impeding our understanding of it has been dispelled: the myth that the founders of the American automotive industry were mostly self-made men.

Chapter One   **The Automotive Paradigm**

■   The basic paradigm for research into American automotive history was first established in the 1920s as a scholarly response to the emergence of mass automobility and to the American conquest of the world automobile market. With more than 80 percent of the world's motor vehicles driving American roads in the late 1920s, it was self-evident that manufacturers in the United States had been uniquely successful in making the transition from producing cars for a wealthy few to turning them out in the millions for the masses. Not surprisingly, the literature of the 1920s emphasized the industry's humble origins and its democratic aspirations. The two books most responsible for creating the paradigm were both published in 1928, and they remain standard works of reference. Their themes so overlap that *The Automobile Industry* by Ralph C. Epstein and *A Financial History of the Automobile Industry* by Lawrence Seltzer can almost be considered as a single treatise. Their concurrence made their message all the more compelling to subsequent historians.[1]

Epstein and Seltzer argued, in the words of the latter, that "the growth of the American automobile industry was characteristically the expansion of originally small enterprises that obtained the bulk of their increasing capital from reinvested profits." Traditional capital markets were closed to the speculative industry, according to Epstein, and as a result the "initial fixed capital requirements were met by the relatively small sums" that the entrepreneurs themselves and "their few backers originally put into the enterprise." How small were these sums? Epstein provided three examples of firms worth tens of millions: only $28,000 of Ford's capital came from "outside sources" as of 1928, only $99,000 of Hudson's, and $144,000 of Reo's. Automobile manufacturing was possible on such a narrow capital base because it was at first little more than an assembly operation: the "owners of existing capital equipment"— namely, the auto parts suppliers—thus provided much of the capital needed for automotive manufacturing. Typically, the parts suppliers offered thirty- to ninety-day open accounts to their corporate customers, which meant that an assembler could with luck construct and sell the car before he had to pay for the material going into it.[2]

Further, since there was a seller's market in automobiles before 1910, manufacturers were able to insist on cash deposits of 20 percent with the initial order, the remainder due in cash upon delivery of the vehicle to the dealer or distributor. In this way a manufacturer was able to conscript the help of his dealers and their hometown banks in providing working capital. Thus automobile companies were doubly blessed: they sold for cash and bought on credit. In the circumstances, the industry posed surprisingly few barriers to entry. As Epstein wrote, the automotive pioneers "were in the main young, and for the most part possessed little or no capital themselves." And yet, given the continuing indifference— even hostility—of the investment community, these self-made men "owned most of the stock, and thus most of the invested capital" of the firms they managed. Epstein thought the auto executive a throwback to the nineteenth-century entrepreneur: "In striking contrast with most modern large-scale enterprises," he wrote, "the executives in the automobile industry were actually owner-managers."[3]

Epstein and Seltzer thus depicted the early American automobile industry as a meritocracy, a glorious affirmation of the success ethic. Barriers to entry were minimal; capital requirements were few; and victory went to those with the keenest entrepreneurial spirit. The appeal of the Seltzer-Epstein thesis lay precisely in this image of an industry led by self-made men committed to democratizing a product that remained more or less the exclusive property of the rich and powerful in other nations before World War II. Thus the entire American nation was seen as benefiting from the openness of its social structure.

Research into the automobile industry since 1928 has been largely paradigm-based. This has been especially true of the work of John B. Rae, who may well be regarded as the head of the paradigmatic community since his first publications on automotive history in the 1950s. Rae, while recognizing that relatively few of the early manufacturers "personified the barefoot-boy-to-millionaire tradition," has stressed the extent to which the early industry "was a classic example of a free market," "entry into the industry was easy and cheap" and "competition was unrestricted." The pioneer manufacturers he characterized as "engineer-entrepreneurs" (close cousins of Epstein's "owner-managers"), "practically all" of whom "came from the middle of the social and economic scale." Rae's own research has demonstrated that "pioneer American automobile manufacturers . . . usually were already in a business that could turn to motor vehicles fairly readily" and that these men tended to be more successful than those who entered the industry without manufacturing experience, yet he has consistently affirmed the main tenets of the Seltzer-Epstein thesis. In 1984 he wrote:

> At the beginning it was easy to enter the industry. All that was required was some mechanical skill and a building where the vehicle could be assembled from parts made elsewhere. The cars were sold for cash . . . and the parts bought on credit, so that if production could be achieved and if buyers could be found, the operation could finance itself.[4]

In a lifetime of research, Rae has of course extended and articulated the paradigm. For our purposes, his most notable contribution to it has been his discussion of the reasons for the industry's localization in Detroit. The Motor City had, Rae has concluded, only one initial advantage not shared with other midwestern manufacturing centers, and that was the ability of its local entrepreneurs: "Geographical location and resources," he wrote in a 1980 essay, were not "a sufficient explanation in themselves." There also "had to be a catalyst, and this catalyst was a remarkable concentration in time and place of a group of individuals" with "exceptional entrepreneurial and technical talent." But not money—Rae has always disputed the contention that Detroit financiers were any friendlier to the nascent industry than those in other communities. Most of the industry's capital requirements, he claims, were met by parts suppliers and dealers. In discounting the importance of local capital, Rae has been faithful to the paradigm, but by arguing that "the real explanation comes down to . . . the fortuitous circumstance that a remarkable group of automobile entrepreneurs appeared simultaneously in the Detroit area," he has inadvertently exposed one of the weaknesses of the paradigm: its tendency to resort to "accident" as an explanatory device.[5]

Even self-professed debunkers of Seltzer and Epstein have accepted their main assumptions. George May, for example, has labored to dispel the myths that have grown up about the careers of Ransom Olds, Henry Ford, and others; through meticulous research he has come to realize that traditional accounts underestimated the financial contribution of Detroit's monied families. Indeed, May has concluded that the interest of the "well-to-do class" was "probably the single most important factor behind Detroit's rise to the top in this new industry." Had he developed this theme, May would have been in a position to challenge the paradigm itself, because he had proof that companies needed access to capital well beyond that provided by their parts suppliers and dealers—evidence, in other words, that the assumptions of Seltzer, Epstein, and Rae about equality of opportunity did not fit the facts about Detroit. But May did not build on this insight; instead, he accepted one of the most important fallacies perpetuated by the paradigm: namely, that not until 1910, at the earliest, were the "days when one could start to manufacture automobiles on a shoestring . . . definitely over." Yet his own findings show that *successful* manufacturing was never possible on a shoestring budget.[6]

Even James Flink, the leading iconoclast of automotive studies, has implicitly endorsed the main tenets of the Seltzer-Epstein thesis. In *The Car Culture*, Flink asserted that "no industry in American history required less capital to enter or promised greater profits," inasmuch as "the requirements for fixed and working capital were met mainly by shifting the burden to parts makers, distributors, and dealers."[7] Clearly, there were industries in eighteenth- and nineteenth-century America that originally required less capital to enter than did automobile manufacturing; in the early 1860s, for example, it took only $300 to $400 to buy a petroleum still. Flink's hyperbole is therefore an ironic tribute to the power of the paradigm: even the industry's critic has accepted its claim that in the beginning it offered unique opportunities for social and economic advancement.

This is not an insignificant concession, especially in the context of the current debate among historians of technology over the politics of innovation. Radical historians have contended that technological innovation is sponsored by one class—the ruling class—and designed for its benefit. The theory adopted by automotive historians obviously contradicts the radical vision: it depicts the American automobile manufacturers as an essentially homogeneous group, with non-elite backgrounds and values, whose concept of the automobile was, as Rae has frequently asserted, not that of a "luxury item, or something to be used for sport" but rather that of a good to be widely distributed to the American public. Automotive manufacturing was, in other words, a "democratic technology" and not an instrument of class hegemony, as radical historians presume.[8]

The radical critique of American technology is not at issue here, but the automotive paradigm is, and it clearly has fundamental flaws. The first of these is its underlying assumption that automobile manufacturers shared a commitment to creating a "democratic technology." This assumption does not jibe with the reality of market segmentation: automobile companies in the United States tended to concentrate until the 1920s on a single price-class in order to achieve volume production. Some companies, among them such Detroit firms as Packard and Lozier, devoted themselves exclusively to the luxury market. Obviously, they made no contribution to the democratization of the automobile and may even have regretted its implications—in the form of traffic congestion and the devaluation of the automobile as a status object—for their wealthy clientele. Presumably, the choice of price-class in some way reflected the social perspective of the entrepreneurs involved; otherwise, we would be left with personal idiosyncrasy and accidents of design as our only explanations for the most important decision most firms had to make. In any case, any theory that fails to take into consideration the phenomenon of market segmentation must be suspect. The development of the cheap utility car was not the project of the entire American auto industry but of a relative handful of companies. And they may well have differed quite radically from the industry norm not only in their model policy but in their social and political outlook.

A second problem with the paradigm is in its conclusion that there were no significant barriers to entry into the early automobile industry, because dealers and parts suppliers provided the bulk of its capital requirements. But who provided the remainder? The sums involved were far from trivial: the typical Michigan automobile company incorporated before 1912 started with authorized capital of $300,000, one-third of it actually paid into its treasury. Either sum was a considerable amount of money to raise in those days, especially when banks were reluctant to help.[9]

Why then has the notion endured that money was only a minor factor in determining who should enter the early auto industry? An answer is suggested by John Ingham's book *The Iron Barons*, a quantitative study of the iron and steel elite in six cities. One of these, Pittsburgh, had developed a reputation for being "the example *par excellence* of the 'rags to riches' rise of the American businessman." Yet on close inspection members of its elite were found to differ "only slightly . . . from American businessmen in general in the late nineteenth century." Why then its reputation for social mobility? Ingham has found the answer in the cultural background of the Pittsburgh iron and steel barons: though typically wealthy and from locally prominent families, they nonetheless seemed like upstarts to the elites of older cities like Philadelphia and New York, particularly since a majority of the Pittsburghers came from "cultural minority groups" who "still faced a certain amount of prejudice and discrimination in seacoast cities." But their way was "unfettered" and their path to success arduous only when viewed from afar. In other words, a group may gain a reputation for having humble origins because it has been consistently compared with the most prominent and privileged families of their era, rather than with the American populace as a whole.[10]

Similarly, the capital requirements of automobile manufacturing have too often been viewed from the vantage point of Wall Street and not often enough from that of Main Street. Historians have downplayed the role of capital in the early industry because they have taken as their reference point either contemporary oligopolies or the auto industry itself after it had reached maturity: $100,000 may pale in significance when compared with the assets of United States Steel in 1901 or those of General Motors in 1929, but for a small business in either year, it was a daunting amount to raise in venture capital. As a result, financially viable automobile companies were generally founded by men already prominent in their own communities. They have been remembered otherwise by historians because the industry's founders have been viewed through the condescending eyes of east coast elites. The midwesterners who controlled the leading firms of the early auto industry may have looked like upstarts to eastern opinion leaders, but that did not preclude their having cut an imposing figure within their own community or region even before they commenced building motorcars.

The myth of equal opportunity has survived as long as it has only because historians have not hitherto undertaken a systematic analysis of the origins of the automotive elite. Obviously, we need to know the backgrounds of as many as possible if we are to make an informed judgment concerning the industry's social origins. To that end, data have been collected for 292 automotive leaders, approximately 80 percent of them senior executives, the remainder either directors or principal investors in a passenger car company active in Detroit before 1930. Table 1 gives the breakdown by category.[11] (The tables are grouped at the end of this chapter.) Studies of elites by Frank Taussig and C. S. Joslyn, Mabel Newcomer, and William Miller restrict themselves to business executives; to facilitate comparison, data are presented here for the executive group alone as well as for the entire community, called hereafter "automotive leaders."[12]

The data confound the notion of the self-made man and industry, revealing Detroit's automotive leaders in the aggregate to have been a typical American business elite of the early twentieth century in that their wealth was more often inherited than acquired. To be sure, Epstein was right about their relative youth (see Table 2), but that may have been due as much to a comfortable head start as to their own talents and ambition. They usually had the advantage of being native-born (typically in the Midwest): less than one-eighth were born outside the country, as opposed to one-third of the general Detroit population in 1900 and one-fourth of the city's industrial elite (Table 3).[13]

Collectively, the automotive elite were also unusually well educated for the times, even by normal elite standards (Table 4), and had generally staked out a successful career before they took up automotive manufacturing (Table 5). Both their educational attainments and their jump-start in business suggest that their families had resources well above the American norm.[14]

Indeed, it appears that 70 percent of their fathers were businessmen or professionals—or about the same percentage as has been found for national business elites in the 1900–1930 period (Table 6). The fathers of more than a third of the Detroit auto leaders were big businessmen (defined here as someone engaged in banking, publishing, or heavy industry—or, failing that, the part owner of three separate enterprises); this would appear to be a much higher percentage than Taussig and Joslyn found for their national sample of corporate executives in 1928 (Table 6). Overall, it appears that the early auto industry, despite a reputation for manufacturing fortunes and careers, provided roughly the same degree of opportunity as the national business community. Moreover, opportunity diminished within the industry as it matured. It increasingly became the preserve of the wealthy and well educated: where 64 percent of those joining before 1906 had fathers engaged in business or the professions, over 74 percent of the newcomers over the next two decades enjoyed this elite background (Table 7).

Obviously, the typical Detroit auto leader did not fit the stereotype of the self-made man; he was more likely to be the son of a prominent businessman. However, there were exceptions, and it is important not to replace one monolithic interpretation with another but, instead, to consider the industry's diversity. It served all classes and markets, and its methods ranged from handcrafted custom work to mass production. It is not surprising, then, that companies serving different clienteles had different sociological profiles. Their diversity becomes self-evident once the data on the 292 auto leaders are disaggregated by company and by price-class.

Epstein provides a precedent for analyzing the industry in terms of price-classes, which he defined as "non-competing groups of cars." They were noncompeting because they differed sufficiently in price to serve different markets. Epstein estimated that there were nine distinct price-classes, which he grouped into three triads for analytical purposes; these he styled the low, middle, and upper price-classes. He thought their boundaries fairly stable over the period he was studying (1903–1928) and so made "no allowance . . . for changes in the purchasing power of money." A car costing $2,000 he placed in the middle price range, whether it sold in 1903 or in 1928.[15]

This book similarly applies a three-class model to the early auto industry and assumes that the lines of class division did not change significantly between 1903 and 1928, as the industry was able to keep its prices stable through increased efficiency despite the inflationary pressures of the period. A standard criterion is thus used in Table 8 for sorting marques by price-class, regardless of the year. The actual dividing lines, however, are set at $675 and $2,775, the placement of each make being determined by the price of its cheapest standard model: a runabout or touring car in 1907, a touring car thereafter.[16] Within each class the makes are arrayed in ascending order of price: thus Hupmobile offered the least expensive model in the middle price-class in 1913 (though still more than $675), and Keeton the most expensive. Several non-Detroit makes are included for illustrative purposes.

Though the table reveals some movement between price-classes as well as rank-jumping within them, most makes retained a distinctive and consistent class identity through the years. It is feasible, therefore, to assort auto manufacturers into a price-class hierarchy, and this has been done in Table 9.[17]

Four companies—General Motors, Chrysler, Maxwell, and Studebaker—have been assigned to a fourth category, one based on ownership rather than on price-class. Though all four bulked large in the local automotive scene, they were nonetheless absentee-owned and -controlled. Because many of their key decision-makers did not live in the Motor City and did not, consequently, play an active role in community affairs, these companies are best conceived of as a distinctive group. Certainly they did not have the same social concerns as the Detroit-owned companies. Moreover, their model policies diverged in varying degrees from the Detroit norm. Of the four, Maxwell came closest to having a consistent, identifiable price-class: from 1913 to its demise in 1925 it targeted the low end of the middle-class range. From 1910 to 1913, however, it was part of United States Motors, a holding company designed to offer cars throughout the price spectrum. Chrysler, a reorganization of Maxwell, originally positioned itself in the middle-class market. But within four years of its incorporation, through the acquisition of Dodge Brothers and the founding of its Plymouth division, it had shed its class identity. Studebaker attempted to make a similar transition after 1925 with its low-priced Erskine and its purchase of Pierce-Arrow, a luxury make; but its models in the late 1920s still covered a fairly narrow price range—at least compared with General Motors, which from 1908 onward filled as many price brackets as possible; classlessness was the secret of its success. Locally owned firms were much more likely to show a class bias in their model policy.

The correlation between the social origins of Detroit's automotive leaders and the cars they built becomes manifest when the four basic groups of producers are compared. For the sake of brevity, the following remarks are limited to the defining features of each set of companies: that is, the points at which they departed most radically from the norm.

The most remarkable aspect of the absentee-owned companies was their reliance on outside talent. Only a sixth of their leaders were born in Michigan, and less than half came from the Midwest (Table 10). The largest segment came from the northeastern states, a reflection of the extent to which Wall Street dominated their affairs. Inasmuch as many financial and marketing decisions were made elsewhere—in New York, in Flint, Michigan, in Wilmington, Delaware—less than half of the leaders relocated to Detroit before 1930. Of those who did, the majority arrived after 1910, the year investment banks in New York and Boston financed the reorganization of General Motors, Studebaker, and Maxwell.

The most remarkable aspect of the leaders of the lower-class companies was their humble origins. They were more likely than other automotive men to be foreign-born—almost a third of Ford's leadership, for example, or about four times the percentage found in middle- and upper-class firms (Table 10). More than two-fifths of them hailed from working-class or farm families, also the highest proportion for any of the four automotive classes (Table 11). There were by extension relatively few business proprietors, executives, or professionals among their fathers. Nor had the leaders of the lower-class firms been markedly successful before joining the auto industry; there were more former workers and clerks in their ranks, and fewer independent proprietors, than was true of leaders in the other price-classes (Table 12). They may well have been held back by an inadequate education: three-fifths had not gone past high school, half again as many as in the industry as a whole; less than a quarter had attended university or college, half the industry norm (see Table 13). Overall, it would appear that the leaders of the lower-class companies came from a more disadvantaged social milieu than those of the rest of the industry and that there was, consequently, a direct correlation between their own standing in the social hierarchy and the original positioning of their cars in the industry's price-class hierarchy.

The same held true for the middle- and upper-class companies. Luxury-car manufacturing was clearly an elite activity: more than 93 percent of the leaders of upper-class companies had been business proprietors, executives, or professionals at the time they entered the industry (Table 12); more than a third had been big businessmen, the highest percentage for any automotive class. A large measure of their success they owed to family advantage: not only had three-quarters of their fathers owned their own business (Table 11), but half had been big businessmen. The wealth of the fathers had meant educational opportunities for the sons, for three-fifths of these leaders had attended college (Table 13). The most revealing statistic, however, concerns their place of birth (Table 10): almost half had been born in Detroit—by far the highest for any automotive class—and this suggests that the leaders of Detroit's upper-class automobile firms came not just from the city's economic elite but from its old, established families. In other words, they belonged to the local upper class. The city's most prominent families controlled such luxury producers as Packard, Lozier, and Lincoln.

The leaders of the middle-class companies occupied an intermediate stratum also within the industry's social hierarchy, their model policy thus conforming to their social standing. In their careers, education, and family background, too, they occupied a middle ground. The most remarkable aspect of this group pertained to their point of origin: relatively few were born in Detroit; they tended instead to come from the rest of Michigan and from adjoining states (Table 10). They were, in other words, typically midwesterners but not native to Detroit. Indeed, the average middle-class leader seems to have moved to Detroit in order to join or organize an automobile company. Only 44 percent of them lived in Detroit in 1905, as opposed to two-thirds of the lower- and upper-class leaders (Table 14).

Inevitably, they were seen as parvenus by Detroit's social arbiters, including those who owned stock in the patrician automobile concerns, yet by the standards of the average American they were a privileged group. After all, more than half had been able to attend college (Table 13), and two-thirds of their fathers had been businessmen or professionals (Table 11). Similarly, the leaders of the lower-class companies were disadvantaged only by comparison with those in other price-classes; almost 56 percent of *their* fathers had been managers, officials, or proprietors at a time (1900) when less than 7 percent of the nation's economically active male population belonged to these three categories (Table 11).[18]

Extremely few automotive executives had lives consonant with either the Horatio Alger myth or the automotive historian's paradigm. Yet even within a world of privilege there were gradations. The leaders of the three price-classes did differ markedly in their social backgrounds, and their model policies did diverge. Granted, the automotive community was at most an attenuated version of the larger society—but then so was the automotive market: before 1920 the majority of U.S. citizens found a new car beyond their financial means. For consumers as well as producers, the price-classes sorted out the rich from the merely prosperous.

Even so, neither group should be lumped together. It makes no more sense to tell the history of the industry in terms of a homogeneous leadership than it does to depict the twelve-cylinder Packard and the Model T Ford as competing in an undifferentiated market. The automotive classes may have been fairly narrow in scope, but they had large consequences for both consumers and producers. And as we shall see, the history of modern Detroit cannot fully be related without taking into consideration the division of the city's leading industry into price-classes.

This chapter has demonstrated (the paradigm notwithstanding) a close correlation between social class and automotive price-class, but the sample data alone do not tell us whether there was a causal relationship between the two. We need to examine the behavior of individual firms to detect whether they did indeed stamp their social biases onto the cars they built. Only through detailed corporate histories, furthermore, is it possible to test the theory of conspicuous production outlined in the Introduction. The data presented in this chapter have portrayed the industry's class structure as being relatively fixed and static. On the whole, that is consistent with the idea of conspicuous production, for most entrants into the early automotive industry would presumably have selected the market most suited to their incomes and status. Even so, we need to know why there was not more rank-jumping (why, for example, every automobile manufacturer did not compete for the upper-class bracket once prosperity had come its way), as well as the circumstances in which companies did forsake their original price-class. To that end, let us go back to the turn of the century, when the Olds Motor Works became not only the first company to manufacture cars in Detroit but also the first to suffer great harm from abandoning its original price-class.

Table 1
Auto Leaders, 1890–1930: Position

Highest Post Attained	Number	% of Sample
Chairman of board	7	2.4
Executive committee of board	5	1.7
President	68	23.5
Vice-president	91	31.5
General manager	7	2.4
Secretary/treasurer	25	8.7
General counsel	4	1.4
Assistant general manager	2	0.7
Manufacturing manager	4	1.4
Sales manager	10	3.5
Chief engineer	7	2.4
Purchasing agent	1	0.4
Director	40	13.8
Large investor	18	6.2
Management	231	79.9
Non-management	58	20.1
Total	289	100.0

Table 2
Auto Leaders and Executives, 1890–1930: Age (1914)

Age	Auto Leaders (%)	Auto Execu- tives (%)	Marquis Auto Leaders[a] (%)	Marquis Non-Auto Businessmen[a] (%)	National Business Elite [b] (%)
Under 30	4.9	5.7	2.3	3.6	1.1
30 to 34	11.4	13.0	14.1	8.9	4.1
35 to 39	17.1	20.2	20.0	14.7	10.1
40 to 44	19.9	21.2	25.9	17.0	12.8
45 to 49	14.2	14.5	18.8	17.5	15.7
50 to 54	12.2	11.4	7.1	12.6	17.1
55 to 59	4.9	4.2	8.2	9.3	15.7
60 plus	15.5	9.9	3.5	16.2	23.4
Under 40	33.4	38.9	36.4	27.2	15.3
Under 50	67.5	74.6	81.1	61.7	43.8
Median age	41	41	42	47	51
Mean age	44	44	41	45	51
Total cases (= 100%)	246	193	85	1,265	7,371

[a] From A. N. Marquis & Co., *The Book of Detroiters* (Chicago, 1914).
[b] From F. W. Taussig and C. S. Joslyn, *American Business Leaders: A Study in Social Origins and Social Stratification* (New York, 1932); data and ages as of 1928.

Table 3
Auto Leaders and Executives, 1890–1930: Place of Birth

	Auto Leaders (%)	Auto Executives (%)	Marquis Auto Leaders[a] (%)	Marquis Non-Auto Businessmen[a] (%)	Zunz, Detroit Industrialists[b] (%)
Detroit	25.0	21.4	12.6	26.2	18.3
Other Michigan	16.1	14.6	28.4	20.3	16.5
Other Midwest[c]	21.4	26.0	21.5	10.5	7.8
Northeast U.S.A.[d]	20.2	21.4	15.8	16.6	29.6
Other U.S.A.	5.6	5.7	5.3	6.1	0.9
Other Countries	11.7	10.9	16.8	20.2	27.0
Total Michigan	41.1	36.0	41.0	46.5	34.8
Total Midwest	62.5	62.0	62.5	57.0	42.6

[a] From A. N. Marquis & Co., *The Book of Detroiters* (Chicago, 1914).
[b] From Olivier Zunz, *The Changing Face of Inequality: Urbanization, Industrial Development, and Immigrants in Detroit, 1880–1920* (Chicago, 1982), app. 6.
[c] Illinois, Indiana, Ohio, Wisconsin.
[d] Census region of New England and Middle Atlantic states.

Table 4
Auto Leaders and Executives, 1890–1930: Education

Highest Level Attained	Auto Leaders (%)	Auto Executives (%)	Marquis Auto Leaders[a] (%)	Business Elite, 1910 (Miller)[b] (%)	Business Elite, 1910 (Newcomer)[c] (%)	Business Elite, 1928 (Taussig & Joslyn)[d] (%)
Public school	41.4	42.3	50.5			
Preparatory school	4.1	4.2	2.0	59.0[e]	60.0[e]	54.7[e]
Business college	7.8	9.0	16.2			
College[f]	44.7	43.4	29.2	41.0	40.0	45.3
Other	2.1	1.1	2.0	0.0	0.0	0.0
Total cases (= 100%)	244	189	99	183	310	not given

[a] From A. N. Marquis & Co., *The Book of Detroiters* (Chicago, 1914).
[b] From William Miller, *Men in Business* (Cambridge, Mass., 1952).
[c] From Mabel Newcomer, *The Big Business Executive: The Factors That Made Him, 1900–1950* (New York, 1955).
[d] From F. W. Taussig and C. S. Joslyn, *American Business Leaders: A Study in Social Origins and Social Stratification* (New York, 1932).
[e] Data not broken down into comparable categories.
[f] Includes nongraduates.

Table 5
Auto Leaders and Executives, 1890–1930: Prior Occupation

	Auto Leaders %	Auto Executives %
Student only	3.9	5.0
Farmer	0.0	0.0
Unskilled worker	0.0	0.0
Skilled or semiskilled worker	5.4	6.8
Salesman	6.1	7.7
Clerk	2.5	2.7
Professional[a]	13.6	14.0
Owner, business	41.2	33.0
Business executive	27.2	30.8
Total business (owners, executives)	68.4	63.8
Owners, big business[b]	28.2	18.5
Total cases (= 100%)	279	221

[a] Includes lawyers, physicians, engineers, teachers, clergy.
[b] Includes capitalists (owners of 3 or more businesses), bankers, and owners of timberlands, public utilities, and newspapers.

Table 6

Auto Leaders and Executives, 1890–1930: Father's Occupation

	Auto Leaders (%)	Auto Executives (%)	Business Elite, 1910[a] (%)	Business Elite, 1870s[b] (%)	Business Elite, 1850–79[c] (%)	Business Elite, 1900[d] (%)	Business Elite, 1925[d] (%)	Millionaires, 1925[e] (%)	Business Elite, 1928[f] (%)	20th-Cent. Steel Men[g] (%)
Farmer	16.7	16.4	12.0	25.0	21.5	20.8	15.0	7.3	12.0	5.0
Public official	4.0	3.6	7.0	3.0	4.7	1.6	2.5	5.2	1.3[h]	5.0
Professional	8.7	10.0	23.0	13.0	18.7	18.9	19.1	10.5	13.0	23.0
Worker	6.7	9.1	2.0	8.0	6.5	4.2	6.2	2.0	10.8	5.0
Salesman	0.0	0.0	0.0	0.0	[0.9	0.7	0.6	0.0	5.3	0.0
Clerk	1.3	1.8	0.0	0.0	0.9]	0.7	3.4	0.0		0.0
Owner, business	59.3	55.5	[56.0	[51.0	[47.7	48.7	47.4	[75.0	34.0	[61.0
Executive	3.3	3.6				2.6	4.1		23.6	
Total business	62.6	59.1	56.0	51.0	47.7	51.3	51.5	75.0	57.6	61.0
Owner, big business	38.7	31.8	—	—	—	—	—	—	14.3	—
Total, business & professional	71.3	69.1	79.0	64.0	66.4	70.2	70.6	85.5	70.6	84.0
Total cases (= 100%)	150	110	167	194	not given	215	203	380	7,361	505

a From William E. Miller, "American Historians and the Business Elite," in *Men in Business*, ed. Miller (Cambridge, Mass., 1952).

b From Frances Gregory and Irene B. Neu, "The American Industrial Elite in the 1870's," in *Men in Business*, ed. Miller.

c From C. Wright Mills, "The American Business Elite: A Collective Portrait," in *The Tasks of Economic History*, supplement to *Journal of Economic History* 5 (December 1945).

d From Mabel Newcomer, *The Big Business Executive: The Factors That Made Him* (New York, 1955).

e From Pitrim Sorokin, "American Millionaires and Multi-Millionaires: A Comparative Statistical Study," *Journal of Social Forces* 3 (May 1925): 627–40.

f From F. W. Taussig and C. S. Joslyn, *American Business Leaders: A Study in Social Origins and Social Stratification* (New York, 1932).

g From John N. Ingham, *The Iron Barons: A Social Analysis of an American Elite, 1874–1965* (Westport, Conn., 1978). Taken from *Poor's Register of Directors* for 1901, 1912, 1921, 1931, 1941, 1955.

h Also includes insurance, real estate agents, hotel keepers, and other miscellaneous categories.

Table 7
**Automotive Leaders, 1890–1930: Father's Occupation
and Son's Entry into the Industry**

Father's occupation	1891–1900 %	1901–1905 %	1906–1910 %	1911–1915 %	1916–1925 %
Farmer	11.8	23.4	15.9	14.8	6.7
Clerk	5.9	0.0	0.0	3.7	0.0
Worker	0.0	10.6	4.5	11.1	0.0
Public official	11.8	0.0	4.5	3.7	6.7
Professional	11.8	6.4	11.4	7.4	6.7
Owner, business	58.8	55.3	61.4	51.9	80.0
Executive	0.0	4.3	2.3	7.4	0.0
Total business	52.9	59.6	63.7	59.3	80.0
Owners, big business	41.2	42.6	34.1	40.7	53.3
Total cases (= 100%)	17	47	44	27	15

Table 8
Makes and Price-Classes

Price-Class	1907	1913	1915	1918	1920	1925
Low ($675 or less)	Brush Ford Reo	Ford	Ford Saxon	Ford Saxon Chevrolet	Ford	Ford Willys Chevrolet
Middle	Maxwell Cadillac Buick Willys Regal Carter Oldsmobile Wayne Thomas Northern	Hupmobile Chevrolet Studebaker Regal Buick Paige Maxwell Willys Oakland Reo King Oldsmobile Chalmers Abbott Cadillac Hudson Keeton	Maxwell Dodge Krit Willys Chevrolet R-C-H Buick Studebaker Briggs Reo King Paige Regal Hupmobile Oakland Carter Oldsmobile Hudson Chalmers Abbott	Dort Maxwell Briscoe Regal Willys Buick Dodge Reo Oakland Studebaker Oldsmobile Hupmobile Scripps Abbott Nash Paige Chalmers Essex Hudson Columbia Liberty	Dort Chevrolet Willys Buick Maxwell Reo Dodge Saxon Nash Oldsmobile Scripps Studebaker Paige Essex Hupmobile Columbia Chalmers Liberty King Hudson	Durant Oldsmobile Maxwell Essex Oakland Studebaker Buick Jewett Hupmobile Hudson Nash Rickenbacker Chrysler Reo Dodge Paige Packard
Upper ($2,775 or more)	Studebaker Packard Lozier	Lozier Packard	Cadillac Lozier Packard	Cadillac Packard	Cadillac Lincoln Packard	Cadillac Lincoln

Sources: The Automobile, October 24 and 31, 1907; Joseph J. Schroeder, Jr., ed., The Wonderful World of Automobiles (Northfield, Ill., 1971), 279–286; Automotive Industries, February 26, 1925, 356–57; corporate histories.

Table 9
Auto Leaders, 1890–1930: Type of Company

Company and Class	Number of Leaders	Percentage (N = 292)
Brush Runabout Co.	2	0.7
Ford Motor Co.	27	9.2
Saxon Motor Car Co.	4	1.4
Lower-class total	33	11.3
Abbott Motor Co.	4	1.4
Briggs-Detroiter Co.	1	0.3
Chalmers-Detroit Motor Co.	12	4.1
Columbia Motor Car Co.	1	0.3
Dodge Brothers Motor Car Co.	9	3.1
Hudson Motor Car Co.	10	3.4
Hupp Motor Car Co.	11	3.8
King Motor Car Co.	6	2.1
Krit Motor Car Co.	3	1.0
Liberty Motor Car Co.	5	1.7
Paige-Detroit Motor Car Co.	12	4.1
R-C-H Corp.	5	1.7
Regal Motor Car Co.	2	0.7
Warren-Detroit Motor Car Co.	4	1.4
Middle-class total	85	29.1
Lincoln Motor Co.	5	1.7
Lozier Motor Co.	16	5.5
Packard Motor Car Co.	22	7.5
Upper-class total	43	14.7
Chrysler Corp.	8	2.7
General Motors Corp.	34	11.6
Maxwell Motor Co.	14	4.8
Studebaker Corp.	11	3.8
Absentee-owned total	67	22.9
Total	228	78.1

Note: 64 leaders are not included in this table: 10 are associated with Cadillac Motor Car Co., excluded by its price-class inconsistency; the rest are involved with too many companies to permit identification with any one of them.

Table 10
Auto Leaders, 1890–1930: Place of Birth and Type of Company

Birthplace	Lower-Class (%)	Middle-Class (%)	Upper-Class (%)	Absentee-Owned (%)
Detroit	26.7	17.9	47.4	9.3
Other Michigan	16.7	23.9	5.3	7.4
Other Midwest	16.7	32.8	15.8	27.8
Northeast U.S.A.	10.0	14.9	15.8	35.2
Other U.S.A.	3.3	4.5	7.9	9.3
Other countries	26.7	6.0	7.9	11.1
Total Michigan	43.4	41.8	52.7	16.7
Total Midwest	60.1	74.6	68.5	44.4
Total cases (= 100%)	30	67	38	54

Table 11
Auto Leaders, 1890–1930: Father's Occupation and Type of Company

Father's Occupation	Lower-Class (%)	Middle-Class (%)	Upper-Class (%)	Absentee-Owned (%)
Farmer	22.2	17.9	7.7	19.4
Worker	22.2	10.3	0.0	11.1
Salesman, clerk	0.0	0.0	0.0	2.8
Public official	0.0	5.1	7.7	0.0
Professional	11.1	15.4	3.8	5.6
Owner, business	44.4	43.6	76.9	61.1
Executive	0.0	7.7	3.8	0.0
Total, business and professional	55.5	66.7	84.5	65.3
Owner, big business	16.7	17.9	50.0	33.3
Total cases (= 100%)	18	39	26	36

Table 12
Auto Leaders, 1890–1930: Career Background and Type of Company

Previous Career	Lower-Class (%)	Middle-Class (%)	Upper-Class (%)	Absentee-Owned (%)
Worker	15.2	2.6	0.0	9.0
Clerk	12.1	2.6	0.0	0.0
Sales	3.0	10.3	4.7	4.5
Student only	6.1	7.7	2.3	1.5
Professional	12.1	16.7	14.0	10.4
Owner, business	15.2	37.2	46.5	43.3
Executive	36.4	23.1	32.6	31.3
Total business and professional	63.7	77.0	93.1	85.0
Owner, big business	12.1	16.7	37.2	23.9
Total cases (= 100%)	33	78	43	67

Table 13
Auto Leaders, 1890–1930: Education and Type of Company

Highest Level	Lower-Class (%)	Middle-Class (%)	Upper-Class (%)	Absentee-Owned (%)
Public school[a]	60.0	40.0	28.9	39.6
Preparatory school	3.3	0.0	5.3	5.7
Business college	13.3	3.1	2.6	3.8
College[b]	23.3	55.4	60.5	50.9
Other	0.0	1.5	2.6	0.0
Total cases (= 100%)	30	65	38	53

[a] Includes high school.   [b] Includes nongraduates.

Table 14
Auto Leaders, 1890–1930: Arrival in Detroit and Type of Company

Date	Lower-Class (%)	Middle-Class (%)	Upper-Class (%)	Absentee-Owned (%)
Before 1891	36.4	30.6	48.8	11.9
1891–1900	15.2	9.4	7.0	1.5
1901–1905	15.2	3.5	11.6	1.5
1906–1910	12.1	28.2	11.6	9.0
1911–1915	12.1	3.5	7.0	16.4
1916–1930	3.0	3.5	7.0	13.4
Before 1901	51.5	40.0	55.8	13.4
Before 1906	66.7	43.5	67.4	14.9
Total cases (= 100%)	33	85	43	67

Note: The figures include those born in the city. The columns do not add up to 100 percent because not all leaders moved to Detroit.

Chapter Two

Detroit's Upper Class Creates an Industry

■ Although Detroiters would eventually have cause to rue their penchant for conspicuous production, it at first worked to their advantage. It helped them to overtake the head start enjoyed by cities with better access to commercial information and hence to technological innovation. Detroit, although ranked thirteenth in population in 1900, was, Webb Waldron reported, a rather "sleepy, middle-western city" with underdeveloped commercial and financial functions. It had once been the principal entrepôt for the upper Great Lakes, but its trading territory had contracted steadily from the 1850s on as the railroads diverted business to Chicago and to other communities located on the main east-west trunk lines. Stranded on the international boundary sixty miles to the north of them, Detroit became increasingly peripheral to interregional trade, and by 1900 its port had slipped to seventeenth place among those on the Great Lakes. According to historian Melvin Holli, the city's "trade preeminence has long vanished" by the time automobiles appeared on the scene. Urban ecologists Beverly Duncan and Stanley Lieberson have also calculated that its banks were of "little more than local significance." Together they formed the nation's thirteenth largest clearinghouse, yet their activities—like those of Detroit's mercantile firms—rarely extended beyond the eastern half of the lower Michigan peninsula, for even within their home state they faced strong competition from businessmen in Chicago, Cleveland, and the Atlantic seaports.[1]

It is not surprising, then, that Detroit's economic elite were not fast off the mark when it came to entering the automobile industry. The city did not even see its first automobile until 1896, ten years after Daimler and Benz had built prototypes in Germany. By the time Charles B. King and Henry Ford had assembled the first two cars to drive the streets of the Motor City—in March and June 1896, respectively—Chicago, the regional metropolis, had already hosted an automobile race; and the *American Machinist* was instructing people, Henry Ford among them, on how to build a horseless carriage at home in their spare time.[2]

Even by midwestern standards, Detroit and Michigan were slow to take up automobile manufacturing. The 1900 (twelfth) U.S. census found only one motor vehicle producer in Michigan, the Olds Motor Works of Detroit and Lansing, whose output it could not reveal for reasons of confidentiality. Michigan thus went on record as having produced none of the 3,901 automobiles manufactured that year in the United States. The leading states in order were Massachusetts, Connecticut, Illinois, New York, New Jersey, Ohio, and Pennsylvania: that is, states enjoying the best communications links with the centers of technological innovation in Europe and New England.[3]

By 1904, however, Michigan had established itself as the leading automotive state, and the following year Detroit was the single most important production center, both in quantity of output and in number of factories. By then, three of the nation's four largest firms—Cadillac, Ford, and Olds—were manufacturing cars in the Motor City. Neither the city nor the state could have achieved such success had they not previously developed the necessary financial and technical expertise. Clearly, it helped that Detroit already had a diversified industrial base: in 1900 the census required 107 headings to categorize the city's manufactures. Many of these firms provided the skilled workers and production experience needed by the new industry; in addition to the obvious—the makers of carriages, bicycles, and gasoline engines for marine and farm use—there were also a host of machine shops and foundries capable of manufacturing auto parts and accessories upon demand. Still, as automotive historians have pointed out, these factories were a necessary but not a sufficient cause for the industry's concentration, for several other locations in the northeast quadrant of the country had comparable assets.[4]

Indeed, cities like Chicago, Pittsburgh, and Cleveland probably offered superior access to consumers as well as local sources of primary and secondary steel. Detroit, remarkably, did not have a single blast furnace in its vicinity at the turn of the century. The city and state did have one advantage, however, and that was their pricing policy. Although data are not available for individual cities, it appears that Michigan companies produced the cheapest motorcars in 1904. Table 15, compiled by G. K. Jarvis from the U.S. *Census of Manufactures*, demonstrates that Michigan automobiles

Table 15
Automobile Production by State, 1904

	Automobiles Produced (#)	Value per Auto ($)	Salaries/ Wages per Auto ($)
California	12	1,134	1,244
Connecticut	832	2,354	1,046
Illinois	205	1,281	618
Indiana	1,020	1,400	546
Massachusetts	2,365	868	310
Michigan	9,125	718	127
New Jersey	51	1,400	1,058
New York	1,808	1,699	718
Ohio	2,808	1,851	565
Pennsylvania	963	1,178	448
Wisconsin	2,390	777	148
All others	113	1,334	801

Source: George Kirkham Jarvis, "The Diffusion of the Automobile in the United States: 1895–1969" (Ph.D. diss., University of Michigan, 1972), 66–67.

had a lower unit value than did those of any other state; in fact, only Wisconsin and Massachusetts came within 50 percent of the Michigan average. Michigan's low prices are best explained by the internal economies of scale achieved by the state's twenty-two automobile companies as they churned out two-fifths of the nation's motor vehicles in 1904. Quantity production gave them a significant advantage in unit labor costs, as Table 15 attests.[5]

Quantity production was possible, as Jarvis has remarked, only because Michigan's manufacturers were originally oriented "toward the mass market rather than the luxury market." At $718, the typical Michigan automobile of 1904 hovered just above the lowest price-class. Given the industry's inexperience in manufacturing automobiles, as well as the relatively low production levels even in Michigan firms, there was only one way to build a car for this price, and that was to offer an outmoded design using obsolete technology.[6]

In other words, one had to build a runabout, a two-seater, which in most instances amounted to a horseless carriage with an engine mounted underneath. Of light, flimsy construction, it was not suitable for use on the rutted highways of the day. Its main competitor, known as a touring car, was much more expensive to produce, especially if it offered all the design features then available in Europe. It was larger, seating four or more, and had a more powerful engine hidden under a hood in front. In short, it looked more like a "real car" than did the runabout; and buyers placed a premium on it. It proved impossible, however, to produce a four-cylinder touring car of standard design for less than $2,000 before 1907. Accordingly, in 1904 touring cars accounted for only 33 percent of American auto production, as opposed to 56 percent for runabouts (the rest comprised a variety of types, some of them commercial).[7]

In 1904, 71 percent of Michigan's production consisted of runabouts, and only the manufacturers of Wisconsin were more committed to building them. The cheap runabout, selling for $650 to $750, accounted for the success of Michigan's automobile industry. Certainly, it powered the meteoric rise of Detroit firms like Olds, Cadillac, and Ford. The latter two eventually became quite innovative (as in Cadillac's introduction of the electric starter and Ford's utilization of vanadium steel), but in 1904 they owed their ascendancy to their success in perfecting an outmoded technology.[8]

Ironically, Detroit's manufacturers seem to have benefited from their own provinciality, as well as that of many of their customers. There was still confusion in more backward regions as to the future direction of automotive design, even though it was apparent to the knowledgeable by 1902 that the touring car would prevail in America, as it had already done in France. The 1905 auto shows demonstrated that the touring car of French design had become the American standard, and the market for runabouts collapsed. Had Detroit ranked higher in the urban hierarchy and had it enjoyed better access to the latest technical and sales intelligence, it is questionable whether its most astute entrepreneurs—the founders of Cadillac, Olds, and Ford—would have staked their capital and reputations on the ephemeral runabout.[9]

Nevertheless, while it lasted, the runabout powered Detroit's rise to the top of the automotive industry, and it was this vehicle that taught local producers the profitability of quantity production for the low and middle price-classes; they appear to have turned their own technological backwardness (and that of their customers) to advantage. Thus Detroit's experience during the first decade of the automotive revolution seems to affirm the contention of Jane Jacobs in *Cities and the Wealth of Nations*, that backward cities develop by trading with other backward cities.[10]

It was not, of course, the runabout's outmoded design that recommended it to either Detroit's manufacturers or their customers but rather its price tag. The single most important factor in Detroit's automotive rise was probably the original choice of price-class. The dynamics of conspicuous production guaranteed that a midwestern city like Detroit would be the one to dominate the low-price market. As historians have noted, the price of automobiles fell steadily as the center of automotive production moved westward. Companies tended to serve the local rich; and eastern firms, though they often had the advantage of priority, had as well the disadvantage of serving the nation's wealthiest elite. The "smart set" in New York City and the vacationers at Newport established the market, and they preferred the latest French fashions. In 1904, imports like Panhard-Levassor, Renault, Darracq, and Clement-Bayard cost between $6,000 and $8,500, which meant that an American company could create a reasonable facsimile, charge half the price, and still find itself in the upper price-class.[11]

However, cars that seemed a bargain on Park Avenue were too expensive for most midwestern businessmen, so the companies that formed to serve them typically opted for a lower price-class, even companies organized by the local elite of the midwestern cities. After all, the midwestern elites belonged to two distinct status systems, local and national. Their original market placement reflected their ranking in the national business and social hierarchies. That is, the elite of a provincial center like Detroit could afford to enter the auto industry in the middle but not at the top of the price-class pyramid; the luxury market required considerably more capital, as companies were expected to do more of their own parts production as well as to open their own distribution outlets. As a result, we find that it was Detroit's pre-automotive elite who organized the city's first entries into the automotive game and who accordingly fixed the city's initial orientation toward the lower end of the market.[12]

Had Detroit's old families persevered with this strategy, they might easily have achieved control of the automobile industry, and Cadillac and Oldsmobile would have remained Ford's main rivals. But the price of these two makes—and others—soared, as the same social dynamics that enabled Detroit's elite originally to undersell their eastern competitors impelled them later to seek a price-class more congruent with their own position in the *local* status hierarchy. In other words, Detroit's manufacturers were constantly abandoning their price-class; what kept the city ahead in the lower end of the market was a succession of new entrants as well as the singular persistence of the Ford Motor Company.

■ 1   The abandonments came after 1904. Until then, it was Detroit's business elite who determined that the city's automotive industry would concentrate on the mass market. The elite did not act as a group but rather as individual investors. Only a minority appear to have become early "automotive leaders," that is, executives, directors, or principal investors in a Michigan automobile company. Thus only 17 percent of the individuals identified by the historian Olivier Zunz as the "leaders of Detroit's industrialization" in 1900 (the president or sole owner of a manufacturing firm employing 100 or more workers) became automotive leaders before 1914. Even when their sons and sons-in-law are considered, family involvement still reached only 26 percent. Similarly, only 9 percent of the individuals listed in the *World Almanac* of 1902 as Detroit's millionaires (and 27 percent of their sons and sons-in-law) became automotive leaders before 1914, or 36 percent overall—a higher figure, as expected of such a wealthy group, but still a minority.[13]

It was only among the city's most powerful capitalists that majority participation occurred. There were twenty-one individuals, representing sixteen different families (see Table 16), who held two or more directorships in the city's eight leading financial institutions between 1899 and 1902. At least 57 percent of this financial elite and 76 percent of their families became major stockholders in one or more Detroit automobile firms before 1914.

Table 16
Financial Elite, 1899–1902: Business Interests

	Nonfinancial Interests, 1900	Automotive Interests before 1914
Barbour, G. H.	stoves	Paige, Lozier
Book, J. B.	real estate	Wayne, E-M-F
DuCharme, C. A.	stoves	Packard
Elliott, W. H.	wholesaling	
Ferry, D. M., Sr.	seeds, real estate	Packard[a]
Flinn, E. H.	law, real estate	
Hecker, F. J.	RR cars, lumber	Detroit Auto
Hendrie, George	real estate, RRs, cartage, traction	
Ledyard, H. B.	RRs, law	Olds
McMillan, Hugh	RR cars, shipping	
McMillan, James	RR cars, shipping, seed, utilities	Packard[a]
McMillan, P. H.	law, RR cars	Packard
McMillan, W. C.	RR cars, shipping	Detroit Auto
Miller, S. D.	law	Reliance[a]
Newberry, T. H.	RR cars, shipping	Packard
Palms, C. L.	stoves, real estate	Wayne, E-M-F
Russel, Henry	law, RRs, real estate	Olds
Seyburn, S. Y.	real estate	
Standish, J. D.	meat-packing	Lozier
White, A. E. F.	paint, seeds	Cadillac
White, H. K.	paint, seeds	King[a]

Sources: Michigan, Report of the Commissioner of Banking for 1900 and 1903, BHC.
[a] Actual investment made by son.
Note: The McMillans, Whites, and Palms–Books constitute three distinct families.

Even within Detroit's business circles, equality of opportunity did not prevail. The financial elite were clearly the group most likely to take a leadership role in the early auto industry. Moreover, the financial elite themselves were, as Table 16 indicates, rather narrowly recruited: of the twenty-one bank directors, fifteen—or 71 percent—were engaged in the provision of stoves, seed grain, or railroad supplies and services. Real estate speculation, either in Detroit itself or in the state's timber and mineral lands, seems to have been the only other major track to financial power in Detroit as of 1900.

The table also reveals the importance of being a member of the McMillan family: Senator James McMillan, his sons Philip and William, and his brother Hugh all held multiple directorships. In addition, the family had representation on the boards of five of the nine largest financial institutions.

In 1910, the *Michigan Manufacturer* described Senator McMillan, by then deceased, as "unquestionably the greatest individual influence in the making of Detroit into a manufacturing city." Olivier Zunz has judged him "the most influential businessman in late nineteenth-century Detroit." Any attempt to understand the composition of Detroit's financial elite at the turn of the century must start with Senator James McMillan. The son of a Canadian railroad entrepreneur, he first came to Detroit in 1855 at age seventeen and through his father's connections signed on as purchasing agent for the Grand Haven Railroad. His most important move came in 1863 when he formed a partnership with an admiralty court attorney, John S. Newberry, an heir to the Walter Newberry estate of Chicago. They worked as a team until John Newberry's death in 1887, accumulating in the process several million dollars in profits from investments in railroad car manufacturing, railroading, public utility promotion, steamship operations, shipbuilding, foundries, forges, seed grain, and banking. Both men translated economic power into social and political leadership: Newberry served a term in Congress, and McMillan built a political machine strong enough to make him United States senator and state "boss" from 1889 until his death in 1902.[14]

Railroad-car manufacturing had been the original inspiration for partnership, and it remained as late as 1899 the keystone of the economic empire assembled by the two men and their heirs. Their original firm, the Michigan Car Company, had merged with Peninsular Car in 1892, and the resulting combine ranked as Detroit's largest employer and single most highly capitalized operation until its absorption by American Car and Foundry in 1899. The merger had the great advantage of creating a community of interest between Senator McMillan and his chief political rival, General Russell Alger, a former governor of Michigan and quondam presidential aspirant who coveted McMillan's Senate seat. A self-made millionaire in the lumber industry, Alger had bankrolled two railroad men, Charles Freer and Frank J. Hecker, when they organized Peninsular Car in 1880. That made Alger a competitor for McMillan in business as well as politics. The merger mitigated their rivalry, however, and Alger settled for the post of secretary of war between 1897 and 1899, before succeeding McMillan in the Senate.[15]

Remaining officially outside the railroad-car combine was Russel Wheel & Foundry, a manufacturer of logging cars since its founding in 1877. It too, however, enjoyed a community of interest with the McMillan coterie, since owners Henry and George Russel were allied with the senator in several business ventures. George, for example, was president and presumably principal stockholder of the city's largest bank, the State Savings Bank, which had been organized by John Newberry and James McMillan in 1883. At the turn of the century it functioned virtually as an adjunct of the railroad-car industry. George Russel had also joined with Senator McMillan in incorporating the Citizens' Street Railway Company in 1891 and Detroit's gas company in 1892. Henry Russel, a member of the financial elite at the turn of the century, had served since 1880 as vice-president and chief counsel for the Michigan Central Railroad. His interests conjoined those of Senator McMillan in the telephone business—they collaborated with the other railroad-car magnates and the Bell system to put together the Michigan State Telephone Company in 1900—and in the steam radiator business. The Russel family had invested in Detroit Steam Radiator, a company organized in 1882 by Henry and Charles Hodges with home heating in mind. In 1891 Senator McMillan helped arrange its merger with a company of his own, Michigan Radiator, plus another in Buffalo to create American Radiator Company, the "largest manufacturer of steam radiators and hot water boilers in the world" at the turn of the century.[16]

The McMillan coterie, obviously, was not limited to railroad-car manufacturers, though they did provide its core. After the death of John Newberry, its most prominent member—aside from the senator himself—was probably Dexter M. Ferry, the seed producer. He had been in business since the 1850s, distributing and then growing seed for local farmers and truck gardeners; by 1879, with the help of financial backers (C. C. Bowen and brothers H. Kirke White and Albert White, both of whom were numbered among the financial elite in 1899–1902), he had driven his main competition, the Detroit Seed Company, to seek a merger. It was, of course, owned by McMillan and Newberry, and thereafter the senator and Ferry operated as close partners in business and politics. Ferry had invested heavily in bank stocks and sat on three of the eight most important bank boards at the turn of the century, where he played a key role in finding financing for McMillan's business deals. He also acted as the senator's chief political lieutenant, succeeding him as chairman of the Republican State Central Committee in 1896.[17]

McMillan's clique was extremely powerful in the 1890s. Only a few of its multifarious activities have been highlighted here. For example, the group also organized or absorbed a host of forges and foundries—producing malleable iron and castings, copper and brass fittings, engines and moving machinery—in their pursuit of vertical integration. Interest in transportation equipment plus expertise in the metal trades, added to financial power, made McMillan and his colleagues the natural sponsors of Detroit's automotive revolution; they played a key role in launching Cadillac, Packard, and the Olds Motor Works. The Ford Motor Company also indirectly benefited from their financial support.

There were few capitalists in Detroit at the turn of the century who did not have some link—usually of dependence—to James McMillan, Dexter M. Ferry, Russell Alger, or George and Henry Russel. Among the financial elite listed in Table 16, two-thirds seem to have been business or political associates of at least one of the railroad-car magnates. In addition to those already named, these included William Elliott, one of McMillan's closest political allies, and three men who had joined McMillan in his street railway ventures: Sidney D. Miller, George Hendrie, and Henry B. Ledyard. Ledyard, also president of the Michigan Central Railroad and a director of two McMillan-dominated banks, seems to have had especially close ties to the McMillan alliance.[18]

What about the one-third of the financial elite who avoided being captured by the gravitational pull of the senator's economic and political influence? What was the source of their wealth and power? Stoves and timberland seem to be the answer. In 1897 five major stove companies, turning out 165,000 stoves a year, made Detroit the stove capital of the United States. The city's second most powerful concentration of capital, stove manufacturing was dominated by a dozen or so families through interlocking boards of directors. The Dwyer brothers, Jeremiah and James, had organized all three of the leading producers; and by the 1890s the Barbour family had gained control over the two largest, Michigan Stove and the Detroit Stove

Works. Judging from their continuity on the boards of these two firms, important investments must also have been made by Francis Palms, Merrill I. Mills, and Charles DuCharme.[19]

The stovemaking families provided three members for the financial elite of 1899–1902: George H. Barbour, Charles L. Palms, and Charles A. DuCharme. They were also the only group, other than the railroad-car manufacturers, to control one of the eight leading banks—People's Savings Bank, the third largest. Since other banks mirrored the mixed base of the city's economy, the stove families came closest of all Detroit's capitalists to achieving independence from the McMillan alliance. They were responsible for three firms that helped to make Detroit the Motor City: Northern, Wayne, and E-M-F.[20]

By now, having mentioned every important automobile company active in Detroit before 1906, I may have given the impression that the railroad-car and stove manufacturers provided almost all the capital required by the industry during its perilous infancy. There was a third source of capital, however, just as there was a third major component in Detroit's financial elite at the turn of the century—the natural resource and land development sector. As Melvin Holli has pointed out, Detroit had little in the way of secondary industry before 1880. As a result, most of the city's nineteenth-century fortunes were accumulated in commerce, railroading, and the exploitation of the state's natural resources. Particularly important had been copper mining and smelting, lumbering and sawmilling, and the land speculation that these promoted. Michigan's pinelands underwrote the membership of at least four individuals within the city's financial elite of 1899–1902: Elisha H. Flinn, Stephen Seyburn, and two brothers-in-law, Dr. James B. Book and Charles L. Palms, both heirs of Francis Palms, who—in addition to his investments in stovemaking—speculated heavily in the pinelands of Michigan, Wisconsin, and Ontario. According to Silas Farmer, a local historian and his contemporary, Palms was "possibly the largest landowner in the United States" before he started selling off his acreage to lumber companies and reinvesting his profits in smaller but more lucrative plots in downtown Detroit. At his death in 1886 his estate was valued at $21 million, and it probably remained the wealthiest in Michigan at century's end. Not all the timber and mining fortunes in Detroit were made so speculatively—some of the city's millionaires had actually supervised the mining of copper and the cutting of timber—but these activities seem to have been less conducive to membership within the financial elite, perhaps because they entailed long absences from Detroit. Even so, a considerable amount of money flowed from the state's mines and forests into the coffers of such pioneer automotive firms as Cadillac and Olds.[21]

The gradually lengthening list of investors in pre-1905 Detroit automotive industry includes bankers, railroad-car and stove manufacturers, railroaders, mine owners, lumbermen, and land speculators. At first glance this may seem quite an inclusive group. Yet it omitted most Detroit businessmen, for the city in 1900 had a far more diversified economy than would be suspected by looking at either the financial elite or at the investors in the early automobile industry. Beverly Duncan and Stanley Lieberson have concluded that Detroit possessed a high number of manufacturing "specialties" in 1900. In nineteen branches of manufacture, they calculated, "the proportion of local workers engaged in industry" in Detroit was "at least double the corresponding proportion in the national work force." By this criterion, only five of the fifteen largest cities had more diversified industrial sectors. Most of Detroit's specialties admittedly did not bulk very large in the local economy, but seven did rank as important employers: druggists' preparations, steam fittings and heating apparatus, foundry and machine shop products, printing and publishing, matches, furniture, and men's clothing.[22]

So diversified was the Detroit economy by 1900 that there is still some doubt as to which industry offered the most employment. Silas Farmer, writing in 1899, deemed railroad-car manufacturing the city's most important employer with about one-seventh of the industrial labor force. He may well have been right: the largest single employer in the city was American Car & Foundry with 2,200 workers on its payroll in 1900. Olivier Zunz, however, on the basis of the twelfth U.S. census, has placed the foundry and machine sector first, followed by clothing and related businesses, and then the construction trades. His ranking, featured in Table 17, would obviously require some adjustment were *all* the manufacturers of Detroit to be included in the data. Several companies, including American Car & Foundry, had to be omitted from the census schedules: their size precluded full reporting to the public for fear of disclosing individual operations. Table 17 should, therefore, be interpreted mainly as an index of the city's economic diversity, for no category apparently occupied more than a seventh of the workers it counted.[23]

The data reveal the extent to which diversity was the most conspicuous aspect of Detroit's industrial life in 1900. As Melvin Holli has observed, "No single industry marked the city's manufacturing or gave it a special character." Even so, some obviously counted

Table 17
Mechanical and Manufacturing Industries in Detroit, 1900

Industrial Sector	Number of Establishments	Number of Employees
Foundry and machine shop	74	6,544
Clothing and related	585	6,359
Construction	505	4,649
Tobacco	192	4,037
Lumber and related	137	3,411
Food and beverages	284	2,952
Printing and publishing	136	2,277
Druggists' preparations	9	2,155
Iron and steel	12	1,630
Transportation and related	139	838
Total	2,847	45,707

Sources: Olivier Zunz, *The Changing Face of Inequality: Urbanization, Industrial Development, and Immigrants in Detroit, 1880–1920* (Chicago, 1982), 98; U.S. Department of the Interior Census Office, *Twelfth Census of the United States, 1900: Abstract* (Washington, D.C., 1902), 357.

more than others in the allocation of economic and political power. The financial elite excluded most of the light industries (tobacco, matches, shoes, and the like), as well as the city's merchants and brokers. Each of these activities produced its millionaires, and many of them would show up in our list of the financially powerful were it expanded to include the directors of the smaller banks. Yet they did not belong to the inner circle: that was reserved for the stove and railroad-car manufacturers, their banking allies, and—as Holli noted—the "real estate speculators and lumber barons."[24]

It was members of this inner group who founded Detroit's automobile industry. Only two companies significantly breached their monopoly before 1905, and both—Ford and Maxwell-Briscoe— were exceptions clearly proving the rule that it was nearly impossible for anyone but the city's financial elite to master the first stage of Detroit's automotive revolution. We would anticipate that the companies founded by the financial elite, especially those controlled by Senator McMillan's associates, would incline toward producing cars for the upper class: that is, for their own kind. Let us now turn to the companies they created in order to ascertain whether the forces of conspicuous production were at work in Detroit from the beginning.

■ 2   Detroit's automotive saga properly begins with the Olds Motor Works, for it not only initiated the local motor vehicle industry but was also the first to prove it a bonanza. Between 1899 and 1903 Olds paid cash dividends of 105 percent *and* raised its capital (through reinvested profits) from $350,000 to $2,000,000. These figures convinced the skeptics, and in the early years of the twentieth century the wealthy of Detroit were scrambling to stake out a share of the new industry.[25]

Although Ransom E. Olds has traditionally received most of the credit for the success of the company and the make bearing his name, research by George S. May suggests that a copper magnate, Samuel L. Smith, actually did more to ensure their survival. As May notes, in a sympathetic biography of Olds, "It was Smith's money and contacts that finally put the Olds horseless carriage operation on its feet and in a new position, the future Motor City." Smith had made his fortune by investing in copper properties in Michigan's Upper Peninsula in the 1860s, his master stroke coming in 1866 when he bought land—adjacent to the Calumet and Hecla mine— atop the world's richest copper lode. Smith eventually organized half a dozen mining companies and in the 1870s branched out into railroad and canal construction in the Upper Peninsula. The following decade he settled in Lansing, the state capital, where he became an associate of Edward Sparrow in several banking and real estate ventures. Though Smith retired to Detroit in the 1890s, the economic interests of the two men remained entangled; and it was probably Sparrow who introduced the copper magnate to Ransom E. Olds, the proprietor of a small gasoline engine business in Lansing and the designer and builder, in August 1896, of that city's first gasoline-powered motor carriage.[26]

Olds lacked sufficient capital to commence production. To attract it, he publicized his vehicle widely and drove around town to show it off to the local gentry. Sparrow finally bit, and in August 1897 he and his friends put up $10,000—enough to buy 48 percent of the voting stock in the newly incorporated Olds Motor Vehicle Company. Smith, who probably invested $2,000, took 10 percent of the shares, his first stake in what he hoped would become another bonanza. Later that same year the new partners bought into Olds's engine works, and over the next few years its profits kept them interested in Ransom Olds's experiments. The automobile company, however, limped along, producing only four cars in 1897–1898. Like most of the pioneer automotive firms, it seemed too anemic to survive. A transfusion of $200,000 in additional capital, however, rescued it from a lingering death in April 1899. The money came from Smith, reportedly because he hoped to find a business in which his sons Frederic and Angus could stake out careers of their own. However, as May has wryly remarked, Samuel Smith had not become a millionaire by letting "family sentiment" outweigh his business sense; it was, accordingly, his desire to gain a larger share of the profitable engine works that prompted the refinancing and merger of the Olds operations. The Olds Motor Works, incorporated May 8 to effect the merger, distributed 12,710 of its 35,000 shares to the Smiths, who became its largest stockholders.[27]

Lansing residents took most of the remaining stock, but 2,500 shares went to four Detroiters: Henry and George H. Russel, Henry B. Ledyard, and Henry M. Campbell. The first three we have already identified as members of the city's dominant business clique, with Henry Russel and Ledyard ranking among the financial elite, and George Russel—the immediate past president of the American Bankers Association—a de facto member. Henry M. Campbell also belonged to the railroad-car group. A son of Michigan's most eminent nineteenth-century jurist, Campbell was Henry Russel's law partner as well as counsel for several major firms, including the Union Trust, one of Detroit's eight major financial institutions, and one that was in 1899 (with Dexter M. Ferry its president, William C. McMillan its vice-president, and James and Hugh McMillan also on its board of directors) clearly a McMillan satrapy. Altogether, Detroiters owned 43 percent of Olds stock, held two-thirds of the executive positions, and obviously dominated the motor company. Less than a week after its incorporation, it purchased five acres on the Detroit waterfront, erected there an assembly plant, and by year's end moved its headquarters as well.[28]

During 1900 the company experimented with eleven models, ranging in price from $1,200 to $2,750, the auto division losing $80,000 in the process. By autumn it concluded that success required greater specialization, that "it would be necessary to throw away all the patterns and commence anew and devote [its] whole energy to one style and finish." Ransom Olds suggested building "a small low down runabout" to sell in the $500 to $650 price bracket. "My whole idea," he later recalled, "was to have the operation so simple that anyone could run it and the construction such that it could be repaired at any local shop." In October he completed and tested a runabout, the first curved-dash Oldsmobile, and it soon went into quantity production. It caught the public's fancy, selling 400 the first year, 2,500 the next, 4,000 in 1903, 5,500 in 1904, and 6,500—its peak—in 1905. During those last three years Olds led the nation in auto sales.[29] Its market mastery of the lower price-class did not go uncontested, but most of its competitors did not have its financial resources and manufacturing experience. Those that did, notably Locomobile and Autocar, "soon abandoned the low-priced field for the production of bigger, more expensive models." This was a path soon taken by Olds itself, with disastrous consequences. But for the moment Ransom Olds was able, thanks to the self-evident profitability of the curved-dash runabout, to constrain whatever impulse his wealthy associates might have felt toward conspicuous display.[30]

By January 1904, however, he had been forced out of the company, his restraining influence removed. The seeds of his departure had been sown during a fire that gutted the Olds factory in March 1901. After shopping around for the best offer, the company resolved to move its home base back to Lansing. But because a scarcity of housing made it impossible to shift the entire business there, the company "decided to rebuild its plant in Detroit and operate it in conjunction with its new facilities in Lansing." It remained in Detroit until 1905 with Frederic L. Smith acting as local plant manager. Smith, a novice in industry, had at first deferred to Ransom Olds. But as he became increasingly involved in the manufacturing end of the business, he began to challenge Olds's credentials and—after two years of bickering over models, standards, and quality control—asserted the prerogative of ownership. Ransom Olds joined the unemployed.[31]

They argued chiefly over model policy. George May has concluded on the basis of their correspondence that this dispute did not itself precipitate Olds's departure, but there is little doubt that it poisoned relations between the two executives. Each adopted the posture that a theory of conspicuous production would predict: Smith, by far the wealthier of the two, advocated a heavier, more powerful—and more expensive—touring car to replace the curved-dash runabout, whose days he saw as numbered. He and Henry Russel, who complained that the "important and intelligent businessmen in Detroit" (presumably the McMillan crowd) considered the Oldsmobile "a cheap machine" unlikely to create permanent "good will for the business," became increasingly convinced that Ransom Olds, committed to the runabout, was dragging his feet on the new model. They were probably correct, for Olds published an article in the *Detroit News* in February 1903 confirming his preference for a cheap, lightweight car while decrying the efforts of some American manufacturers to make "the automobile, the child of luxury, instead of the child of necessity."[32]

May tends to discount the significance of this rhetoric, pointing out that Ransom Olds, when he organized the Reo Motor Car Company in mid-1904, opted to build the very car he had earlier disparaged. He apparently no longer thought a $1,250 touring car a luxury, and he featured it in his advertising, even though for a time he also offered a runabout. The strategy worked at first: Reo ranked among the industry's top ten producers between 1905 and 1915 before commencing its long slide into bankruptcy and abandonment of the passenger car business in 1936. However, Ransom Olds never returned to the low-priced field, having "lost the urge," as his biographer put it, "to make a determined bid for a share of the cheap car market." In other words, the medium price-class more accurately reflected the *Weltanschauung* of an individual who, with his second automobile company, had become a millionaire proprietor and Lansing's most prominent citizen.[33]

Oldsmobile was still producing some runabouts as late as 1907, but the emphasis had shifted to four-passenger, four-cylinder touring cars. At first, these were modestly priced—perhaps reflecting Ransom Olds's contribution to their development—but in 1907 Fred Smith hitched the company's fate to a cumbersome four-cylinder touring car selling for $2,250. He was closer now to building cars for his social and economic peers but also closer to bank-ruptcy, for the "shift from the production of low-priced vehicles to high-priced, high-powered ones," as May has remarked, "apparently came too fast for the public," and sales plummeted. Smith "allowed his obvious enthusiasm for the bigger cars to cloud his judgement of what the public was prepared to buy."[34]

It was a common error; most of the automotive manufacturers, it seems, allowed social values to obscure their vision. In any case, the new class strategy cost the company money, and S. L. Smith was compelled to advance another million dollars to keep it afloat. Even then, it would probably have gone under had not General Motors rescued it in November 1908. Organized just two months before, GM needed a "name" company to add luster to its own reputa-tion and so was willing to bail out the Smiths by paying $3.04 million (all but $17,000 of it in GM stock) for the Olds factories and the Oldsmobile trademark. The name thus survived, but Olds-mobile would never again be the sales leader.[35]

■ 3   Although it failed to learn from its own exam-ple, Olds taught the rest of the Detroit auto industry, as Christy Borth remarked in 1954, that big profits could be made from the "mass distribution of a moderately-priced, easily operable, readily-serviceable transport tool" and thus prepared the way for Ford, Chevrolet, and Plymouth. More important, its early success gave heart to the financial elite, keeping them interested in the auto industry at a time when their other companies—including Packard and Cadillac—seemed to be foundering. By persevering, they assured Detroit's eventual automotive supremacy.[36]

Packard, the most patrician of Detroit's automobile firms, traced its origins to the experiments of James W. Packard, a prosperous manufacturer of electrical appliances in Warren, Ohio. In 1899 he designed a one-seat, one-cylinder motor buggy with wire wheels. To manufacture it, Packard organized the Ohio Automobile Com-pany on September 10, 1900, with an announced capitalization of $250,000, of which only $10,000 actually went into the corporate treasury.[37]

Auto manufacturing required considerably more capital than that, and so Packard welcomed the interest of Henry B. Joy, a Detroit millionaire, in the fledgling enterprise. The latter's father, James F. Joy, had been a prominent railroad attorney and promoter who had for a time occupied the presidency of both the Michigan Central and the Burlington line. In one of his last ventures before his death in 1896, James Joy constructed the Union Depot to serve as the Detroit terminus of the Wabash and Pennsylvania railroads. These ventures brought him into frequent contact with the railroad-car clique, and his family's full admission into the alliance came in 1892 when Henry Joy married Helen Newberry, daughter of Senator McMillan's erstwhile business partner.[38]

Henry Joy had, therefore, no difficulty in finding $25,000 to invest in Packard's company or in locating ten friends willing to put up an additional $225,000. Their names—Richard P. Joy, Truman H. Newberry, John S. Newberry, Jr., Fred Alger, Russell Alger, Jr., Philip McMillan, Dexter M. Ferry, Jr., Charles A. DuCharme, and Joseph Boyer—read like a who's who of Detroit's establishment. With the exception of Boyer, a recent arrival from Saint Louis, the partners belonged to Detroit's most patrician families. Their fathers were the core of the financial elite, the McMillan alliance incarnate. And now the sons, most of them in their mid-thirties, were seeking to extend the scope of the alliance by exploiting the main chance of their own era.[39]

The Detroiters gained control of the Ohio company in October 1902 when it reincorporated as the Packard Motor Car Company and assigned them half the capital stock and a majority on the board of directors. At first they had no intention of assuming command. None of them had any experience with auto manufacturing, and so they were content to elect James W. Packard president and general manager. Joy, however, immediately began to meddle. He deluged Packard with letters, suggestions, adjurations, and proposals that usually read like orders. Packard soon had enough, and when the company moved to Detroit in late 1903, he remained behind to manage his electrical appliance business. He held on to his investment and served as chairman of the board until 1915, but his resignation as general manager in October 1903 effectively ended his active participation in the firm's affairs.[40]

Suddenly bereft of a manager, Joy's colleagues forced him to take the position. "He got us into this scheme," they reasoned. "Let him get us out." Thereafter, until his resignation from the presidency in 1916, Joy ruled the corporation, becoming the "personification of the firm and the automobile." Joy himself noted in 1920: "I never failed during all the years I was connected with Packard to ultimately win the support of the directors for plans of action which might advance the interests and welfare of the corporation . . . except as to financial policy."[41]

Financial control rested securely in the hands of his friends. The second stock issue in 1903 left the Ohio investors with less than 30 percent of the voting stock. In 1910 the corporation went public, selling more than a million dollars' worth of stock on the New York exchange. But in 1920 four families—the Joys, Newberrys, Algers, and McMillans—still held two-thirds of the voting stock and largely dictated its finances from their positions on the board of directors.[42]

■ 4 Packard, car and company, epitomized the patrician, conservative world view of its sponsors. Theirs was a very genteel form of conspicuous production. From James and William Packard the Detroit capitalists had inherited a fine car. The Packard brothers, Arthur Einstein has related, "were not backyard inventors or mechanical inventors or mechanical cranks. . . . The fact that they were well-to-do almost certainly influenced their early concentration on a machine which was well-appointed and as completely reliable as the technology of the time would permit. . . . Cost was secondary to quality." Henry B. Joy continued the policy; under his regime Packard was a "gentlemen's car, built by gentlemen." The company sought an extremely exclusive clientele: its first four-cylinder model, completed in 1903, carried a price tag of $5,000. This proved too rich even for the wealthy blood, and the company lost $200,000. The price then dropped to the $3,500–$4,500 range, where it stayed for the next seventeen years.[43]

Pride hampered Packard's quest for profit. Refusing to "compete on prices," it priced itself out of the mass market. Alvan Macauley, then its president, summed up the company's attitude in 1922 when he wrote a board member that "to be consistent with our history, we must always finish up a job a little better than our closest competitors, and get an extra price for the added attractiveness." On occasion the company tried to break loose from its upper-class strait jacket. In 1918 Truman Newberry told his fellow directors that they "should abandon the so-called Packard policy of supreme excellence and high cost, and get down to brass tacks and produce a vehicle that will compete with the Dodge car." Richard Joy agreed, reminding Macauley that the board was "at least as much interested in making money as in building reputation."[44]

Newberry and Joy had their way: in 1920 the company introduced a six-cylinder model, the "Single Six," lighter and less powerful than earlier offerings. Retailing for $3,000, it was inexpensive by traditional standards, and by mid-decade its sales enabled Packard to overtake Cadillac and Pierce-Arrow to become the nation's leading luxury car manufacturer. But $3,000 was three times the price of a Dodge and more than $1,000 above the company's original target. Try as it might, Packard found it impossible to build a plebeian car.

Richard P. Joy almost immediately regretted the decision to manufacture the Single Six, especially as it forced the company to rely on parts suppliers. "There was a time," he wrote the general counsel in 1921,

> when Packard cars were "made in the Packard shops" in order that the very highest standard of skilled workmanship might be maintained under direct Packard supervision. . . . Today the Packard car is practically an assembled car. . . . I would prefer less earnings and higher quality, believing that policy would bring more lasting prosperity to the Packard company.[45]

Even though they were capitalists, the Joy, Alger, McMillan, and Newberry families tempered their pursuit of profit with aesthetic and class considerations. Standing atop the social pyramid, they refused to risk their hard-earned reputations on shoddy, lower-class merchandise. Just as "dependability" became the catchword at Dodge Brothers and "service" at Ford, "reputation" summed up Packard's self-image. "Reputation," the company claimed,

> is never completely earned. . . . It is always being earned. It is a reward . . . but in a much more profound sense it is a *continuing responsibility*. . . . That which has been accorded a good reputation is forever forbidden to drop below its best. It must ceaselessly strive for higher standards. . . . There is an iron tyranny which compels men who do good work to go on doing good work. The name of that beneficent tyranny is reputation.[46]

Gripped by the "iron tyranny," Packard adopted the most conservative manufacturing and model policies of any of the major producers. As a result, the Packard car looked stodgy, respectable, and slightly old-fashioned—just like the clothing and homes of the American upper class. Reluctant to innovate and unwilling to shed its patrician sensibilities, Packard retreated to the loftiest but smallest corner of the automobile industry. Mass production, and mass profits, it left to those less obsessed with reputation.

■ 5　　　　　　　Cadillac, Packard's main competitor in the luxury market in the 1920s, was also initiated by members of the McMillan clique. It should not surprise us, then, that it ended up in the same price-class. Yet the two companies had strikingly different histories. The Packard investors had been prepared to search far afield in order to find a well-appointed car to their taste: Henry Joy had even scouted New York City before choosing Packard. The Cadillac group, apparently, did not look beyond the boundaries of Detroit and, their options limited, settled for a much more humble vehicle, one that took years to metamorphose into a luxury marque.

Cadillac's story started with the Detroit Automobile Company, which was organized to commercialize a horseless carriage that Henry Ford—then chief engineer for Edison Illuminating Company of Detroit—had been working on since 1896. A farmer's son, Ford had received a broad technical training, first as an apprentice in the James Flower & Brothers Machine Shop and subsequently as a mechanic with Detroit Drydock, Detroit Shipbuilding, and Westinghouse. After supervising a sawmill near the family farm in Dearborn, Michigan, he had joined the electric company in 1891. By the late 1890s he was giving increasing attention to developing a horseless carriage. His skill with engines and his father's friendship with William Maybury, Detroit's mayor, brought him to the attention of the McMillan clique, and Detroit Automobile was incorporated on August 5, 1899. Along with Olds, it established 1899 as the date the automobile industry commenced in Detroit.

Yet Detroit Automobile contributed so little to that industry— making only two cars during its brief life-span—that it would now be totally forgotten had Henry Ford not become involved in two additional companies: the Ford Motor Company and the Henry Ford Company—or Cadillac, as the latter was renamed in 1902. Detroit Automobile was severely hampered by Henry Ford's inexperience as a manufacturer and by its own undercapitalization: its only assets were $15,000 in cash and a prototype designed by Ford. It should have started with more, considering the wealth of its stockholders. They belonged to Senator McMillan's immediate circle and included his son William, whom historian Sidney Olson has described as "the key backer" of the enterprise; Frank Hecker, a partner in the railroad-car business; Frank W. Eddy, a chemical and rubber manufacturer who served as "director of several McMillan-controlled companies"; Safford S. Delano, whose father had been associated with the Newberry and McMillan clans in the railroad-car and steel-parts business since the late 1860s; and Mark Hopkins, a close political ally. Two other investors, Lem W. Bowen and Albert E. F. White, like the senator, were officers and directors of the Ferry seed company. White, Hecker, and William C. McMillan also counted among the financial elite. The most prominent names or fortunes among the other stockholders belonged to William Maybury, the city's mayor; Clarence A. Black, a millionaire from investments in hardware, sugar, salt, banking, and real estate; Frederick S. Osborne, head of Cameron Currie & Company, Detroit's most prestigious brokerage; and William H. Murphy, son of Simon Murphy, a millionaire lumber merchant who was reportedly Detroit's biggest landlord at the turn of the century.[47]

It was an elite group: "No other pioneer automobile company," Sidney Olson has written, "began with backers of such stature, such influence, and so much cash in reserve." But the stockholders, anxious for a quick, speculative return on their investment, refused to give Henry Ford the time or money to perfect his prototype. Frank Hecker gave up first, Fred Strauss (Ford's assistant) later recalled; he "wanted to throw in the sponge. He said everything was going too slow." By the spring of 1900, with $86,000 spent and only one delivery truck built and sold, most of the stockholders were inclined to agree. But William Murphy and Mark Hopkins convinced them to keep the company alive by scaling down expenses and returning to an experimental basis. By November, even this proved too much for the disgusted stockholders, and the company "surrendered its charter and went out of business."[48]

In January 1901 the Detroit Automobile Company was formally dissolved, but Black, Bowen, Hopkins, White, and Murphy, purchasing its assets at the receiver's sale, continued to underwrite Henry Ford, whose experiments now focused on a racing car. On October 10, he bested Alexander Winton, an established manufacturer, in a race staged at the Grosse Pointe track, thus becoming "something of a national celebrity." Hoping to capitalize on this publicity, Ford and his five partners filed papers on November 30 to incorporate the Henry Ford Company with an authorized capital of $60,000, half of it paid in cash. The stock they divided evenly, six ways.[49]

Ford, apparently dissatisfied with the split, concentrated on perfecting his racer rather than on building the commercial model his partners expected. The world's speed record squarely in his sights, he wrote his brother-in-law Milton Bryant that in racing "I expect to make $ where I can't make ¢s at Manufacturing." William Murphy, fearful of another fiasco, ordered Ford's staff to leave the racing car alone. "He told me . . . he would fire me," Oliver Barthel claimed. "If I valued my job, I'd better not do any work on it." When Ford persisted, Murphy resolved to ease him out of the company; he directed the staff to "pay no attention to Henry at all."[50]

Ford got the message and resigned on March 10, 1902, taking with him $900 in cash, his drawings for the racer, his name (the company agreed not to use it), and the resolve "never again to put [himself] under orders." His prospects then looked bleak: he had alienated Detroit's most powerful capitalists (Lem Bowen, the future president of the D. M. Ferry company, vowed "never to ride in a Ford"— a pledge he kept until 1924, the year before his death), and when he sought backing for his third venture in 1903, he found most of the city's doors closed to him. Yet he had profited from his association with Detroit's financial elite: they had paid for his early mistakes, thus allowing him, later, to organize a company without their help. In effect, they had subsidized his march to independence. The Ford Motor Company was the only sizable firm before 1906 to breach the local elite's monopoly over the auto industry. It succeeded, despite a shoestring budget during its first six months, because its product incorporated the results of seven years (since 1896) of costly research. It thereby avoided trial and error and thus beat the financial elite at their own game.[51]

■ 6   The Henry Ford Company became the Cadillac Automobile Company in August 1902 after Ford had resigned and Henry Leland had convinced the remaining four stockholders that he could build a better engine for their car than either Henry Ford or Ransom Olds could. The stockholders originally approached Leland in despair, asking him "to appraise their automobile plant and its equipment" in advance of liquidation. Leland then managed and owned a substantial minority interest in the machine shop of Leland & Faulconer, one of the city's major employers, with 251 people on its payroll in 1900. Since the Olds fire he had been supplying that company with gasoline engines. Applying the techniques of precision engineering he had learned from the New England armories, he trebled the engine's efficiency, making it too powerful for the flimsy Olds runabout. In August 1902, Leland told Murphy and his partners that they were foolish to give up: with the powerplant he had perfected, they could outstrip Olds and beat its prices. When Leland & Faulconer agreed to supply the engine and other machined parts, the four partners changed their minds about quitting. On August 22 they reorganized the Henry Ford Company, raised its capital to $300,000, and changed its name to the Cadillac Automobile Company in honor of Detroit's founder.[52]

Cadillac faltered in 1904, forcing yet another reorganization. Bowen and Murphy told Henry Leland and his son Wilfred that "either you boys will come and run the factory for us, or we will go out of business." They consented; Leland & Faulconer merged with the auto concern; and the combine, now capitalized at $1.5 million, was renamed the Cadillac Motor Car Company. William Murphy emerged as the largest stockholder with 6,600 shares; Albert White, Lem Bowen, and Clarence Black followed with 5,500 each; and William Metzger, Cadillac's first distributor, had 3,000. Henry Leland, receiving 2,500 shares for his holdings in Leland & Faulconer, took charge of production. Clarence Black, the president, frequently patroled the factory, however, to make sure Leland avoided the exotic racing-car bug that overtook Henry Ford.[53]

Cadillac at first offered more competition for Olds than it did for Packard; its main product until 1907 was a one-cylinder runabout for which it charged, depending on the year, between $750 and $850. In other words, it occupied the bottom of the medium-price bracket. Better built than cars twice its price, however, the runabout powered Cadillac to second place in national sales between 1904 and 1906. Even so, the company's "interest was centered in higher-priced cars" from about 1905 onward. That year it introduced a four-cylinder touring car selling for $2,500; in 1906 it staked out a position in the upper-class market with a $3,750 model. The company's profits continued, however, to hinge on the sales of runabouts until 1907 when, with the public increasingly disdainful of one-cylinder makes, these fell off 37 percent. The company itself almost failed, being sustained only by short-term loans underwritten by the personal notes of four directors.[54]

Cadillac surmounted the crisis by transferring its sales effort to four-cylinder models costing about $2,000. In 1909 it discontinued the one-cylinder car. It was clear by then that Cadillac was well on its way to serving its stockholders' social and economic peers. It had negotiated the transition more successfully than had Olds, but the passage had been rough, especially during the nationwide financial panic in the autumn of 1907; and Cadillac's controlling group proved ready to sell when approached by General Motors. On August 20, 1909, GM bought Cadillac for $4.75 million, all but $75,000 of it in cash. Only the Lelands accepted GM stock as partial compensation. Their partners, mindful of the uncertainty of auto manufacturing, demanded full payment in cash. Collecting a clear profit of $4 million, they severed all ties to the industry.[55]

Their departure left Henry Leland, now president, and his son in sole command of the Cadillac organization, for General Motors, then strictly a holding company, allowed its subsidiaries to retain "their corporate and independent operating identities." William Durant, GM's founder, was primarily interested in high finance; he left manufacturing to experts like Henry Leland, whom he told, "I want you to continue to run Cadillac exactly as though it were still your own. You will receive no directions from anyone." To ensure that Durant stuck to his word, Leland put it on the record by issuing a press release: "We have the written assurance of the purchaser that the Cadillac Company will continue to carry on its business as though it were an entirely independent organization. . . . Cadillac standards, Cadillac policies, Cadillac methods . . . will be carried without alteration, and exactly as though the transaction recently consummated had never taken place."[56]

Until they left GM in 1917 the Lelands ruled Cadillac much as they wished. Its product and organization became physical extensions of their biases and ideals. In 1917 the *Detroit News* decided that "the whole factory, the entire business . . . [voiced] the inner convictions of father and son on certain fundamental facts of life."[57] To understand Cadillac's policies it became necessary to understand Henry M. Leland and, through him, his son Wilfred, his alter ego.

Sixty years of age in 1903, Henry Leland belonged to an older generation than most of the automotive pioneers. They inherited the engineering profession; he helped to create it, being a charter member of the American Institute of Weights and Measures, the National Foundries Association, and the Society of Automobile Engineers. A devout Presbyterian, he regarded his profession as a quasi-religious calling, perhaps the twentieth-century equivalent of the old New England ministry. In 1914 he told his fellow automotive engineers that "all the really great achievements which the world enjoys today may justly be placed to the credit of the engineering profession." The builders of ships, bridges, and subways, he said, were the true benefactors of mankind.[58]

Alfred Sloan, Jr., president of General Motors, once remarked of Henry Leland that "quality was his God." More accurately, he regarded it a moral obligation of the manufacturer to his public. Leland almost always thought in absolutes: a product or an idea or a man was either totally "right" or totally "wrong." According to his son, he had an absolute passion to make things "R-I-G-H-T," for "if it is right," he claimed, "then it is perfect." At Cadillac, rightness meant perfect standardization, interchangeability of parts. Leland brought to it his "long production experience in metalworking on a precision basis," gained in the machine shops of New England, where he had learned to machine to tolerances of one millionth of an inch. He set the same standards for the automobile, Cadillac becoming the first car company to use the Johannson gauges and to banish files from its assembly room: a part was made "right" the first time or it was discarded.[59]

Cadillac's emphasis on precision engineering paid immediate

dividends: in 1908 it won the Dewar Trophy, donated by the Royal Automobile Club, by proving it could dismantle three of its cars, scramble their parts, reassemble them, and then complete a distance run. It never forgot this victory; years later, long after Leland's departure, it reminded the public that Cadillac was "First to produce a standardized car, a car in which all parts are exact duplicates of other parts of the same kind." It called itself the "Standard of the World," the firm where "Craftsmanship [was] a Creed and Accuracy a Law."[60]

Leland's emphasis on quality and engineering inevitably channeled Cadillac sales toward the luxury market, for only the rich could afford a car built to his exacting standards. Like Packard's four families he maintained that "price should be considered last by a manufacturer in selecting material for his product." In 1915 the average price of Cadillac jumped to $3,000, and it thereafter topped the General Motors line.[61]

Thus two of the three companies financed by the McMillan clique rose, appropriately enough, to the peak of the industry's price-class pyramid. The third, Oldsmobile, never quite reached it, though a bid for the summit would probably have come in due course had the Smiths stayed in charge. Packard was a paragon of conspicuous production; Cadillac and Oldsmobile were apparently equally intent on transposing their social values to their companies. Whether they would both have wound up permanently in the upper price-class is impossible to know, given their financial difficulties and sale to General Motors by 1909. Overall, however, their behavior seems to fit the model of conspicuous production, even though the correspondence between the price-class of Cadillac and Oldsmobile and the social position of their masters is not perfect.

This chapter has examined the companies founded by Detroit's railroad-car families and their associates. They were the dominant group in Detroit's economy, and it is not surprising—given the high cost and high risk of auto manufacturing—that they dominated the early local automotive scene as well. As we would anticipate, their main competition locally (aside from Ford, always the exception) came from lesser segments of Detroit's economic elite. Chapter Three is accordingly devoted to the automotive ventures of those businessmen who belonged to the economic elite but not to the McMillan alliance. We shall have abundant opportunity to observe there the extent to which Detroit's elite succumbed to the temptation of conspicuous production.

Chapter Three   The Upper Class Exits the Industry

■   So far as the average Detroit investor was concerned, the prospects for making money in assembling automobiles had never looked better than they did in 1909 and 1910. The latter year saw at least thirty-one new Detroit entries into the auto industry, a record never surpassed. Many firms immediately failed; even so, the size of Detroit's auto community continued to expand until 1913 (when it peaked at some forty-three companies). Interest during these years was at fever pitch: when Detroit's postmaster, Homer Warren, announced a new automobile company, he was "literally deluged with letters from clergymen, physicians, lawyers and . . . businessmen, all . . . willing to pay a premium to secure small blocks of the stock." These would-be investors did not, however, include Detroit's pre-automotive elite. Although fifty of them did pay to move the Lozier Motor Company to Detroit, by 1910 they were as a group more intent on liquidating their automotive investments than adding to them. The old families cut back on their involvement just as the passenger car industry entered its most remarkable period of expansion, with output rising from 181,000 units in 1910 to more than 1.5 million in 1916.[1]

As its title suggests, this chapter relates the decision by members of Detroit's upper class in 1909–1910 to reduce their involvement in the local auto industry. To understand that decision, one must review the history of the firms they controlled. The preceding chapter examined the three ventures of the railroad-car manufacturers, the core group in Detroit's financial elite at the start of the automotive era. The primary investment of Detroit's stove families—the second most important element within the financial elite of 1899–1902—was E-M-F, which in 1909 ranked fourth in sales nationwide. Old money also went into Reliance, Maxwell-Briscoe, Paige-Detroit, and Lozier.

■ 1   E-M-F brought together two older companies: the Northern Motor Car Company (originally Northern Manufacturing) and the Wayne Automobile Company. Northern was incorporated in 1902, the same year that Henry Joy and his associates brought Packard to Detroit and that Cadillac emerged from the ashes of the Henry Ford Company. It was organized by William T. Barbour, president of the Michigan Stove Company (and first cousin of George H. Barbour, then a member of Detroit's financial elite), to capitalize on a runabout designed by Jonathan D. Maxwell, chief engineer at Olds. Their "compatriots in the venture" included G. Bert Gunderson, secretary-treasurer of Michigan Stove; William E. Metzger, whom we have already seen at Cadillac; and in the design department the pioneer inventor Charles B. King.[2]

Maxwell had originally designed an improved Oldsmobile, and Northern at first specialized in building runabouts whose price dropped from $800 in 1904 to $650 in 1906. The company placed most of its bets, however, on a touring car advertised as "the highest-priced two cylinder car in the world," a claim largely substantiated by its $1,700 price tag. Predictably, the car found few takers, and Northern's difficulties in this period seem to have been directly attributable to its attempt to climb the price-class ladder before it had a suitable vehicle. In October 1906 it finally introduced a four-cylinder touring car, for which it charged more than $3,000. Northern, in other words, was now in the business of serving the social peers of the stove families. But it was not in business for long: in 1908, to stave off bankruptcy, it procured a merger with the E-M-F Company, another firm with ties to the stove manufacturing sector.[3]

E-M-F was itself a reorganization of Wayne Automobile, another failing company. Wayne had been founded in late 1903 by Charles L. Palms, stove manufacturer, publisher, banker (and member of the financial elite), and one of the principal heirs of the Palms real estate fortune. His fellow investors included his uncle, Dr. James B. Book; Edward A. Skae, a dealer in coal and coke; and the heads of the production staff—Roger J. Sullivan and William Kelly. Predictably, Palms decided to build an expensive automobile. "A high-power car of the general type of the Packard," the Wayne cost $2,500 in 1907. Production reached 1,000 that year, but Palms, displeased with poor earnings, handed the presidency over to Barney F. Everitt, a veteran body manufacturer, in September. Everitt, however, left the Wayne factory—the chief source of its troubles—unchanged: it continued to paint chassis by hand and assemble each car in a single stall. Palms and Book decided they needed a production expert, someone who knew the latest techniques. They went after the best, hiring Ford production manager Walter E. Flanders and two of his assistants, Max Wollering and Thomas Walburn. These men immediately rearranged the plant, but the company still lost money—$400 to $450 on every car shipped.[4]

Concluding that Wayne's price was too low, the directors calculated that they could make a profit by building a bigger, more expensive model. Flanders told them this would only inflate their losses. Their salvation, he insisted, lay in mass-producing a medium-priced ($1,250) thirty-horsepower touring car. The directors were dubious, but Flanders finally convinced them that volume manufacturing, despite its low profit margin, was ultimately more lucrative than luxury production. They disbanded Wayne and organized the E-M-F Company on August 1, 1908, to build the smaller car. In so doing, they temporarily defied the logic of conspicuous production. Here was a company with a difference.[5]

Leadership of the new corporation passed to the production staff. Its name in fact celebrated the heads of the functional departments: Everitt, Metzger, and Flanders. Metzger's participation in the project carried a high price tag: he insisted that E-M-F salvage his investment in the Northern Motor Car Company. On October 2, 1908, E-M-F purchased Northern for $200,000 and assumed its debts. The purchase was really a merger, for Metzger, Gunderson, and Barbour agreed to lend E-M-F the funds needed to retire Northern's obligations.[6]

The accession of Northern further strained E-M-F's already tight finances. While capitalized for $500,000, it actually started with only $50,000 in its treasury and a credit line of $200,000 from the local banks. It remained shaky until Flanders worked out a marketing arrangement with Studebaker Brothers, the giant South Bend, Indiana, wagon factory. Studebaker had been making automobiles in a small way since 1904, but its conservative management hesitated to plunge deeply into the industry. Instead, it decided to sell the E-M-F and Garford cars (the latter from a Cleveland firm) through its retail wagon outlets, thereby testing the water without any risk of going under themselves.[7]

The arrangement worked out too well. As E-M-F's assets increased (ninefold between its organization in August 1908 and December 1909), Metzger and Everitt became eager to cut the Studebaker connection. They argued that it left E-M-F too vulnerable and undercut attempts to build an efficient, independent sales network. As early as March 1909, Everitt was urging the Board to decide "once and for all that we are through with the Studebaker outfit."[8]

Studebaker, too, was getting nervous; it feared being left in the lurch. Frederick S. Fish, its general counsel, expressed his fears in a letter to Flanders. "I recognize," he wrote in April, "that you have the whip end in the entire transaction, and that the more we exploit your car, the more we build up your business . . . and make a strong competitor in the future." Fish proposed a merger; if they remained divided, he predicted they would both fall prey to "the recent large combination in the medium-priced automobile business." The specter of General Motors haunted Flanders as well, and he seconded Fish's appeal for amalgamation. Since he dominated the board, he left Everitt and Metzger little recourse but to sell their shares to Studebaker Brothers for $800,000. On April 29, 1909, Studebaker acquired one-third of E-M-F's stock and the right to name two directors. It also undertook to market E-M-F's entire output.[9]

It was a fragile quasi-merger; both parties realized that Studebaker could not continue for long in the anomalous position of minority stockholder and jobber. Flanders and Studebaker maneuvered for advantage, each trying to accumulate bargaining chips for the final showdown. According to Flanders, Studebaker sought to build up the rest of its automobile business at E-M-F's expense; he alleged that Studebaker dealers were required to order Garford cars if they wanted to get the E-M-F "30." He responded by deliberately forcing up production beyond the level Studebaker could handle. In December 1909, with Studebaker technically failing in its contractual obligations, Flanders rescinded the April agreement, announcing that E-M-F would go it alone. Over the next weeks he backed up his threat by putting together a viable sales organization.[10]

Studebaker now faced the prospect of an independent E-M-F Company, one in which it retained a sizable financial stake yet exercised no control. It went through the motions of initiating a lawsuit, but Flanders knew it had no desire to air the deficiencies of its retail network. As Max Wollering observed, "Studebaker had to buy the E-M-F Company to save face." In the driver's seat, Flanders and his Detroit associates drove a hard bargain. In March 1910 they sold out for $3.8 million, bringing a handsome return on their original investment. Dr. Book alone cleared $1.3 million on an investment of $120,000.[11]

The leading factions of Detroit's 1899–1902 financial elite had now sold three of their four automobile companies. They retained only Packard, the firm whose model policies most closely conformed to the owners' social rank. Was this outcome merely a coincidence? Or does it suggest that elite entrepreneurs may have regarded an exit from the industry as preferable to producing cars in the wrong price-class?

Consider E-M-F: by 1910 it had achieved financial success, but only as a consequence of surrendering control to hired managers, especially to Walter Flanders. He dominated E-M-F for most of its brief existence; in fact, Barney Everitt accused him of forgetting that he owed his position to the board of directors. Thrusting the Detroit capitalists into the background, he tried to make E-M-F's factories the most progressive in the trade, complete with a moving assembly line and a metallurgical laboratory. Inspired by Ford's success, Flanders wanted to compete for the mass market. In early 1909 he concluded that the E-M-F "30" was too big and expensive to compete with the smaller Fords, Buicks, and Maxwells. He asked the board, therefore, to approve the development of a twenty-horsepower model designed by James G. Heaslet. When the board balked, Flanders resorted to a squeeze play: he resigned as general manager on February 19, 1909, and proceeded with plans for the independent manufacture of the Flanders "20."[12]

In its origins the crisis was essentially a reprise of the struggle for control of Oldsmobile in 1904, but the outcome here was quite different. This time the elite investors feared to exercise the prerogative of ownership, for they deemed Flanders, whom they paid $25,000 a year (five times what Charles Palms received as treasurer), indispensable. They therefore capitulated, rehiring Flanders and giving him carte blanche to use the twenty-horsepower runabout to enter the bottom end of the low-priced field. By forcing Palms, Book, and Barbour to set aside their natural predilection for luxury manufacturing, Flanders made a striking success of the E-M-F Company: in 1909 and 1910 it ranked fourth in the nation in sales.[13]

Then why were his wealthy backers eager to sell out to Studebaker? Was it to regain control over their own economic destiny? Were they bothered by the emphasis on a lowly runabout that sold for $750? Other firms—including Northern—had started out by making cheap cars, but was it quite another matter in an industry so influenced by conspicuous production to revert to them? Or was the decision to sell out simply a recognition that mass production entailed unacceptable financial risk for a group of entrepreneurs who had become conservative with wealth and family tradition? We cannot know for certain which factor predominated because the men involved never described their motivation. Given the industry's behavior as a whole, however, it is reasonable to assume that among their probably mixed motives was the will to power, prestige, and security, as well as to profit.

■ 2   The other companies founded by Detroit's old families were a mixed bag, none of them as successful as those already discussed. Reliance Motor Car Company was the only other automotive producer organized in Detroit before 1905 with the help of a member of the 1899–1902 financial elite: the lawyer Sidney T. Miller was one of Reliance's directors, and presumably among its principal stockholders, when it filed its articles of association in November 1903. Nevertheless, the company did not have the kind of patrician sponsorship that we have by now come to expect. Its largest stockholder apparently was J. M. Mulkey, a dealer in salt and portland cement, and the rest of its leadership did not move in the same circles as the McMillans, Algers, and Barbours. They included Fred O. Paige, an insurance broker and former paper manufacturer; Hugh O'Connor, president of Michigan Wire Cloth; George Wetherbee, a manufacturer of woodenware. Though clearly members of Detroit's economic elite, they lacked the power and resources of the railroad-car and stove combines. Reliance accordingly did not have sufficient capital to compete with them in the automobile industry, which it quit in July 1907, but it did persevere in the motor truck business until February 1909, when the company was sold to General Motors and became its truck division. Reliance, in other words, performed much as expected: it prospered, though perhaps not as handsomely as it might have had Miller brought more of his banking associates on board, and it sold out to General Motors on schedule—that is, between late 1908 and early 1910.[14]

With the founding of Reliance, the resources of Detroit's financial elite had been apparently fully engaged by the infant automobile industry. Maxwell-Briscoe, for example, was forced to look outside Detroit for capital even though it brought together Jonathan D. Maxwell of Northern and Olds, a proven engineer-inventor, and Benjamin Briscoe, a businessman of considerable stature in Detroit at the turn of the century. His sheet-metal firm employed 100 workers in 1900—and that was before its business rapidly expanded, thanks to contracts from Olds for radiators, fenders, and the like. By late 1903 Briscoe had already been briefly involved in the Buick Motor Company, whose affairs he oversaw just long enough to effect its transfer to Flint, Michigan. And now he was seeking backers for a car of Maxwell's design. He was able to raise only $42,000, however, of which $15,000 constituted a loan from Theodore D. Buhl, who received $25,000 in common stock in partial compensation.[15]

Buhl, a millionaire whose family owned two major metal-fabricating companies—Buhl Stamping and Buhl Malleable—with a combined work force of 700, had taken control of Parke-Davis, a major pharmaceutical firm, in 1896 and served as its president until his death in 1907. He had impeccable credentials, yet he was neither a member of the city's financial elite, as defined, nor a partner of the railroad-car and stove cliques. As an independent capitalist he apparently lacked the connections to finance Maxwell-Briscoe. As Benjamin Briscoe explained in his 1921 memoirs: "There was a feeling on the part of the capitalists that the business was growing too fast, and that the automobile had reached the limit of its possibilities." In other words, the financial elite already had their investments in place, and not even a Buhl could induce them to raise their stake. Briscoe later recalled: "After some weeks spent in a vain attempt to secure sufficient subscriptions to our stock to justify us in beginning operations, we gave up trying to do [it] in Detroit, shipped the car to New York City and followed it." Maxwell-Briscoe was thereafter controlled by Wall Street interests.[16]

The Buhl family finally found its niche in the Paige-Detroit Motor Car Company. Paige merits close attention; it had the wealthiest backers of any Detroit company persisting in the middle-class field after 1910. How was Paige-Detroit able to escape the snare of conspicuous production? The answer is highly revealing of the extent to which class considerations did in fact shape the entrepreneurship of the pioneer Detroit companies. Paige was organized in October 1909 and took its name from Fred Paige, whom we have already seen at the helm of Reliance. Its first car was, typically, a two-cylinder runabout (with an unusual two-cycle engine designed by Andrew Bachle) priced at $800, or the bottom of the middle price-class.[17]

Paige's stockholders were young, mostly in their late thirties and early forties, wealthy and powerful. E. D. Stair published two of the largest local dailies, the *Journal* and the *Free Press*. Charles B. Warren, an eminent lawyer, had organized the Michigan Sugar Company, an adjunct of the Havemeyer "sugar trust," and now served as its president and general counsel. Its vice-president, Gilbert W. Lee, had also organized a wholesale grocery with branches in five Michigan cities. Warren's law partner, William B. Cady, had sizable investments in Detroit's Outer Belt Line railroad, the Cheboygan Paper Company, and the American Twist Drill Company. Charles H. Hodges was president of the Detroit Lubricator Company and vice-president of the American Radiator Company, two firms founded by his father. Sherman Depew, son of a biscuitmaker who teamed up with Nabisco, married into the shoe manufacturing firm of Pingree & Smith. Harry and Edward Jewett headed a coal mining and wholesaling outfit. Arthur and Willis Buhl had split up their family's business empire when their father, Theodore D. Buhl, died in 1907. Alex McPherson, aged seventy-three—more than twenty years older than any of his partners—had occupied the presidency of the Detroit National Bank since 1891.

Almost all the Paige investors were inheritors, by birth or marriage. Warren, whose father owned two newspapers and several sugar mills in the Saginaw Valley, made the most advantageous match politically, for he wed Helen Wetmore, niece of Senator James McMillan. Lee, by capturing the hand of George Hammond's daughter, probably gained the most money, however, for Hammond owned one of the largest meat-packing companies in the Midwest. It was this firm that underwrote James Standish's membership in Detroit's financial elite at the turn of the century. Cady also married well: his wife was the daughter of Hoyt Post, a banker who also served as president of Peninsular Electric Light.[18]

With backers like these, two of whom had marital ties to Detroit's financial elite of 1899–1902, Paige-Detroit seemed destined to seek the upper price-class or, if frustrated in this ambition, to sell out to a firm more comfortable with the mass market. Predictably, Paige-Detroit responded to its first sales crisis, in 1910, by seeking a higher price-class. But first it shook up the management: Fred Paige left, and Harry M. Jewett (the coal dealer) replaced him as president. Jewett saved Paige-Detroit by junking the runabout, whose two-cycle motor had proved unpopular, and by concentrating on touring cars whose floor price gradually floated upward from $1,075 in 1914 to $1,595 in 1920. Paige thus achieved a modest success in the middle stratum of the industry, its sales peaking at 39,380 in 1925.[19]

Most of the companies owned by Detroit's economic elite started in the middle class; only Paige-Detroit persisted there. Why the aberration? The clue to Paige's staying power may be found in its association with the Lozier Motor Company, a luxury manufacturer that absorbed the attention of Paige's principal stockholders after 1910. Lozier was defiantly patrician, boasting that it sold "at a Higher Average Price Than Any Other Car in the World" and that "PRICE has always been the LAST CONSIDERATION." At $5,000, it was the only Detroit-made automobile to compete with the European cars for the very pinnacle of the upper-class market. For Detroit's elite, ownership of Lozier stock became the ultimate status symbol.[20]

Originally located in Plattsburgh, New York, Lozier came to Detroit in 1910 after fifty local capitalists put up $1 million to acquire control. At the center of the group were several Paige-Detroit stockholders, and most of the investors belonged to their immediate circle of friends, family, and close business allies. With Gilbert W. Lee, Charles B. Warren, Fred Paige, Charles Hodges, E. D. Stair, Willis and Arthur Buhl, Harry and Edward Jewett, and Sherman Depew interested in both companies, Lozier and Paige competed in the industry virtually as a double entry. The Lozier satisfied its stockholders' passion for luxury manufacturing, thus undoubtedly helping to keep the price of the Paige down.[21]

But Lozier cured them of the big-car bug. In June 1911 they spent a million dollars to finance the development of its six-cylinder model. When even this proved inadequate, they reluctantly turned to Wall Street for help. The bankers demanded two places on the board of directors and the appointment of Harry M. Jewett as president, making Lozier an adjunct of Paige-Detroit. It still failed to make a profit. Despite additional capital of $2 million in March 1913, it went into bankruptcy in September 1914. Under new owners it sputtered through 1915 and 1916 before passing into history. An expensive object lesson, Lozier taught the Paige stockholders that the middle-class market, while not glamorous, was at least preferable to losing millions.[22]

With the demise of Lozier, only two automobile concerns of any size or importance remained under the command of Detroit's pre-automotive elite. Both Packard and Paige were solid companies, but both still operated on the limited scale of a luxury manufacturer. Paige, though it priced its cars to sell to the average car buyer, was outsold by Cadillac every year between 1909 and 1924; even in its best seasons, 1925 and 1926, it barely squeezed by the upper-class producers. Neither Paige nor Packard allowed Detroit's pre-automotive elite to retain much clout in the automotive industry.[23]

■ 3   How different the situation had been in 1905. Then, the city's pre-automotive elite had dominated the automobile industry not just of Detroit but of the nation as well. The five companies in which the railroad-car and stove cliques had become involved contributed 55 percent of the nation's motorcar production in 1905 (Tables 18 and 19). Five years later, despite the addition of Paige-Detroit, their share of the market had fallen to 2 percent. Their retreat within Detroit's automotive sector had been just as decisive, from a near monopoly over local output in 1905 down to 3 percent by 1910.

It was an extraordinary reversal and one difficult to explain. The firms involved enjoyed several advantages over most of their competition—including a head start and superior financial resources—and with the exception of Oldsmobile, their sellout does not seem to have been forced by defeat in the marketplace. Cadillac and E-M-F were experiencing the best years in their history and ranked among the industry's leaders in sales and profits when sold, respectively, to General Motors and Studebaker. The prices paid, though attractive, were by no means compelling: Cadillac's shareholders, for example, received only $4.75 million, an amount General Motors recovered in just fourteen months out of Cadillac's subsequent net earnings.[24]

Some historians have argued that the sales were forced by rumors then circulating about impending horizontal combinations in the automobile industry. Cadillac and E-M-F may have feared competing as independents against "trusts" financed by Wall Street or its allies. That possibility added to past difficulties would explain their eagerness to sell. The argument is plausible, especially as it fits a behavioral pattern already observable in Detroit's business circles. Since the early 1890s the city's financial elite—particularly the McMillan alliance—had responded to the country's first merger movement by selling out to would-be monopolists. The first important sale came in 1891, when American Radiator absorbed two Detroit manufacturers of steam radiators. Though the Detroiters retained a financial stake, the combine's headquarters was thereafter located in Chicago. In the traction sector the key merger came in 1900: Detroit United Railway emerged with a local monopoly and eastern (primarily New York and Cleveland) ownership. Similarly, the city's privately owned electric utilities were consolidated into Detroit Edison in 1903 with control passing to an eastern group headed by the North American Company of Boston.[25]

The most significant merger occurred in 1899 when William C. McMillan, the senator's elder son, arranged for the sale of Detroit's railroad-car combine to American Car & Foundry of Saint Louis. While Detroit's capitalists received stock in the car "trust," they did not control it; American Car & Foundry was in fact part of J. P. Morgan's community of interest. With a stroke of the pen, Detroit's financial elite had been decapitated. The city's workers also im-

Table 18
Output of Companies Owned by Pre-Automotive Elite

Company	1904	1905	1907	1909	1910
Packard	250	481	1,403	3,106	3,084
Cadillac	2,457	3,942	2,884	7,868	
Olds	5,508[a]	6,500[a]	1,045[b]		
Northern	750	750	unknown		
Wayne	<620	unknown	1,000		
E-M-F[c]				7,960	
Paige				few	500
Total	9,585	11,673	6,332	18,934	3,584

[a] Includes Lansing output.   [b] All output in Lansing.   [c] Merger of Wayne and Northern.
Sources: See Table 19.

Table 19
Relative Output of Companies Owned by Pre-Automotive Elite

	1904	1905	1907	1909	1910
Total elite output	9,585[a]	11,673[a]	6,332[b]	18,934	3,584
Total Detroit output (all companies)	9,000	10,736	15,000	45,000	114,120
Elite percentage of Detroit total	106%	109%	42%	42%	3%
Total U.S. output	22,419	21,321	40,558	102,698	158,103
Elite percentage of U.S. total	43%	55%	16%	18%	2%

[a] Elite output in Detroit alone is not known; figure includes Olds's Lansing production.
[b] Includes Olds's Lansing production.
Sources: Automobile Quarterly, *The American Car since 1775* (New York, 1971), 138–39; *Automotive Industries* 46 (February 16, 1922): 326; *Cycle and Automobile Trade Journal* 14 (December 1909): 122–25; Detroit *News*, August 7, 1910; Lawrence Seltzer, *Financial History of the American Automobile Industry* (Boston, 1928), 76, 156; L. V. Spencer, "Detroit, the City Built by the Automobile Industry," *Automobile* 28 (April 10, 1913): 793.

mediately paid a price: American Car & Foundry reduced employment at its Detroit works by 44 percent in the year after consolidation.[26]

What would account for these deals, as well as the decision to sell Cadillac, E-M-F, and Oldsmobile? Three answers suggest themselves; none of them can be considered conclusive, however, for they are inferred more from the financial elite's behavior than from their pronouncements. The first emphasizes the vulnerability of an elite from a minor trading and banking center when confronted by pressures, born of improvements in transportation and communication, toward the development of a nationwide business system. The advantages enjoyed by Detroit's financial elite were only local or at most regional advantages. By 1900 these financiers, observed from afar, were less imposing figures. The city to whose fortunes they had linked their own had not kept up with regional growth. Between 1890 and 1900 it had slipped a notch in the population hierarchy: Milwaukee had claimed its position as the fourth largest city on the Great Lakes.[27]

Detroit's eclipse as a wholesaling center undercut the power of the city's financial elite to some degree; so too did the decline of opportunity for moneymaking in the state's mines and forests. Lumbering had created many local fortunes, some of which transfused money into the automobile industry, but as Rolland Maybee has observed, "the Golden Age of Michigan Pine was coming to a close at the turn of the . . . century." Lumber companies had cut 160 billion board feet, leaving only 5 billion standing; and it "was plain to be seen," as Arthur Hill remarked in 1899, that Michigan had nearly "reached the end of the God-given resource." The state's mining industry continued to grow but at a slower pace; by 1898 it had entered its stable, mature phase. Big eastern outfits owned the copper range, leaving little room for local initiative or profit.[28]

As opportunities diminished elsewhere in the Michigan economy, automobile manufacturing beckoned; and the original decision to gamble on the risky new industry may have been as much a sign of economic vulnerability as was the later decision to disinvest once the stakes mounted. Motor manufacturing became progressively riskier as it became more heavily capitalized. Where once $100,000 had sufficed to float a company, by 1910 it took at least $2 million to initiate even limited production. Detroit's financial elite were perhaps unnerved by these sums, especially as there was no guarantee that autos, like bicycles in the 1890s, were not merely a fad whose sales would stagnate as the public turned to other novelties. Besides, it is doubtful that either as automakers or as bankers they had the wherewithal to survive a recession in which the sales of all their marques collapsed simultaneously. And that had already come close to happening in the winter of 1907–1908. The decision to sell may have been induced, in other words, by a fear of being caught overextended in a recession. Detroit's financial elite perhaps had sufficient capital to enter the automobile game but not enough to persist in it—at least not without unacceptable risk.[29]

An alternative explanation would focus on management. We have seen that each of the elites' automobile companies underwent a severe management crisis, typically ending with the expulsion of the hired manager (often himself a minority stockholder) and the assumption of more direct control by the financial backers themselves. The ouster of Ransom Olds, Henry Ford, Fred O. Paige, and James W. Packard are cases in point. The one major exception to the rule was E-M-F, where Walter Flanders steadily increased his power until the company was sold out from under him.

Overall, Detroit's financial elite appear to have resisted sharing control with salaried managers. They were empire builders rather than organization builders; they preferred to own a stake in many businesses rather than to develop any one of them into a large, vertically integrated concern. Even the most exceptional companies— for example, the railroad-car combine before 1899—were closely held corporations in which family members remained active in senior management. Detroit's financial elite believed in family as opposed to managerial capitalism; they tended to enter into partnership with members of their own extended families or with friends who had through long acquaintance become surrogate relatives. In each enterprise they insisted on complete control: at Packard, "capital expenditures in excess of $200" required the approval of the board of directors.[30]

Packard could be run as a family business because it did not transcend the lessons learned by the financial elite (or by their families) in Detroit's traditional industries. Building Packards was not all that different from building railroad rolling stock or stoves, and though finding a market for them might have been slightly more difficult, it was considerably less daunting a task to open a handful of elegant showrooms in the wealthier metropolises than it was to establish a sales presence at thousands of village crossroads. The middle and lower price-classes required constant innovation in the mechanics of production and distribution, and their designs changed more rapidly than did those in the highest price-class. All in all, the two lower price-classes demanded more managerial and technical expertise than did the luxury market. It is not surprising, then, that the financial elite persevered with Packard but bailed out of Olds, Cadillac, and E-M-F after it became apparent that they could not manage these firms successfully themselves. Paige-Detroit, a special case, survived because its scale of operations were those of a low-volume, luxury producer and therefore susceptible to owner management.

The two foregoing explanations for the retreat of 1908–1910 are not mutually exclusive. Indeed, they seem complementary: a group that felt itself vulnerable and unable (as the stakes rose) to take a multimillion dollar gamble on automobile manufacturing might also be anxious to maintain family control over its enterprises and to prefer to sell out rather than to share that control. In both instances we are speaking of an entrepreneurial style that revolved around family, region, and personal supervision and that could under economic duress produce a laager mentality, a circling of the wagons for defense.

A third possible explanation for the great démarche of 1908–1910 reprises our main theme of conspicuous production. It notes the survival of Packard, the company that came closest to serving the social peers of Detroit's financial elite; the upward striving of Olds, Paige, and Cadillac; and the tensions that the $750 runabout brought to E-M-F. None of these facts is by itself conclusive, but together they constitute plausible evidence for conspicuous production. Yet is it likely that families who already occupied the top rung of Detroit's social ladder would be so fearful of losing status by building an inferior automobile that they would indulge in conspicuous production? After all, they were the ones who determined the city's pecking order, were they not? Packard's gentlemen had an answer: reputation is easily lost. If "we . . . put [the Packard] reputation on the bargain counter . . . how long would there be a bargain, a reputation or a Packard?" a 1919 truck advertisement rhetorically asked. The answer was obvious: not even the McMillans could be certain that they would stay atop the city's social hierarchy.[31]

Moreover, the financial elite—the inner core of Detroit's business class that oversaw the city's first automotive investments—appear to have been especially anxious to define and preserve Detroit's social order. Their families had taken the lead after 1880 in organizing Detroit's first men's clubs, which, as in other American cities, helped to define the boundaries of the upper class. As Max Weber noted after a tour of the United States, "Affiliation with a distinguished club was an essential above all else. He who did not succeed in joining was no gentleman." In Detroit, two clubs had the power to ascribe upper-class status: the Yondotega and the Detroit Club, both founded by the city's financial elite of 1899–1902. The Yon-dotega, one of the city's smallest clubs, maintained a steady membership of 100 after its organization in 1891. During its first thirty years its board of trustees always included Charles Freer, who made his fortune in railroad cars, one of the McMillans or Newberrys, and Cameron Currie, an investment banker and one-time "fixer" for George Hendrie in the traction business.[32]

The Detroit Club, with several hundred members, was less exclusive but probably more influential than the Yondotega; indeed, its dining and conference rooms served as unofficial headquarters for Detroit's economic leaders. Founded in 1882, the club chose Hugh McMillan, the senator's elder brother, as its first president; its roster of chief executives thereafter faithfully reflected the composition of Detroit's financial elite. Most of its presidents engaged in railroad-car or stove manufacturing (for example, George H. Russel, George Barbour, Russell Alger, Truman Newberry) or in railroading and public utilities. One might well conclude that the families who took time off from the task of making money to help institutionalize the city's social hierarchy were indeed status-oriented. It stands to reason that they would have difficulty treating as powerful a status object as the automobile in an entirely detached fashion.[33]

■ 4   Their retreat from automobile manufacturing, effected between 1908 and 1910, was a momentous occasion for Detroit's financial elite and for the city whose affairs they had hitherto dominated. It is difficult to exaggerate the extent to which members of the upper class opted out of the city's leading industry: not only did they sell three major companies to General Motors and Studebaker, but they declined to accept stock as compensation. E-M-F and Cadillac had demanded and received cash. Olds, a failing company, had been forced to accept GM stock—largely preferred—as an initial payment, but most of this was sold off the following year. As a result, General Motors by 1910 had *no* important Detroit stockholders; nine years later not one Detroiter had holdings of more than 2,000 shares of GM common; and Studebaker had not a single Detroit stockholder after 1910.[34]

This disengagement was bound to have serious consequences, for neither Packard nor Paige-Detroit gave the pre-automotive elite much say in the automobile industry after 1910. It became difficult, then, for that elite to retain their local preeminence. And yet it would be years before the full implications of their retreat from the automobile industry would be known, for their fate would in large measure depend on their success in co-opting the leadership of the middle- and lower-class companies into their own ranks. In other words, they could sustain their socioeconomic position if they could successfully recruit the individuals and families who controlled the new industry. The next chapter examines the middle-class companies to see, first, whether their leaders were likely candidates for admission into the city's upper class and, second, whether they would add much strength to it, once admitted.

Personalizing the Automobile

Early auto manufacturers often attached their own personal prestige to their product in an effort to distinguish it from hundreds of competing cars, many of them produced by individuals with minimal technical background and financial resources. Early automotive advertisements thus sported photographs, personal pledges, and brief biographies that intertwined the reputation of the car with one or more of the individuals responsible for its production.

These illustrations (except the first and the last) are from the National Automotive History Collection, Detroit Public Library, and are reproduced here with permission.

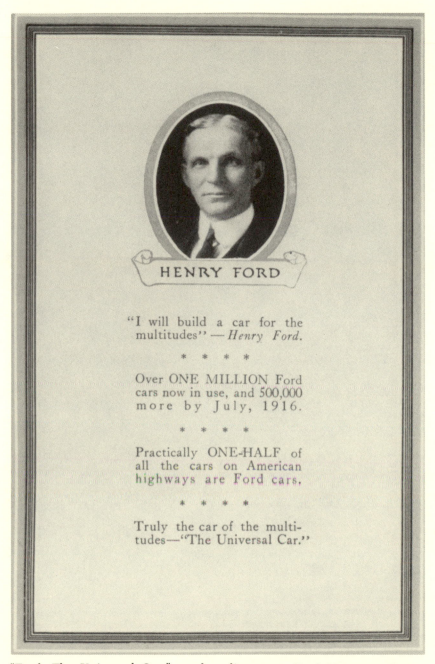

HENRY FORD

"I will build a car for the multitudes" — *Henry Ford*.

* * * *

Over ONE MILLION Ford cars now in use, and 500,000 more by July, 1916.

* * * *

Practically ONE-HALF of all the cars on American highways are Ford cars.

* * * *

Truly the car of the multitudes—"The Universal Car."

"Ford, The Universal Car," product literature, Ford Motor Company, 1915. From the collections of Henry Ford Museum & Greenfield Village.

Raising the Curtain

In the near future this curtain will be removed and disclose the latest product of the world's greatest Automobile designer

Mr. R. E. OLDS

The new cars will be manufactured by the REO CAR CO., of Lansing, Mich., of which Mr. R. E. Olds is President and General Manager, and whose initials furnish the name.

That the cars will be strictly high-class and embody many new features in Automobile construction, no one who is familiar with the past efforts of Mr. R. E. Olds will doubt.

We want live agents, and those making early application will be first in line for consideration.

The entire sales management of the REO MOTOR CAR CO. will be in charge of Mr. R. M. Owen, with Eastern offices at No. 138 West 38th Street, New York.

REO MOTOR CAR CO.
138 West 38th Street

Factory-Lansing, Mich.   **NEW YORK**

The Horseless Age, November 16, 1904.

The Car with the Half-Million Dollar Motor

Benjamin Briscoe
President
Briscoe Motor Corporation

Benjamin Briscoe, one of the foun-ders of the automobile industry, contributes the greatest car of his many successful models.

THE name of Benjamin Briscoe is indelibly written in the annals of motor car history. He has won fame both as a designer and a manufacturer of high-grade, quality automobiles. From the first, Mr. Briscoe has produced motor cars that could be bought and run by the man of modest income, at the same time fully satisfying the taste and pride of ownership of people of the greatest wealth and refinement.

Thousands upon thousands of motor cars traveling the roads of the world at this moment are living testimony and absolute proof of his rare skill and his wonderful creative and inventive genius.

He it was who taught an industry, which boasted many of the greatest inventors of all times, how to manufacture efficiently and in a large way, not only motor cars, but also many of the important accessories.

Cars bearing his name have won many of the most hazardous endur-ance tours ever contested and recorded.

Truly the automobile business and the motoring public at large have been the gainers from the efforts of this master designer and manufacturer.

And the Half-Million Dollar Motor!

It is the result of an experience covering the life of the motor industry and four years of untiring effort and labor.

Mr. Briscoe has told the story of how the Half-Million Dollar Motor came into existence in his own inimitable way in his booklet, "The Half-Million Dollar Motor." The story bristles with human interest and breathes the spirit of men accustomed to doing big things in a big way.

He tells how he and fourteen of the world's greatest engineers created and developed this marvelous engine—the engine which powers the Briscoe 4-24—

The Car with the Half-Million Dollar Motor

Briscoe 4-24 Catalogue, 1917–1919.

A PERSONAL MESSAGE

BY
WALTER P. CHRYSLER
CONCERNING THE NEW
DODGE BROTHERS SIX

Ever since the first Dodge Brothers car made its notable appearance some 15 years ago, the name of Dodge Brothers has enjoyed commanding prestige.

Hence, in acquiring the Dodge Brothers Corporation, and in undertaking to plan, produce and protect the products which will bear the Dodge name, we are mindful of our profound personal obligation to the vast Dodge Brothers public and the host of Dodge Brothers dealers throughout the world.

It is our sole aim to add so consistently and conspicuously to the present acclaim of Dodge that every Dodge owner and every Dodge dealer will feel even greater pride and have cause for greater satisfaction.

We are utilizing every element of progressive engineering, scientific manufacturing and outstanding value which has contributed to the success of all other Chrysler-built cars and to the general and rapid progress of the Chrysler Corporation.

In creating these new Dodge Brothers cars, we have striven to make them distinct additions to Dodge prestige and worthy exponents of every fine tradition associated with both Dodge and Chrysler good will.

We have embodied such evident value, such surpassing performance, such engineering supremacy and so much of originality, beauty and luxury that by every comparison, the intrinsic value of Dodge Brothers cars will remain unchallenged.

The new Dodge Brothers Six furnishes unassailable evidence of the unlimited capabilities of the great, organized forces of the Chrysler Corporation when they are marshalled to full strength in any enterprise.

From an engineering standpoint, this new Dodge Brothers Six is a supreme achievement by a group of engineers whose scientific accomplishments have revolutionized automobile design.

We believe that in performance, in new measures of comfort, in long-lived excellence, and in persistent and inherent value it surpasses every previous conception of what a car at this price could possibly be.

The utmost we would ask is that you actually see, examine and test the car itself—demanding of it more than you ever before have asked of any motor car at or near its price.

In the higher-price field, the new Chrysler-built Dodge Senior has already won preference among the buyers of large, fine cars.

It marks a notable advance in style, in performance, in luxurious comfort and in its wealth of refinements.

We are proud to be the creators and sponsors of these two fine cars—the new Dodge Brothers Six and the new Dodge Senior—and present them in the sincere conviction that they offer the high values, dependability and distinction which a discriminating public expects always of Dodge Brothers.

We believe that in these first two products of the new era of Dodge under Chrysler management will be found the strongest pledge it is possible for me and my associates to offer that the future of the Dodge Brothers Corporation is in safe hands.

W. P. Chrysler

Motor Age, January 1929.

Warren-Detroit "30"

These are the men in charge—the men whose skill, integrity and experience has made the "Warren-Detroit" take instant place as the most highly standardized automobile ever presented as an initial product.

When you know these men and their records you know why the "Warren-Detroit" is already a demonstrated success.

HOMER WARREN, *President*
Prominent in Detroit's Real Estate and Manufacturing interests. Known from one end of the country to the other as a man who "does things."

JNO. G. BAYERLINE, *Vice-President and General Manager*
Has been in the automobile manufacturing business for TEN years. Was with The Toledo-Pope-Hartford Co., then in Engineering and Purchasing Depts. of Olds Motor Works and latterly Purchasing Agent for Hudson Motor Car Co.

W. H. RADFORD, *Chief Engineer and Designer*
Been connected with the industry since 1903 when he was with Northern Motor Car Co. Later acted as independent consulting engineer for several well-known automobile companies. For two years was designer for the Olds Motor Works. For the past year was Assistant Chief Engineer of the Hudson Motor Car Co.

R. W. ALLEN, *Secretary*
With Olds Motor Works for six years. For a year was Assistant Purchasing Agent at Hudson Motor Car Co.

T. A. BOLLINGER, *Factory Superintendent*
A thorough Mechanic with experience in every department. Formerly in charge of assembling work at Olds Motor Works and Hudson Motor Car Co.

Our entire organization including all factory and office men are experienced automobile men.

ANOTHER IMPORTANT POINT

We have a *double* source of supply on all materials. Further, among our principal stockholders are a number of prominent automobile parts manufacturers. This means not only highest quality workmanship and materials but in combination with our perfect organization assures you that deliveries will be made on time—but get your order in at once.

Warren Motor Car Co., Detroit

Warren-Detroit "30" Catalogue, 1910.

Climbing and Price—Class Hierarchy

The automobiles, once personalized, tended to promote the social ambitions of their makers, climbing upward with them through the community's prestige hierarchy. Pierce-Arrow, a Buffalo company, ran an advertisement in 1912 that vividly captured its own "progress" in class and size. An automobile's ascent typically came in spurts as new models were introduced; and the rapid and radical shift upward in the price—class hierarchy displayed in the paired advertisements for Oldsmobile, Hudson, and Paige-Detroit was the norm for an industry whose leaders seemed to believe that the whole world was becoming richer with them.

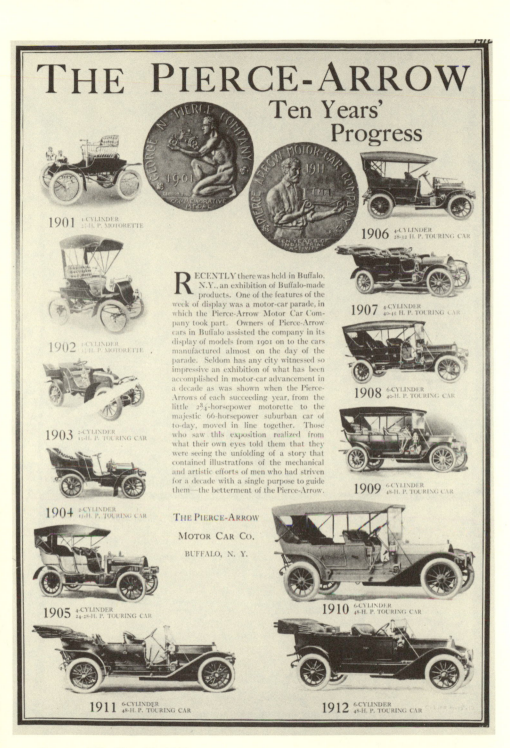

THE PIERCE-ARROW

Ten Years' Progress

1901 1-CYLINDER 2¾-H. P. MOTORETTE

1902 1-CYLINDER 4¾-H. P. MOTORETTE

1903 2-CYLINDER 15-H. P. TOURING CAR

1904 2-CYLINDER 15-H. P. TOURING CAR

1905 4-CYLINDER 24-28-H. P. TOURING CAR

1906 4-CYLINDER 28-32 H. P. TOURING CAR

1907 4-CYLINDER 40-45 H. P. TOURING CAR

1908 6-CYLINDER 40-H. P. TOURING CAR

1909 6-CYLINDER 48-H. P. TOURING CAR

1910 6-CYLINDER 48-H. P. TOURING CAR

1911 6-CYLINDER 48-H. P. TOURING CAR

1912 6-CYLINDER 48-H. P. TOURING CAR

RECENTLY there was held in Buffalo, N.Y., an exhibition of Buffalo-made products. One of the features of the week of display was a motor-car parade, in which the Pierce-Arrow Motor Car Company took part. Owners of Pierce-Arrow cars in Buffalo assisted the company in its display of models from 1901 on to the cars manufactured almost on the day of the parade. Seldom has any city witnessed so impressive an exhibition of what has been accomplished in motor-car advancement in a decade as was shown when the Pierce-Arrows of each succeeding year, from the little 2¾-horsepower motorette to the majestic 66-horsepower suburban car of to-day, moved in line together. Those who saw this exposition realized from what their own eyes told them that they were seeing the unfolding of a story that contained illustrations of the mechanical and artistic efforts of men who had striven for a decade with a single purpose to guide them—the betterment of the Pierce-Arrow.

THE PIERCE-ARROW

MOTOR CAR CO.

BUFFALO, N. Y.

Country Life, May 15, 1912.

Oldsmobile
in the Hall *of* Fame

Delivery Wagon	Touring Runabout	Standard Runabout	Light Tonneau Car
$850	$750	$650	$950

Five years of unparalleled service have enshrined the Oldsmobile forever in the Hall of Fame; proclaimed it in every land—*the best thing on wheels.*

The superior merits of our line of cars are acknowledged by automobile experts. They are the standard by which others are tested. If you are interested and wish full particulars call on our nearest sales agent or write direct to Dept. 21.

Olds Motor Works, Detroit, U. S. A.

Member of the Association of Licensed Automobile Manufacturers

The Oldsmobile of 1904 from *Scientific American*, June 18, 1904, and the Oldsmobile of 1908 from *The Automobile*, July 9, 1908.

OLDSMOBILE

The Oldsmobile is a reliable car, the necessity for even minor adjustments has been reduced to the minimum.

Thus, while its beauty and luxury appeal to women, its everyday efficiency has a particular fascination for busy men,—who want to step into a car that is ready to go—and keep on going—at all times.

Light the lamps and start off; your evening's recreation is at hand,—return when you will.

You cannot buy more efficiency with more money; you cannot buy Oldsmobile efficiency with less; it is "the logical car at the logical price."

Model M, fully equipped, • • • • $2,750
Model MR, "Flying Roadster," fully equipped, $2,750
Model Z, Six Cylinders, 130 inch wheel base, $4,200

Member Association
Licensed Automobile
Manufacturers

OLDS MOTOR WORKS
Lansing, Michigan, U.S.A.

THE OLDSMOBILE CO.,
of Canada
8o King Street East
Toronto,   Ontario

Hudson Twenty
$900

$900
Strong–Speedy–Roomy–Stylish

There have been many low priced cars, but never one so big, strong, speedy and good looking as this one. In the Hudson "Twenty" you get the best automobile value ever offered for less than $1000. In this car you find that something called *class*—that something which other cars at or near this price have lacked.

Most low priced cars have been too small. In the Hudson "Twenty" you get a *big* car. Note the long wheel base—100 inches. Note the big, strong wheels, the large radiator, big hood, staunch, clean-made frame.

This car looks a big car. It *is* a big car. Other cars selling under $1,000 have not been roomy. One felt cramped after riding in them. The Hudson "Twenty" has ample leg room. There is no Roadster made, regardless of price, that affords more comfort to those who ride in it. From the front seat to the dash there is a space of 31 inches.

Designers of other cars selling around the price of the Hudson "Twenty" have not seemed to realize that it is as easy to make a *good looking* car as it is to make another kind.

Here is a car that is good looking. It is big and racy looking. Note the graceful and harmonious lines. Observe the sweep of the fenders and the frame. There is no car with better lines. None from this standpoint more satisfying.

A man who can afford a half dozen cars will enjoy the Hudson "Twenty" as well as the man who can own but one.

Judged by every mechanical and engineering standard this car is thoroughly up-to-date without embodying any experimental features. It is a car that looks and acts like the more expensive. It is big, roomy, stylish, satisfying.

Some High Grade Features

The Hudson "Twenty" has a sliding gear transmission, selective type, three speeds forward and reverse, such as you find on the Packard, Peerless, Pierce, Lozier and other high grade cars. No other low-priced cars do not have this type of transmission.

All the Power You Need

The motor is vertical, four cylinder, four cycle, water cooled, known as the Renault type. And Renault motors are the pride of France.

The Hudson "Twenty" motor develops all the power you can want. Any Hudson "Twenty" will do 50 miles an hour. On the Grosse Pointe race track one of them has been driven a mile a minute.

The frame of the Hudson "Twenty" is of the best open hearth stock. It is 3½" x 1½" section, accurately and carefully riveted together with hot rivets, and braced against all possible strains. Our frames are made by the Hydraulic Pressed Steel Company of Detroit, the company which makes frames also for the high-priced Stearns cars.

Single Piece I-Beam Axle

The front axle is a one piece drop-forged I-beam section, of the best grade of open hearth steel, carefully heat treated. The Peerless, Pierce, Matheson, Lozier and other high grade cars use drop forged front axles.

The rear axle is of the semi-floating type, shaft-driven, proved out by a score of makers.

Perfect Comfort Here

There is more rake to the steering post than is found on the average car. This allows the driver a comfortable position. The generous diameter of the steering wheel makes the car easy to handle.

The springs are of special steel, semi-elliptic in front, and three-quarter-elliptic in the rear, such as you find in the Renault, Chalmers-Detroit, Pierce and others.

Lubrication is of the pump circulated, constant splash system, which has proved so satisfactory on the Oldsmobile, Chalmers-Detroit and other highly successful cars.

The body is composed of the best grade of ash, carefully placed and securely bolted to the frame. The seats are large and roomy and well upholstered.

It Pleases the Eye

In color the "Twenty" is a rich maroon, with mouldings and edges of bonnet striped in black. Leather is blue black. Fenders, fender irons, pedals, and top irons are enameled black. The radiator, steering column, side lamp brackets, hub caps, and side control levers are of brass. Steps are aluminum.

The tires are 32"x3" in front and 32"x3½" in the rear. The crank shaft has a tensile strength of 100,000 pounds; the clutch is leather faced, cone type; the clearance is 12½ inches under the steering knuckles.

Worm and segment type steering gear, with extra large bearings, is used, and the control is of the accepted standard sort, shifted by lever on the right hand side.

Fulfills Every Demand

The Hudson "Twenty" not only looks like the more expensive cars, but it *acts* like them too.

It can go faster than most careful drivers want to ride, it can climb all of the hills, and stand up on all sorts of roads, and it will do this work on a small amount of gasoline, and at a low cost of repairs and tires.

The Hudson "Twenty" is the ideal car at the price. It leaves nothing to be desired.

Nothing experimental about it. Nothing untried.

The "Twenty" has been recognized by the Association of Licensed Automobile Manufacturers. It is the only four cylinder *licensed* car selling for less than $1,000.

Deliveries will begin in July, and orders will be filled in rotation as received. Please wire or write for catalog and name of nearest dealer.

The Men Behind the Hudson

J. L. Hudson, President—Mr. Hudson is a leading, conservative business man and capitalist of Detroit.

Hugh Chalmers, Vice President—Mr. Chalmers is president of the Chalmers-Detroit Motor Company. He was formerly vice-president and general manager of the National Cash Register Company.

R. B. Jackson, Treasurer and General Manager—Mr. Jackson is a mechanical engineer. He was factory manager of the Olds Motor Works from 1903 to 1907.

Geo. W. Dunham, Chief Engineer and Designer—Mr. Dunham was chief engineer of the American Motor Carriage Company from 1901 to 1904. In the latter year he became associated with the Olds Motor Works in a designing capacity. He was chief engineer of the Olds Motor Works from early in 1907 until March 1st, 1909. Mr. Dunham's success in the past as a designer of high-grade motor cars that gives satisfaction to their owners is the best proof that the Hudson "Twenty" will give satisfaction.

R. D. Chapin, Secretary—Mr. Chapin is treasurer and general manager of the Chalmers-Detroit Motor Company.

H. E. Coffin, Vice President and Chief Engineer of the Chalmers-Detroit Motor Company, is a member of the board of directors.

Hudson Motor Car Company, Detroit, Michigan
(Members A. L. A. M.)

The Hudson "Twenty" of 1909 from *The Saturday Evening Post*, June 19, 1909, and the closed Hudson of 1912 from *Life*, October 17, 1912.

*Luxury, Beauty, Comfort and Quality
without Extravagance*

Hudson Closed Cars

*Finest Limousine and Coupe Bodies on Chassis Designed by 48 Master Builders
A Four—the "37," and the "54"—a Six*

If you seek beauty, comfort, quality, richness and appointment, and do not especially care for exclusiveness which is obtained only by paying a high price, these cars will appeal to you.

The bodies were designed by men who have done similar work for the builders of the most expensive cars. No expense has been spared in material or workmanship. By larger production than is possible with cars of much higher price, we are able to include all in appointment, in finish, completeness and other essentials that is to be had in any closed body automobile.

Designed by 48 Leading Engineers

HUDSON cars are designed and built by 48 expert engineers, at the head of which body is Howard E. Coffin, America's leading automobile designer.

These men were gathered from 97 leading factories of Europe and America and have had a hand in building more than 200,000 motor cars.

They have contributed all their experience and skill to the production of the HUDSON "37" and the "54" HUDSON. These cars are the best they know.

Just as much skill and experience is incorporated into the building of the bodies.

The imagination of the most fastidious buyer can suggest nothing in appointment, tone, character or completeness that these cars do not possess. Every thought has been anticipated. In choosing a HUDSON the only detail that you do not get which is found in other cars, is that uncertain quality which cost alone suggests but does not assure.

Electric Self-Cranking—Electrically Lighted

The Limousine and Coupe bodies used are identical for both chassis. The former seats seven—the latter three passengers. Limousines are finished in imported Bedford cord, over-stuffed upholstering. The Coupe is upholstered in pebble grain leather.

The Limousine on the "37" chassis is $3250, and on the "54"—the Six—chassis—is $3750. The Coupe on the "37" is $2350, and on the "54" $2950. Prices are f. o. b. Detroit. Open bodies—either Touring, Torpedo or Roadster Type—are furnished at extra charge.

HUDSON MOTOR CAR COMPANY

7531 Jefferson Ave., Detroit

See the Triangle on the Radiator

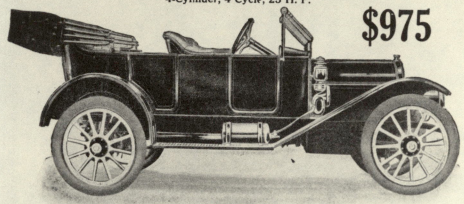
The Paige-Detroit of 1911 from the Automobiles File for Paige-Detroit for 1911, and the Paige sedan of 1916 in the Advertisement File, Paige-Detroit, 1916.

PAIGE

The Standard of Value and Quality

The SEDAN $1900
F.O.B DETROIT

Closed Car Models

Cabriolet	-	$1600
Sedan	-	1900
Town Car	-	2250
Mounted on "Six-46" Chassis		
Fairfield "Six-46" -	$1295	
Seven passenger		
Hollywood "Six-36"	1095	
Five passenger		

THE Paige Sedan is the highest type of "year 'round" car.

Cozy and warm for winter service, it can be instantly converted into an open car by lowering the window panels into the lower casements.

Whipcord, broadcloth or Bedford is used in the upholstering. The appointments throughout are luxurious and distinctive.

With the two side doors—with the wide aisle between the front seats—with the two auxiliary folding chairs—the Sedan is as commodious as a luxurious salon.

And—most important of all—this handsome body is built upon the famous Paige "Six-46" chassis. The price, complete, is $1900.

The Paige-Detroit Motor Car Co.
1210 McKinstry Ave.   Detroit

(1)

The Social Extremes

Though they aimed for the top of the price—class pyramid, most automotive leaders had to settle for a less-lofty market niche as they failed to find the capital or customers needed to gain the summit. Some wisely abandoned the ascent when they realized it was hurting their company's prospects; others persevered into bankruptcy.

Two Detroit cars that reached the summit of the price—class hierarchy were Lozier (shown here and on the jacket) and Packard. They sold to wealthy buyers who hoped that an upper-class automobile would give them a "reputation" for being "quality people." At the far end of the price—class hierarchy was Ford, a utility car for the masses, especially farmers. The social extremes were echoed in Detroit's community affairs where the owners of Packards and Loziers often opposed the owners of Fords. They simply had two different models of how the world should work.

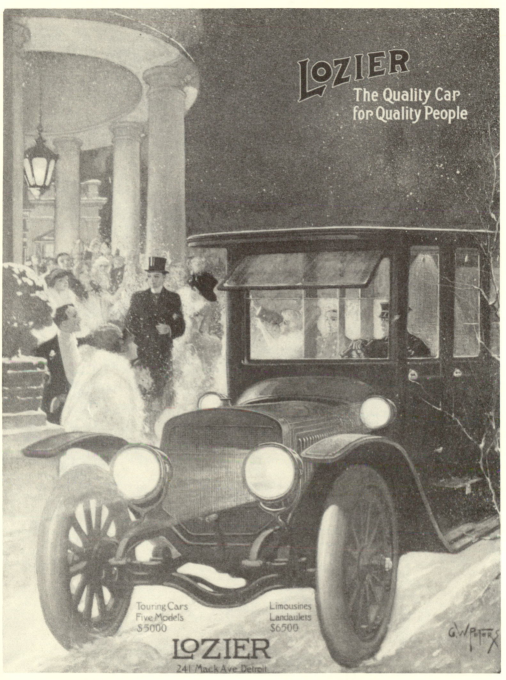

Life, January 9, 1913.

"The supreme combination of all that is fine in motor cars."

The Restful Car

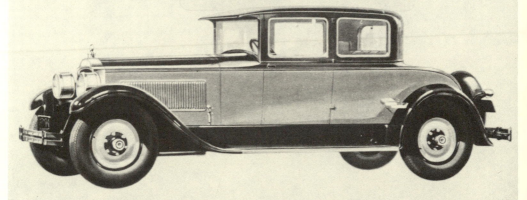

Reputation · Enduring fame is a sufficient reward to many for a lifetime of effort and great accomplishment. Certainly a well deserved and outstanding reputation is even more difficult to achieve than financial success.

Packard has achieved both. But Packard reputation today, after twenty-seven years of service to the public, is an even greater asset than Packard's absolute financial independence.

For Packard is a name which means superlatively fine motor cars in every quarter of the globe. And this reputation, so laboriously and deliberately built up, is more jealously guarded than all the gold in Packard's surplus.

It means more. For it reflects the confidence of the world in Packard vehicles—in Packard engines. Packard power has won international renown on the land, in the air and on the water. A generation of uninterrupted success and constant leadership is the best guarantee that that excellence of reputation will be sustained.

PACKARD

ASK THE MAN WHO OWNS ONE

The portrait is of General John J. Pershing, the most famous general in World War I. *Scientific American,* March 1927.

THE UNIVERSAL CAR

Farmers' dollars are big dollars—because they are hard earned dollars. It is because the American farmer is ever a careful and painstaking buyer that he is today the happy and proud possessor of more than half the Ford cars in existence.

75,000 Ford cars already sold this season— one-third of America's product. Five passenger touring car—torpedo runabout —delivery car—town car. Get Catalog from Ford Motor Company, Detroit, Mich.

Ford Times, September 1912. From the collections of Henry Ford Museum & Greenfield Village.

Chapter Four

Middle-Class Entrepreneurs and Their Firms

■ Until 1903, Detroit's old families had almost a complete monopoly over the quantity production of automobiles in the Motor City. That year, however, saw fourteen local companies organized; eleven more started up the following year. The influx did not slacken until the country's entry into World War I in 1917. By then, at least 214 different automobile companies had come to Detroit. Most of them had, however, quickly failed: the population of automotive manufacturers, after peaking in 1913 at forty-three, fell steadily thereafter, dropping below thirty in 1917 and below twenty in 1923. By 1933 only seven companies remained independent and still manufacturing motor vehicles in Detroit out of the 239 or more that had attempted to build cars there since the late 1890s (Table 20).[1] The survivors were Ford, General Motors, Chrysler, Hudson, Hupmobile, Packard, and Graham-Paige (formerly Paige-Detroit).

Even a vintage car buff would have difficulty recognizing the names of many of the automobiles enumerated and some of their names are in any case best forgotten. Certainly, few modern drivers recall the Tyro, Tom Thumb, Wiffler, Bi-Car or S&M. It would be unfair, however, to leave the impression that all the also-rans were misconceived. Some are included in the thirty-one Detroit automobile companies that realized at least a moderate success; that is, they either ranked among the industry's ten leading producers nationwide at least once before 1925 or demonstrated better than average durability by surviving into their fifth season—a feat achieved by less than a seventh of the total. These superior companies are listed in Table 21, as are the dates during which they operated as independent enterprises in the Motor City. Six of them belonged to Detroit's pre-automotive elite (and, more narrowly, the financial elite); of the remainder, the great majority were founded between 1907 and 1914. These years witnessed a brief moment of

84

opportunity for entrepreneurs with more courage than capital. Until then the industry had been so volatile, its design and engineering requirements so unpredictable from one year to the next, that only the most established firms and families could raise sufficient capital to persist in it.

As of 1905, Ford and Pungs-Finch were the only non-elite exceptions to this rule. The latter, however, cut such a minor figure that it merited only a single, brief reference in George May's detailed history of Michigan's auto industry; John Rae, the leading chronicler of the national industry, ignored it completely. So the Ford Motor Company was in fact one of a kind, its success built upon the expensive research and development financed by members of the McMillan alliance during Henry Ford's first two, failed automotive ventures.[2]

After 1907 the industry became temporarily much easier to enter because it settled upon a universal design—the four-cylinder touring car—that could be assembled from standard parts bought from specialists like Continental Motors, Timken-Detroit Axle, Kelsey Wheel, and Fisher Body. Assembling required relatively little capital, for the parts companies assumed most of the financial burden: "Many of the so-called motor car manufacturers," a Timken veteran later recalled, "in reality owned nothing but a name plate and an assembly building." These companies would be hard pressed to survive after 1913 when their sources of supply began to dry up (through vertical integration and merger), the public soured on "assembled cars," and the industry's leading firms—notably Ford—started to achieve significant economies of scale. But for a brief interlude the barriers to entry lowered sufficiently to enable middle-class entrepreneurs to organize viable automobile companies.[3]

It is not possible, for lack of space and sources, to deal with all these newcomers; this chapter examines only the five most successful. Case studies of Chalmers, Hudson, Hupmobile, Dodge, and Saxon demonstrate that the middle-class entrepreneurs and their companies were no more able than Detroit's upper class to ignore the status connotations of the automobile. Thanks to their limited resources, they did not have the option of starting off expensively in the luxury market with a Packard or Lozier. They had to build a more modest, generic model, a runabout or touring car for the medium-priced market. Yet as their companies became more firmly established and the entrepreneurs themselves grew wealthy, later models began to ascend the price-class hierarchy. These cars announced the social arrival of their owners, a group that encompassed the manufacturer as well as the purchaser.

Table 20
Detroit Automobile Industry: Entries and Exits

Year	Companies Entering	Companies Exiting	Net Gain or Loss	Total at Year's End
1897–1900	4	1	+3	3
1901	3	2	+1	4
1902	5	1	+4	8
1903	14	1	+13	21
1904	11	13	−2	19
1905	11	7	+4	23
1906	9	6	+3	26
1907	10	12	−2	24
1908	8	11	−3	21
1909	14	9	+5	26
1910	31	27	+4	30
1911	16	13	+3	33
1912	12	12	0	33
1913	18	8	+10	43
1914	26	31	−5	38
1915	12	17	−5	33
1916	10	15	−5	28
1917	3	5	−2	26
1918	0	5	−5	21
1919	2	2	0	21
1920	2	0	+2	23
1921	7	5	+2	25
1922	5	8	−3	22
1923	1	9	−8	14
1924	2	4	−2	12
1925–1929	2	6	−4	8
1930–1933	1	2	−1	7
Total	239	232	+7	7

Sources: Automobile Quarterly, *The American Car since 1775* (New York, 1971); Automobile Manufacturers Association, *Automobiles of America* (Detroit, 1968); automobile trade journals; the Detroit press.

Table 21
Major Detroit Motor Vehicle Companies before 1925

Companies in Top Ten U.S. Producers (any one year)	Years in Detroit	Additional Companies Surviving Five Years or More	Years in Detroit
Oldsmobile	1899–1905	Northern	1902–1908
Packard	1902–1954	Detroit Electric	1907–1923
Brush Runabout	1907–1910	Abbott	1909–1916
E-M-F	1908–1910	Paige-Detroit	1909–1928
Hupmobile	1908–1940	Carharrt	1910–1916
Studebaker	1910–1926	King	1911–1923
Saxon	1913–1922	Grant	1913–1922
Chrysler	1924–	Liberty	1916–1923
Cadillac	1902–1909	Pungs-Finch	1904–1910
Ford	1903–	Regal	1907–1918
Chalmers	1908–1917	Krit	1909–1914
General Motors	1908–	Warren	1909–1914
Hudson	1909–1954	Grinnell	1910–1916
Maxwell	1913–1925	R.C.H.	1911–1916
Dodge	1914–1928	Columbia	1916–1924
		Doble	1917–1924

By producing conspicuously, the middle-class companies lost their original markets and momentum. As a result two of our five, Saxon and Hupmobile, went bankrupt; two others, Chalmers and Dodge, had to be sold to avert bankruptcy. Hudson fared better but only because in 1918 it created a subsidiary, Essex Motors, to reoccupy the niche that Hudson had forsaken in the lower end of the medium-priced market.

In the end, none of the five companies was able to reach the upper price-class. They were, in other words, less successful at "social climbing" than their own proprietors had been. By 1918 the auto industry's new men had become part of Detroit's upper class, their rapid social ascent demonstrating the extent to which these new men and Detroit's old families must have shared fundamental values. One of these values was, to borrow a phrase from Thorstein Veblen, a tendency to attach social prestige to the conspicuous production of prized commodities. A shared commitment, within their respective means, to the conspicuous production of automobiles helped to unify old and new money in Detroit, undoubtedly accelerating the formation of a new, more inclusive upper class. Ironically, however, it also ensured that the addition of the auto industry's new men would do little to strengthen that class, for their emphasis on the middle price-class—the most crowded and competitive segment of the automotive market—gave the middle-class entrepreneurs insufficient economic clout to offset the growing influence of Ford, General Motors, and Chrysler, three companies less prone to produce conspicuously.[4]

■ 1   Chalmers-Detroit, the oldest of the five most successful middle-class companies, might never have been founded had Oldsmobile not decided to abandon the lower price-class. In opting for the heavier, more expensive models beloved by the patrician Fred Smith, Olds ignored a light, four-cylinder model designed by its chief engineer, Howard E. Coffin, as a replacement for the curved-dash runabout. Coffin therefore joined with three colleagues—sales manager Roy D. Chapin, purchasing agent Fred O. Bezner, and traffic manager James J. Brady—in organizing a company to produce Coffin's prototype. The four, all from middle-class backgrounds, lacked the financial and social connections necessary to start up an automobile company, and they made little headway until Roy Chapin conceived the idea of looking for a financial "angel" in the California resorts. There Chapin made the acquaintance of auto magnate Erwin R. Thomas of Buffalo, who manufactured the Thomas "Flyer," winner of the celebrated "Great Race" of 1908. Thomas agreed to finance a Detroit subsidiary with the four former Olds executives as his junior partners and managing directors. On May 8, 1906, they incorporated the E. R. Thomas–Detroit Company with a capitalization of $300,000, one-tenth of it paid in at the organizational meeting. Two-thirds of the capital stock went to Thomas, who put up an additional $100,000 and undertook to market Coffin's small car through his sales network. His four partners split the remaining stock.[5]

Thomas-Detroit, like E-M-F, prospered from its alliance with an established firm, selling 500 cars in its first year. Chapin, however, fretted over absentee rule; he knew that E. R. Thomas, controlling the sales network and two-thirds of the stock, had the power to shut down the business at will, leaving his partners in the lurch. Chapin therefore looked for a new investor with sufficient money and influence to offset the Buffalo capitalist and the ability to build an independent sales organization for the Detroit concern.[6]

He found him in Dayton, Ohio, at National Cash Register (NCR), a firm famous both for its high-pressure sales techniques and for its summary dismissals of senior executives. In 1907 NCR's vice-president, Hugh Chalmers, got the sack, and he agreed to take the presidency of Thomas-Detroit for a salary of $50,000 a year and a chance to become his own boss by purchasing half of E. R. Thomas's controlling interest. By June 1908 Chalmers was firmly in control, and Thomas-Detroit was renamed in his honor.[7]

His experience with NCR convinced Chalmers that success in the durable goods sector depended more on salesmanship than on technical proficiency. Accordingly, he devoted most of his energies to marketing, and under his personal leadership Chalmers-Detroit became celebrated for such promotions as its annual award to baseball's leading batter and for the triumphs of its "Blue Bird" racing team, but its reputation as a manufacturer steadily declined. In 1909 it lost the core of its production staff when Chapin, Coffin, Bezner, and Roscoe B. Jackson left to organize the Hudson Motor Car Company. In December of that year Hugh Chalmers bought their stock for just under a million dollars, thus becoming the unchallenged authority in Chalmers-Detroit. He then surrounded himself with salesmen, many of them—Lee Counselman, E. C. Morse, and Harry W. Ford, for example—trained at NCR. Between 1909 and 1917 eight different men held the post of assistant manager or general manager; not one had had any manufacturing experience.[8]

The rule of the sales staff made the Chalmers car stylish but technically outmoded. Perhaps the Chalmers "30," as its advertisements proclaimed, "afford[ed] more eye delight" than cars selling over $5,000, but it also went "basically unchanged" from 1908 to mid-1913. It sold in the $2,000 range, placing it among the rarefied ranks of the upper-middle-class makes—an ambiguous position that corresponded to Hugh Chalmers's social origins and ambitions. In 1915, selling only 7,500 of its expensive cars, Chalmers-Detroit ran into financial difficulties and turned to New York for financial assistance. J. S. Bache, a major brokerage, stepped in to reorganize it as the Chalmers Motor Car Corporation.[9]

When sales still failed to pick up, Chalmers sought additional relief through merger with the Maxwell Motor Company, which needed additional plant facilities. In September 1917 Maxwell leased Chalmers's property for five years on a profit-sharing basis. The agreement—a recognition of defeat—ended Chalmers's independent existence. It was "practically a liquidation," a banker noted, for the assets were "pressed down to a minimum figure" to induce Maxwell to lease them. For the next five years Maxwell tried to retrieve the Chalmers market, but the name no longer sold automobiles. The Chalmers line lost more than a million dollars, and was dropped in 1922. Eugene W. Lewis, a parts supplier, provided its best obituary: "If Hugh had been as fine a manufacturer as he was a salesman, his car would probably be well known today."[10]

■ 2   Hugh Chalmers had another opportunity to build an enduring name for himself in the automotive industry: had he not sold his stock in December 1909, he might now be remembered as one of the founders of the Hudson Motor Car Company, forerunner of American Motors. Chapin and Coffin had organized Hudson the previous February after Chalmers had refused to produce a small car for the medium-priced market. Coffin had designed such a car, a twenty-horsepower model, and wanted to put it into production. Once again, as at Olds, he found himself stymied by the ambitions of his wealthier associates. Clearly, it was still difficult to raise capital for the manufacture of a low-priced car.[11]

Fortunately, one of Coffin's engineering assistants, Roscoe B. Jackson, had recently married the niece of J. L. Hudson, Detroit's wealthiest bachelor, and this marriage offered Coffin and his partners a chance to raise the needed money. Hudson, a department store magnate and "emblem of integrity, civic-mindedness and material success" in Detroit, was the perfect sponsor, especially since he also had excellent banking connections with Wall Street through the E. Naumberg Company of New York. Through Jackson's efforts, he met with Roy Chapin and together they mapped out the Hudson Motor Car Company. J. L. Hudson gave it his name and most of the $15,000 in its treasury, receiving in return 18 percent of the stock. Hugh Chalmers took 15 percent, and Coffin, Chapin, Bezner, Jackson, and Brady split the rest. For the first time Chapin and his closest allies controlled an automobile company, and even though Hudson was considerably smaller than Chalmers-Detroit, they decided to stake their automotive futures on its success. They feared—quite rightly, as it turned out—that Hugh Chalmers would go the big-car route, and they knew they lacked the muscle in Chalmers-Detroit to restrain him. Therefore, Chapin, Coffin and Bezner approached Chalmers and suggested a stock swap. In December 1909 they completed the deal, with Chalmers paying an additional $788,000 to cover the difference in the value of the stock traded.[12]

Hudson was an instant success: within a year its profits had made Coffin, Chapin, and Bezner millionaires, permitting them to take early retirement. In 1911 they handed the company over to Jackson and his assistants: "We have faith in the future of the company under your control," Chapin told him. The trio chose well: under Roscoe Jackson and William J. McAneeny, their stock appreciated 450 times between 1909 and 1926. The company's success attested to the excellence of the organization that Chapin had assembled and to the passion for engineering excellence that Coffin had bequeathed the firm.[13]

Hudson's cars appealed to a middle-class clientele who wanted technical precision but could not afford elite styling. Rarely did its advertisements stress beauty; rather they boasted that "the Hudson car is the simplest, most clean cut" on the market and that it represented "good, sound, automobile design." Leaving out expensive frills, Hudson built first-class automobiles at a reasonable price. Its greatest triumphs included the first moderately priced six-cylinder automobile, in 1912; eight years later the first closed body to go into mass production; and in 1926 the first all-steel body manufactured "on a production basis in the manufacturer's own plant."[14]

Though Hudson's first model sold for $900 in 1909—the price of a comparably equipped Model T Ford—the pursuit of engineering excellence drove its price skyward until it reached $2,200 in 1918. Obviously, the company had forgotten that its founders had quit both Olds and Chalmers-Detroit in order to pursue their ambition of making a low-priced car; the higher price was more in keeping with their own higher social status and income. In short, Hudson was now serving the peer group of its founders. There were not enough of these to keep the company healthy, however, and between 1916 and 1918 sales fell by half. Hudson responded to the crisis by forming a subsidiary to market the less expensive Essex. At $1,395 the Essex occupied a considerably higher notch in the price-class hierarchy than had the original Hudson, but it was, even so, sufficiently popular to power the corporation into the ranks of the industry's eight leading producers during the 1920s.[15]

■ 3   Both Chalmers and Hudson suffered for their price-class inflation. And they were not alone, as we shall see from the histories of three other leading firms. Hupmobile (or more properly the Hupp Motor Car Co.) had the distinction of being the most humbly financed of Detroit's major automobile companies; it came closest to filling the main contours of the automotive paradigm (Chapter 1). Its story began in 1908 when two brothers, J. Walter and Joseph R. Drake, and John E. Baker invested $3,500 in a prototype being developed by Robert C. Hupp, a one-time assembler and car tester for Olds who was then head of Ford's repair and accessory department. Hupp completed the first Hupmobile the night before Detroit's annual auto show, but it seemed pointless to display it when the partners had no further money to invest. Fortunately, at this juncture Charles D. Hastings intervened. Formerly Olds's office manager, he now held the same position with Thomas-Detroit. He knew how to sell cars: he took the Hupmobile to the show, got orders for 500, and collected $25,000 in cash deposits. This was enough to begin production, and additional money came in as cars were delivered. Edwin Denby, a lawyer and congressman from Detroit, paid in another $7,500, thereby gaining an equal share with Hupp, Baker, and the two Drakes. Hastings joined in 1909 and soon rose to the post of general manager and vice-president.[16]

Hupmobile later emphasized its penurious origins, and parts of its history did read like a Horatio Alger tale. By industry standards, its founders were poor. At the age of thirty-two Robert Hupp, the son of a railroad freight agent, had no money; his partners, very little. The Drakes came from an immigrant family: their father was a small-town merchant; Joseph, a retail jeweler, sold his store to invest in Hupp. Walter had been a Detroit lawyer with a solid though not spectacular practice before becoming president of Hupmobile in 1908. He apparently met Denby while both served during the Spanish-American War aboard the USS *Yosemite*.[17]

Denby had by far the most illustrious social credentials of the Hupp investors: grandson of a United States senator and son of the first American ambassador to China, he came from patrician stock and was a member of the Sons of the American Revolution. Still, he had only modest assets; according to E. G. Pipp of the *Detroit News*, Denby was so poor when he first ran for Congress in 1904 that he had to beg the paper for "free publicity." However, his investment in Hupp and his 1911 marriage to Marion Thurber, daughter of President Grover Cleveland's private secretary, laid the foundations for his fortune: by 1923 his assets topped $300,000, and he had for some time been traveling in the same social circles as Packard's well-heeled investors.[18]

The Hupmobile stockholders were bent on getting rich as quickly as possible: from 1908 onward they paid out 60 percent of profits as dividends, leaving the company with inadequate financial reserves to ward off hard times. These arrived in 1915 as the company encountered consumer resistance to its ever-rising prices. Originally, it had offered a $750 runabout, but by 1911 it had opted instead for a larger, more expensive touring car.[19]

The firm's decision should by now occasion no surprise, nor should Robert C. Hupp's reaction. In 1911 he and Hupmobile parted company: he said he quit; the owners said he was fired. Whatever the case, he left because of his continued commitment to small cars, a commitment no longer shared by his now wealthy associates. His new company, the R.C.H. Corporation, offered a $700 car that sold well at first, but as a trade journal later recalled, "the car did not stand up well in users' hands." By 1913, R.C.H. was bankrupt; its creditors lost more than a million dollars; and Robert Hupp's auto career was effectively over.[20]

By 1915, Hupmobile's big-car strategy had brought it to a similar crisis. To save themselves, the stockholders sold a controlling interest for $6.5 million to a syndicate of New York and Chicago banks, which then placed three representatives on the board of directors. Thereafter, the firm was a hybrid: though absentee-owned and -controlled, it still acted like a local business concern, for J. Walter Drake continued as president, and his old associates remained active in the organization. Hupp's time of troubles reversed the previous trend toward building ever more costly and prestigious automobiles. Adversity taught the company its proper place in the industry's price-class hierarchy, and it restricted its sales to the lower half of the middle-class market, boasting thereafter that it made "the best car of this class in the world."[21]

■ 4   Evidently, middle-class entrepreneurs were as loath to build cars for the lower-class market as were Detroit's patricians. Though they commonly started off at the bottom of the middle price-class, they almost inevitably made a bid to join the industry's more glamorous upscale producers. This was true even of Dodge Brothers, Inc., although its two controlling stockholders, John and Horace Dodge, had at one time been willing to risk their entire careers in backing Henry Ford, the chief proponent of manufacturing utility cars for the masses. But the Dodge brothers, too, raised their sights as prosperity came their way. The sons of a skilled mechanic, John and Horace had served their apprenticeship as machinists in Detroit before crossing the river to Windsor, Ontario, in 1894 to open a bicycle factory; it was a small operation and brought only $10,000 when sold in 1899 to a Canadian bicycle combine. They then recrossed the Detroit River to start a machine shop, which in 1901 received its first big order: 1,000 engines and transmissions for the Olds runabout. In 1903 the Dodge brothers, taking a giant gamble, turned down lucrative contracts from Olds and Northern to join the infant Ford Motor Company as minority stockholders and manufacturers of the engine and chassis for the "Fordmobile."[22]

Until 1903 the brothers had proceeded conservatively. Why, then, did they risk their hard-earned independence on Henry Ford, a two-time loser who had offended most of Detroit's financial elite? Allan Nevins has suggested that "faith in Ford's engine designs and the hope of a larger profit" lured them into Ford's net. The engine may have attracted them, but the profit argument seems plausible only by hindsight. The deal with Ford, as John Dodge later admitted, was not all that advantageous for the two brothers. In return for 10 percent of the capital stock of the Ford Motor Company they had to invest $3,000 of their own money, forgive $7,000 in debts owed them, and retool their machine shop to produce 650 chassis and engines ordered by Ford. Though the latter advanced $15,000 to help meet the cost of producing the first batch of engines, retooling actually cost Dodge Brothers between $60,000 and $75,000—which meant that the machine shop would soon have been bankrupt had not Ford, one of the most undercapitalized of the industry's major firms, been an instant success.[23]

It would seem that the rationale behind the Dodges' alliance with Ford lay not in the fine print of the contracts they signed but in the nexus of shared aspirations and prejudices. Socially, John and Horace Dodge belonged to Ford's world rather than to the rarefied climes inhabited by the Olds and Northern stockholders. Uneducated and rough-hewn, they did not fit into an automotive world still controlled, in 1903, by Detroit's financial elite. Even in 1914, when the Dodges—now multimillionaires—set out to establish their own independent automobile company, they still proved an unappetizing nostrum for Detroit "society" to swallow.

John Dodge, in particular, gained notoriety for his public drinking and rowdyism. His most celebrated brawl took place in his favorite saloon: in the midst of a serious drinking bout he suddenly ordered its proprietor to dance. When the latter indignantly refused, Dodge pulled out a revolver and barked, "I mean what I say, and I want you to get up on that table and dance!" While the frightened saloonkeeper complied, the auto manufacturer hurled shot glasses at the bar mirror by way of applause. On another occasion he reportedly smashed all the light bulbs in the chandelier gracing the banquet room of Detroit's finest hotel. He got away with these pranks because he paid handsomely for damages and because he belonged to the "City Hall gang" during the mayoralty of Oscar Marx (1913–1919). As Marx's chief bankroller, Dodge was the "unquestioned 'Warwick' of the . . . dominant section of the local Republican [party]," who made its members "do his will by a mere word."[24]

Money and connections kept the police blotter unstained but did not at first buy the Dodges' way into polite society. John Dodge apparently was the most important automobile executive ever blackballed by the Detroit Club; even the auto-dominated Detroit Athletic Club accepted the two brothers only with "deep misgivings." In time, the Dodges' millions prevailed. In June 1920, shortly before his own death and five months after his brother had passed away, Horace "arrived" in a grand manner. The marriage of his daughter Delphine into a prominent Philadelphia family preoccupied the local press for a week, in part because the Detroit Symphony Orchestra, out of gratitude for his financial support, played at her reception. All of that lay in the future, however; in 1903 the Dodge brothers felt far more at home in the company of Henry Ford, a farmer's son, and they probably sympathized with his plans to build an inexpensive vehicle for the common man. In any case, they rejected the blandishments of elite companies like Olds and Northern in favor of helping Ford launch his automotive revolution.[25]

Their perspective had by July 1914 subtly altered. Thanks to their share of Ford's profits they had become multimillionaires, able to provide virtually all of the $5 million in capital needed by their newly incorporated Dodge Brothers, Inc. Like so many of the middle-class entrepreneurs enriched by the auto industry, they wanted to develop a car superior to the one that had launched them on the path to fortune. Believing that a "man's work is but an expression of the character of the man," they wanted to "build a product they might deem worthy of themselves." That meant an upgraded Model T. The first Dodge sported several features the Ford automobile conspicuously lacked: an all-steel body, independent suspension, sliding gear transmission, and electric starter. This was a package calculated to appeal to Ford's more prosperous customers; as John Dodge exclaimed, "Just think of all those Ford owners who will someday want an automobile."[26]

In many respects, the Dodge "chugger" and the "Tin Lizzie" were close cousins. Like Ford, the Dodge company set as its primary goal the building of an "honest, good car" offering "comfortable and dependable transportation at the lowest possible price." To keep costs low, both companies settled upon a standard model and avoided making cosmetic changes. Dodge started with only one type of chassis and thereafter resisted enlarging its product line, operating on the slogan "Constant improvement but no yearly model change." Dodge also kept mechanical changes to a minimum: "So thoroughly were the Dodge Brothers sold on the simplicity and dependability of their four-cylinder engine . . . that this power plant remained the only one used in . . . the 1914–1920 period—and for a number of years after the founders' passing." When change became inevitable, it was deliberately disguised so that "older model Dodges could be updated by using genuine factory parts."[27]

Though closely related, the Dodge and the Ford differed in one vital respect: price. Dodge was clearly the rich relation. At $785, even the first Dodge cost $300 more than a Model T touring car, and thereafter the gap widened: the price of Dodge's cheapest model rose to $1,085 in 1920. Along the way it exchanged position in the price-class hierarchy with several other firms, including Reo, Buick, Chevrolet, and Willys-Overland (see Table 8, Chapter One). The brothers claimed that they wanted to serve the "average citizen," a mythical individual they deemed three times as wealthy as did the Ford Motor Company. Despite their rhetoric, despite the many points of convergence between their manufacturing philosophy and Ford's, the Dodge brothers in the end behaved like the typical middle-class auto entrepreneur. They were so wealthy by 1914 that they had perhaps lost touch with the economic reality of life in America for the "average citizen."[28]

Even less in touch was the Wall Street investment house of Dillon, Read, which bought control of Dodge in 1925 from the brothers' widows. As *Fortune* magazine later recounted, "They began prettying up their products and they deserted their price class." By 1928 it was possible to buy a Dodge priced as high as $2,000. The bankers' model policy almost ruined the company: from third place in 1924 it slipped to ninth in 1928, its impending bankruptcy averted only by a timely sale to the Chrysler Corporation. Dodge was so badly bitten by the big-car bug that it was not even able to meet its payroll at the end.[29]

In the final analysis, Dodge was not all that different from the rest of the companies founded by middle-class auto entrepreneurs. They all seemed to fit a common pattern: they started off by manufacturing or assembling a small car whose price put it at the boundary of the lower- and middle-class markets. For most of them it would have been difficult, if not impossible, to raise the capital necessary for a more expensive make, especially if it required more in-house manufacturing. The elite investors in Packard could afford to erect a self-sufficient plant, but that was not an option for the middle-class entrepreneurs. However, as their companies prospered, they became more ambitious; their cars grew in size, and it was clear that the entrepreneurs wanted to crown their careers by making a prestige automobile. In each case, albeit to varying degrees, their ascent through the price-class hierarchy ended in crisis. The survivors, much chastened, generally traded in their prestige models for more humble revenue-producers.

■ 5   By raising their prices, the middle-class entrepreneurs ran counter to the industry trend. Most of them started off selling cars for less than $875. In 1910 these cars captured 13 percent of sales by volume; six years later their share had risen to 71 percent. Detroit's middle-class companies had in the meantime boosted their prices so that their cheapest models cost between $875 and $1,775—while the market share of this price-class was falling from 68 percent in 1910 to 25 percent in 1916. The middle-class producers, operating in an overpopulated field, had a high mortality rate (remember, we have been dealing with the *success* stories here) and low profit margins.[30] The obvious question arises: why did they not move to contest the low-priced field where most of the industry's growth took place after 1910?

Hupmobile's general manager Charles Hastings had an answer: Ford had that market sewn up. "It was almost a prohibitive proposition," he claimed, "for anyone to . . . compete with Ford. I think a man would have been a fool to go into the automobile industry with that in mind." Paige's president Harry Jewett concurred: "It was an acknowledged fact among all the local manufacturers that to endeavor to compete against Ford you might just as well go against a brick wall."[31] It was not quite that simple: the Saxon Motor Company proved in 1914 that it was possible to meet Ford head on and survive. Its subsequent fate, however, revealed the limited horizons of the middle-class auto entrepreneurs.

Saxon started in 1913 with $100,000 in capital subscribed equally by Hugh Chalmers and nine executives of Chalmers-Detroit. Under the presidency of Harry W. Ford, Chalmers's general manager, it built a four-cylinder, two-passenger automobile priced under $500. That is, it targeted the same market as Ford, and its advertising copy, stressing the car's utility and economy, read like Ford literature. The formula worked: Saxon sold 53,000 cars from 1914 to 1916, placing it eighth in the industry. At the end of its first year it declared a 1,200 percent dividend in cash and stocks. Then—in a familiar crisis—the board of directors split into warring factions over prices and models. In 1915 Harry Ford bought out Hugh Chalmers and the Chalmers-Detroit group; apparently they had never been particularly interested in serving the lower-class market and were only too willing to accept a 1,400 percent profit for their brief investment. Ironically, Harry Ford himself introduced a six-cylinder model that same year and gradually shifted the company's emphasis toward the middle-price range. Predictably, sales fell off, and in 1917 the company's creditors forced their way onto Saxon's board of directors. With Harry Ford's death late the following year, one of these—Benjamin Gotfredson, president of American Auto Trimming—took charge. He oversaw Saxon's demise in 1922.[32]

Saxon clearly fell victim to the industry's penchant for conspicuous production. It failed because Harry Ford succumbed to the big-car bug and because its erstwhile backers had little faith in the original plan of competing head-on against the Ford Motor Company in the lower-class field. All five of our case studies have featured entrepreneurs who could not resist the impulse to build more expensive, more prestigious makes as their own fortunes improved. Perhaps they lost touch with the market, believing that the whole world was getting wealthier with them; or perhaps, as they became wealthier, money became a less powerful incentive than pride in manufacturing a fine automobile—one that their newly acquired acquaintances at the country club would admire. Whichever the case, they obligingly vacated the lower-class market, leaving it to Henry Ford almost by default.

■ **6**　　　　This chapter has been dealing with the most successful of the middle-class companies; it is likely that the minor companies displayed a similar pattern of prestige behavior. One indication that the big-car mania was almost universal in Detroit's automotive circles was the marked tendency for middle-class entrepreneurs to move upward in price as they moved between motor ventures. We have already seen this phenomenon in the careers of Ransom Olds, Roy Chapin, Howard Coffin, and the Dodge brothers. Also noteworthy for their corporate social climbing were three executives—Percy Owen, R. E. Cole, and H. M. Wirth—who left lowly Saxon in 1916 to manufacture the Liberty, a car in the upper-middle-class bracket; and three others—J. G. Bayerline, T. A. Bollinger, and W. L. Daly—who stopped producing the middle-priced King car in 1916 in order to launch the Columbia, a considerably more expensive make.[33]

Meanwhile, William Metzger was proceeding upward from low-priced Cadillac and Northern runabouts to the mid-range E-M-F and Everitt touring cars (the latter produced by the Metzger Motor Car Company from 1909 to 1912) and then finally to the Rickenbacker roadster in 1921. This last was the most exciting and luxurious make with which he was associated; it was, therefore, a fitting capstone to his career, even it its life-span was fairly brief. Joining him at Rickenbacker was his one-time E-M-F partner Walter Flanders, whose career also seemed to lead him ever upward in the price-class hierarchy. There were exceptions to the rule: obviously, not every senior executive had the luxury of a choice. Enough of them did, however, for conspicuous production to characterize movement between companies as well as within them.[34]

The corporate and personal biographies of middle-class entrepreneurs, then, added to the statistical profiles in Chapter One, offer compelling evidence—admittedly circumstantial—that conspicuous production played a decisive role in the manufacture of middle-priced American automobiles before 1929. However, the case is not complete until the social behavior of these men has also been examined. A theory positing that industrialists allowed their social ambitions to intrude on their business decision-making must demonstrate that they did indeed have social ambitions.

The rest of this chapter therefore surveys the social and civic activities of the middle-class entrepreneurs with a view to establishing, first, that they were social beings with lives and ambitions outside the office; and second, that they quickly came to regard Detroit's upper class as their peer group. It argues that the social ascent of Detroit's middle-class automakers came with stunning rapidity: after all, it was not until 1906 that they founded their first company, Thomas-Detroit (later Chalmers), and it took another four years for success to buy them the time and resources to become involved in the world outside their offices. Yet by 1918—less than a decade later—the new men of the auto industry and Detroit's old families had coalesced into a new upper class.

Some observers will object that it is impossible—by definition—for any group to attain upper-class status within a generation, never mind a decade. E. Digby Baltzell, for example, has asserted that upper classes are always the product of two or more generations: "An upper class," he wrote in *Puritan Boston and Quaker Philadelphia*, "is nothing more or less than a *group of consanguine families* whose ancestors were elite members and family founders one or more generations earlier."[35] But this definition, stressing inherited status, would seem to have little application to the midwestern cities at the dawning of the automotive era. It may be a useful concept for the study of Boston and Philadelphia, but it appears to be of limited utility for an understanding of Detroit's social structure. Few members even of the McMillan alliance would have qualified under it as "upper class" in 1900, though they patently dominated the city's life.

Those who stress intermarriage, as does William Domhoff, might also have difficulty accepting the thesis of this chapter. It is true that three auto executives did marry nieces of J. L. Hudson, the department store magnate (Roscoe Jackson, Edsel B. Ford, and Ernest Kanzler), but they were very much the exception to the rule; besides, the willingness of Hudson's relations to wed social parvenus calls into question (according to some theorists) his own family's social status. Moreover, too much stress can be placed on marriage patterns. As John Ingham has pointed out in *The Iron Barons*, they may identify a city's "core families," but it is still possible to be a member of the upper class—albeit a "marginal" one—without such kinship ties.[36]

A definition that does encompass Detroit's new men within the city's upper class is provided by Frederic C. Jaher in *The Urban Establishment*, a study of the elites of five nineteenth-century American cities. Few if any American historians have devoted more attention than Jaher to the study of urban elites. His book, the culmination of his life's work, defines any group whose members "exercise authority, accumulate wealth, and command respect" as an "elite." The elite, he observes, tend to be functionally specialized; they develop into an "upper class" by expanding "their hegemony latitudinally." An upper class thus is characterized neither by inheritance nor by longevity (Jaher seeing the extension of dominion "longitudinally" as the hallmark of an urban "aristocracy") but rather by its multifaceted leadership. It was in this sense—of developing into a multifunctional elite—that the auto industry's new men can be regarded as "upper class" as early as 1918. By then, as we shall see, they were operating as partners and intimates of Detroit's old families in almost every aspect of community life.[37]

The co-optation of the owners of the middle-class automobile companies began about 1910. It was made possible by an increase of 175 percent in local, non-Ford automobile production between 1909 and 1911, an increase that transformed several harried executives into industrial statesmen. Hugh Chalmers, for example, decided in 1910 that Chalmers-Detroit no longer required his personal supervision; he surrendered the general managership to Lee Counselman and threw himself into the committee work of the Detroit Board of Commerce, serving as a director for the next two years. The following year Roy Chapin and Howard Coffin concluded that Hudson had reached a similar state of self-sufficiency. Roy Chapin, exploiting his newfound liberty, embroiled himself in Republican politics (an appropriate choice for an upwardly mobile Detroiter), agitated for an improved highway system, and co-founded an important downtown men's club.[38]

Once freed from their management responsibilities, the industry's leaders proved exceptionally active in community affairs. They were joiners. Data from the 1914 *Book of Detroiters* indicate that automotive leaders were twice as likely to belong to a social club and 22 percent more likely to join the local Board of Commerce than were other business leaders. A full listing of their multifarious activities would require a separate book; here there is space only to mention the highlights.

In becoming involved in the city's core financial institutions, the Board of Commerce, the Employers' Association, the municipal reform movement, state politics, Detroit's charities, and finally the downtown men's clubs, the automotive executives made a two-stage assault on Detroit society: between 1910 and 1912 they became junior partners in the city's leading institutions; over the next six years they gained a full partnership. Not all the activists were "new men"; Packard's patricians played a pivotal role in both industry and community affairs. But distinctions between old and new money had little meaning in the industry by 1918, for the newcomers—with the major exception of the Ford executives—readily accepted the old families' interpretation of what was best for Detroit.

In banking, an area central to the power of Detroit's pre-automotive elite, the 1910–1914 period was the turningpoint in the ascent of the industry's new men. Until then the lower- and middle-class companies found it extremely difficult to obtain credit locally. Even an established firm like Studebaker (E-M-F) frequently complained that the "conservative attitude of the Detroit banks to the automobile industry" forced them to "secure banking facilities outside of the city of Detroit." There was, to be sure, the occasional exception: William Livingstone of Dime Savings Bank climbed aboard the Ford bandwagon in 1906 by lending Henry Ford $100,000 to buy out his principal partner; and John T. Shaw of First National Bank (Detroit) rescued Cadillac twice from bankruptcy—in 1907 and 1910.[39]

Yet the banking community in general was so unsupportive that even the well-heeled Packard investors wanted to create an alternative source of credit. In March 1907 three Packard stockholders—Richard Joy, John Newberry, Jr., and Frederick Alger—attended a meeting chaired by Charles B. Warren, who had several automotive investments. The meeting spawned the city's first "automobile bank," the National Bank of Commerce, with Richard Joy as president. At first dominated by Detroit's pre-automotive elite, the bank soon added James Couzens of Ford to its board; and by 1917 Edsel Ford, John Dodge, Alvan Macauley (Packard), and A. R. Demory (Timken-Detroit) had also represented the automobile industry's new wealth within its councils.[40]

By 1916 four additional "automobile banks" had emerged, three of them organized by Henry Ford and James Couzens to service Ford and its employees (see Chapter Five). John and Horace Dodge took the initiative in organizing the fourth, Merchants' National Bank, in August 1914. Their partners included David Gray, a Ford heir, and three of the industry's new men: Hugh Chalmers, autoparts manufacturers Eugene W. Lewis (Timken-Detroit), and W. O. Briggs (Briggs Mfg.).[41]

Economic power that sprouted banks like dandelions could not be ignored by the railroad-car, stove, and timber families who controlled Detroit's major financial institutions. In 1910 the old-line banks began to add an automobile tycoon or two to their boards of directors. Between 1910 and 1912 Henry Ford collected four bank directorships; James Couzens and Paul Gray (Ford), Standish Backus (General Motors), and Roy Chapin (Hudson) also acquired passkeys to Detroit's financial establishment.[42]

The timetable governing the entry of the industry's nouveaux riches into Detroit's financial elite also dictated the pace at which they joined the city's associational life. Consider their growing involvement in the Detroit Board of Commerce, then the central command post for the civic activities of the business community. In 1910 the names of automotive leaders began to appear on its board of directors, with Henry Ford—the wealthiest and most powerful of the new men—the first elected. Very quickly the industry turned the board into its private preserve: between 1911 and 1917 the board's president came from either a passenger car company or an auto parts concern, with Homer Warren (Warren), James Couzens (Ford), Charles B. Warren (Paige), and Edwin Denby (Hupmobile) serving back to back. Throughout this period the board's leading figure was Hugh Chalmers: from 1910, when he headed its membership drive, until his company began to falter during World War I, his boundless energy suffused the organization and helped set its goals.[43]

It was also Chalmers who orchestrated the entry of the auto companies into the Employers' Association of Detroit (EAD), thus laying the foundation for the industry's subsequent domination of the local open shop movement. Once again, 1910 was the pivotal year. To be sure, Henry Leland of Cadillac had helped organize the Employers' Association in December 1902, but for the next eight years most automobile concerns paid only lip service to its union-busting goals. The Ford Motor Company typified the industry's lackluster support before 1910: it joined the EAD in 1903 but did not pay any dues before 1908; like most companies it became active only after Hugh Chalmers created the Automobile Division in 1910. By 1916, however, the auto industry controlled the association: its roster of officers included Allan Templeton, an autoparts supplier, as president; F. F. Beall of Packard as vice-president; and A. L. McMeans of Dodge Brothers as treasurer.[44]

Involvement in business organizations like the Employers' Association and the Board of Commerce helped to persuade the industry's parvenus that they and the pre-automotive elite shared a community of interest. They had, as well, a common interest in municipal reform. In May 1912, Henry Leland, president of Cadillac, organized the Detroit Citizens League to promote "moral and civic betterment in general, including politics where and when necessary." The league's secretary, William Lovett pronounced it a "merger of business and religion," inasmuch as it depended on the Protestant brotherhoods and men's clubs for the bulk of its officers and membership, while the automotive industry supplied approximately half of its finances.[45]

The industry's participation also constituted a merger of sorts (though not one spotlighted by league literature): the reform movement allied old and new money, bringing together patrician families like the Joys, the Ferrys (both Packard), the Buhls, and the Barbours (both Lozier) with the four Detroit-based directors of General Motors and the leaders of middle-class companies like Chalmers and Hudson. The alignment certainly demonstrated that the goals of structural reform of Henry Leland and the industry's new men were sufficiently conservative to rally the old guard. In their hands, the revolutionary new technology was not going to produce a political upheaval.[46]

In fact, the reform movement culminated in a referendum in June 1918 in which a small turnout of voters overwhelmingly endorsed a new city charter incorporating reforms first approved by the National Municipal League almost two decades before. The Municipal League's 1899 program was by 1918 more conventional than controversial, and it found ready support in the business community. As for the auto industry, it provided almost all the money spent by the Citizens' Charter Committee (an organization created by the Citizens League and headed by Hugh Chalmers) on the referendum campaign. Once again, old and new money came together (including donations from Edsel Ford, C. Harold Wills, and Horace Rackham of the Ford Motor Company) to promote a common vision.[47]

The new charter gave Detroit a strong mayor, with broad powers of appointment and dismissal, and a small council elected at-large. To expunge politics from city government, the charter made most offices appointive and separated municipal elections (thereafter nonpartisan) from state and federal voting. The charter, in other words, reconstructed municipal government as a board of directors for administration of the city's business. In Detroit, as elsewhere, structural reform tended to reduce the responsiveness of municipal government to non-elite groups and to increase, marginally, the influence of big business. However, the impact of the reforms should not be overstated: tinkering with political structures did little to affect the basic distribution of power in Detroit, as can be seen from the fact that the reform coalition failed to elect its choice for mayor even at the height of its influence in November 1918. For our purposes, reform was less important for what it accomplished than for the opportunity it afforded the old families and the new men to work together toward a common goal. A cooperative venture such as municipal reform undoubtedly facilitated the fusion of the two groups into a new upper class.[48]

So, undoubtedly, did politics in general; uniformity of status came naturally to a business elite with almost uniform political sentiments. Detroit's businessmen tended to be staunch, standpat Republicans of decidedly protectionist views. There was the occasional Democratic exception, usually for ethno-religious reasons, but Republicanism made good business sense in a town dominated by Senators McMillan and Alger and their associates. Even in 1914, with both senators deceased and the Republican party riven by the Progressive schism, Republicans still outnumbered Democrats among the business elite by five to one. As for auto manufacturers, they were—with the usual exception of Henry Ford—ardent protectionists and voted Republican in even greater numbers than the business community as a whole, as Table 22 indicates.[49] (Tables 22–26 are grouped at the end of the chapter.)

Auto money began to flow into the party's coffers, as well. At first it came from Packard's families, notably the Algers and the Ferrys, both seeking to prolong the life of the McMillan alliance. By 1916, however, the seven largest Detroit contributors to the National Republican Congressional Committee (for Michigan) included three men enriched by auto manufacturing: John Dodge (Dodge Brothers), Edwin Denby (Hupmobile), and James Couzens (Ford). Large contributions also came from industry stalwarts Roy Chapin (Hudson), Hugh Chalmers, Charles B. Warren (Paige), and John Kelsey (Kelsey Wheel), as well as from the five Packard families. By 1916 the industry also provided executive leadership for the Michigan GOP: almost two-thirds of the Detroit Committee of the Republican National Committee and four-fifths of the committee in charge of the November advertising blitz had close ties with the automotive business. Obviously, political institutions proved convenient in the ceaseless quest by automotive leaders for privilege and place.[50]

■ 7   Through their economic, political, and civic activities, Detroit's upper class and the industry's new men learned that they shared a community of interest, but these activities did not in themselves make the two groups social peers. The social life of the upper class, a relatively private realm, was more difficult to enter than the public sphere we have just been examining—but social equality, as it turned out, could be bought. In the case of the Dodge brothers, the price of admission to polite society was an orchestra. Horace Dodge joined William H. Murphy and Paul Gray as the principal benefactors of the Detroit Symphony after its opening season in 1914. In 1919, they each furnished $150,000 toward construction of a concert hall. All three had drawn large dividends from the automobile industry, as had such small donors as Jerome Remick and Charles H. Hodges. The orchestra, then, constituted the automobile's first important boost to Detroit's cultural life. It justified the auto elite's social pretensions, especially those of the Dodges, much as the construction of Detroit's art institute had sanctioned the "arrival" of Senator McMillan's generation.[51]

Money contributed to the philanthropies cherished by Detroit's upper class could also buy respectability. In Detroit, as elsewhere, the funding of charitable institutions had helped to legitimize the social privileges of the local upper class, but the city's explosive growth in the auto era generated a charity bill larger than its members could handle; by 1910 they had no choice but to entreat the "gasoline kings" to help shoulder the burden. They looked first to Henry Ford, whom they pressured into contributing $25,000 to Harper Hospital's building fund in 1909.[52]

The other auto manufacturers also became involved: as early as 1909 to 1911, twenty-two of the thirty-four largest contributions to Associated Charities of Detroit came from persons, families, or firms engaged in the automotive business. Old wealth—represented, for example, by the Packard families—still predominated, but the names of Ford's senior managers and stockholders were also beginning to appear on the list (Table 23).

By 1914–1915 more than two-thirds of the twenty-seven largest contributions to the Associated Charities came from the auto sector, with almost two-fifths of the contributions now coming from individuals, families, and companies whose fortunes had been made by the industry. It was at this juncture that the leaders of the middle-class companies (Hudson especially) joined the list (Table 24).

During World War I the formation of the Community Fund (originally the Detroit Patriotic Fund) greatly upped the scale of charitable giving in Detroit; it now took $50,000 to win a place among the top twenty-four donors. The automotive community, with almost three-quarters of the major benefactions, almost completely dominated the list for 1918–1920. Most of the old families able to contribute $50,000 or more had had—like the Packard families—their fortunes replenished by motor manufacture, and the industry's new men (and firms) accounted for almost half of the list. By war's end it was clear that so far as charitable giving was concerned, a new upper class had taken shape (Table 25).[53]

By then the automotive leaders had also acquired entry to Detroit's exclusive social clubs. As of 1914 the proportion of industry executives belonging to both the Detroit Club and the Country Club of Detroit exceeded that of the general business elite (Table 26).

Membership did not always mean total acceptance: the old

families did refuse to share the management of the Detroit Club with the industry's new money. As of 1930 the middle- and lower-class auto firms had yet to provide a single director or officer for the club. Even the auto parts companies had provided just one individual, Hal H. Smith of Hayes Mfg., president in 1923–24. The auto industry's new men responded by creating an elite establishment of their own, the Detroit Athletic Club (DAC).

Legend has it that Henry B. Joy of Packard was the prime mover behind the organization of the new club in November 1912. Both Malcolm Bingay and George W. Stark, two of Detroit's leading journalists and raconteurs, agreed that the new club had its genesis in Joy's desire to "civilize" the industry's more rambunctious young executives; both quoted Joy as saying, "The only place these men in the automobile industry have to meet is the Ponchartrain Hotel Bar. Let us organize a club to get them out of the saloons of Woodward Avenue."[54]

Certain elements of the legend are correct: several motorcar pioneers did describe the bar of the Ponchartrain Hotel as the auto industry's social "club" before 1912. Alfred Sloan, Jr., of General Motors wrote: "The Ponchartrain was where motorcar gossip was heard first. New models customarily had debuts there. . . . Even on ordinary days . . . the tablecloths would be covered with sketches: crankshafts, chassis, details of motors . . . and all sorts of mechanisms. Partnerships were made and ended there."[55] In a similar vein, LeRoy Pelletier, who served Ford and E-M-F in advertising and sales, once jocularly proposed to the Ponchartrain's proprietor: "I would take up this handsome Turkish rug which covers the floor of your lobby. I would then get some red paint . . . and I would have a great circle drawn in red paint and within that circle I would have inscribed this legend: 'The Heart of the Auto Industry.'"[56]

Tales about the old Ponchartrain held more than a grain of truth, but Stark and Bingay exaggerated the part played by Henry Joy in leading the auto elite from the Woodward Avenue drinking establishments into the subdued Italian Renaissance lobby of the Detroit Athletic Club. The record shows that it was an advertising executive, Charles A. Hughes (who had worked for the Hudson car company) who on November 27, 1912, summoned "a party of sixteen men to meet at the Ponchartrain Hotel to talk over the prospects of building up a real athletic club." Joy was too busy to attend, though he was subsequently elected to the organizing committee and served as a charter member of the board of directors. Yet the most energetic figures in the new organization were Hughes, its secretary; Hugh Chalmers, its president; Roy Chapin, head of the membership committee; and the clothing manufacturer Abner Larned, who conducted the fund-raising drive for the clubhouse. The auto industry dominated the early DAC; in fact, it accounted for 32 percent of the charter members and 73 percent of the men elected to the vice-presidency or presidency before 1922.[57]

As the names Chalmers and Chapin imply, the DAC constituted not the condescending gift of a Detroit patrician but rather the middle-class executives' own quest for social respectability. Full acceptance by Detroit's upper class depended upon their acquiring a more sedate, responsible life-style, in conformity with the traditional values of the city's prominent families. The organization of the Detroit Athletic Club helped many of the industry's new men to settle down, facilitating their assimilation by the social elite. A passion for conformity pervaded the automobile industry after 1910; even junior executives, a trade journal noted in May 1914, were beginning to "behave" themselves:

> The bar receipts of the Wolverine Club are said to have fallen away $400 in the course of one month recently while many automobile men who formerly gave their evenings over to innocent roisterings in public places, now conduct themselves in the strictest decorum, lest their merriment be ascribed to alcoholic rather than animal spirits.[58]

Once established, the DAC grew with stunning rapidity: in less than ten weeks it gained 1,400 members; in 1921, as William Metzger (E-M-F) assumed the presidency, the membership stood at 3,250. Metzger attributed the club's spontaneous success to the "salesmanship" of its organizers: "A very cleverly handled campaign of subtle publicity created the impression that no Detroiter of standing could well afford to remain out of the new club." Metzger held that "membership in the DAC [had become] . . . almost as important as a rating in Dun & Bradstreet." Even earlier, in 1918, stove manufacturer (and Packard stockholder) Charles A. DuCharme agreed that "more men . . . in the membership of the DAC [were] . . . active in the affairs of the city . . . than [in] all the rest of the organizations put together."[59]

There were more exclusive clubs (the Yondotega, after all, was limited to 100 members), but the DAC had undoubtedly become the city's premier social club within a decade of its founding. Yet its preeminence did not constitute a setback for the pre-automotive social elite, for they had helped to boost its fortunes: Henry B. Joy and Emory W. Clark, a banker as well as a director of General Motors, had been members of the organizing committee. In fact, the club appears to have been conceived by both sectors of the auto industry—both old and new money—to promote the emergence of a new, revitalized upper class.

By 1916, Dau's *Blue Book*—the Detroit equivalent of the *Social Register*—listed the names of most of the industry's new men, including Roy Chapin, Howard Coffin, and Fred Bezner (Hudson), James Heaslet (Studebaker), Harry Jewett (Paige), Horace Dodge, and Henry Ford. It had taken remarkably little time for Detroit's upper class to be transformed by the automotive revolution. By the end of World War I the industry's parvenus had become part of the city's new multifunctional elite.

The rapidity of elite circulation in this period is mainly explained by the transforming power of the auto industry itself. It was almost impossible to deny civic and social preeminence to the leadership of an industry contributing one-quarter of the city's manufacturing output in 1909 and two-fifths five years later. It was especially difficult for Detroit's upper class, already industrial in character, to dispute the social pretensions of the automotive elite. Besides, with the city's population increasing by 282 percent between 1899 and 1919, Detroit's upper class no doubt realized the inevitability—indeed, the necessity—of augmentation if they were to retain class leadership.[60]

Thus we do not find Detroit's middle-class entrepreneurs having to force their way into Detroit's upper social echelon. Rather, their membership was sponsored by individuals like Henry B. Joy, who helped organize the DAC; his brother Richard, who presided over the first "automobile bank"; and J. L. Hudson, whose nieces' marriages made him thrice an uncle to the industry's nouveaux riches. Through their automotive investments these individuals and their families personally incorporated the new wealth into the old and naturally took the lead in merging the two. They were Detroit's most exclusive matchmakers.

The middle-class automotive leaders found Detroit's social pyramid an easy climb, the way to the top mapped out for them by the older monied families who shared their financial interest in motorcars. It also helped, however, that the middle-class entrepreneurs were so anxious to be co-opted into Detroit's upper class that they demanded minimal change in the existing structure. They paid such exaggerated fealty to the hegemonic values of Detroit's pre-automotive elite that the first "automobile banks" (leaving Ford's institutions aside for the moment) sported names—the National Bank of Commerce, Merchants' National Bank—that harked back to a commercial era predating even the McMillan alliance. Not until

1933, and then only at the initiative of Henry Ford, did a "manufacturers" bank emerge.

A group too easily co-opted adds little to the strength of an existing elite, as Vilfredo Pareto pointed out in his classic *Treatise on General Sociology*. Pareto argued that the circulation of elites—that is, interclass "mixing"—is essential to the survival of any dominant group, the alternative being decadence and eventual overthrow. True circulation depends, however, on offering admission to "any individual potentially dangerous" to the elite and in allowing "the new members [to bring] in their opinions, traits, virtues, prejudices." Indeed, these variations from existing elite norms are essential prerequisites for elite revitalization. Elite circulation does *not* occur, Pareto asserted, in those instances where the doors are open "only to individuals who consent to be like it, and are indeed driven by their ardour as neophytes to exaggerate in that direction." Such recruits, he argued, do "nothing to replenish" the "inner strength" of an elite; indeed, they confound it, for they "intensify traits that already prevail to excess in it." Harold Lasswell, the noted political scientist, made a similar point in a 1965 book on revolutionary elites: "Extremes of seeming conformity constitute innovations of as much danger to sound elite formation as deviations in an obviously nonconformist direction."[61]

In Detroit the danger came from excessive conformity in business practice. The leaders of the middle-class companies were easily accommodated by Detroit's pre-automotive elite because they had so many values in common—including a tendency toward conspicuous production. A new upper class could emerge in less than a decade because both groups placed high value on social status and concurred on its determinants. However, the prestige behavior of the middle-class entrepreneurs ensured that they would add far less strength to Detroit's establishment than their early careers had promised. We have already noted how little Hugh Chalmers and Henry Leland were able to contribute after their companies, Chalmers and Lincoln, failed. Others, though more successful in the long run, could nevertheless offer only the resources of middle-rank companies like Hudson and Hupmobile, which were insufficient to rescue Detroit's old families at the moment of supreme danger in 1933.

What increasingly mattered after 1910 was control of the "Big Three" of the automobile industry: Ford, Chrysler, and General Motors. By 1929 they accounted for 75 percent of industry sales; thus it was essential to Detroit's upper class to have some input into their decision-making. Yet these firms, owned by outsiders, did not become an integral part of Detroit's upper-class social system before the Great Depression.

The same dialectic that guaranteed that Detroit's upper class would recruit those elements within the auto industry which added least to its strength—that is, those most prone to mix their social and price-class aspirations—also assured that the Big Three would be built and controlled by those manufacturers who were least susceptible to conspicuous production. General Motors and, to a lesser degree, Chrysler avoided defining themselves in class terms by adopting an organizational structure that enabled them to have more than one social identity. Ford was the one company suffi-ciently able to surmount the impulse toward conspicuous produc-tion to specialize in the lower-class field. As William Stout, sales manager for the Scripps-Booth automobile company noted in his memoirs, "The only one who did not have the idea that he was in the luxury business was Henry Ford."[62] Why did he and his com-pany deviate so radically from the industry norm? The answer, we shall discover in the next chapter, lies in the unique circumstances of the Ford Motor Company's birth and formative years. Henry Ford had the great advantage of being the first automotive entrepreneur in Detroit to violate substantially the monopoly position of the pre-automotive elite. They never forgave him—nor he them.

Table 22
Political Affiliation of Auto Elite, 1896–1930

Party	Auto Executives (%)	Auto Leaders (%)	Marquis[a] Auto (%)	Marquis[a] Non-Auto (%)
Republican	31.2	36.6	51.5	45.4
Democrat	3.8	4.1	7.1	9.0
Other	0.8	1.0	6.1	6.5
None	64.2	58.2	35.3	39.1
Total cases (= 100%)	234	292	99	1,272

[a] Sample from A. N. Marquis & Co., *Book of Detroiters* (Chicago, 1914).

Table 23
Top Contributors, Associated Charities of Detroit, 1909–1911

	Amount ($)	Automotive Connection
J. L. Hudson	1,207	Hudson
Emory L. Ford family[a]	841	
Whitney family	645	
Alger family	350	Packard
Newberry family	325	Packard
Joy family	225	Packard
Joseph Boyer	200	General Motors
Mrs. F. E. Carter	200	
Henry Ford	200	Ford
Henry Leland	200	Cadillac
E. P. Wenger	200	
Barbour family	190	Paige, Lozier, E-M-F
Ferry family	175	Packard
Hiram Walker family	175	E-M-F (Canada)
M. J. Murphy	150	General Motors
Dodge brothers	125	Ford
Philip McMillan	125	Packard
Buhl family	100	Lozier, Paige
Fred M. Butzel	100	
Detroit City Gas	100	
J. W. Drake	100	Hupmobile
J. S. Farrand, Jr.	100	
Bernard Ginsburg	100	Grabowsky
Norval Hawkins	100	Ford
Frank J. Hecker	100	
James S. Holden	100	
James Inglis	100	American Blower[b]
Kelsey Wheel	100	mfr., car wheels
McCord Manufacturing	100	mfr., car radiators
Michigan Carbon Works	100	
Newcomb, Endicott	100	
Benjamin Siegel	100	
Charles B. Warren	100	Lozier, Hupmobile, Paige
C. Harold Wills	100	Ford

Source: Associated Charities of Detroit Papers, Box 1, Walter Reuther Library, Wayne State University.
[a] No relation to Henry Ford, the "chemical Fords" made their money in soda ash and glass-manufacturing.
[b] A manufacturer of sheet metal auto parts.

Table 24
Top Contributors, Associated Charities of Detroit, 1914–1915

	Amount ($)	Automotive Connection
Emory L. Ford family[a]	2,000	
Gray estate	2,000	Ford
Tracy W. McGregor	1,750	
Leland family	1,512	Cadillac
Joy family	1,210	Packard
Joseph Boyer	1,000	General Motors
Willard D. Pope	813	
Whitney Realty	800	
Horace H. Rackham	700	Ford
Dexter M. Ferry, Jr.	650	Packard
Herbert W. Alden	500	Timken-Detroit Axle
Alger family	500	Packard
Fred O. Bezner	500	Hudson
Walter O. Briggs	500	Briggs Mfg. (car bodies)
Roy D. Chapin	500	Hudson
Howard E. Coffin	500	Hudson
Fred J. Fisher	500	Fisher Body
Frank J. Hecker	500	
Roscoe B. Jackson	500	Hudson
Newberry family	500	Packard
Newcomb, Endicott	500	
Timken-Detroit Axle	500	mfr., car axles
Barbour family	425	Paige
Philip H. McMillan	400	Packard
Mrs. W. R. Parker	325	
Fred M. Butzel	300	
Hugh Chalmers	300	Chalmers

Source: Associated Charities of Detroit Papers, Box 1, Walter Reuther Library, Wayne State University.
[a] No relation to Henry Ford.

Table 25
Top Contributors, Detroit Community (Patriotic) Fund, 1918–1920

	Amount ($)	Automotive Connection
Henry Ford interests	670,000	Ford
Emory L. Ford family[a]	522,000	
James Couzens	350,000	Ford
Packard investors[b]	254,200	Packard
Gray family	245,000	Ford
Hudson investors[c]	219,500	Hudson
Whitney interests[d]	199,000	
Dodge brothers	150,000	Dodge, Ford
General Motors	116,000	General Motors
Buhl family	115,000	mfr., auto parts
Scripps-Booth interests[e]	106,700	Scripps-Booth
Burroughs investors[f]	106,000	Lincoln
Fisher Body interests[g]	102,000	Fisher Body, GM
Horace H. Rackham	100,000	Ford
American Shipbuilding	100,000	
American Car & Foundry	92,500	
John W. Anderson	85,000	Ford
Detroit Edison	75,000	
W. H. Murphy family	65,000	Lincoln
Timken-Detroit interests[h]	60,500	Timken-Detroit Axle
Great Lakes Engineering	55,000	
Solvay Process	50,000	
Studebaker	50,000	Studebaker
C. Harold Wills	50,000	Ford

Source: Associated Charities of Detroit Papers, Box 1, Walter Reuther Library, Wayne State University.

[a] No relation to Henry Ford.

[b] Packard Motor Car; Alger, Ferry, Joy, McMillan, and Newberry families.

[c] Hudson Motor Car; R. D. Chapin, H. E. Coffin, R. B. Jackson, W. J. McAneeny, R. H. Webber.

[d] D. C. Whitney, Whitney Realty, T. W. McGregor.

[e] G. G. and R. H. Booth, W. E. Scripps, Anna Scripps Whitcomb, Scripps-Booth Motor Corp., *Detroit News*.

[f] Burroughs Adding Machine, Joseph Boyer, Standish Backus.

[g] Fisher Body, C. T. and F. J. Fisher, Aaron and Louis Mendelssohn.

[h] Timken-Detroit Axle, A. R. Demory, E. W. Lewis.

Table 26
Elite Membership in Social Clubs, 1914

	Auto Elite (% in club)	Non-Auto Elite (% in club)
Detroit Club	20.2	17.3
Detroit Athletic Club	32.3	15.6
Yondotega Club	2.0	2.5
Detroit Country Club	23.2	11.9
Detroit Yacht Club	6.1	4.1
Detroit Boat Club	28.3	17.4
Detroit Golf Club	8.1	4.9
Detroit Automobile Club	15.2	4.2
Total cases (= 100%)	99	1,272

Source: A. N. Marquis & Co., *The Book of Detroiters* (Chicago, 1914).

Chapter Five

An Isolated Survivor in the Lower Class

■   In 1922 Henry Ford, looking back over two decades, explained why he left the Henry Ford Company. His partners, he alleged, betrayed "a speculative turn of mind" wherein "the whole thought was to make to order and get the largest possible [price] for each. . . . I found that the . . . company was not a vehicle for realizing my ideas but merely a money-making concern—that did not make much money." In effect, he charged them with wanting limited, high-priced production for the wealthy—with planning a company like Packard, Cadillac, or Lozier. The charge was highly credible, as his associates at the Henry Ford Company—William Murphy, Albert White, Lem Bowen, and Clarence Black—all belonged to the pinnacle of Detroit society and were therefore unlikely to be long satisfied with building Ford's lowly motor wagon. Their company, the inventor perceived, was destined—like Cadillac—to drift into the higher price brackets. The pre-automotive elite were not the people to implement his dream of providing inexpensive transportation for the common man.[1]

No one knows for certain when the dream first fired his imagination. Ford himself claimed in 1915 that he recommended to his partners in the Detroit Automobile Company that they manufacture a single model in large quantities. In October 1902 he talked about building a "family horse." A year later John W. Anderson, a partner in the Ford Motor Company, recorded in his diary a conversation in which Ford declared, "The way to make automobiles is to make . . . them come through the factory all alike, just like . . . one match is like another match when it comes to a match factory." Anderson, shocked, asked how cars could ever be sold in such quantities, and Ford replied, "You need not fear about the market, the people will buy them all right, because when you get to making them in quantities, you can make them cheaper, and . . . the market will take care of itself."[2]

117

Ford had trouble raising money to finance his dream because by 1903 he had alienated Detroit's financial elite, some of whom had lost money on his two failures. To find backers for the Ford Motor Company, therefore, he had to look within a lower economic and social stratum. This had its disadvantages: the new company was so underfinanced that it almost failed during its first year. Still, his new partners proved receptive to his plan to build for the mass market.

The key man in Ford's third venture was Alex Y. Malcomson, a Scottish-born coal dealer. He had emigrated to Detroit in 1880 at age fifteen, started out as a grocery clerk, and soon saved enough money to open his own store. Branching out into coal, he organized Detroit's largest coal company and, integrating backward, bought several West Virginia mines. Malcomson was an inveterate gambler. Occasionally his promotional schemes clicked—as had his booming coal business—but they often backfired. For example, he lost several thousand dollars on a scheme to manufacture iceboxes. Undaunted, Malcomson decided to try the riskiest but most lucrative game in Detroit, if not the country—automobile production. Scouting around for an inventor, he settled upon Henry Ford, whom he knew as a customer at the colliery. Through the summer and fall of 1902 Malcomson financed the development of Ford's prototype. By November, his resources exhausted, Malcomson sought additional capital by organizing a joint-stock company, but Ford's reputation made it impossible to sell its stock. Detroit's capitalists understandably wanted to see the car running before investing in it. Ford completed it the following May, thus enabling Malcomson to assemble a ragtag little band of investors—most of them his close friends and business associates—and on June 16, 1903, they incorporated the Ford Motor Company.[3]

Though it issued $100,000 in capital stock, the corporation began with only $28,000 in cash. Ford and Malcomson, as payment for past efforts, each received 25.5 percent of the stock, so that together they held a controlling interest. Another 10 percent went to John and Horace Dodge in exchange for $7,000 in materials and a note for $3,000. A further 5 percent was sold to Charles H. Bennett, vice-president and a major stockholder in the Daisy Air Rifle company, for a promised $5,000. He appears to have been impressed by Ford's engine.[4]

Yet another 10.5 percent went to John S. Gray, Malcomson's uncle, for $10,500 in cash, which his nephew virtually extorted from him. Gray, a Scottish immigrant who had made his fortune manufacturing candy, headed the German-American Bank, a small institution to which Malcomson owed considerable money. It had financed the expansion of his coal business and had a vital stake in his continued prosperity. Because Gray, like most bankers, heartily disapproved of the auto game, Malcomson kept his partnership with Ford secret until March 1903. But then, realizing that he could not afford to keep his commitments to Ford's parts suppliers, Malcomson entreated his uncle to invest in the infant auto concern. Gray, trapped, reluctantly agreed; if he were to refuse, Malcomson would likely go bankrupt, crippling the German-American Bank. Nevertheless, Gray drove a hard bargain, extracting from his nephew a pledge to reimburse him for any loss he incurred during the Ford company's first year.[5]

Albert Strelow showed little more enthusiasm for the Ford venture. A general carpenter and contractor, he first encountered Malcomson in December 1902, when the latter purchased a coal company that held the lease on a wagon shop he owned. Malcomson wanted to use the building for assembling automobiles and offered Strelow $5,000 to make the necessary renovations. By the time these were completed, Malcomson was hovering on the brink of bankruptcy, and Strelow—to keep his tenant—contributed the $5,000 paid him to Ford's capital stock. But he never prized the investment very highly, selling out in 1907 for $25,000.[6]

The remaining stockholders were more enthusiastic but could afford to invest only a few thousand dollars. John W. Anderson, "a struggling young graduate of the University of Michigan Law School," bought 5 percent of the stock with $5,000 cash borrowed from his father, a prosperous surgeon and one-time mayor of La Crosse, Wisconsin. Anderson's law partner, Horace H. Rackham, a farmer's son, put up another $5,000, paid in two installments. Anderson and Rackham, aged thirty-seven and forty-five in 1903, had not achieved much success in their law practice, for their major account, the Malcomson Fuel Company, chiefly used them to collect bad debts. Auto manufacturing offered them a chance to retrieve their momentum, and turn their careers around.[7]

Some of the stockholders lacked even the grain of success and financial security the two lawyers had achieved. Malcomson's cousin Vernon Fry, manager of the notions department of a large downtown store, contributed $5,000 in three installments. C. J. Woodall, a junior clerk in Malcomson's coal company, gave his note for $1,000. Another Malcomson employee, James Couzens, was the most sanguine of Ford's investors; he was determined to "beg, borrow, or steal" enough money to purchase a decent stake in the company. But he raised only $2,500, and three-fifths of that was a bank loan arranged by Malcomson. Thirty-one in 1903, Couzens, like most of his partners, had not achieved much success in business. A native of Canada, he grew up in Chatham, Ontario, where his father, an English immigrant, owned a small soap factory. After graduating from business college, Couzens moved to Detroit in 1889, where he worked as a car checker in the yards of the Michigan Central Railroad. Six years later he joined Malcomson and by 1903 was acting as his factotum, with the responsibilities—though not the title—of general manager.[8]

■ 1   Starting with only $28,000 in cash, the Ford Motor Company flirted with disaster during its first month: after four weeks of operations, it was down to its last $223.65. But then orders started coming in, each with a deposit attached, and by August 1903 the company had weathered its first crisis. Its survival could be attributed to the popularity of the first Model A Ford, a two-cylinder runabout that sold for $850. It offered more power than usual for the money, for most runabouts, including Cadillac's, had to get by on one cylinder.[9]

For its 1904–1905 sales season Ford offered three models, two of which—the runabout and a new touring car—used the original two-cylinder engine; they sold for $800 and $1,000 respectively. At Malcomson's insistence, the company also offered a heavier, four-cylinder car for $2,000, the Model B. The now familiar pattern was already emerging: Henry Ford was pushing the company toward the $500 car that workingmen and farmers could afford, while Malcomson—to Ford's disgust—was intent on converting the company into a luxury manufacturer; he saw his social and economic peers as the most promising automotive market. As Allan Nevins put it, Malcomson—like Fred Smith at Oldsmobile—"believed in the rich man's market." The outcome of the struggle over price-class was, however, markedly different at Ford, in part because Malcomson lacked overall control but mostly because Henry Ford was a master of corporate maneuver.[10]

In November 1905 Ford organized the Ford Manufacturing Company to supply engines, axles, and transmissions for the Model N, a four-cylinder runabout he had designed. Its stockholders, drawn from the Ford Motor Company, excluded Malcomson and his closest allies: Fry, Woodall, and Gray. By manipulating its prices, the subsidiary was poised to siphon off the profits from the new runabout, leaving Malcomson to sink with the elephantine models B and K. The latter, priced at $2,800, occupied so lofty a spot in the industry's price-class hierarchy that Malcomson was competing with companies that were, at least in Detroit, out of his social league.[11]

The competition did not have long to run. In December 1905 Malcomson undercut his position on the board of directors by organizing the Aerocar Company to manufacture a four-cylinder, air-cooled touring car. His associates at Ford balked at the idea of financing a rival firm, and when Aerocar fared poorly, Malcomson lacked the financial resources to refuse when Henry Ford offered to buy his shares for $175,000.[12]

His departure triggered an exodus: Woodall, Fry, Strelow, and Bennett also sold out to Ford and Couzens. Bennett said he quit to save his reputation: "I felt that in my own community, if it was known that I was in with a crowd of fellows that had frozen out somebody . . . and fouled his credit, I wouldn't stand quite as high as I would like." The same month that Malcomson sold out, John S. Gray passed away; his four heirs, though they kept his stock, left the running of the auto business to Ford, who became president. A year later, when the last of the Malcomson group sold out and Aerocar failed, Ford gleefully reported to James Couzens, his chief cohort, "The enemy is completely whipped." Ford, with 58.5 percent of the stock, now had absolute control; Couzens, with 11 percent, led the minority stockholders.[13]

Malcomson's eclipse enabled Ford to concentrate on his dream of building a "light, low-priced car . . . powerful enough for American roads and capable of carrying its passengers anywhere that a horse-drawn vehicle will go." He was looking to the rural market; farmers were the peer group he intended to serve. As early as 1906 the Model N's popularity in rural areas made Ford the nation's leading manufacturer, a ranking the company kept until 1927.[14]

In November 1908, Ford introduced the Model T, "the farmer's car." It was, Richard Crabb has noted, the first automobile "with the size and power to outperform a good team of horses and still come within the financial reach of most people." It could pull itself out of the springtime gumbo, and its abnormally high undercarriage cleared the mountainous ruts in rural roads during the dry season. Most farmers had the mechanical knowledge to repair it, and Ford dealers stocked inexpensive spare parts. The Model T was almost perversely utilitarian—by all accounts the plainest and perhaps ugliest car of its era. Yet its lack of adornment and pretense attracted rural buyers, who distrusted knickknacks and frills.[15]

The Model T was at first too expensive for most farmers; its original pricetag of $850 put it in the middle price-class. But Henry Ford was still, as he explained to the founder of General Motors in 1908, "in favor of keeping prices down to the lowest possible point, giving to the multitude the benefit of cheap transportation." And so he kept pushing the price downward—even in 1916, when demand for the Model T had already outstripped supply—and by August 1924 the price of a Model T touring car had fallen to $260, the lowest price in history for a four-cylinder automobile. By then Ford's profit was less than two dollars per unit, and only 5 percent of the company's earnings came from the Model T that year; the rest stemmed from "by-products, freight charges, bank balances, securities, and spare parts." In his zeal for volume production, Henry Ford was almost giving the car away.[16]

■ 2   In an industry marked by extravagant displays of conspicuous production, Ford's corporate behavior was truly exceptional. The company evinced as much zeal in forcing prices downward as its competition did in hoisting them upward. As John Rae has remarked, Ford "was not alone in having the idea" of a low-priced car for the "great multitude," but "he was alone in sticking to it with grim persistence."[17] Why did this company and this man depart so radically from the auto industry's well-worn path?

Any answer must be speculative; the Ford model policy after 1906 depended on the whims of its autocrat and founder, and his motivation has defied easy analysis. Charles Sorensen, for twenty years head of production at Ford, claimed, "I knew him better than did members of his own family," yet "it was useless to try to understand Henry Ford. One had to *sense* him." Sorensen's experience was common: Dean Marquis, for a time the head of Ford's Sociological Department (that is, personnel), wrote: "There is about [Henry Ford] the fascination of an unlimited uncertainty. No living being knows what he is likely to do or say next." Allan Nevins, who wrote the definitive biography, was equally perplexed by the man, noting that "veterans of the Ford Company frequently remarked that [Henry Ford] was not one man, but half a dozen, and they never knew which one they would meet next." Thus no interpretation of him can be considered definitive.[18]

Indeed, one cannot even be certain that Henry Ford entirely resisted the impulse to produce conspicuously. After all, he did acquire a luxury car producer in 1922, the Lincoln Motor Company. This purchase may well demonstrate that no one could resist the temptation to build fine cars, and that while Henry Ford may have had uncommon resistance to the big-car bug, he was not in the end entirely immune to it. Or it may simply mean that Henry Ford was at age fifty-nine finally allowing his son Edsel, who had by then been president of the Ford Motor Company for four years, a share in the decision-making.

The Lincoln story properly begins with its incorporation on August 29, 1917, by Henry and Wilfred Leland—one month after they had "resigned" from Cadillac following a series of disputes with GM president William C. Durant. The Lelands raised $850,000 in capital and quickly organized Lincoln to manufacture Liberty aircraft engines. Its stockholders included the Dayton Metal Products Company; John Trix, president of the American Injector Company; and two former associates of the McMillan family in the automobile business: William H. Murphy, the real estate heir who had helped finance Cadillac, and Joseph Boyer, president of Burroughs Adding Machine and a founder of Packard.[19]

At war's end, Lincoln issued $1.75 million in preferred nonvoting stock (control remaining with the original investors) in order to retool for the manufacture of a "super Cadillac," to be priced between $4,600 and $6,600. Here was conspicuous production with a vengeance: with their second car, the Lelands wanted to outdo the Cadillac. It was a natural progression, for the Lelands were by 1917 worth $1.5 million, and Henry Leland was widely regarded as Detroit's leading reformer, its most eminent citizen since the death of J. L. Hudson. It was not surprising, then, that he was moving upmarket and that two intimates of the McMillan family were associated with him in launching Detroit's most socially ambitious auto project to date.[20]

Plagued by labor unrest and shortages of men and materials, Lincoln completely missed the auto boom of 1919–1920; its debut in September 1920 coincided instead with the beginning of the postwar depression. The company's fortunes rapidly slid downhill: the government hit Lincoln with a claim for $4 million in back taxes; its board started feuding; and its banks refused to renew their loans. In November 1921 Lincoln went into receivership; the following February, with great fanfare, Henry Ford bought Lincoln at auction.[21]

Ford's move stunned Detroiters, who had seen him cling tenaciously to a policy of manufacturing a single, low-priced model. In an interview, Edsel Ford denied that his father sought any financial advantage from the transaction. He depicted the purchase as a simple gesture of Christian charity toward the beleaguered Leland family: "We do not need the Lincoln as an automobile," Edsel averred:

It's way out of our line. But also, we do not wish to see a great industry like the Lincoln wrecked and its control lost to Detroit. The Lelands, for a generation, have done so much for, and meant so much to Detroit that it would be a shame . . . if Detroit let the Lincoln company go to ruin. . . . Rather than see . . . [its stockholders] lose all hope for their money—in many cases all they have in the world— . . . we will buy it.[22]

The statement touched all the bases: charity, loyalty, gratitude, and civic pride. It even went on to allude to impoverished widows and children. The elder Ford's comments followed the same lines, although he credited his wife Clara with making him see the importance of saving the Lelands from losing "everything they've got." He promised to work out "some way . . . to even do a little something for those stockholders like school teachers . . . who put their money into the stock of this company . . . and lost it."[23]

By promising to rescue the Grand Old Man of Detroit and the small stockholders, Henry Ford gained reams of favorable publicity. So great was his yen for fame in these years that he may have bought Lincoln solely for the headlines it generated. Certainly, it is difficult to accept his "humanitarianism" at face value. Far from admiring the Lelands, he more likely detested them, since they were linked to his forced departure from the Henry Ford Company and were political rivals who had opposed his Senate candidacy in 1918 (see Chapter Eight). Ford, a vindictive man, was one to crush his opponents; he did not normally offer them charity. And in fact, the Lelands lasted only four months as Ford employees. Although Allan Nevins and Frank Hill have blamed their dismissal on a "failure to harmonize," one cannot help thinking that it gave Ford great satisfaction to discharge them.[24]

Henry Ford may also have wanted to cap his career by building a luxury automobile. A more plausible explanation, however, is that Edsel Ford was the prime instigator. The son, aged ten in 1903, had grown up with the Ford Motor Company. Its fabulous success had affected him far more than it did his father, who—ostentatiously ignoring Detroit's social elite—secreted himself some fifteen miles away in a gloomy mansion in Dearborn. But Edsel, over his father's protests, moved to Grosse Pointe to hobnob with the city's upper class. Unlike Henry, who evinced a farmer's distrust of high culture, Edsel became the leading patron of the Detroit Institute of Art in the mid-1920s. Always attracted more to design than to construction, Edsel found the Model T old-fashioned and aesthetically unappealing. He longed to build a prestigious automobile to compete with Packard; as he told his golf partner, John Bell Moran, "Father made the most popular car in the world. I would like to make the best car."[25]

The acquisition of Lincoln reflected the social maturation of the Ford family, yet it was surely Edsel who recognized and welcomed the social implications of entry into the luxury field. Henry Ford was too attached to his lower-class car and his populist ideals to convert to the Cadillac-Packard way of looking at the world, and he scorned social climbing. But Edsel, who married into one of Detroit's leading families, strove to achieve a status commensurate with his great wealth. The younger Ford was not in a position, however, to dictate the purchase of Lincoln; he needed his father's approval, which he probably got by stressing the "publicity and acclaim that saving the Lelands would bring" the elder Ford. The latter's essential lack of interest in luxury manufacturing can be seen in the fact that he allowed Edsel far more leeway in managing Lincoln than he ever permitted him with the Model T Ford.[26]

There is an essential ambiguity to the Lincoln purchase (due in part to the media hype surrounding it) which makes it difficult to characterize. There seems little doubt that Henry Leland and Edsel Ford both indulged in prestige behavior, but the motivation of Henry Ford is more difficult to ascertain. Moreover, even if he was by 1922 not averse to building a luxury automobile, the Lincoln purchase would not by itself explain why he had for the preceding two decades been, as William Stout said, "the only one who did *not* have the idea that he was in the luxury business."[27] The Lincoln deal simply came too late to have had any influence over Ford's persistence in the lower-class field.

■ 3   And so we return to our original question: what was it that caused Henry Ford and his company, at least before 1922 and probably after that as well, to depart so radically from the industry norm? The question is not original, for while the social prejudices of his competitors have been scarcely noticed in automobile history (perhaps because they favored the status quo), Ford's behavior has been endlessly dissected and the relationship noted between his model policy and his antipathy toward the rich. Roger Burlingame expressed the consensus: "Above all else, this man suspected and despised the rich and shied away from anything that smacked of luxury. It would have been wholly out of character for him to favor the production of expensive cars."[28]

There has been considerable speculation as to where this animosity against the rich and identification with the "common man" originated. Typically, Ford's attitudes have been ascribed to his farm upbringing or to the Populist ideology his generation of rural Americans presumably imbibed. But fully one-sixth of Detroit's automotive leaders were farmers' sons, and some of them came from hardscrabble farms, whereas Ford's father was, as Henry himself remarked, "well-to-do." And, as has been pointed out, Michigan was scarcely a Populist stronghold.[29]

Indeed, Ford's social background was not sufficiently unusual to explain in some straightforward, mechanical way his persistence in the lower price-class. To be sure, the company's overall social profile was (as we saw in Chapter One) appropriate for the leading producer in the lower-class market, which is not surprising, since Ford was inclined to hire people who shared his social values and to fire those (like Ernest C. Kanzler, a vice-president who left in 1926) who did not. However, the social composition of the Ford management team, while suggestive, did not necessarily affect its model policy; that was Henry Ford's undisputed domain after 1906. And he was certainly not the most underprivileged of the industry's founders. Charles Nash, an orphan who spent his youth as a migrant farm laborer, had a far better claim to that distinction, yet he eventually felt quite comfortable with bankers and in building the Nash for them to drive. Henry Ford's social origins are not, therefore, a sufficient explanation for his lifelong animosity towards the socioeconomic elite.[30]

Are we left then with history by accident? Was the evolution of Detroit and the early auto industry purely serendipitous, the result perhaps—as Anne Jardim has argued—of Ford's narcissistic delusion that the Model T, a "farmer's car," would prove that he had not forsaken his parents' way of life? Was Ford alone immune to the big-car bug because he had already succumbed to a more serious mental condition? We cannot say. With the subject deceased, it is too late for psychological testing.[31]

Similarly, one cannot *prove* that personal whim and idiosyncrasy did not decide the outcome of the early car wars. There was, as we have seen, a close correlation between the social background of entrepreneurs and their model policies, but people did not rank themselves in the price-class hierarchy in exact correspondence with their place in the social order. How could they? Not only was each individual involved in several different status systems (national, state, and local, just for starters), but some individuals —most notably Henry Ford—appear to have had a faulty consciousness. Given the intensity with which he inveighed against the "rich," Ford evidently did not regard himself as one of them

—even after he became a billionaire. He considered himself a successful workingman; they, on the other hand, were "non-producers"—"social parasites" who "got lots of money for doing nothing." As he explained to a biographer, Ford believed that

> every manufacturer should be able to go into the shop and with his own hands make the thing that he wants to manufacture. If he cannot do this, he is no manufacturer at all. . . . His workingmen are the real manufacturers, and he is but a parasite that lives upon them.[32]

So completely did he distance himself from the capitalists of his day that he could without conscious irony tell the press after a visit to the home of J. P. Morgan, an individual less wealthy than Ford himself, that "it was very interesting to see how the rich live." The statement read better then than it does now, for as Reynold Wik has pointed out, almost none of his contemporaries thought of Ford as a rich man; he did not conform to the popular image.[33]

The attempt to apply the concept of conspicuous production to Henry Ford and the Ford Motor Company is not, then, an attempt to impose a deterministic straitjacket on the past. Rather, it is an effort to extricate our understanding of Ford from the premise of exceptionalism that has heretofore governed the literature on the early automotive industry. Too much emphasis on Ford's idiosyncrasies—or madness, as some would have it—has obscured the extent to which the individual and the company did fit the industry-wide pattern.

Half a century ago Charles Beard called on historians to make an "act of faith" that there is indeed an order to history, and that written history is not mere chaos.[34] This book accordingly assumes that the behavior of even an eccentric like Henry Ford can be seen as part of an intelligible pattern. For that reason, his resistance to conspicuous production is not going to be explained away as a personal eccentricity; rather, this apparent exception to the rule will be used to refine our understanding of the concept of conspicuous production.

The concept holds that manufacturers endeavored, until and unless threatened with ruin, to build cars for their social peers. Their product thus scaled the price-class hierarchy even as the producer climbed socially. The two usually rose in tandem, with the social ascent taking the lead and model policy responding to the entrepreneur's changing perception of what constituted his peer group. The choice of price-class correlated, in other words, with the various stages by which the industry's founders were co-opted into

Detroit's local upper class. If that was the normal pattern, then it follows that Henry Ford's persistence in the lower price-class must to some degree reflect his estrangement from Detroit's upper class, even long after he had the financial means to buy and sell most of them. In other words, his continued allegiance to the lower price-class probably owed more to a miscarriage in the elite recruitment process than to his social origins.

Typically, Ford is seen as the architect of his own social isolation. Often he is accused of a suspicious nature bordering on (or crossing the border of) paranoia, which made his co-optation virtually impossible. Here was an individual who carried a gun and surrounded himself with armed bodyguards out of fear that "Wall Street" was so intent on crushing his company that it would balk at nothing, including murder, to achieve its goals. Similarly, he refused to allow his son Edsel to enlist during World War I, out of fear that "certain interests" opposed to the "Ford system" would "have seen to it" that he never returned. And American entry into World War II he interpreted as a New Deal conspiracy against his company.[35]

Such a man was obviously not an easy person for the local elite to co-opt. In fact, the local upper class was far from anxious to add Ford to their number. But the evidence of his "paranoia" has obscured the fact that he did have real enemies; they were not all the product of his own perfervid imagination, and there were indeed several attempts to drive him from the industry. Yet historians have tended to downplay the threats to Ford, partly because of his exaggerated fears but also because the reigning paradigm—the image of the self-made auto executive—has led them to underestimate the revolutionary nature of the Ford Motor Company.

The essential fact is this: Ford's company was the first to breach the monopoly held by Detroit's pre-automotive elite over local motorcar production. From our present vantage point, all the early companies blur together; they appear to have entered the industry more or less simultaneously. But if we work forward from 1899, the year Ransom Olds started manufacturing in Detroit, then Ford's achievement stands out in stark relief: he was the first one locally to surmount the monetary barrier that had made auto manufacturing a preserve of the financial elite. Not until 1906, with the arrival of Thomas-Detroit, did Detroit's pre-automotive elite encounter another local threat to their motor primacy. To be sure, there were several firms that announced, and even occasionally built, a prototype before they failed; but in terms of a real company and a real challenge, at first there was only Ford. That singularity alone would have augured trouble for him, but given the circumstances of his departure from the Henry Ford Company and the feeling in elite circles that he had not behaved honorably in his dealings with his patrician backers, Ford had good reason to be "paranoid" about their possible response to his third automotive venture.

■ 4   In fact, Detroit's elite immediately tried to put Ford out of business. The Association of Licensed Automobile Manufacturers was their weapon of choice. The ALAM claimed to control the basic patent for the gasoline-powered motorcar, which it had acquired from George Selden, a Rochester patent lawyer and inventor, by way of the Electric Vehicle Company. Two Detroiters —Henry Joy of Packard and Fred Smith of Olds—had taken the lead in organizing the association in February 1903, just a few months before Ford's incorporation. First it decreed that no one could manufacture cars without its license; then it used its licensing authority to restrict entry into the industry, rejecting two-thirds of the forty-three companies who applied in May 1903.[36]

After six years, the Association of Licensed Automobile Manufacturers remained a very select club with only thirty-one members, just four more than when it began. Typically, its members built expensive cars: the ALAM included the makers of almost every model retailing for more than $3,000, but it never encompassed more than four makes selling for less than $1,000; it deliberately excluded producers of low-priced cars in an attempt to keep prices high and the market stable. A club for the wealthy, it threw open its doors to companies owned by the upper class, like Cadillac and Northern, but resisted the overtures of outsiders and social climbers.[37]

Even in 1903, therefore, Ford knew that it would be difficult to get a license. During the spring and summer the company badgered Fred Smith, then president of ALAM (and the capitalist who, having fired Ransom Olds, drove Oldsmobile to the brink of bankruptcy), for a promise to consider its license favorably. Smith, citing Ford's past failures, advised the company to "go out and manufacture some motor cars and gain a reputation and prove [it] wasn't a fly-by-night producer before . . . [asking] for membership." According to Smith, he assured Henry Ford and James Couzens that "when they had their own plant and became a factor in the industry, they would be welcome." But a Ford stockholder, John Wendell Anderson, remembered his message as being considerably more hostile. Smith reportedly told him that the ALAM intended to force small assembly plants like Ford to fold: "Well, we are disposed to be fair," Smith loftily assured Anderson. "We will take an inventory of their stocks, machinery, equipment, whatever they may have, and give them fair value for it. Then they quit business."[38]

Henry Ford resolved to fight and publicly dared the ALAM to test the validity of its patent in the courts. The association's directors hesitated, for they themselves doubted it would survive judicial scrutiny. But Henry B. Joy, "inflexibly opposed to admitting Ford . . . threatened to withdraw Packard from the A.L.A.M. unless legal action were taken." The social context of the court action could not be more obvious: Packard versus Ford, an inner member of the McMillan alliance trying to smite the local upstart.[39]

In the winter and spring of 1904 the association sued the Ford company, its American dealers, and its European distributors. The legal battle lasted more than seven years, not ending until the United States Circuit Court of Appeals finally found in favor of the Ford Motor Company by ruling in January 1911 that Ford was "neither legally nor morally bound" to purchase a license from the plaintiffs, since their patent did not "cover the modern automobile." The legal contest had cost Ford close to a million dollars, but it was money well spent, since it established him as the champion of the common man against the "trust" and further identified him in the public mind as the manufacturer of a people's car. In vanquishing the ALAM, Ford had won his battle against key elements in Detroit's upper class; they did not thereafter have the power to harm his company.[40]

The New York banking community had greater financial resources, however. As the Ford Motor Company prospered, Wall Street became increasingly eager to gain control of it; they deemed the company too important to the American economy to be left in the hands of a man they considered unpredictable and unstable. The company transcended "the ordinary manufacturing proposition," Seward Prosser, president of the Bankers Trust of New York (a Morgan bank) explained in 1915. "It is, in effect, a very large and important financial institution, and it needs the guiding hand of a man with . . . balance and sound judgment." He fretted that with Henry Ford in charge it would "come to naught." The following year Ford received offers from both the House of Morgan and the brokerage firm of Hornblower & Weeks, the latter for $500 million. He refused to sell, even though he suspected that the bankers were exploiting the war emergency to dry up his steel supply (presumably through Morgan's influence at U.S. Steel).[41]

Wall Street made another bid for control in January 1921, when the postwar recession temporarily closed the Ford plants. Word went out that the Ford Motor Company needed an additional $40 million to meet its obligations. Several Detroit and New York banks offered to lend the money, provided they could name the company's treasurer. But Ford had no intention of borrowing; he raised the necessary funds by cutting costs and dumping unwanted cars on his dealers. Nevertheless, the banks kept shoving loans at him. On one occasion Joseph Bowers, vice-president of the Liberty National Bank of New York, a "Morgan-controlled institution," showed up unsolicited; he asserted that Ford needed a loan and insisted on naming not only the treasurer but also one of the directors. These safeguards were necessary, he said, because "some prominent Grosse Pointe men, all bankers" had warned against making loans to Henry Ford, whom "they deemed . . . erratic and irresponsible." Ford, his suspicions about bankers and Grosse Pointe confirmed, brusquely showed Bowers the door.[42]

Both Wall Street and Griswold Street, its Detroit counterpart, would definitely have preferred a world without Henry Ford and probably also without the Ford Motor Company. For a while there was the possibility that Ford, though sales leader from 1906 onward, might—like Oldsmobile and Locomobile before it—falter; and, gratifyingly, Ford's production did decline in 1908 as it made the transition between the Model N and the Model T eras. But then it charged ahead, leaving the pack far behind: its output increased tenfold between 1909 and 1912. As Ford asserted dominance over the automobile industry, Detroit's upper class came to the painful realization that it could ill afford to show unremitting hostility toward either the man or his company. They would have to be co-opted.[43]

There were several gestures of confraternity. For example, the ALAM, deciding to accept its legal defeat graciously, treated Henry Ford and James Couzens to a magnificent banquet. "The pipe of peace was smoked literally and figuratively," a trade journal reported, "by Colonel Charles Clifton, President of the A.L.A.M., and Mr. Ford while the banqueters cheered." Congratulatory telegrams poured into Ford headquarters, including one from Richard P. Joy, a Packard director and brother of Ford's great antagonist. And the Ford Motor Company was at last asked to join the ALAM—to become an insider.[44]

Detroit's business elite also did their best to bring the Ford team on board. In 1910 they made Henry Ford a director of the Board of Commerce as well as of one the city's largest banks. Within two years he had been elected to the boards of three more major financial institutions. Two of these boards had also welcomed Ford's general manager, James Couzens; a fifth bank had added Paul Gray, a Ford director, to its board. The year 1910 also saw Henry Ford receive a signal honor: the chairmanship of the finance committee of the newly organized association to build a general hospital for Detroit. Hospitals had previously been the principal focus for the charitable contributions of Detroit's upper class; in cooperating with Ford in the fund-raising drive, they were in effect recognizing him as a social peer.[45]

But the attempt at co-optation miscarried, and by 1918 both Henry Ford and James Couzens had been completely alienated; any prospect of their cooperating with Detroit's upper class had been extinguished, and their self-identification with the "common man" was by then stronger than ever. In identifying the issues that drove a wedge between the Ford leadership and Detroit's elite, one must keep in mind the question of responsibility: were Ford and Couzens simply too deviant to be assimilated? Or did Detroit's upper class exhibit in their dealings with the Ford leadership the same kind of self-defeating conservatism that had already lost them the auto industry?

Henry Ford's appointment as chairman of the hospital fund-raising drive constituted his first important social coup—but if it was designed to co-opt him, the honor backfired terribly. The problem, according to historian William Greenleaf, was simply that Ford proved to be an "inept and absent" fund raiser. He obviously did not have the right contacts. What he did have was money, but after contributing $110,000 in land and cash, he resented suggestions from Detroit's elite that he save the hospital project by putting even more into the kitty and huffily withdrew his support. His elite associates responded by trying to unload the half-completed hospital onto the municipal government; one of them, George G. Booth, used his newspaper, the *Detroit News*, to blame Ford for the collapse of the project. Stung by this attack and anxious to forestall public ownership, Ford paid off his fellow subscribers in June 1914 and assumed the debts of the hospital, which received a new name the following year—the Henry Ford Hospital. As Greenleaf has shown, it then adopted an egalitarian fee policy that turned a sizable portion of the medical community against it—and, by extension, against Henry Ford.[46]

The attempt to incorporate Ford into Detroit's financial elite proved equally abortive; he simply was not willing to obey the informal rules of the banking fraternity. For example, in February 1909 he organized the Highland Park State Bank to handle the company payroll and the savings of employees living in the vicinity of his new plant in suburban Highland Park. Fearful of the "money trust," Ford was determined to exclude the big Detroit banks from the suburb, then virgin territory. As the mechanics of banking held no fascination for him, he left the management of the new bank to James Couzens. (Years later Couzens boasted, "I ran [the bank] from across the street, in my office at the Ford plant.")[47]

It was not the decision to found a bank that upset Detroit's financial elite: the city's economy was expanding rapidly; the Highland Park State Bank was but one of several that were organized to serve the auto industry; and it remained quite small. What infuriated them was the announcement in December 1913 that the Ford Motor Company henceforth would pay its suppliers by crediting amounts owed them to accounts in the Highland Park State Bank. Though suppliers had little choice but to accept this dictum, the city's bankers loudly protested so flagrant an attempt to steal their business. For this offense, and other less serious improprieties, the Detroit Clearing House Association denied its facilities to Ford's banks. He was literally being ostracized by the city's financial elite.[48]

Within a month, the industrial elite were also looking for ways to punish Ford, now quickly taking on pariah status. Detroit's industrialists were sorely distressed by the announcement of the "five-dollar day": on January 5, 1914, James Couzens told a news conference that the Ford Motor Company intended to double its minimum wage to five dollars a day. It was, he exulted, "the greatest revolution in the matter of rewards for its workers ever known to the industrial world." Ford's plan, hatched in secret, dropped like a bombshell on an industry already beleaguered by rising labor militancy. Publicly, his competitors dared not criticize the pay hike, for it immediately found near universal support in labor circles and the media. The most pointed statement, by Hugh Chalmers, merely rebuked Ford for taking such a radical step without consulting his fellow industrialists.[49]

In private, however, the other auto manufacturers fumed about Ford's "treason" to his industry and class. Alvan Macauley of Packard phoned up to protest, "We are not running a philanthropic business like you." Studebaker, "flabbergasted" by the news, prepared for renewed labor unrest in its Detroit factories; vice-president Albert Erskine informed his board of directors, "It is believed in the city that [Ford's] plan contravenes all economic laws and must in the end fail because of competition." Elliott G. Stevenson, attorney for the Dodge brothers, probably summed up the attitude of Detroit's automotive community toward Ford's *coup de main* when he sourly observed, "Many wise men think it is wrong to so undermine the whole substrata of organized society by paying such wages to common labor and spreading discontent . . . in those industries which cannot pay $5 per day."[50]

Several small manufacturers fled the city rather than match Ford's wages. They should have waited awhile, however, for it turned out that Detroit's employers easily weathered the economic storm stirred up by Ford's announcement. The notoriety of the five-dollar day lured so many workers to Detroit that the local Employers' Association was able to keep wage increases to a minimum, and by year's end the war and inflation had further discounted the practical impact of Ford's pay hike.[51]

Yet Ford's heretical labor policy had symbolic import. Once again he had flouted the status quo; he had departed from the common front mounted by local employers in their dealings with the working class and appeared to threaten every industrial concern with labor discontent, strikes, and the union shop. For public relations reasons the economic elite, like the auto industry, had to acclaim the five-dollar wage. The *Michigan Manufacturer* even called it the "most generous stroke of policy between captain of industry and worker that the country has ever seen." But in the privacy of their corporate offices and social clubs, they strove to punish the Ford Motor Company for its renegade actions. James Couzens found the climate in the Detroit Club so inclement that he pulled the company out of the Employers' Association in retaliation.[52]

Couzens also responded by trying to embarrass employers who were unwilling or unable to emulate Ford's labor policies. In a memorable speech in December 1914 he lectured the Board of Commerce for failing to cope with the city's unemployment problem:

> You fellows sit back, smug and complacent, and don't give a damn what becomes of your workmen. You ask for more patrolmen to guard your property; but what do you do for your workmen? . . . You kick them into the street. . . . You can't give these men work during the summer and then discharge them in the winter while you take your golf sticks and go to California, and do your full duty.

The speech got results—the Board of Commerce, energized by the rebuke, rounded up several hundred new jobs for the unemployed—but Couzens's invective permanently alienated "a good number of Detroit businessmen."[53]

Even less popular was a letter-writing campaign in which Couzens not very subtly suggested that subsistence wages were driving employees to vice and crime. In a letter to S. S. Kresge, for example, Couzens derided the dime store magnate for his ostentatious fund raising for a rescue home for unfortunate girls: "I think you can do much more for girls and women by paying them better wages," Couzens advised, "than you can by subscribing $1000 to rescue them after they have gotten into trouble." Kresge never forgave or forgot the insult. Nine years later the press reported, "To this day he has left unturned no stone he could place in the road of James Couzens."[54]

■ **5**   By 1915 that sentiment, widely held in elite circles, had made life perilous indeed for James Couzens and Henry Ford. They were not—Ford's fancies aside—in any physical danger, and the company itself was unassailable as long as the Model T found favor. But Detroit's upper class, unable to strike at the two multimillionaires economically, exacted retribution in the social realm. There they took dead aim at the reputations of Ford and Couzens, using public ridicule as their weapon.

They mocked Henry Ford most for his pacifism. Detroit's business elite was by the summer of 1915 ardently pro-preparedness, with majority opinion favoring an arms buildup, universal military training, and an assertive foreign policy. The preparedness movement thus offered another opportunity for automotive leaders to affirm their loyalty to upper-class norms; they were, Roy Chapin said, "heart and soul behind the preparedness movement," a cause that brought together patrician automakers like Philip McMillan and Henry Joy and newcomers like Roy Chapin, Hugh Chalmers, Harry Jewett, and John Dodge.[55]

A sizable minority passed beyond the advocacy of strong defensive measures to call for war: "I felt many, many months ago," Henry Joy wrote a Packard distributor in February 1916, "that it was our duty to bear our share of the burden, and not let England and France . . . fight battles alone which are . . . the battles of America." Occasionally, a venal note was heard: Packard's advertising manager fretted that failure to support the Allies would cost the United States dearly in lost trade after the war. Still, most of the war lobby seemed more concerned that the United States would forfeit its honor if it acquiesced in Germany's "outrages" against its shipping. Some of the auto executives became, in fact, obsessed with the need to fight. In May 1917, for example, a friend recalled the "passion and fervor—the almost agony" of Edwin Denby's long-standing "fear that the country was too steeped in the lethargy of gain and self-seeking to realize its danger."[56]

Henry Ford's position on the war made for quite a contrast: not only did he vociferously denounce preparedness; he also used his fortune to finance the peace movement. To reporters he explained his motives as follows: "I hate war, because war is murder, desolation, and destruction, causeless, unjustifiable, cruel, heartless to those of the human race who do not want it." When challenged to identify the cause of war, he had a ready answer: "It is capitalism, greed, the dirty hunger for dollars." In April 1915 he vowed to burn his factory to the ground rather than convert to war production; the following September he labeled professional soldiers "lazy or crazy" and boasted that only ten of his employees belonged to the National Guard. In November he started financing the antiwar movement.[57]

In espousing pacifism, Ford was deliberately throwing down the gauntlet to Detroit's business elite, as he made clear in press releases:

> It's a pathetic sight and positive fact that most men who pose as standing for the best things in life and pray to God in churches on Sunday for peace . . . are busiest nowadays in obtaining orders that will enable them to convert their factories into workshops for making shot and shell for destroying mankind.

The Detroit business elite fought back, led by the president of Packard. Henry B. Joy did not mince words; in a typical salvo he blasted "loud-mouthed bleaters for peace at any price" who, he stated, "ought to be shot or punished in some proper manner." Ford retorted that Joy's preparedness activities made him a "Detroit briefholder" for murder.[58]

Nor did Ford's pacifism remain in the realm of rhetoric. In December 1915 he chartered the *Oscar II*, the famous "Peace Ship," to transport an unofficial American peace commission to The Hague. Though a hostile American press professed to find the peace ship merely amusing, Ford quite certainly made new enemies in Detroit by marking himself—with the expenditure of almost half a million dollars on this venture alone—as an important obstacle to intervention.[59]

In October 1916 Ford again broke ranks with the vast majority of Detroit businessmen, who voted Republican, by endorsing Woodrow Wilson's reelection. Ford still claimed to be a Republican, but he announced his support for the incumbent because Wilson had "saved the United States from the horrors and desolation of international war." This endorsement undoubtedly helped Wilson throughout the Midwest, where the Model T had made Henry Ford a regional saint, and in California, a key swing state where Ford spent three-fifths of the $55,000 he contributed to the president's campaign. When California provided Wilson his margin of victory, Ford gained a reputation as a "kingmaker" and additional ill will in the Detroit business community. Even though he changed his tune once the United States entered the war—by October 1917 he was pronouncing American involvement "the best thing that ever happened in the world"—Detroit's upper class did not forgive his previous apostasy, for it had, after all, involved the ultimate "life and death" issue.[60]

■ 6   Ford's politics of war attested to a heterodoxy so profound that even a broad-minded elite might have had difficulty accommodating him. Couzens's fate, on the other hand, revealed how narrow was the orthodoxy to which the Ford associates were expected to conform. The five-dollar day behind him, Couzens did his best to behave "responsibly." He announced in favor of "preparedness in a moderate and sane way" and supported the Republican Party against Ford's challenge in 1916. Admittedly, his Republicanism was tainted by a refusal to endorse party conservatives and by his declaration that he preferred to be "called an Independent or a Progressive than to be called a Republican," but much could be forgiven the party's largest contributor in Michigan. If the Detroit business elite sought additional evidence of his fundamental soundness, they could find it in his election to the board of directors of the United States Chamber of Commerce in February 1916.[61]

Yet he too was targeted for public humiliation. Consider the fate that befell him when he agreed, in September 1916, to become Detroit's police commissioner. He was offered the position by Mayor Oscar Marx in order to confound those critics who blamed the administration for the city's rising crime rate. Everyone expected Couzens to be a hard-nosed "law and order" policeman who would protect property and enforce public morals. Instead, Couzens's empathy with the poor led him to contest the justice of enforcing the Sunday closing laws against workingmen's saloons as long as the "rich" were permitted to drink in their clubs. "There are in statute books and among city ordinances so many obsolete and absurd laws," Couzens declared, "that it would be foolish for an official to announce that he intended to enforce the law strictly."[62]

Couzens, assailed in the press and from the city's pulpits for his moral laxity, soon had to backtrack and affirm that he would enforce the letter of the law. The statement sounded platitudinous, but Couzens meant what he said: there would be but one law for rich and for poor. "Effective at once," he informed the superintendent of police, "I want every man in the department instructed to absolutely enforce all laws twenty-four hours of the day. . . . From now on, I want every law and ordinance complied with. . . . No excuses will be accepted."[63]

In promulgating his edict, Couzens must have hoped to ally himself with responsible elite opinion. Instead, he became the butt of their jokes, his reformism dismissed as the prattling of a village fool. His tenure as police commissioner proved to be a fiasco, the press publicizing his misadventures as they would a serial melodrama: they treated their readers to stories about the police commissioner issuing parking tickets to the Common Council, having his own car stolen, and himself ending up in jail on a contempt citation. Typical of the ridicule that buffeted him each week were the headlines: "Couzens Fails Even to Regulate Motorists" and "Police Keep Right on with Their Bungling."[64]

The gales of laughter swept away any prospect of Couzens's alignment with the upper class. He blamed the elite for his embarrassments and accused them of hypocrisy toward urban reform: "When they asked me to clean up Detroit, they didn't mean it," he said. "They wanted me to make it nice enough to appease the reformers and let it stay rotten enough to appease the bums. It was all confusing." For Couzens, in other words, the social world of his economic peers was an inexplicable terra incognita whose rules he found too "confusing" to comprehend. He genuinely had not expected them to ridicule his attempts to deliver evenhanded justice.[65]

■ 7   It would appear that the two automotive leaders (and their company) simply did not know how to behave in a socially "correct" way. Whatever the issue—charity work, banking, labor relations, national politics, or war and peace—they seemed unerringly to take a position offensive to the limousine set. It is therefore tempting to regard Ford and Couzens as the architects of their own exclusion, to say that they declined to make the concessions necessary to gain admission to Detroit's upper class and thus earned for themselves social opprobrium and for Couzens the epithet of "scab millionaire." Years later Couzens explained, "They [the upper class] hate me because I won't conform. I'm still a poor man as far as they are concerned."[66]

Both he and Henry Ford responded to their social isolation by accentuating their original, primary identification with the country's working poor. Increasingly, both broadcast encomiums of the virtues of those who worked for a living—as opposed to Detroit's coupon clippers. Couzens, for example, contended that he would "rather take the judgement of 40,000 average workmen than the judgement of the 40,000 biggest businessmen in the United States." He and Ford constantly referred to their humble origins, Couzens saying, "I worked twelve hours a day, year in and year out, for poor pay. . . . I think I know how the average man feels on most questions." The constancy of their devotion to the lower-class market brought the two men popularity and a vicarious sense of belonging, both of which were denied them by their presumptive peers in Detroit's business elite. To gain further approval from the masses, they increasingly trumpeted their estrangement from the traditional values of the establishment, making a rapprochement at the top even less likely.[67]

It would appear, then, that Ford's persistence in the lower price-class was inextricably linked—in a feedback loop—to continuing alienation from Detroit's upper class and its value system. There can be no question that Ford and Couzens constantly affronted the sensibilities of the old families and that in economic, political, and community affairs they did not take sufficient pains either to ascertain or to accede to the will of Detroit's upper class. It is not surprising, then, that the latter made them feel like outsiders.

If we look at consequences—at the fortune that their class orientation brought Ford and Couzens and at the financial ruin that their animosity wreaked upon Detroit's upper class in 1933 (see Chapter Eight)—then there can be but one conclusion as to who bore the greater responsibility for the botched recruitment of the two major stockholders of the Ford Motor Company. Ford and Couzens ultimately did not need to adhere to Detroit's upper-class social system; their fabulous wealth and power effectively put them outside it and above it. Detroit's upper class, on the other hand, needed Ford—not only, as it turned out, for protection against more powerful elites situated in Chicago and New York but also for day-to-day help in administering Detroit's affairs. S. S. Marquis, dean of Detroit's Episcopal cathedral, understood this dependency and epitomized it in the following passage from his 1922 memoir of Henry Ford:

> Wherever he goes the crowds press upon him as if he were a king out for an airing and thrust their petitions, not into his hands, but into his ears. I once took him to a reception at which a large

> number of high dignitaries of the church were present. They
> formed in a line, like purchasers of tickets at a circus, and in turn
> made their wants known for schools, colleges, missions, and strug-
> gling parishes. . . . I have seen him besieged in a similar manner by
> business men at club receptions.

No wonder Ford had come to suspect that every offer of friendship
masked an "ulterior motive." Couzens had reached the same conclusion: "Every man who comes near me wants something," he once
informed a small group at the Detroit Athletic Club. "They are
all alike. If I were poor they wouldn't speak to me. It's never Jim
Couzens. It's always Jim Couzens' money."[68]

How could an upper class composed of mendicants expect to
discipline the multimillionaires of Ford, to teach them to respect
their class norms? Yet they attempted to impose a strict code of
rectitude on the Ford magnates and, in so doing, revealed the same
kind of myopic conservatism that had already undermined their
efforts to sustain class rule through continued domination of the
city's economic life. By 1910 their entrepreneurial limitations had
cost them control of Detroit's dominant industry; in the decade that
followed they failed to appreciate the *necessity*, for them, of con-
ciliating and co-opting the leaders of the Ford Motor Company, the
only one of the automotive Big Three to be locally owned and
controlled. They seemed not to realize that the goodwill of Henry
Ford and James Couzens had—given the motorization of Detroit's
economy—become essential to their continued class rule. They
did not perceive, in other words, that the economic situation dictated that they, not Ford, should make fundamental concessions on
values.

■ 8   It is "axiomatic," as the political scientist Heinz
Eulau has observed, that elites "seek to perpetuate themselves, their
goals and their ways of doing things." But it is also true that the
revitalization of an elite group, such as Detroit's old families, requires it to understand that in the final analysis "elites . . . are not
'recruited' but *emerge* in the process of societal transformation as
new values come to constitute the bases of power." In Detroit,
power after 1910 increasingly depended on coming to terms with
the emerging ethos of mass production. This accommodation the
pre-automotive elite were reluctant to make—not only, as we have
seen, in their automotive strategies but also in their negative reaction to Henry Ford's expression of the values implicit in the new
production technology.[69]

Consider Ford's two unpardonable "sins" against the established order: the five-dollar day and the pacifist campaign. From an elite perspective these Ford initiatives struck at the foundations, respectively, of class and nation; Detroit's upper class felt it had to retaliate, but in retaliating, its members squandered whatever possibility had existed of co-opting Henry Ford and James Couzens into their ranks. It is important, then, to appreciate that the Ford initiatives obeyed the logic of mass production and that the upper class, in opposing them, was in effect quarreling with the future.

In retrospect, even Ford's pacifism seems more compatible with the mass production era than does the bellicosity of Detroit's upper class. To be sure, automotive executives did not in early 1917 realize the threat posed by modern war; indeed, Hugh Chalmers assumed that the "motor industry would be stimulated" by it. Hudson, adopting as its "war slogan" the challenge "Business as Usual—and More of It!," predicted that "war would not curtail the demand for pleasure automobiles," for "the part this country would play in the great war would be that of an economic arsenal to the fighting forces already engaged." The industry believed, in other words, that its greatest contribution to the war effort would lie in automotive manufacturing and that only a portion of its capacity would be needed for military production.[70]

Wall Street had less roseate expectations, however, and the price of automobile shares fell sharply once war was declared. The investors proved the better seers: the federal government slapped a 5 percent luxury tax on passenger cars in May 1917, and the following November the War Industries Board attempted to cut off the industry's supply of alloy steel on the grounds that it was engaged in a "nonessential" activity. The industry's lobbyists—headed by Hugh Chalmers, the representative of the National Automobile Chamber of Commerce—did their best to fend off regulation, yet by August 1918 they had been forced to agree to restrict production of passenger cars for the last six months of the year to 25 percent of the 1917 level. As a result, an industry that had set new production records each year experienced its first setback, with overall production (including trucks and buses) falling by 38 percent. Though prices rose in partial compensation, most companies reported reduced profits. Studebaker, its "war business . . . nowhere near as profitable as [its] regular commercial work," netted only 4.8 percent on sales. Packard, its profits down sharply, paid no dividend in January 1918. Hudson and General Motors, finding their dealer networks disrupted, tried to save them by finding new products—such as tractors and refrigerators—to sell, but even so, some marginal dealerships did fail.[71]

The industry found it difficult to compensate for drooping sales by switching to war contracts because mass production, an inflexible technology, relied on special-purpose tools and fixed conveyor systems, both of which had to be redesigned to accommodate a new product. Asked to manufacture the Liberty aircraft engine, Detroit's auto manufacturers were proud, as Howard Coffin said, that it had taken them less than six months to get it "from the first scratch on paper in June [1917] to the beginning of production of quantity manufacturing tools," but critics wondered where the *engines* were. Eventually, the industry geared up to mass-produce aircraft engines—24,000 of them by the armistice—but not in time to avoid being charged with incompetence by the Senate Committee on Military Affairs, which reasoned that the traditional handwork methods of the aviation industry would have gotten far more planes into combat. The loss of prestige was probably not as painful as the financial losses incurred when the government canceled its aircraft orders in 1919, leaving several manufacturers—notably Lincoln, Packard, Ford, and General Motors—with a major investment in specialized tools for the manufacture of engines that no one now wanted.[72]

The industry's experiences during World War I suggested that mass producers should pray for peace. In 1915–1916 Henry Ford's pacifism conformed to the objective needs of the new production technology, but his sympathies were apparently shared by only one other Detroit auto leader: William C. Durant, the founder of General Motors. It is surely more than coincidence that Durant also shared Ford's vision of a future defined by mass automobility. Durant did not broadcast his beliefs in Ford fashion; nevertheless, his associates have testified to his opposition to war. According to the Lelands, Durant had no sympathy for the war or for "patriotic platitudes." They told a Senate committee that he had opposed Cadillac's undertaking military contracts. John Lee Pratt, Durant's assistant, told a similar story: GM's chief "was very much opposed" in 1916 to Buick's "taking on war work." Though Durant, like Ford, saw the wisdom of supporting the war once the United States had entered it, his stance in 1915–1916 is highly suggestive: with the founders of the two most successful and innovative automobile companies agreed on the necessity for peace, it would appear that Detroit's upper class was unwise to make bellicosity a test of orthodoxy.[73]

Similarly, had its members been less conservative, the upper class would have been more forgiving of the five-dollar day. Had they fully appreciated the revolutionary nature of Ford's factory, they would have understood that mass production demanded a substantial increase in the wages paid to semiskilled and unskilled labor.

The five-dollar day was not, as they thought, a "charitable gift" from a wealthy demagogue. Rather it had a twofold rationale: first, a major wage increase was needed to induce Ford's employees to accept the assembly line and the enhanced management control over production that the line entailed. Mass production methods demeaned workers' skills and reduced their independence on the job; Ford realized that the new technology could be sold to his employees only if it came with higher wages attached. Second, Henry Ford realized that workers' wages would have to rise if they were as a class to have the means to purchase the output of mass producers like the Ford Motor Company. At the time of the five-dollar day, most major American manufacturers made producers' goods: that is, products for use by other corporations. Ford was looking ahead to a consumer society whose economic vitality would depend on a substantial augmentation in the purchasing power of the masses.[74]

In proclaiming the five-dollar day, Ford and Couzens were heralding the future industrial and economic order; in seeking to punish them for their modernity, Detroit's business elite were in effect rejecting the future. They took refuge in traditional values and, as is typical of a decadent elite, limited their recruitment efforts to those who—like the middle-class auto entrepreneurs—endorsed the status quo. But in rejecting Ford and Couzens, Detroit's upper class lost two potential paladins. As a result, in 1933 it would find itself desperately looking for help from General Motors and Chrysler, two companies whose indifference would prove almost as deadly as the outright hostility of the Ford leaders.

The next chapter shows that both companies owed their success (by 1929 they had joined Ford in the Big Three) to their creative response to the challenge of mass-producing motor vehicles. They realized, as Bernard Weisberger has said of GM's leadership, that "the instrument of mass production . . . merited . . . a new kind of business organization, the supercorporation."[75] Through management structures that made them more bureaucratic, decentralized, and impersonal than their Detroit competition, they were able to resist the industrywide impulse to stamp their owners' social aspirations onto their product. Indeed, their organizational reforms permitted them to offer a full range of models, and thus to evade the trap of conspicuous production. Like Ford, these two companies excluded Detroit's upper class, even after it had been reconstituted in the years from 1910 to 1918. And once again, the city's old families proved unable to recruit the leaders of those firms that most faithfully incorporated the spirit of the new production technology.

Chapter Six
The Absentee-Owned Firms

■   Versatility paid large dividends in the automobile industry. Only Ford built a giant enterprise by serving a single price-class. Chrysler and General Motors joined Ford in the Big Three because they muted their class-consciousness and adopted a multimodel policy that generated sales across the entire price spectrum. General Motors in 1925 comprised five automaking divisions with models selling from $525 to $4,350. Chrysler, a late starter, achieved a full line in 1928 by adding Dodge and Plymouth. Their Detroit competitors limited themselves to a narrow range of models and prices.

There were obvious advantages to building a full line. It reduced the possibility that a bad model year would prostrate sales and improved the odds of finding a car that could capture the public fancy. With a model for all economic seasons, a company was less susceptible to the vagaries of the business cycle. Moreover, it ensured customer loyalty by providing models to express every nuance and shift in income and career. No matter how they fared in life, customers returned to Chrysler and General Motors to shop. GM also discovered that by placing its cars "at the top of each price range," it could lure auto buyers into higher brackets where its profit margin widened. Similarly, the prices of the divisions overlapped to facilitate upward movement.[1]

A full product line made economic sense, as the success of General Motors demonstrated. In 1925 it captured one-third of the industry's net profit; in 1926, one-half. Its earnings that year reached $190 million—a peacetime record to that date for all industries. Yet the GM money machine had few imitators. The owners of the class-defined companies like Packard and Hudson molded the firms in their own image. Where ownership and control coincided, few escaped the trammels of personality. Companies owned by the old families and by middle-class entrepreneurs were each an extension of the personality of the dominant executive and therefore wore a mental straitjacket that restricted it to a narrow, self-defeating model policy. General Motors and Chrysler, by contrast, depersonalized their organizations, bureaucratizing them and separating ownership from control. That was the secret of their success and of their ability to market a full line of products in defiance of class barriers within the industry.[2]

■ 1   Billy Durant's combination of genius and folly made General Motors the first company to evolve a multimodel policy. His tale has been amply recounted in two major biographies as well as several corporate histories. Briefly, then, he was the son of a ne'er-do-well but grandson of H. H. Crapo, a lumber millionaire and onetime governor of Michigan. He hailed from Flint, the "Vehicle City," where he began building road carts in 1886. By 1904 his company, Durant-Dort, was the largest carriage manufacturer in the United States. As it prospered, Durant lost interest, and by 1901 he had left its management to take up stock speculation in New York City.[3]

His attention reverted to Flint in November 1904, however, when he received an appeal for help from the Buick Motor Company, at that time "almost a family firm" of Flint's tightly intermarried elite. Buick was nearly bankrupt and threatened to drag down Flint's three banks with it; its president therefore entreated Durant to rescue the company as a favor to his native city. Durant agreed and immediately raised $500,000 by public subscription, most of it from Flint's vehicle companies, who joined the banks as Buick's sponsors.[4]

As a community project Buick prospered: in 1907 it ranked second nationally in sales. Its success stoked Durant's ambitions; he began to dream of making Buick the cornerstone of a giant automotive combine. Consolidation held considerable allure, for it offered protection against a capricious buying public. Durant "wanted to have a lot of 'makes,'" A. B. C. Hardy explained, "so that he would always be sure to have some popular cars." Durant told him, "I was for getting every car in sight, playing safe all along the line." The idea behind General Motors, Durant informed John Lee Pratt, was to reduce the "gamble in changing models"; a company with several divisions would never have to make a complete model changeover.[5]

A second, equally compelling incentive came from the stock market, which tended to regard a combine as worth more than the sum of its parts. "Billy never thought that General Motors would become the big manufacturer that it did," commented Durant's attorney, John J. Carton. "What . . . he desired, most of all, were large stock issues in which he, from an inside position, could dicker and trade." Though his biographers tend to downplay stock speculation as a motive, the House of Morgan concluded otherwise and after two years of negotiations dropped its plans to finance his combine. It simply did not trust him.[6]

Durant's combine thus lacked a Wall Street sponsor. He consequently had to build it on a narrow capital base, and within two years it had collapsed into near receivership. Incorporated on September 16, 1908, General Motors—with the notable exception of Cadillac, which received $4.4 million in cash—was able to acquire only those companies willing to accept GM stock in payment for their own. By 1910 General Motors had acquired stock in twenty-five companies, ten of them manufacturers of passenger cars. Of these, only Buick, Cadillac, and Olds were established producers; the rest operated, according to A. B. C. Hardy, "heads over heels in debt."[7]

Durant, interested primarily in empire building, did not care to manage the companies he acquired; he organized General Motors as a holding company, which it remained until January 1917. Each of the operating companies was allowed, as Henry M. Leland phrased it in the press release announcing GM's purchase of Cadillac, to "continue to carry on its business as though it were an entirely independent organization." Leland promised no alteration in "Cadillac standards, Cadillac policies, Cadillac methods and the entire Cadillac organization"—in short, no diversion from the company's ascent into the upper price-class. Each of GM's subsidiaries would be allowed to carve out its own class niche. As a holding company, General Motors was thus able to contain and diffuse the negative effects of conspicuous production among its various car divisions.[8]

That no single vision would be imposed on General Motors became even clearer when Buick's sales difficulties cost Durant control of the holding company in 1910. In exchange for a five-year loan of $12.75 million, a banking syndicate led by Lee, Higginson and Company of Boston and two New York houses—J. and W. Seligman and the Central Trust Company—received the right to vote a majority of GM's common shares for the duration of the loan. Ownership and control were thus sharply divided, further reducing the likelihood that General Motors would become a vehicle for social climbing by its principal stockholders.

The bankers' takeover somewhat paradoxically gave Detroit's capitalists a greater say in the management of General Motors. Durant's operations had rotated about a Flint–New York axis, and his board of directors, reflecting that bias, had included only one Detroiter—Wilfred Leland, representing Cadillac. The bankers, in contrast, reconstructed the corporation as a Detroit-based enterprise; the Motor City was, after all, easier to reach from the East than Flint.[9]

In their search for allies in Detroit, the bankers naturally settled upon the city's upper class. GM's presidency they awarded to Thomas Neal, a Detroit paint manufacturer and banker; as treasurer they installed James T. Shaw, a private banker from Dearborn; as corporate secretary, Standish Backus, a young lawyer and the son-in-law of Joseph Boyer, president of Burroughs Adding Machine. Boyer himself joined the board of directors, as did Michael J. Murphy, a Detroit furniture manufacturer; Emory W. Clark, president of the First National Bank of Detroit; and Andrew H. Green, Jr., regional manager for the Solvay Process Company. The appointments strengthened GM's ties with Detroit's most powerful commercial bank—First National—of which Neal, Clark, and Murphy were three of the "most active directors." The bank had already proved a useful ally, with timely loans to Cadillac during the 1907 and 1910 crises.[10]

For the next five years after the 1910 reorganization Detroiters graced GM's board and executive offices. During that period they helped the eastern bankers to retrench. General Motors began to concentrate on its profitable makes, dropping the rest, and by 1916 there were only four survivors among its automobile subsidiaries: Oldsmobile, Buick, Cadillac, and Oakland—the last a smaller outfit acquired in 1909 and subsequently renamed in honor of its hometown of Pontiac, Michigan. The GM line still covered a large part of the price spectrum but not the lower price-class, which it had forfeited by failing to replace Buick's cheapest car, the Model 10. From their respective vantage points neither Detroit's upper class nor the eastern bankers could perceive the market potential of an economy car; indeed, as Bernard Weisberger has pointed out, Durant's predictions about the future size of the automobile market had convinced the bankers that he was a "wild man" whom they could not trust to head a major industrial company. The conservatism of this period bore mixed results: a quadrupling of sales but also a halving of market share as General Motors failed to keep up with the industry's frantic rate of expansion.[11]

Excessive caution also led the bankers to refuse to pay dividends on GM's common stock. When investors, in exasperation, began to unload it, their disenchantment offered Billy Durant the opening he needed to retake control. But he could not hope to defeat the bankers without powerful allies, and to attract them he had to prove that he retained his automotive mastery. This he amply demonstrated by incorporating Chevrolet in November 1911 and leading it to tenth place in the industry less than four years later. Though originally located in Detroit, Chevrolet represented—as was increasingly typical of Durant's ventures—a mixture of Flint and New York capital.[12]

Chevrolet's success attracted to his banner a host of wealthy allies: they included Louis G. Kaufman (president of Chatham-Phenix National Bank of New York), the Rockefellers, and the Du Ponts. By May 1916 this syndicate controlled more than half of GM's voting shares, and Durant took over as president, the original set of bankers retiring from the corporation's affairs. But Durant did not, in this second ascendancy, have the kind of unfettered power that he had enjoyed in 1908–1910. He now shared command with Du Pont, manufacturer of munitions and chemicals, which in 1917–1919 used its extraordinary war profits to acquire 28.7 percent of GM's shares; only Durant held more.[13]

To safeguard its investment, Du Pont insisted that its executives "assume charge and be responsible for the financial operation" of General Motors. It installed a Du Pont executive, John J. Raskob, as chairman of GM's finance committee but soon discovered that this committee, while required to raise money for the corporation, lacked an effective voice in spending it. That remained the preserve of the executive committee, then controlled by Durant and the operating divisions. Though General Motors had ceased to be a holding company in 1917, its subsidiaries becoming divisions, the managers of the producing units still jealously guarded their autonomy.[14]

Meetings of the executive committee resembled a summit of heads of state, each placing the interests of his principality ahead of the system as a whole. The division chiefs indulged in a "sort of horse-trading": "When one of them had a project . . . he would get the vote of his fellow members," John Lee Pratt observed. "If they would vote for his project, he would vote for theirs." Durant, an ardent exponent of expansion, undercut attempts to trim their budgets. When division managers received less money than requested, he told them "to go on and spend what money they needed without any record of it being made."[15]

From 1917 to 1919 Durant masterminded a spending spree that

tripled the corporation's paper value and added four automobile divisions: Sheridan, Scripps-Booth, Chevrolet, and General Motors of Canada. The company also integrated backward, to control its supply of parts and accessories, and diversified into tractors and refrigerators. Durant finally decided to slow down in late 1919 but found it impossible to circumvent the barter system on the executive committee. Moreover, the finance committee refused to abandon a multi-million-dollar project of its own: the construction of a massive headquarters building on Detroit's Grand Boulevard, a circumferential road three miles from downtown.[16]

Sales slipped in the spring of 1920, but the division heads, still committed to expansion, kept buying. By October, inventories amounted to $210 million, and the corporation for the second time bordered on bankruptcy. Durant's personal difficulties threatened to push it over the brink: he had borrowed heavily, using his stock as collateral, in a vain attempt to prop up the price of GM's securities. In November he informed the Du Pont company that he could no longer meet his margin calls. Du Pont acted quickly, forming a holding company to take over his assets and debts. To close his accounts, it advanced $7 million of its own money, borrowed $20 million through J. P. Morgan & Company, and put up $1.3 million of its GM shares as additional collateral. Its financial muscle pulled General Motors through the storm, but Durant personally was considerably less fortunate, losing—by his own reckoning—$90 million and control of General Motors.[17]

His final exit left Du Pont, with 36 percent of the voting shares (as of June 1921), master of General Motors. Only the House of Morgan, its principal banker and creditor, had the power to restrain it. The board of directors, reshuffled, reflected the new alignment: eight of its twenty-eight members were named by Du Pont, three by the Nobel Company (Du Pont's partner in the Canadian explosives market), and six by the House of Morgan. Durant's group, much diminished by his defeat, had only two representatives. Five directors fit the category of owner-managers: Charles S. Mott, Fred J. Fisher, Alfred P. Sloan, Jr., Charles F. Kettering, and R. Samuel McLaughlin owned companies absorbed by General Motors. Thus, they were large stockholders as well as senior executives.[18]

Overall, the board reflected the domination of eastern capital. Michigan had few spokesmen; Detroit's old families, none. Fred Fisher was the only Detroiter; self-made and rough hewn, he was considered unlikely to defend their interests. The Michigan elite viewed the new setup with alarm, and Pierre S. du Pont, Durant's successor as president, undertook a goodwill tour to reassure them of GM's continuing commitment to the state. He calmed them down, but there was no disguising the fact that Detroit and Michigan had suffered a serious loss of economic independence.[19]

■ 2   Under Durant, General Motors escaped the limitations of personality by decentralizing. It was able to pursue a multimodel policy by giving division heads a free rein, in effect allowing them to act as entrepreneurs in their own right. The company paid a heavy price for this flexibility, however, almost failing in 1910 and 1920. The new regime realized it had to tighten the organization while preserving the autonomy and individuality of the operating units. They wanted, according to Alfred P. Sloan, Jr.—the executive who dominated GM after Durant's departure—"a happy medium . . . between the extremes of pure centralization and pure decentralization." As executive vice-president, he proposed a policy of "decentralized operations with coordinated control" or—as he described it in 1926—"centralization of policy and decentralization of management."[20]

Sloan accorded the division managers an "altogether free hand" in running their enterprises. They reported to the executive committee through a group vice-president who had authority to advise but not command. Similarly, the sales, financial, and technical staffs at headquarters were limited to proferring advice to their counterparts within the operating units. Interdivisional committees brought together line officers, advisory staff, and general executives to pool ideas. Again, the heads of the operating companies remained free to go their own ways. Sloan, committed to decentralized management, kept a low profile. He later claimed that while he was president, from 1923 to 1937, he only once issued a direct order to a division manager; and that occurred in 1924 when the car producers resisted suggestions to curtail production in the face of a deepening recession.[21]

Sloan wanted General Motors itself to be an "objective organization" free from the toils of personality. The general office therefore developed a system of statistical controls that allowed it to compare the performance of the divisions and thus to determine how resources should be divided among them. As long as they performed well according to objective criteria—for example, by achieving a satisfactory rate of return on investment—the division managers were given free rein. As Sloan commented, "Men capable of getting the results we want will not work under orders. . . . Their methods of getting things done are too personal to themselves to be brought

under rules and regulations." He wanted the car divisions to develop and to sustain personalities of their own under the umbrella
of an impersonal "objective" corporation. He thus created a dualism
that enabled GM to escape the constraints of class consciousness
in the 1920s and 1930s as it had done in the past. Individual divisions had their own class images, and executives could seek social
prestige by moving between them. The corporation itself was classless and therefore relatively immune to the status obsessions of its
rivals. As a result, by 1927 it held a large enough share of the mass
market to move into first place in the industry—to stay.[22]

General Motors built its striking success on the twin pillars
of decentralization and bureaucratic planning. Together they
made possible a viable multimodel policy. The corporation made
the organization, rather than the product, its hallmark. Frequent
changes in ownership and command between 1910 and 1920 facilitated these innovations by reducing the personal factor in GM's
operations. Wide distribution of stock separated ownership from
control, and the early interest of eastern capital also helped to
ensure that General Motors would set profits rather than local
prestige as its ultimate goal. Besides, GM provided Cadillacs as
well as ephemeral marques (for example, the Rainier, the self-styled
"Pullman of Motor Cars") for those of its shareholders and executives who needed a moving testament to their own high social
status.

An impersonal money machine, General Motors operated outside
the nexus of Detroit's upper-class social system. Indeed, the company scarcely existed for most Detroiters before 1919. Everyone of
course knew about Cadillac and its ubiquitous president, Henry
Leland, but Cadillac operated like an independent company and
was not especially associated with General Motors in the local view.
It was only in April 1919 when the corporation announced plans to
build its gigantic headquarters on Grand Boulevard that Detroiters
awakened to the growing importance of General Motors to their
city's well-being. The announcement followed on the heels of a
decision to shift part of Chevrolet's production to Detroit from Flint
and preceded by a few months the purchase of a controlling interest
in Fisher Body, a locally owned firm. For the first time, General
Motors in Detroit bulked larger than the outline of Cadillac's factories.

Even so, the corporation still had an amazingly low profile in the
city, given its awesome power. However, it adopted a more aggressive stance after consumer studies revealed that "people throughout
the United States, except at the corner of Wall and Broad streets,

didn't know anything about General Motors." The corporation responded by creating an institutional advertising committee and hiring Bruce Barton to conduct a splashy advertising campaign.[23]

Locally, the campaign revolved around well-publicized contributions to the Citizens League and the Board of Commerce. Its beneficence seemed to work: the latter's official journal, the *Detroiter*, once scarcely aware of GM's existence, in May 1923 devoted an entire issue to the theme of Detroit as the "Home of General Motors." Typical of its tone was Robert Adams's observation: "Take away every General Motors interest here, and Detroit would not today be the city it is. Stop the wheels in General Motors plants, and Detroit is struck a blow from which no community can soon recover."[24]

The Board of Commerce itself, so close to failure in the mid-1920s that it had to sell its headquarters building, survived the decade only through the largesse of the major automobile companies, which after 1922 bought "plural memberships" on behalf of their employees. General Motors purchased 300, twice as many as Dodge Brothers, its closest rival in this regard. A grateful board heaped accolades on GM, calling its contribution the "largest single [contribution] given by any business in the world to help sustain and operate any commercial organization."[25]

By the mid-1920s General Motors and its executives had become major bankrollers of civic causes in Detroit. For example, GM, Fisher Body, and their allied families and interests gave $317,000 to the Detroit Community Fund in 1926–1927—twice the contribution of Packard and its six families, an amount exceeded only by Ford and its stockholders, past and present. Yet although the corporation met its financial responsibilities, it did not offer leadership to Detroit. Like any absentee-owned corporation, it shied away from controversy in the 1920s and 1930s, taking refuge in the familiar and the conventional. Its executives were more likely to offer leadership in the smaller communities—Charles Mott to Flint, Charles Kettering to Dayton, Ohio—where GM built plants. And though most of the corporation's offices were installed in the mausoleum on Grand Boulevard, its president after 1921 lived in the East, and it was to New York and Wilmington that the executive staff looked rather than to Detroit. The corporation operated on an international basis and was reluctant to become embroiled in Detroit's local affairs.[26]

GM's headquarters eloquently expressed its isolation from the main currents of city life. The corporation apparently expected Detroit's capitalists to follow it from downtown to the "New Center" on Grand Boulevard. Only Fisher Body obliged, erecting a sky-scraper across the boulevard from GM's headquarters. For more than half a century the two buildings stood in lonely splendor amid a morass of auto dealerships and one-story retail outlets—evidence that General Motors, though it operated in Detroit, did not belong to it. It was instead a bureaucratic, impersonal transplant of eastern capital.

■ 3   Chrysler, always laboring in the shadow of Wall Street, had even fewer ties to the city. It started as the Maxwell-Briscoe Motor Company (we surveyed its Detroit origins in Chapter Three), whose organizer, Benjamin Briscoe, lacked the necessary backing from the city's financial elite to raise sufficient capital in Detroit. He therefore went east, raised $360,000 in New York City, and rented an assembly plant a few miles to the north in Tarry-town. J. P. Morgan and Richard Irvin & Company put up most of the capital, but Briscoe also borrowed $150,000 from W. L. Hamilton, Morgan's son-in-law.[27]

In three years Briscoe built the company into the fourth largest auto manufacturer in the country, but he found his more grandiose ambitions impeded by Morgan's foot-dragging. Hamilton apparently demanded 20 percent interest on his loan, thus drawing off capital needed for expansion and leaving Maxwell-Briscoe so strapped for cash that it had to issue debentures to its dealers to finance the 1907 model year. In addition, Morgan quashed several merger plans in 1908 and 1909. Briscoe, consequently, sought a new backer to offset the banker's conservatism.[28]

He found Anthony N. Brady, a New York traction and electric utilities magnate, who promised to invest $1 million if Briscoe would salvage his investment in the Columbia Motor Car Company. In February 1910, Briscoe, Brady, the Morgan partners, and Eugene Meyer, Jr., a New York banker, floated the United States Motor Company with a capitalization of $30 million. Within a month it gobbled up nine automobile assemblers and parts manufacturers, including Columbia, Maxwell-Briscoe, and three Detroit companies: Brush Runabout, Briscoe Manufacturing, and Gray Motor Company.[29]

The combination ran through its working capital in a few months and then issued $6 million in debenture bonds through Eugene Meyer & Co. Even this proved inadequate when Maxwell-Briscoe alone among the motorcar subsidiaries won public favor. In September 1912, with Brady and Morgan failing to agree on a rescue plan, the corporation passed into receivership and reverted to the bondholders, led by Eugene Meyer, Jr. These also included representatives of the Chase National Bank, the Guaranty Trust, the Central Union Trust, and the Bankers Trust Company, all of New York, as well as James Cox Brady, representing his father.[30]

This group made Briscoe the scapegoat, replacing him with Walter Flanders, late of E-M-F, who proposed junking the corporation's unprofitable models and concentrating on the Maxwell-Briscoe line. In a few months Flanders reduced the number of chassis offered from 164 to 4. In addition, he centralized production in Detroit. The United States Motor Company, reincorporated January 1913 as the Maxwell Motor Company, became a middle-class producer, its cars selling in the $1,085–$2,350 range. Under different leadership, Maxwell might have retained its product diversity and thus posed more of a threat to General Motors. But Flanders insisted on injecting his presence and personality into the organization, and Maxwell as a result developed into a latter-day E-M-F. The directors, none of whom lived near the head office and plants in Detroit, were willing to give Flanders carte blanche as long as Maxwell earned the dividends necessary to recover the millions they had lost on United States Motors. His one opponent on the board, Eugene Meyer, Jr., obliged by selling out in December 1916, and the Bradys confirmed Flanders's rule the following year by giving him the board chairmanship.[31]

His position secure, Flanders let the company drift. Its production facilities aged; engineering standards declined; the automobile soon gained a poor reputation; and the company, its sales falling by 10,000, slipped from fourth place in 1915 to eleventh in 1920. By then it was moribund, enfeebled not only by its sales decline but also by a crushing load of inventory built up as a hedge against wartime inflation. The sudden deflation of 1920 pushed it over the brink; by the summer it was bankrupt, its shares unmarketable. The Bradys, in desperation, entrusted the company in August 1920 to a management committee headed by Walter P. Chrysler, a former vice-president of General Motors.[32]

Chrysler, son of a locomotive engineer, had followed a career in railroad maintenance and manufacturing until he joined Buick as works manager in 1910. He quickly transformed it into GM's leading moneymaker and was rewarded by promotion to vice-president in charge of operations for the whole corporation. Growing dissatisfied with Durant's leadership, however, in August 1919 he retired from GM and, he said, from business. His retirement was brief: the following spring he answered the appeal of Ralph Van

Vechten, president of the Continental and Commercial National Bank of Chicago, to take charge of the Willys Corporation, the first of the automotive combines to falter during the 1920–1921 recession.[33]

One rescue mission led to another, and Chrysler also consented to head Maxwell's reorganization committee. Composed of creditors, the committee brought together Van Vechten; James Cox Brady; J. L. Butzel of the First and Old Detroit National Bank; Hugh Chalmers for the Chalmers Motor Company; Barney F. Everitt for the merchandise creditors; and three New York bankers—George W. Davison of the Central Union Trust, Jervis R. Harbeck of the Industrial National Bank, and E. R. Tinker of Chase National.[34]

In the spring of 1921 Chrysler cut his connection with Willys to devote full attention to Maxwell's recovery. He arranged a "friendly" receivership and reorganized it in May as the Maxwell Motor Corporation. With the original common stock written down to zero, control passed to Chrysler's bankers, and Chase National displaced the Brady family as the dominant interest. Even so, Chrysler, chairman of the board and later president, steadily concentrated decision-making in his own hands.[35] He upgraded Maxwell's engineering standards and aggressively marketed the "Good Maxwell," doubling sales between 1920 and 1923. But the corporation, remaining in ninth place in sales, gained no ground in the industry. Figuring that Maxwell needed a completely new model to improve its position, Chrysler lured three young engineers—Fred Zeder, Owen Skelton, and Carl Breer—away from Studebaker and set them to work designing a light-weight motorcar with a high-compression engine.[36]

Maxwell unveiled its prototype, named the "Chrysler," at the New York auto show in January 1924. It caused such a sensation that Chase National Bank agreed to underwrite a $5 million bond issue to finance its mass production. By 1925, with the Chrysler outselling the Maxwell two to one, the directors decided to reorganize the company as the Chrysler Corporation in June. Several of Maxwell's banking allies at this juncture unloaded their stock while Walter Chrysler himself bought heavily; he thus emerged as the largest single stockholder, with 2.5 percent (in 1937) of the shares.[37]

In the 1920s Chrysler operated as a public corporation with widely dispersed stock ownership. But the New York financial community, with ten of the fifteen positions on the board of directors in 1925, still dominated its affairs. The core group consisted of Walter Chrysler and four directors representing investments of at least twelve years' duration: E. R. Tinker of Chase National,

James Cox Brady, Harry C. Bronner of Hallgarten & Co., and Henry Sanderson of Charles D. Barney & Co. Detroit had only two spokesmen, Allen F. Edwards and Hugh Chalmers. The latter represented the creditors of the former Chalmers Motor Company (absorbed by Maxwell in 1922). Edwards, a director of the Union Trust who was linked by marriage to the Russels and McMillans, spoke for the financial interests of Detroit's old families.[38]

Walter Chrysler, like Durant and Sloan, paid little heed to Detroit. He operated out of New York, even though the corporation kept its headquarters in the Motor City. Until he retired in 1935, Chrysler dominated the board of directors, thanks to his large stock interest and his role in transforming the corporation. Between 1923 and 1928 the company's common stock appreciated 2,000 percent, leaving the bankers very satisfied with his stewardship.[39]

In most respects, Chrysler implemented the management precepts he had learned at General Motors. Fighting the temptation, as James Flink put it, to see "the corporation that bore his name as an extension of his personal genius," Chrysler wanted to "eliminate the human equation and command all operations with scientific, mechanical precision." Therefore, he fostered development of an impersonal, bureaucratic organization. Instead of price-class, the corporation built its identity around a "reverence for engineering." The phrase became its talisman, the equivalent of Dodge dependability and Ford economy. In a sense, engineering excellence became Chrysler's claim to status.[40] Dodge and Ford offered basic transportation; Chrysler, heralding the arrival of the "rapid-transit era," emphasized speed and power. Its 1924 model, priced at $1,500, was the first "high performance" car in the medium-price bracket. Mark Howell called it the first modern automobile: it had a "brand new kind of smoothness," he wrote, "so utterly lacking in effort that it reached the senses as a dynamic flow."[41]

The car captured Walter Chrysler's personality in steel; it immortalized his name, and he may have been tempted to focus the corporation's energies solely on its production. But at General Motors he had seen the profitability and security of the multimodel approach. As a result, in 1928 he bought Dodge and introduced the low-priced Plymouth, thereby giving the corporation a complete line ranging over $3,180 of the price spectrum; it thus escaped the limited horizons of the single-class company. The following year Chrysler joined Ford and General Motors in the Big Three.[42]

By 1929, Chrysler and General Motors alone had succeeded in establishing modern, bureaucratic organizations. They built their corporate personality around an administrative ideal rather than a particular type of car or price-class; in other words, they escaped the class-consciousness of their rivals. They managed this feat by divorcing ownership from control. Companies owned by Detroit's upper- and middle-class entrepreneurs lacked the flexibility of General Motors and Chrysler because they let personal and class considerations shape their decision-making.

The city's upper class had almost no say in managing GM and Chrysler. Neither corporation belonged to Detroit, even though they planted their general offices there. Their true focus was in New York, where their key executives resided. They answered to eastern capital and the internal needs of their bureaucracies. Not much is known about Chrysler's civic activities, perhaps because they were so limited: the corporation apparently had less interest in Detroit's affairs than did General Motors. For example, in 1926–1927 Chrysler announced donations of only $6,000 to the Detroit Community Fund—though it may have given more to Hamtramck and Highland Park, the suburban communities that housed its plants.[43]

Neither Chrysler nor General Motors had any real stake in the persistence of Detroit's upper-class social system in general or in the fate of the city's old families in particular. In normal times this did not matter, inasmuch as the leaders of the two corporations had, as we saw in Chapter One, social backgrounds similar to Detroit's business elite as a whole. Born to wealth and privilege, they were unlikely to behave like "a commercial Savonarola," as the *Detroit Journal* accused James Couzens of doing.[44] In a severe crisis, however, the interests of Detroit's upper class and the two absentee-owned corporations could and would diverge. And the Detroit elite, suddenly deprived of the assistance of the Big Three at the moment of greatest peril, would have ample reason by mid-1933 to rue their earlier penchant for conspicuous production, which—as we have seen—by 1910 had cost them control of the auto industry. Without access to the industry's largest treasuries, they were unable to protect their most basic economic interests during the bank crash of 1933.

In observing that the social ambitions of Detroit's automotive leaders influenced, even dominated, their entrepreneurship, we have seen that the near-universal impulse to produce conspicuously almost guaranteed that the most successful motor companies, that is the Big Three, would be those least interested in conforming to the norms of Detroit's upper class—and, therefore, the most difficult to recruit into that class. The result was the long-term enfeeblement of Detroit's upper-class social system. Even before the bank crisis the industry's social cleavages (as incorporated in its various price-classes) affected Detroit's civic affairs. Among these, the politics of municipal transportation drew the most sustained attention from the members of Detroit's automotive community in the generation after their rise to municipal preeminence around 1910. As major employers, they were necessarily interested in how the labor force commuted to work; as self-styled transportation experts they inevitably became embroiled in Detroit's long-standing feud over public transit. From 1913 onward the initiatives of local automotive leaders largely set the terms of debate. Despite their prestige and power, however, they were not able to dictate the final outcome; as the next chapter shows, they allowed their internal disputes, which grew out of the industry's class divisions, to spill over into municipal affairs. The results were satisfactory neither for Detroit nor for the automotive leaders, some of whom devoted more than a decade trying to resolve the city's transportation difficulties.

Chapter Seven

The Auto Community and Mass Transit

■   In 1974, Bradford Snell, appearing before a subcommittee of the Senate Judiciary Committee, charged that the "Big Three car companies [had] used their vast economic power to restructure America into a land of big cars and diesel trucks." They had, he averred, "eliminated competition among themselves, secured control over rival bus and rail industries, and maximized profits by substituting cars and trucks for every other competing method of ground travel, including trains, streetcars, subways, and buses." Snell accused the auto industry of having deliberately conspired to destroy mass public transit.[1]

So far as cities were concerned, he alleged that the industry, or more narrowly General Motors, undertook after 1932 to substitute motor buses for streetcars, knowing full well that rubberized mass transit was less efficient, more costly, and less acceptable to commuters, many of whom were left with little choice but to drive to work. Since 1973, these allegations have been widely circulated and accepted, and they have recently received a book-length exposition from David J. St. Clair.[2]

These charges have been disputed, principally by transportation historians aware of how sickly American street railways had become by 1923, the year their ridership peaked and well before the putative automotive "conspiracy" had begun. These historians emphasize the destructiveness of government regulation; they depict as well the demise of the street railways as a tragedy brought on by the corrupt practices and arrogant behavior of their private owners during the era in which rails still monopolized mass transit. The traction companies accordingly had few friends when rubber-wheeled competition set in. Indeed, many Americans looked to the motor bus, the jitney, and the automobile to exact revenge against a hated monopoly. Buses, far from always being as unpopular as the conspiracy thesis supposes, were as ideologically acceptable in the 1920s as fixed-rail rapid transit became in the 1970s.[3]

Much of the debate between these two schools comes from differences in basic research strategies. Those who find a conspiracy also tend to take an economistic approach, while Snell's critics are inclined to agree with A. S. Lang and R. M. Soberman that "the ultimate test of a transportation system lies not in any technoeconomic indices of efficiency, but in the extent to which it finds acceptance within the total value scheme of the community it serves." These critics stress the importance of such intangible values as the quest for novelty (motorized transit had this going for it in 1920 and against it in 1970), the reelection efforts of politicians, and the stockpiling of resentments over time. Public mass transit, Paul Barrett has observed, always made enemies as the most blatant "symbol of coercion and of the power of big business." Also, as Christopher Armstrong and H. V. Nelles have pointed out for Canadian traction, many North Americans made their first encounter with industrial discipline and large, impersonal technical systems when they boarded a streetcar. Inevitably, they rebelled and would not listen to the accountants telling them what a bargain they had. Traction has always made economic sense, but by the 1920s few were prepared to deal with the public transit issue in strictly economic terms.[4]

In Detroit, for example, the street railway question had become extremely politicized by the time automotive leaders became involved. Mayor Hazen Pingree had won an 80 percent majority for a municipal takeover as early as 1891, and the subsequent success of the privately owned Detroit United Railway (and its antecedents) in foiling the popular will made traction the city's hottest political issue. By 1912 three mayors had gone down to defeat for daring to propose a compromise short of municipal ownership, and it had become downright foolhardy to run for city council without first declaring for "M.O." *Detroit Saturday Night* observed:

> It has come to pass in Detroit that we cannot talk street cars and keep our minds clear for any other question at the same time. The street car question is our hereditary and perpetual hoodoo. Only the weather excels it as a medium of introducing conversation. Only religion can inspire longer or more bitter or less lucid dialogues.

Detroit by the eve of World War I was not a city where transit issues were limited by the economic parameters assumed by the conspiracy theorists. Municipal politicians had little option but to favor public ownership, irrespective of its financial merits.[5]

What was the position of Detroit's automotive leaders on municipal ownership? Were they already in 1914 plotting the demise of the
nation's street railways, starting with the vulnerable Detroit United
Railway? The answer is that Detroit's automotive entrepreneurs
actually promoted mass public transit for their home community,
at least before 1930. They were, it is true, divided as to the relative
merits of motor buses and street railways, and a majority in the
1920s probably wanted to eliminate surface rail transit. But these
same individuals also championed underground rapid transit.
Contrary to the conspiracy theory, they did not see rail and rubber
as diametric opposites. They promoted variants of both electric and
gasoline-powered transit.

It should not surprise us that Detroit's automotive companies
wanted to improve the local transit system, for by the late 1920s
they needed to attract and maintain labor forces of as many as
98,000 men at a single factory site. Though companies like Ford
naturally would have preferred their employees to commute in
company-built cars, the fact was that no more than 25 to 30 percent
did come by auto, even in the late 1920s after new car prices had
dropped appreciably and a lively used car market had emerged.[6]

How were auto workers to get to work? The commuting crisis had
begun as early as 1908, when auto producers bought land six miles
from downtown along the Detroit Terminal Railway, the outer belt
line. A suburban location offered Ford, Hudson, Chalmers, and
General Motors, among others, an opportunity to make innovations
in plant design and layout to accommodate mass production. The
key shift came in 1910, when Ford moved his operations to suburban Highland Park.[7]

Inevitably, manufacturers on the periphery became concerned
with the state of local public transit. To be sure, skilled workers
could afford to buy or rent housing within walking distance of
suburban plants, but line workers had to settle for cheaper, older
housing on the near east side or adjacent to one of the aging factory
districts. As the city spread out, their journey to work became
increasingly onerous; by 1929 some Ford workers had to travel as
long as two hours each way. The inevitable result was increased
absenteeism, tardiness, and labor turnover, all of which were in-
compatible with efficient assembly-line production. As the automotive revolution pushed out the geographic frontiers of metropolitan Detroit, it became obvious that without some compensating
breakthrough in transportation technology, the local automotive
industry could be strangled by its own success. Understandably,
then, automotive executives were public transit enthusiasts.[8]

Even had they not had an incentive as major employers to improve Detroit's public transit, industry executives would have been drawn to transportation reform by their own social position. To an unusual degree for a city its size, Detroit's wealthy families maintained a preindustrial residential pattern: they still lived in the vicinity of the central business district. With the automotive revolution, however, the elite neighborhoods came under extreme pressure, and mansions along Woodward and Jefferson Avenues (each formerly a prime address) either gave way to automobile dealerships and garages or were converted into cheap rooming houses. In such circumstances, the elite readily agreed on the need for transportation reform. Most were anxious to decamp to one of the fashionable new districts in Grosse Pointe, Indian Village, and the North Woodward area, and they wanted to reduce their own commuting time along the city's congested arteries. Whether they traveled by streetcar or by motorcar, they stood to benefit from improved traffic flow. Everyone with money to invest in suburban real estate also had a significant stake in resolving the city's transportation crisis.[9]

Automobile executives thus had no reason to plot the demise of public transit in Detroit and many reasons to improve it. In addition to economic benefits, they also stood to gain considerable social prestige and political advantage (for those who sought it) if they could resolve the city's most enduring public controversy.

Unfortunately, they could not agree on a single strategy for improving Detroit's public transit. Inevitably, the internal feuds of the city's automotive community spilled over into the transportation arena. The primary debate pitted the champions of municipal ownership of the existing street railways, led by James Couzens, against those who sought to supplant the street railways with motor buses, superhighways, and fixed-rail rapid transit. Prominent among the latter were two successive presidents of Packard, Henry B. Joy and Alvan Macauley, as well as Henry Leland, founder of Cadillac and Lincoln. Once again, members of the local upper class, including now the more prominent of the auto industry's new men, were rejecting the proposals and values championed by the Ford leadership and in doing so were forfeiting an opportunity to co-opt them; the attempt to improve Detroit's traffic circulation helped to occlude the circulation of elites.

Moreover, the transit policy standoff prevented the construction of a rapid transit system in the 1920s, when the local economy was perhaps still vibrant enough to pay for it. But there was certainly no plot involved—merely a clash of values that reflected and accentuated the divisions within the automotive community itself.

■ 1   It was in 1913 that the automotive community
assumed the primary responsibility for solving the city's festering
transportation crisis. The Detroit United Railway (DUR), its financial strength eroded by the incessant debate over its future, had by
then abjectly failed to keep pace with the city's mushroom growth;
as a result, track mileage per capita had fallen by almost half since
1899. Most businessmen, despite an instinctive predilection for
private enterprise, had reached reluctant agreement that municipal
ownership alone could, by ending the political wrangling, raise the
necessary capital for expanded track and service.[10]

Yet a significant minority remained ideologically opposed to
public ownership, including several upper-class leaders of the early
auto industry: Fred T. Moran (Welch); George H. Barbour (Paige
and Lozier); J. L. Hudson (Hudson); and C. A. DuCharme, Russell
Alger, Jr., and Henry B. Joy (all of Packard). In general, however,
most auto executives before 1913 quietly supported any plan that
offered an end to the street railway controversy.[11]

The Verdier Act of March 1913 offered a way out of the impasse:
through it the state legislature finally empowered the city of Detroit
to form a commission to acquire and operate a street railway within
its boundaries. On July 29, 1913, Mayor Oscar Marx appointed two
Ford stockholders, John Dodge and James Couzens, along with
William D. Mahon (representing the street railway employees)
to the Board of Street Railway Commissioners. John Dodge, the
mayor's chief financial backer, doubtlessly dictated the membership
of the commission and the inclusion of Couzens.[12]

That same summer the Street Railway Commission made a purchase offer on Detroit's behalf, but the DUR rejected it because
the offer amounted to less than the sum of the company's outstanding bonds. The company proposed, however, a compromise—and
it was seconded by the commission—that the voters approve the
principle of municipal ownership in a special election to be held
in November 1915. That done, the Circuit Court of Wayne County
would set the purchase price, its decision binding on both city and
company.[13]

Couzens and Dodge carried the banner for municipal ownership
in the ensuing referendum campaign. They had few allies: the
Detroit News, a handful of Common Council members, and, within
the business community, only Abner Larned, a clothing manufacturer; Alfred Lucking, counsel for both the commission and the Ford
Motor Company; and Henry Ford. Even the Municipal Ownership
League, the socialists, and the labor unions denounced the proposal
as a "pig-in-a-poke" plan whose ultimate price tag no one dared

predict; they declared that the people had a "right to vote on the price," which alarmists predicted would be as high as $40 million.[14]

The Ford Motor Company, thus almost isolated in its support for municipal ownership in 1915, found its prestige at stake: not only had the much-derided plan been drawn up by two of its principal stockholders and the company counsel, but Henry Ford had given it his public benediction, calling it "one of the safest business propositions I have ever heard of." Ford said he had "so much confidence in the integrity and judgement of . . . Messrs. Couzens, Dodge, and Lucking that [he] would not hesitate to favor it on their word alone." This statement was the crux of the municipal ownership debate in 1915. As the *Detroit News* pointed out under the headline "The Wizards of the Ford Motor Co. Agree on the D.U.R. Purchase Plan," the question had become whether the voters agreed that the municipal ownership proposal "must be a good sound business document or Mr. Couzens would not be a party to it."[15]

The founders of the Ford Motor Company were on trial. The *Detroit News* asked each day through the last month of the campaign whether the voters intended to "repudiate the work" of James Couzens and John Dodge. With the help of the *News*, the municipal ownership vote became a referendum on the Ford Motor Company and its leadership. In effect, people were asked to follow the lead of the "master minds of the great Ford Motor Company" in civic affairs. The returns, therefore, were crushing to the company's political and social ambitions: needing 60 percent to pass, the purchase plan received less than half the vote. It fared especially poorly in three "silk-stocking" wards (the first, second, and fourth), Detroit's upper class thus gaining a measure of revenge against the Ford Motor Company and its presumptuous executives.[16]

Taking his cue from this defeat, John Dodge mended his fences with the city's establishment. He was, after all, a man whose cars were already beginning their social ascent; there would be no further talk of municipal ownership from John Dodge. But Couzens was more determined than ever: "Somebody had to make [municipal ownership] a practical business proposition," he later remarked, and "that seemed to be my job. The logic was so plain that I couldn't possibly have escaped it."[17]

■ 2   As police commissioner from 1916 to 1918, Couzens temporarily set aside his dreams of municipal transit ownership to follow the will-o'-the-wisp of his anti-vice crusade. In

March 1918—with the common council demanding his resignation and Mayor Marx deciding not to stand for reelection—Couzens realized that his string with the police department was running out and began desperately looking for an alternative career. Remarkably, he decided to run for mayor. The experts scoffed at his prospects; in fact, Couzens subsequently stated, "I was kidded into standing for Mayor. Some of my friends said I was so unpopular I couldn't be elected dogcatcher. Indeed, it did look that way."[18]

No one, not even Couzens, could hope to be elected mayor without some organized support; his came largely from his friends at Ford and its banking affiliates and from the Detroit Board of Commerce, an organization he had once headed. He reportedly had the backing of a third of the board's membership—those individuals known as "live wires," recognized more for their hustle than for their wealth or social prominence.[19]

Political pundits assumed that Couzens would trail the four-candidate field in the August 27 nonpartisan primary. His motley band of supporters appeared no match for John Gillespie, who had inherited John Dodge's political machine; or for William Connally, who controlled the local branch of the Democratic Party; or finally, for the candidate favored by Detroit's municipal reformers—Divie B. Duffield, the library commissioner. Duffield, the Harvard-educated scion of an old Detroit family, had served as president of the city's Charter Commission and so received the backing of Henry Leland, the Michigan Anti-Saloon League, and the Detroit Citizens League, as well as most of the automotive industry.[20]

Couzens was facing the concerted opposition of his economic peers as Detroit's upper class closed its ranks against the "scab plutocrat" who had in the past shown little interest in the cause of municipal reform. Now that the charter was in place and the city's first "strong mayor" was to be elected, the elite wanted one of their own kind. W. P. Lovett, the secretary of the Citizens League, stated that it "did not support Mr. Couzens because he is too stubborn for us" and too independent. He was a social outsider who was proving difficult to co-opt. Most of the wealthy—including "practically all of the members of the [socially exclusive] Yondotega Club," according to Couzens—endorsed Duffield.[21]

Though spurned by the business elite, Couzens nonetheless ran as a "business" candidate. He made just one specific campaign promise: "If I am elected Mayor," he announced, "I will get rid of the D.U.R., and if I don't the people ought to rail-ride me down Woodward Avenue and throw me in the river." Couzens had a lot of company in attacking the DUR in 1918; even Duffield asserted that "municipal ownership is no longer a campaign issue; it is, as far as Detroit is concerned, an accepted municipal principle, the application of which has been demanded by the people." Yet Duffield, like Gillespie and Connally, did not seem overly eager to apply the principle. It was too controversial an issue, he claimed, to discuss while the United States was at war.[22]

Couzens thought otherwise. On August 7 he deliberately had himself thrown off a streetcar to dramatize his own war against the Detroit United Railway. The company had attempted to hike its basic fare a penny to six cents, and Couzens—in a move evocative of Hazen Pingree's battles in the 1890s—boarded a streetcar that morning and refused to pay the new fare. The exasperated conductor finally pushed him off the car in full view of photographers brought by the mayoral candidate.[23]

It was a magnificent stunt; however, it set off several days of rioting, which tied up the city's traffic until the company capitulated. Duffield's elite constituency was outraged by Couzens's "playing to the grandstand." Henry Leland wrote the *Free Press* that "any candidate for mayor who so far belittles himself as to advocate physical resistance on the part of the passengers is certainly lacking in the qualities which ought to be embodied in the next mayor." He suggested that Couzens might even be guilty of treason, a theme *Detroit Saturday Night*, the city's patrician weekly, picked up when it fumed, "To bellow about tearing up street railway tracks . . . and disorganizing the entire street railway traffic in times when the boys [are] over there . . . is little short of treason."[24]

But the wealthy lacked the votes to stop Couzens. He led the first round of balloting on August 27, with Duffield finishing a distant third behind Connally, who brought out the Democratic vote. Couzens carried fifteen of the twenty-one wards, winning the support of the city's minorities: that is, its Poles, blacks, Jews, socialists, and independent laborites. He lost the "silk-stocking" wards to Divie Duffield, but once Duffield was out of the running, Detroit's Republican establishment threw its support to Couzens, and he defeated Connally handily in the runoff election in November.[25]

In his inaugural address Couzens announced that he would propose a different plan for municipal ownership "every six months, until one was adopted." Then, with a swiftness unprecedented in Detroit's hoary street railway war, he opened negotiations with the DUR and by February 1919 had made an offer of $26.7 million for its Detroit lines. With a little prodding from the Common Council, which passed an ordinance authorizing construction of a competing system, the DUR agreed on March 18 to sell for $31.5 million. While that price was admittedly high, Couzens decided to submit the purchase plan to the voters on April 7, 1919, on the assumption that they were prepared to pay that much and more to rid themselves of the hated monopoly.[26]

Couzens belatedly discovered that he had fallen behind public opinion in the turbulent postwar years. Judging from the silence of traditional critics like Henry Leland and Henry Joy, he apparently now enjoyed the grudging if tacit support of conservative businessmen, but this time the traditional supporters of M.O. deserted him. Led by the Municipal Ownership League, they refused to pay the DUR anything beyond the bare condemnation price and advocated legal proceedings to oust the company from the streets. Even Henry Ford rejected the purchase proposal. His lieutenant Charles E. Sorensen noisily maintained that the private company's rolling stock was too expensive at any price, since the Ford Motor Company was developing a gasoline-powered streetcar. Sorensen's statement, "posted all over Detroit in handbills and printed in full-page advertisements," became a major component in the defeat of Couzens's plan.[27]

The purchase plan really never had a chance; it was effectively trapped in an electoral no-man's-land by the reversal of the usual battle lines on M.O. Even the DUR could not make up its mind: first it supported the plan and then, convinced that Couzens would lose the referendum, unleashed a torrent of handbills to help defeat it. The street railway war had apparently reached a stalemate: "The people have had a fair proposal put up to them twice," John C. Lodge, a future mayor, lamented. "It seems as if they are for municipal ownership in the abstract, but when a concrete proposal comes before them they balk at the price."[28]

The street railway commissioners in October 1919 prescribed a way out of the impasse: taking their cue from Cleveland's successful Tayler Plan, they proposed a new franchise for the DUR based on "rides-at-cost." Businessmen (including auto executives) immediately rallied to the commission's suggestion, since it offered a viable alternative to municipal ownership. Alvan Macauley of Packard described the Tayler Plan as "one thing which would be sure to give quick results" and announced the formation of a committee to lobby for it. The committee had close ties to the auto industry: it included—in addition to Macauley—Harry M. Jewett of Paige-Detroit; W. Ledyard Mitchell of Maxwell; Andrew H. Green, Jr., and Emory W. Clark, two former directors of General Motors; and F. W.

Dennis of the Joy Realty Company. According to the *Detroit News*, Dennis was fronting for Henry Joy, the real genius behind the industry's support for rides-at-cost.[29]

The Common Council approved the Tayler Plan, but Couzens immediately vetoed it and fired the street railway commissioners for proposing it. Maintaining that "municipal ownership is dead when this plan is adopted," he insisted that the city bring the DUR to terms by building a competitive system. He then placed a $15 million bond referendum on the April 1920 ballot to give the city government sufficient capital to begin construction. His opponents within the auto industry determined to bury Couzens and municipal ownership once and for all; even William Durant of GM now declared himself opposed—the first time, apparently, that he had taken a public stand on a local Detroit issue. Orchestrating the attack was Henry Joy, erstwhile president of Packard, who put together an industry coalition extending from John Dodge to Alvan Macauley, including en route the Board of Commerce and the Real Estate Board.[30]

The almost perfect isolation of Couzens within the automotive community on this issue may explain why Henry Ford now suddenly backed his former general manager. Ford had no great love for municipal ownership, regarding it as intrinsically inefficient, yet he was not prepared to watch Couzens fight alone against the Detroit establishment. Ford signaled his reconciliation with Couzens by allowing his chief engineer, William Mayo, to join the Street Railway Commission. By 1920 the M.O. battle had deteriorated into a power struggle between the Ford millionaires and the rest of the auto industry. "For years [Couzens] had been stepping on sacred toes," recalled Jay Hayden, one-time secretary of the commission. "If he won this battle, it was clear that he would be even more firmly entrenched. The myriad of interests that he had thwarted moved as one in a supreme effort to stop this man."[31]

Yet Couzens prevailed, despite the opposition of the auto industry, most of Detroit's press, and the DUR, which spent $500,000 to attack his plan. Streetcars began rolling on the city's lines the following February, which meant that the new municipal Department of Street Railways would soon be able to take over those lines on which the former monopoly's franchise had already expired. In April 1921 the voters authorized purchase of these lines for $2.3 million, the transaction being completed the following December. That same month the DUR, faced with the threat of ouster from the streets (Couzens was finally brandishing this ultimate weapon), reluctantly agreed to give the city running rights over its tracks and to accept universal transfers.[32]

With that concession, the onetime street railway monopoly forfeited its best bargaining position; in March 1922 it meekly consented to sell its remaining property in Detroit for $19.9 million. This was a bargain-basement price, one to which the company would never have acceded in its prime. Its general manager claimed that the "price paid is over $10,000,000 below [the system's] actual present day worth." Overwhelmed by Couzens's string of *faits accomplis*, resistance to municipal ownership collapsed, and the purchase plan swept the April 1922 referendum with 89 percent of the vote. At midnight on May 14, 1922, the city became the owner of 373 miles of track. After nine years and two major rebuffs, Couzens's crusade had ended in total victory, and Detroit became only the third major American city—following San Francisco and Seattle —to own its entire street railway system.[33]

■ 3 In the climactic debate over municipal ownership in 1919 and 1920, opinion within the auto community had been sharply divided; indeed, the battle seemed at times an extension of traditional trade rivalries. With executives from Packard and Lincoln leading the attack on a plan championed by the Ford Motor Company, the 1920 referendum assumed the guise of a social conflict between Detroit's establishment and an upstart, rebellious outsider.

Yet there was an additional dimension to the M.O. battle after 1919. Henry Joy, Sidney Waldon, and Henry Leland considered themselves as expert in transportation matters as Couzens, and by their reckoning his passion for municipal ownership was an anachronistic throwback to Pingree's era; they held Couzens guilty of ignoring changes in technology over the preceding thirty years. These three regarded streetcars as outmoded and saw no rationale for buying a system that had deteriorated under private ownership. Regarding the motorbus and the subway train as the solution to Detroit's transportation crisis, they fought Couzens's attempt to saddle the city with a white elephant.

The Street Railway Commission had echoed these sentiments when it presented the Tayler Plan to the Common Council. They depicted the plan as a stopgap measure to give Detroit time to build a subway system. As a start, they recommended construction of a subway under Woodward Avenue in the business district. Pointing out that the municipality lacked the resources to finance both a subway and a street railway system, they said that municipal ownership of streetcars had to be set aside. "We considered the plan of having the city build the surface lines and subways," Sidney

Waldon, a commissioner, advised the press, "but we dropped it when we saw that the present bonding limit of Detroit precluded any extensive rapid transit system and surface lines at the same time."[34]

Most of the automotive industry's activists endorsed the subway proposal in 1919. Henry Leland and John Dodge were already on record as preferring subways. In December 1919 Leland took the next step and "expressed the hope that surface lines would be abolished entirely in favor of subways with motor buses taking care of the short jumps in the downtown section." Henry Joy, Alvan Macauley, and auto manufacturers of similarly conservative complexion decided to counter Couzens's crusade with a campaign of their own: "The city's demand for a subway will be jeopardized by the expenditure of fifteen millions of its credit which can better be saved for initiating a subway system."[35]

The street railway elections of 1919–1922 thus revolved around the relative merits of surface and underground rail transportation. Couzens declared the subway issue a red herring to distract the voters. In March 1920 he asserted, "The subway agitation is an effort to obscure the real question which is—shall we have more streetcars and a more extended street railway system or not?" Couzens argued that his M.O. plan should logically precede the subways: "The city is in no position to develop a subway project until it controls surface transportation, as the two must be considered together."[36]

Couzens pushed the subway cause into the background until November 1922. Then, his cherished M.O. safely in hand, he created a Rapid Transit Commission (RTC) composed of five prominent businessmen: Herbert W. Alden, vice-president of Timken-Detroit Axle company; Clarence W. Hubbell, former city engineer; Willard Pope, vice-president of Canadian Bridge Company; Andrew H. Green, Jr., president of Charcoal Iron Company and a former director of General Motors; and as chairman, Sidney D. Waldon, the retired auto executive.[37]

From the start Waldon dominated the commission, appropriating the subway cause as his own personal crusade in the same way that Couzens had monopolized the battle for municipal ownership of the street railway. A British immigrant trained as a locksmith, Waldon had joined the automobile industry as a car tester but swiftly rose to the vice-presidency first of Packard, then of Cadillac. In 1916, though only forty-three, he retired from business a millionaire, determined to "return to society some of the things that he . . . owed it." He devoted his retirement to promoting automobiles, highways, motor buses, air travel, and rapid transit—anything that would increase "transportation efficiency."[38]

Above all, he wanted to maximize the usefulness of the automobile. To him it was "the magic carpet of transportation for all mankind," yet "its great efficiency for rapid transit" was, he complained, "defeated by the very great numbers trying" to use it. Civilization had to choose, Waldon said: it must either accept a "gradually reducing efficiency of the motor vehicle" or "set itself squarely to the problem of providing the increased facilities essential to its best use."[39]

To unclog Detroit's choked traffic arteries, Waldon and the RTC proposed widening the major thoroughfares and clearing them of streetcars, with public transit going underground or—beyond a five-mile radius—down the median strip of 204-foot-wide "superhighways." The commission's "master plan" envisioned twenty such superhighways stretching over 240 miles and three counties, with space on each for surface rapid transit. While admitting that the system exceeded Detroit's current needs, the RTC argued the financial importance of acquiring rights-of-way for future development while suburban land remained cheap.[40]

Superhighways appealed to the Motor City. Little opposition arose, and the Common Council adopted the master plan in April 1925. Seven months later a referendum decisively approved a financial plan for land acquisition and street widening within Detroit. Beyond the city boundaries two superhighway commissions oversaw implementation of the master plan, using revenue raised by the state gasoline tax. By 1929 authorities had purchased more than one third of the needed rights-of-way, and Detroit was well on its way toward freeway development.[41]

Subways had a different fate. The principal problem was their cost. Most of the superhighway system lay outside the city and county and so had little direct impact on Detroit taxpayers, but the city would have to assume most of the subway burden. The RTC spent two years searching for a financial formula that would pay for rapid transit without undermining Detroit's municipal credit. It finally decided that subways should be financed by those who benefited most from them: that is, their users and the owners of abutting property. It wanted riders to pay for the rolling stock—approximately 32 percent of the total cost—through ten-cent fares. And as the RTC saw no reason to enrich a few fortunate property holders, it assigned 51 percent of the cost to landlords within "proximity assessment" zones extending a half-mile on each side of the subway lines. They were to pay a special tax assessed against the appreciation in the value of their property. A city-wide tax would cover the remaining 17 percent. As the financial report mentioned no dollar figures, it easily carried a referendum held in September 1924. Detroiters obviously liked the idea of subways, at least in the abstract.[42]

Still, people balked at paying for them. Certainly there was little support for the plan announced in August 1926 to build a 47-mile system at a cost of $280 million. Detroiters were suffering a heavy tax burden in the mid-1920s as a result of the municipalization of the street railway and the cost of providing municipal services for a rapidly expanding population. The city had an inadequate tax base because so many of the largest employers had escaped its jurisdiction by planting their factories in independent suburbs. There was not, as a result, much enthusiasm for the RTC's ambitious subway program; vocal support came only from the downtown merchants and from Henry Ford, who hoped to improve access to their stores and factories, respectively.[43]

It took the Rapid Transit Commission three crucial years to realize that Detroit's subway system would have to be built piecemeal, one line at a time as money became available. The commission was also slow to appreciate the need to conciliate the city's street railway department. Any subway plan that seemed to threaten the city's street railway investment would be stillborn. The RTC could have ignored a private monopoly; indeed, it would have been easier to sell rapid transit to Detroiters had it still been possible, as in 1919, to see the new system as retribution for the DUR's past misdeeds. But James Couzens had deprived the subway lobby of its bogeyman, and the proposals of the RTC had to be sold on their—primarily financial—merits.[44]

In April 1929 the commission sought voter approval for a $91 million, thirteen-mile system consisting of short streetcar tunnels downtown "built to rapid transit specifications" (in order to win over the street railway department) and a double-track line crossing the city via the Vernor Highway from the east-end factory district to Ford's plant in the western suburbs.[45]

The new plan won the support of a powerful coalition of business interests, including the downtown property-holders, the retail and wholesale merchant bureaus, the Employers' Association, the Board of Commerce, the Detroit Engineering Society, the Real Estate Board, and the Citizens League. The grouping was not unusual: throughout the United States similar business coalitions had formed behind transit projects designed to avert the threatened decline of the central business district by improving its accessibility to outlying residents and reducing traffic congestion. Detroit's downtown, however, was in especially deep trouble because the city's commercial and financial sectors were so underdeveloped and because General Motors had since 1919 been promoting a rival "New Center" three miles from the core.[46]

The automobile industry added its weight to the subway campaign. It made its position clear in 1925 when John Lovett, general manager of the Michigan Manufacturers' Association (an organization dominated by auto interests), told reporters that industrialists, though alarmed by rising taxes, nonetheless wanted rapid transit because they saw no other way to change the fact that "it takes an hour and a half for the average worker to get to his place of employment." Auto manufacturers also probably agreed with Sidney Waldon that traffic congestion hurt automobile sales and reduced Detroit's appeal as a factory site. Some perhaps even shared his vision of a "new kind of city . . . where there will be sunlight and air, [and] rapid transit on rails and rubber with . . . far greater . . . safety than now exists anywhere."[47]

The Ford Motor Company had an additional reason to embrace the plan: the proposed subway would link its principal plant at the River Rouge in Dearborn with twenty-seven of Detroit's twenty-nine streetcar lines, thus promising to solve its workers' commuting problems at a single stroke. It is not surprising, then, that Edsel Ford joined senior executives from Briggs (an autobody manufacturer), Packard, Hudson, Chrysler, and Timken-Detroit Axle on the Citizens' Better Transportation Committee organized in February 1929 to direct the subway cause for the April 1 referendum. As usual, General Motors kept aloof from the campaign except to announce that it approved of a subway, provided that Detroit passed a zoning law to forestall overbuilding along the route.[48]

Subways had formidable sponsors. The automobile industry was unusually united behind them. An opponent labeled the subway coalition the "biggest lobby Detroit [had] ever known." Yet the proposition went down to a "crushing defeat," winning only 28 percent of the vote and 55 of 852 precincts. "The defeat of the project," the Detroit Free Press observed, "was more decisive than that received by any project in recent years." Although Waldon kept the RTC alive and even came close in the late 1930s to winning federal financing for a Woodward Avenue subway, rapid transit as a local cause was prostrated by the 1929 debacle.[49]

Subways evidently appealed to a fairly select group of people. The RTC identified them as "people who lived in hotels and apartment houses . . . and tenements" within the circle of Grand Boulevard. The wealthy, whether living in downtown hotels or in such elite residential districts as Indian Village and North Woodward, gave a narrow majority to the plan. Their vote was no longer very important, however, for the suburbs had by 1930 lured away more than half of Detroit's "substantial families."[50]

Homeowners in the "zone of emergence" surrounding the central business district resoundingly rejected the proposal by margins as high as ten to one; the farther out they lived, the more likely they were to oppose the subway plan. The RTC accused the residents of the outlying neighborhoods of voting their own selfish interests: they apparently "did not believe the east and west subway offered them any advantage." But the response of the entire city beyond the three-mile radius was so uniformly hostile, even in areas promised service, that an additional factor was clearly at work.[51]

That factor was the fear of "heavy assessments," the fear that homeowners and small businessmen would be taxed on purely putative gains in the value of their property. These two groups found leadership in neighborhood improvement associations and from real estate operator Howard Starret and the Property Holders' Protective Association. Thus the proposal was defeated by a tax revolt, by the objection of Detroit's middle- and lower-income neighborhoods to the high cost of subways. They preferred a less expensive solution to the city's transit problems, something called the Miller-Schorn system. Harry Miller, a realtor, and Nicholas J. Schorn, a tanner, had proposed to the Common Council in March 1925 that Detroit use its streetcars to provide rapid transit over express routes. Try as it might, the RTC could not shake the Miller-Schorn alternative; nor could it persuade Detroiters that its engineers knew more about transportation than the two amateurs. As Paul Barrett has observed of Chicago, transit engineers squandered their moral authority by attempting to give a scientific gloss to political compromises. Detroit's RTC itself had denied the utility of piecemeal construction of rapid transit; it was difficult, then for the commission to insist in 1929 that its stripped-down plan was scientifically superior to Miller-Schorn.[52]

■ 4   As Mark Foster has noted, the outcome of Detroit's subway crusade was not unusual for the 1920s. In Los Angeles, rapid transit promoters had not even been able to arrange a referendum. The lineup of forces was also quite typical: nowhere, it seemed, did small property-holders living on the urban periphery warm to the idea of paying higher taxes to revitalize downtown areas. What made Detroit's subway politics somewhat unusual, however, was the existence of a municipally owned street railway, a rarity in American big cities before World War II. The Department of Street Railways constituted an additional obstacle for the subway promoters to surmount.[53]

The subway proposal would obviously have fared better had it been put to voters in the early 1920s, before they had spent $40 million on surface street railways and before the luster of the automotive boom had begun to fade. Detroiters were in an incredibly expansive mood before the automotive market became saturated and smaller companies like Lincoln were squeezed out. Aware that their traditional rivalry with Cleveland had ended in undisputed demographic victory, the city's boosters were setting their sights on Philadelphia and Chicago. It was natural, then, to underline their ambitions by acquiring transit facilities hitherto found only in the nation's principal metropolises. Rapid transit could probably have been sold to Detroit before 1922 by the right salesman—by a James Couzens or some other politician with a populist image.

It is impossible, of course, to know what the consequences of a successful subway campaign would have been. Nor is it entirely clear to what extent municipal ownership of the street railways benefited Detroit. It would, however, appear that both municipal ownership and rapid transit have generally strengthened transit systems by retarding the decline in ridership that has beset every American transit system since the 1920s (excepting the unusual wartime traffic).[54] There is no credible scenario, however, by which Detroit could have achieved both municipal ownership of surface traction and rapid transit in the 1920s, at least not with the automotive community so divided before 1922.

Public transportation was, if we can judge from their own private papers as well as those of the corporations they headed, the municipal issue that auto manufacturers found most salient from 1913 to 1929; no other issue seems to have engaged them in such endless controversy. In the end, their combined efforts—often working at cross purposes, as we have seen—gave Detroit a municipally owned transit system but failed to deliver on the promise of rapid transit. It would appear, then, that they were neither as omnipotent nor as hostile to public mass transit as the conspiracy theorists believe. Certainly, it is difficult to see their various activities as a concerted plot to eliminate alternatives to the automobile.[55]

Their efforts to uncork Detroit's transportation bottleneck produced considerable internal disagreement at times, most notably in 1914 and 1918–1922. These disputes further estranged James

Couzens and Henry Ford from Detroit's old families and the auto industry's new men. Once again the founders of the lower-class car company were made to feel like pariahs. The conservatism of Detroit's upper class, of the individuals who had organized most of its automobile companies, was so narrow that Couzens's brand of civic populism was no more acceptable to them in the early 1920s than Hazen Pingree's had been in the 1890s, when the McMillan alliance ostracized him for initiating the municipal ownership debate.[56]

Yet municipal ownership of the street railways was—especially viewed from a distance—a small price to pay to accommodate Couzens, who through a combination of great wealth and political savvy was rapidly becoming one of the most powerful individuals in Michigan. Chapter Eight begins by returning to 1918, the year that both James Couzens sought election as Detroit's mayor and Henry Ford as United States senator. By opposing the political ambitions of both Ford millionaires, Detroit's upper class forfeited its last chance to transfuse the new blood needed to build up its strength for the travails of the Great Depression. The chapter ends with the Michigan bank crash of 1933, which was disastrous for the old families of Detroit and debilitating to the city's economy. Couzens and Ford alone could have averted the collapse, but the dynamics of conspicuous production ensured that the two individuals with the greatest power to save Detroit's old families would also be the least likely to try.

Chapter Eight

The Price Paid for Conspicuous Production

■ Although Detroiters believed that they had proprietary rights to one of Michigan's two Senate seats, the "Detroit" seat was in fact held between 1907 and 1919 by a Grand Rapids publisher named William Alden Smith. In 1918, when Smith announced his retirement, the remnants of the McMillan alliance thought the time was ripe to restore the *status quo ante*. James McMillan and General Russell Alger had held the seat for them between 1889 and 1907; now, after an unfortunate hiatus, it was to go to their rightful political heir, Truman Newberry—who, in addition to having served Theodore Roosevelt as secretary of the Navy was also the son of McMillan's principal business partner, Congressman John S. Newberry. Granted that he was not even currently residing in Michigan, having moved to Manhattan to take up a naval command, his election nonetheless seemed natural, even inevitable. As treasurer of Packard, he even had automotive credentials. Who would stand in his way? Only Henry Ford.[1]

Ford was, to be sure, an unlikely candidate for political office. He was so uninterested in politics that he had probably never even voted. And throughout his quixotic Senate campaign in 1918 he evinced little interest in winning. He spent no money and made not a single campaign appearance; moreover, his supporters waited until October to put together an organization. It was not surprising, then, that Ford lost, especially as he was running as a Democrat in a Republican state. Under the circumstances he might even have accepted defeat graciously, if only Detroit's upper class had not gone so far out of their way to make him and his kin feel like social pariahs. Detroit's old families and their allies in the auto industry ran a scurrilous campaign against Ford; it guaranteed that he would seek revenge—in politics and beyond.

Ford must have been surprised by the intensity of the vituperation, for he considered his candidacy an act of selflessness. President Woodrow Wilson had personally told him that it was his "patriotic duty to come to the Senate from Michigan," that in wartime "men must sacrifice themselves for their country," and that Ford was "the only man in Michigan who [could] be elected and help to bring about the peace [Ford] so much desire[d]." What Wilson meant was that Michigan Democrats had calculated that Ford, a nominal Republican, was the only Wilsonian internationalist who could be elected in 1918, a year in which many Americans wanted to vote against Wilson's war policies. Certainly, the second year of the war did not offer much prospect for a regular Democrat in Michigan, a state that had not elected a Democrat to the Senate since the 1850s.[2]

But Ford was not originally supposed to run only as a Democrat. William Connally (Couzens's mayoralty rival) arranged for Michigan's Democratic State Central Committee unanimously to endorse Ford's candidacy and to propose that the Republicans also nominate him as a wartime gesture toward national unity. Ford magnanimously—and naively—offered to run as candidate for both parties. But the Republican regulars, citing his position on tariffs, war preparedness, and international affairs, would have none of him; in the party's primary they delivered the Republican nomination to Truman Newberry. Ford easily won the less valuable Democratic nomination, even though Newberry's campaign committee funded a nuisance candidate.[3]

Newberry's victory in the general election in November should have been a foregone conclusion, given Michigan's normal Republican majority of 100,000–150,000 votes. In fact, the final result was unusually close: Ford, running strongly in Detroit, came within 4,334 votes of victory. His remarkable showing doubtless owed something to the goodwill he had earned from the Model T and the five-dollar day.[4]

More significant, however, was the scandal that broke out over Newberry's excessive campaign spending. In their zeal to defeat Ford, the Newberry forces admitted that they had spent at least $176,568 on the primary campaign (Ford alleged that it was over $500,000), despite the limit of $3,750 set by state and federal Corrupt Practices Acts for both the primary and the general election. In September a grand jury began investigating the Newberry campaign, and by election day several prominent Republicans had appealed to Newberry to withdraw from the race for the good of the party and the state. It came as no surprise, then, that he received 36 percent fewer votes than had the Republican candidate for president two years previously.[5]

In October 1919 the grand jury announced that it had evidence of "fraudulent expenditure of between $500,000 and $1,000,000 in connection with the election," undoubtedly more than was needed. The excess reflected the symbolic importance of the election for Newberry's camp. They justified their violation of the electoral laws by saying that the money was not "used so much to obtain a seat in the Senate as for triumph of the principle of Americanism." In other words, Ford by 1918 was so much an outsider in Detroit's elite circles that even his patriotism was suspect. Henry B. Joy of Packard, for example, explained his contribution of $25,000 as an "effort to give the people of the State of Michigan an opportunity to vote for a man in opposition to Ford pacifism and slackerism." The election was "purely a case of 'defeat Henry Ford,'" he contended.[6]

Similarly, Colonel Frank Hecker, a retired railroad car manufacturer, held that every Michiganite had a duty to oppose a candidate who had once had the temerity to assert that "the word 'murderer' should be embroidered on every soldier's uniform. . . . If Ford could spend a million dollars in advertising to prevent and delay American's 'preparedness' for the war," the Colonel thundered, "we ought to [be allowed to] raise whatever amount is necessary to counteract that vicious, wicked, treasonable campaign against our country's welfare." To Truman Newberry himself, Ford symbolized all that was wrong with America: behind Ford's candidacy he espied "Anti-preparedness, Slackerism, Pro-Germanism, I.W.W., Non-Partisan League" advocates and socialists of every hue. Newberry averred that he was proud of his role in keeping "a pacifist free-trader masquerading as a Republican" out of the Senate and was prepared to accept political martyrdom to defeat "Capitalized Pacifism."[7]

Newberry's backers in Detroit were unwilling to forgive Ford's antipreparedness activities. To them, he had in 1915–1916 been a traitor to his city and country. His pacifism was just one aspect of a total mind-set making him, in the words of Russell Alger, Jr. of Packard, "one of the most dangerous characters that the country has today." In other words, the wealthiest man in Detroit did not have the backing of the local wealthy. Indeed, most of them detested him.[8]

Newberry had the overwhelming support of Detroit's economic elite. Allan Templeton, president of the Board of Commerce, chaired his campaign; Frank W. Blair, president of Union Trust, acted as treasurer. Newberry's business support cut across party lines:

the city's two most prominent Democrats—Sidney T. Miller and Andrew H. Green, Jr.—both declared for Newberry, Green contributing over $12,000 to the campaign. Henry Leland and the Detroit Citizens League also quietly worked against Ford, as they had against Couzens.[9]

The automotive community lined up en masse behind Newberry's candidacy. Two companies founded by Detroit's upper class, Packard and Paige-Detroit, were especially prominent, and Newberry attracted support as well from Hupp, Maxwell, Hudson, and even General Motors. Walter Flanders and William Durant (the presidents of Maxwell and General Motors, respectively) signed an advertisement endorsing Newberry; Durant personally contributed $5,000. Roscoe Jackson of Hudson also took the election very seriously: he wrote Roy Chapin begging him to "come out to Detroit to vote . . . against Henry Ford."[10]

Ford's business support was basically limited to the *Detroit News*, his parts suppliers (most notably Harvey Firestone and George Holley), and his banker, William Livingstone of Dime Savings. James Couzens, despite his distaste for pacifism, also announced that he was "strong for Henry Ford for senator"; given the lineup of forces, he had little choice. Only a handful of independents agreed with George H. Barbour, the stove manufacturer (and investor in Lozier and Paige-Detroit), that Ford deserved their vote because "no one [had] been more instrumental in assisting the growth of Detroit."[11]

Had this viewpoint been more prevalent in business circles, Ford, even if not endorsed, would at least have been treated with respect. Instead, the 1918 election was particularly vicious: Ford's foes concentrated their fire on his son Edsel, accusing him of "slackerism"—cowardice—because he had permitted his father to procure a draft exemption for him to run the Ford Motor Company. Members of the Detroit Club affixed to the bumpers of their Packards, Cadillacs, and Paiges banners proclaiming, "Our son is not a slacker." Newberry's supporters asked whether voters were ready to elect a candidate whose son was sitting out the war "in ignoble safety." These slurs stung. Ford had overlooked the jibes that he himself lacked the mental equipment and temperament to be senator, but the slanders against his son spurred him to seek revenge on Newberry and his associates.[12]

■ 1   On November 15, 1918, Ford announced his intention to demand a recount "for the purpose of showing how our elections are manipulated by the moneyed interests." He alleged that "Wall Street interests" had bought Newberry's nomination for $176,000, and that they were prepared to spend $176,000,000 to "clean up the country." Ford went beyond mere words: he gave an initial $40,000 to his general counsel, Alfred Lucking, and to Bernard Robinson, Firestone's attorney, to pay for finding proof that Newberry and his cohorts had conspired to steal the election. Robinson put together a team of private detectives—100 of them, according to Keith Sward—and dispatched them to every county in Michigan to track down rumors of electoral corruption.[13]

Robinson took the evidence they gathered to the federal Department of Justice and persuaded it to appoint a special assistant to the attorney general, put a team of federal investigators at his disposal, and impanel a grand jury. In one final coup, Robinson arranged to have a personal friend named chief prosecutor. All this took considerable time and money, and it was ironic that Henry Ford, who had been unwilling to spend a cent to win the Senate seat for himself, was now spending as much as $100,000 to deny it to Newberry.[14]

The grand jury began its deliberations in October 1919, and on November 29 it indicted Senator Newberry, Allan Templeton, Frank W. Blair, and 132 leading Michigan Republicans on six counts of electoral fraud. Over the course of the trial the number of defendants and charges gradually diminished; but when the verdicts were read on March 20, 1920, seventeen persons were found guilty of conspiring to spend more than $3,750 on a primary campaign. The court sentenced Senator Newberry to two years in a federal penitentiary and a fine of $10,000. The convictions were, of course, appealed and on May 2, 1921, were overturned by the U.S. Supreme Court, which ruled that Congress had acted unconstitutionally in attempting to regulate primary elections. The substance of the government's case against Newberry and his sixteen co-defendants went unchallenged; still, Newberry claimed vindication and returned to the Senate the following week after a self-imposed exile of one and a half years.[15]

He had avoided prison but still faced a Senate trial. His campaign stood condemned of violating the letter and the spirit of the elections laws. Ford and the Democrats pressed for his expulsion from Congress. To confirm his election, they argued, would "establish the precedent that hereafter a man . . . can by the expenditure of $200,000 to $800,000 purchase a seat." The Republican majority in the Senate, unable to ignore the mounting outcry against "Newberryism," finally agreed to a full-scale debate and vote in January

1922 on Newberry's claim to the Michigan seat. The debate was heated: Democrats castigated Newberry and his campaign committee as a "band of money marauders . . . making common barter of a seat in the United States Senate." Democrats thundered, but Republicans had the votes; on January 12, 1922, the Senate voted 46 to 41 to confirm Newberry's victory. Nine Republicans voted against Newberry, and more would have bolted had not the resolution also included an amendment by which the Senate "condemned and disapproved" his excessive spending.[16]

Even this public humiliation did not appease Henry Ford. Newberry still had his seat. "I don't think the people will stand for it," Ford advised the press. "They will make known their decision later. It will be through those Senators who run for office this Fall." He then helped the people to voice their displeasure by funding the opposition to Charles Townsend, senior senator from Michigan, who had incurred Ford's wrath by defending Newberry.[17]

Townsend defeated Ford's candidate, Congressman Patrick Kelley, in the Republican primary in another expensive campaign. Townsend's bills for the primary topped $30,000, thus fueling the charges that he too was guilty of "Newberryism." The money came from the friends of Senator Newberry and from the auto industry, which was in part rewarding him for his leadership of the congressional highway lobby. As well, establishment executives—Roy Chapin, Alvan Macauley, Sidney Waldon, J. Walter Drake, Dexter Ferry, Jr., and Fred Alger—saw this election as a referendum on "Fordism." Chapin, for example, pointed out that the real issue was not Newberry's campaign expenditures but whether the "Ford crowd and the [Detroit] *News*" were "going to run Detroit forever."[18]

When Townsend prevailed in the Republican primary, Ford threw his support in the election proper to the Democratic candidate, Woodbridge Ferris, a former governor. With Ford's return to the Democratic fold, 1922 shaped up as a reprise of 1918, Ferris and Townsend merely standing for the real combatants: Henry Ford and Truman Newberry. Ferris wrapped himself in Ford's colors: he mentioned the five-dollar day as often as possible and praised Ford as a "manufacturer who had effectively solved the question of capital and labor." Ferris also attacked "Newberryism," denouncing it as "worse than Bolshevism, worse than anarchy, worse a thousand times than any political heresy the world has ever known." He warned that the "honor of the state and the preservation of the republic" would be hanging in the balance on election day.[19]

Ferris defeated Townsend by 20,000 votes, running more than

125,000 votes ahead of the Democratic candidate for governor. Ferris owed his victory—the first for a Democrat in sixty-five years —both to a split in the Republican party (as many ranking Republicans distanced themselves from "Newberryism") and to the powerful political machine that Ford's minions built for him around the company's dealerships and parts suppliers. It was, according to Townsend, "the most extensive organization ever known to . . . [Michigan]. It extended into every hamlet. It was held together by business contacts and obligations."[20]

It was not only Townsend who suffered from the taint of "Newberryism" in 1922: the corruption issue influenced the outcome in several other states as well. In all, nine pro-Newberry votes disappeared from the Senate. The *New York Times* calculated that a majority were now prepared to expel Newberry, and Senator Robert La Follette promised a vote as soon as the Senate convened.[21]

Newberry had, he said, since 1918 "suffered the tortures of hell"; Townsend added that the Packard executive "no doubt would give every dollar he has if he had not entered the race at all." Even his family name—one of the oldest and most prominent in the Great Lakes region—had by 1922 become synonymous with political corruption and fraud. One senator suggested that "Newberryism" should be defined as that which is "bad, wicked, dangerous to the State."[22]

Newberry, indicted as a perjurer by a grand jury, convicted of electoral corruption, and condemned by the Senate as a threat to "the perpetuity of a free government," spared himself the ultimate indignity of expulsion from the Senate by resigning on November 18, 1922. Detroit's upper class shared in his humiliation, for he had been their champion against "Fordism."

It was now up to Governor Alex Groesbeck to appoint someone to serve out the rest of Newberry's term. Since the choice would determine the magnitude of his defeat, Newberry lobbied Groesbeck for a "real Republican": that is, someone who shared his own conservative values as well as those of Detroit's upper class. Henry Ford was out of the question—his selection would have insulted too many in the Republican Party—but there was a danger that Ford's alter ego would get the call. Newberry pleaded against naming Mayor James Couzens, the now notorious champion of municipal ownership. Couzens could not be trusted, Newberry warned, for he was "rather overwhelmed by his wealth and the fleeting popularity he has achieved through the *Detroit News*." Believing that he had obtained the necessary assurances from the governor, Newberry felt doubly betrayed when he learned on November 28 that Couzens had indeed been appointed to complete his term.[23]

Couzens's appointment was logical, however: Groesbeck was aligned with the Ford–*Detroit News* wing of the Republican Party and had supported Ford in 1918 versus Newberry. He did first offer the seat to George Booth, the publisher of the *News*, but when the latter declined it, the Senate mantle passed almost inevitably to Couzens, one of the few politicians in Michigan acceptable to both Ford and the *Detroit News*. Henry Ford hailed the appointment, calling Couzens the "best man who could have been picked for the job" because he was "independent and fearless and like[d] nothing better than a fight for the common people against the special interests."[24]

In Washington, Couzens harassed Detroit's upper class, doing much to enfeeble them politically during the fourteen years in which he represented Michigan in the Senate. He seemed to take special delight in embarrassing his foes from the auto industry. In 1923 he accused Henry and Wilfred Leland of having been war profiteers and openly called on the federal government to charge them with tax fraud. In 1925 he accused two of Hupmobile's founders, Edwin Denby and J. Walter Drake, of "influence peddling" in the tax case of a prominent Detroit capitalist. The political star of Denby, who resigned as secretary of the Navy over the Teapot Dome scandal, was already fading; but Drake, the assistant secretary of commerce, had hitherto avoided the kind of front-page, negative publicity that Couzens now gave him.[25]

The year 1925 also saw Couzens and Ferris help to defeat (in a tie vote) the nomination of Charles B. Warren for United States attorney general. This was the first rejection of a presidential cabinet nominee since 1868. It was explained by Warren's unsavory reputation as a member of the "sugar trust," as well as by the surprising decision of Michigan's senators to vote against one of their own. Warren, former ambassador to Mexico and Japan, was well connected to Detroit's upper class: he had married into the McMillan family and had invested in three elite automobile companies (E-M-F, Lozier, and Paige). Inasmuch as he had represented Michigan for eight years (1912–1920) on the Republican national committee, he could normally have counted on both Michigan votes and therefore on victory. But the Newberry-Ford feud had put two individuals in the Senate who rejected the values of Detroit's Republican business establishment, and Warren lost.[26]

This rebuff, coming hard upon the heels of the forced resignations of Newberry and Denby, left Detroit's establishment without a voice of their own in Washington's inner circle until Roy Chapin of Hudson became secretary of commerce in 1932. Even then, it was clear that the most powerful Detroiter in federal politics between 1926 and 1933 was James Couzens. A man they had done so much to antagonize (and who frequently replied in kind) would be called upon to play the key political role in their defense when they became economically vulnerable during the Great Depression.

■ 2 Ironically, Detroit's old families helped to increase their vulnerability to an economic crash by banking too heavily on a single giant corporation, the Detroit Bankers Company, to protect them from financial adversity. Detroit Bankers was a response to the rapid, automobile-fueled ascent of another banking group, the Guardian Detroit Union Group.

Though the motor industry had, as we have seen, started to spawn new banks as early as 1907, it was only with the emergence of the Guardian Group in 1924–1929 that the auto industry's new men came to dominate one of Detroit's principal financial institutions. Until then, bank directors and officers still "were substantially all local businessmen and shares were in the possession of a large number of old residents." The roster of the governing boards of the three largest institutions "read almost like a page from the Detroit social register." General Motors contributed only one director, Fred J. Fisher, and Ford and Chrysler went totally unrepresented.[27]

The Guardian Detroit Union Group started small, with the formation of the Guardian Trust Company in December 1924. Yet it already had several automobile companies behind it (General Motors, Ford, Maxwell-Chrysler, Packard, and Hudson), and in June 1927 it was joined by the Guardian Detroit Bank and an investment affiliate. Given its sponsorship, Guardian Detroit was inevitably dubbed the "automobile bank." The "Ford bank" soon became a more correct designation: with Edsel Ford on the board of both the bank and the trust company some measure of Ford control was perhaps inevitable, but the strongest link binding the emerging group to Ford was forged in March 1928 when the bank took almost one-third of the capital stock in the Universal Credit Corporation, Ford's new credit agency. Universal's subsequent decision to invest most of its capital in Guardian Detroit stock further strengthened their mutual ties.[28]

In 1929 a series of mergers created Guardian Detroit Union Group, Inc., in control now also of the National Bank of Commerce (Detroit), Ford's three suburban banks, and the Union Trust Company. Union Trust, once the financial control center for the McMillan alliance, brought several of the city's old families into the group. (It brought trouble, too, for it was the bad accounts of the Union Trust that ultimately bankrupted the group.) The Guardian Group also began to "acquire bank shares in institutions in . . . the principal cities of Michigan . . . where industry was closely allied with the industries of Detroit." By mid-1931 its empire included twenty-three banks (twelve of them in metropolitan Detroit), seven investment affiliates, and a mixed bag of subsidiaries ranging from a safe deposit company to a travel bureau. By Michigan standards the Guardian Group was awesome in size, with resources over half a billion dollars.[29]

It threatened to overwhelm the old-line banks, who accordingly responded with a holding company of their own. Organized in October 1929 but incorporated the following January, Detroit Bankers Company brought together five major financial institutions, including First National and the Peoples Wayne County Bank. Capitalized at $50 million, Detroit Bankers controlled $725 million, or 60 percent of the city's banking resources. Though it had more than 8,000 shareholders, the dominant interests belonged to Detroit's old families (see Table 27). By 1932 their banks, most of which predated the automobile, had merged into a giant institution, First National Bank–Detroit. Its only important competition locally then came from Guardian National Bank of Commerce, an institution fashioned from the Detroit banks acquired by the Guardian Group. Together the two banks controlled 93 percent of the city's banking resources. Only four small competitors survived.[30]

Although deeply suspicious of each other, the two groups had similar goals: first, rationalization of local banking to improve efficiency and profits; second, promotion of Detroit as a financial center. The Guardian Group, the more expansive and aggressive, sought to "gather together, under unified ownership" the smaller Michigan banks "whose business had flowed to New York and Chicago and which could be handled just as well or better through strong Michigan banking institutions, thus retaining that business within the State." Its motto frankly particularistic—"Incorporated in Michigan for Michigan"—it strove to make Detroit the financial center of both Michigan and the automobile industry. To block any attempt by outside interests to gain control, the Guardian Group made certain that its stock was widely distributed and forced Goldman, Sachs—New York investment bankers—to sell their holdings in one of the constituent banks. As of December 31, 1929, 89 percent of the group's shares were owned in Michigan, with no one individual holding more than 2 percent of the total.[31]

Table 27
Principal Stockholders in Detroit Bankers Company as of February 13, 1933

	Shares Held	Decade of Family's First Wealth
Alger-Shelden family	33,741	1860s
Heirs of James McMillan	30,413	1860s
Heirs of Dexter Ferry	27,432	1860s
Seyburn-Stoepel family	27,255	1840s
Heirs of John Newberry	25,455	1860s
Standish-Backus family	24,090	1850s
Heirs of Simon Murphy	23,485	1840s
James C. McGregor family	22,657	1890s
"Chemical" Fords	17,304	1880s
Christina A. White	14,303	1860s
Barbour family	13,950	1870s
James E. Davidson	13,533	1880s
Mendelssohn family	13,000	1900s
Russel-Edwards family	11,712	1850s
Heirs of Henry B. Ledyard	11,218	1800s
Michael J. Murphy	10,600	1880s
Livingstone family	10,282	1870s
Hugo Sherer estate	10,000	1890s
Total shares represented		340,440
Total shares outstanding		1,775,598
Percentage held by principal stockholders		19.2

Sources: *Detroit Times*, March 31, 1933; *Detroit News*, August 1, 1933.

Detroit Bankers also feared an outside takeover. Its "moving spirit," Julius Haass, a conservative career banker who had married into a wealthy meat-packing family, told his successor that he organized the holding company "to prevent . . . the possibility of an attack on Detroit by any large interests elsewhere." To protect Detroit Bankers from infiltration by the "interests," Haass insisted that he be "absolutely in control" during the group's formative years. He therefore named a twelve-man board of trustees composed of local bankers, the majority of them representing families prominent in Detroit since the Civil War, to hold the entire voting stock for five years (see Table 28). Thomas G. Long, general counsel for First National–Detroit, later claimed that he suggested the arrangement to Haass: "It was felt that New York interests might buy in heavily enough to get control," Long told a grand jury. "By having trustee stock, they could not get control." A community holding company, its aims chiefly defensive, Detroit Bankers nonetheless consciously promoted Detroit as a financial metropolis, for it conceived of First National as a giant magnet to attract deposits from correspondent banks throughout Michigan. The plan succeeded to a degree: by 1932 First National–Detroit was the "third largest separate bank outside of New York City" and eleventh largest overall.[32]

Superficially, Detroit Bankers was a match for any one of the automotive Big Three, for it had resources of $800 million in 1930, as compared to $1.32 billion for General Motors, $925 million for Ford, and $225 million for Chrysler (1929 figures). Detroit Bankers thus offered Detroit's pre-automotive elite the hope of continuing to have as much influence over Detroit's economy as any of the Big Three auto companies, all of which, as we have seen, were owned by outsiders of one sort or another. The Guardian Group, though many of its shares were held by old-family interests, did not offer the same hope for successful resistance, since within it the old families had already taken a back seat.[33]

In placing more than half of Detroit's banking resources in a single basket, Julius Haass had not anticipated anything as severe as the Great Depression. Between 1929 and 1933, as the sales of locally made automobiles fell by two-thirds, industrial employment in Detroit plummeted 58 percent. The population declined by 83,000; the unemployed streamed out of the city, abandoning homes and mortgages but taking their meager bank deposits with them. Detroit's banks had invested too heavily in mortgages—First National alone held $150 million in mortgage loans in 1933—and inevitably came under severe pressure as the rate of withdrawals

Table 28
Trustees of Detroit Bankers Company, 1930

	Source of Family Wealth	Decade of First Wealth	Founder of Family Fortune
Ballantyne, John	soda ash	1890s	John B. Ford
Barbour, William	stoves	1860s	William Tefft
Bodde, J. R.	banking	1910s	same
Browning, McPherson	banking	1840s	William McPherson
Chittenden, H. L.	unknown	unknown	unknown
Clark, Emory W.	banking	1850s	Myron H. Clark
Douglas, D. D.	law, utilities	1850s	S. T. Douglas
Fisher, Fred J.	auto bodies	1910s	same
Haass, Julius	meat-packing	1860s	Peter Henkel
Livingstone, T. W. P.	banking	1870s	William Livingstone
Seyburn, Wesson	real estate	1840s	W. B. Wesson
Stone, Ralph	banking	1910s	same

Source: Senate Committee on Banking and Currency, *Hearings: Stock Exchange Practices*, 73d Cong., 1st sess., 1933, 5061.

accelerated. Between 1929 and 1932 Detroit's banks lost 50 percent of their deposits. Even so, the two major banks, despite some impairment of capital, continued to be solvent, at least by the liberal standards then applied by the federal comptroller of currency.[34]

The same could not be said of the Guardian Group's Union Guardian Trust Company, whose unencumbered assets in January 1933 fell almost $14 million short of its deposit liabilities. Over the preceding two years it had exhausted its credit, first with its principal guarantor, Edsel Ford, and latterly with the Reconstruction Finance Corporation (RFC), the agency established by the Hoover administration to prop up faltering financial institutions. By law the RFC had to demand full and adequate security for its loans, something neither the trust company nor the Guardian Group, itself in dire need of a government loan to restore liquidity, could offer.[35]

Fully aware that failure of the trust company might trigger a statewide bank panic, the RFC contemplated bending its regulations to grant the Guardian Group the required assistance. Operating on the assumption that the Ford Motor Company, already deeply committed financially to the group's survival, would (if left no alternative) agree to subordinate its deposits of $7.5 million held by the trust, thereby converting them from a liability to a capital asset, the RFC calculated that a "gap" of $6.38 million was all that prevented resolution of the crisis.[36]

The amount was so small that it was tempting to find it by reassessing the collateral offered by the Guardian Group upward beyond its current market value. Yet the RFC hesitated, fearful of the political and legal repercussions of an unsecured loan. The agency was even then under heavy political attack in Congress and the press for making a suspicious loan the previous year to Central Republic Bank of Chicago, an institution headed by Charles G. Dawes, former vice-president of the United States and onetime head of the RFC. There had been inadequate security but the agency had hastily authorized a loan to prevent a run on Chicago's banks, already underway in the suburbs, from spreading to the major institutions in the Loop. That the loan bailed out Dawes, an influential Republican, may have been immaterial to the agency but not to the public; and the RFC dared not, with Congress threatening to cut off its funding, risk further controversy.[37]

It therefore passed the buck to President Herbert Hoover. On February 9, 1933, he assumed personal command of the Detroit crisis. First, he "secured an agreement from the officials of the General Motors and Chrysler companies to deposit $1,000,000 each" in Union Guardian Trust, subordinate presumably to the RFC loan. Then he summoned Michigan's two senators, Arthur Vandenberg and James Couzens, to the White House to ascertain their positions. Hoover had, according to his *Memoirs*, already decided that "the Detroit issue was so great in its ramifications throughout Michigan and Ohio" that he "wanted to take the risk" of granting an unsecured RFC loan "even if we lost a few millions." He thought that the Guardian Group's assets were undervalued and that the RFC, if assured political protection, could safely reappraise them. But first James Couzens would have to be neutralized.[38]

Couzens was a severe critic of the RFC: that very week he had reaffirmed that "he was not in favor of trying to save any banks that were not sound and solvent." He had also been using his Senate subcommittee on banking to berate the agency for the Dawes loan. Hoover anticipated a change of heart when Detroit's banks were at issue, but Couzens was consistent. He was "definitely opposed" to an unsecured loan and threatened to "shout against it from the rooftops and on the floor of the Senate!"[39]

His opposition left Hoover and the RFC no safe option but to raise the required capital privately in Detroit. The following day Hoover's emissaries—Arthur Ballantine, undersecretary of the treasury; and Roy Chapin, the Detroit automotive entrepreneur turned secretary of commerce—departed for the Motor City, reaching it on February 11, just as the banks closed for the holiday weekend; thanks to Lincoln's birthday, they were not scheduled to reopen until February 14. That gave Chapin and Ballantine approximately seventy hours to scrape together the $6.38 million needed to save the Union Guardian Trust. News of its insolvency was now spreading through Detroit's business community, and a run was inevitable without a massive infusion of new capital. Even Detroit Bankers now learned of its rival's distress as the RFC attempted to give the holding company an opportunity to prepare its bank for the impending storm.[40]

Two days were wasted in desultory talks at the offices of the Union Guardian Trust while Detroit's financial elite awaited the arrival of the New York train carrying Walter Chrysler, president of Chrysler Corporation; Donaldson Brown, chairman of the General Motors finance committee; S. Sloane Colt, president of Bankers Trust, representing J. P. Morgan and Company, GM's banking associate since 1920; and senior executives of the Central Hanover Bank & Trust, Guaranty Trust, and Chase National Bank, the New York correspondents of First National Bank–Detroit, who came to assess its collateral for an emergency loan. A delegation of bankers also headed for Detroit from Chicago, apparently in response to an appeal from S. Sloane Colt, the Morgan representative. Already it was clear that Detroit's bankers had lost control over their own destiny.[41]

■ 3   With the arrival of Chrysler, Donaldson Brown, and the out-of-state bankers, the talks took a backward step. The two automotive companies now hedged on their earlier pledge of $1 million each for the Guardian rescue fund, insisting on full security for their loans to the trust company. Rebuffed, they scaled down their proposed contributions: Chrylser to $274,000, General Motors to $619,000. Moreover, they made the loans contingent on "reasonable participation by Mr. Edsel Ford in the furnishing of the new capital." Other Detroit industrialists and bankers took the same tack. "Nobody else was going to subordinate if Mr. Ford did not." The meeting became "completely disorganized," a treasury official recalled. "Everyone talked, yet no one said anything." By the end of the day, pledges amounted to only $1.6 million, far short of the $6.38 million required. That left the fate of Detroit's banks in Henry Ford's hands.[42]

But Henry refused to budge from Fairlane, his Dearborn mansion. Like supplicants at the court of an oriental potentate, Chapin and Ballantine drove out the morning of February 13 for a private audience arranged by President Hoover in an earlier phone call. They were an unfortunate choice for their delicate mission. Chapin, political spokesman for Detroit's establishment, had clashed frequently with Ford over the previous two decades; a Republican stalwart, he had lent his name to the scurrilous Senate campaign in 1918 that had impugned the elder Ford's patriotism and the younger Ford's bravery. Ballantine, though temporarily in government service, was a Wall Street lawyer with ties to New York Trust, New York Life, and Bowery Savings—the kind that Ford instinctively mistrusted. The arrival of Chapin and Ballantine probably clinched the case in Ford's mind: he was now convinced that the Guardian's troubles stemmed from "some kind of deal between Treasury officials, Wall Street and his competitors to wreck him."[43]

Perhaps his paranoia had finally gotten completely out of hand. But he was not the only prominent Detroiter to interpret the bank crisis as a conspiracy. The memoirs of one banker called it "The Plot to Give the Cream of the Banking Profits of the Entire Country to the Customers of the New York Investment Bankers"; another told a grand jury that the crisis "was a plan to strangle or cripple Mr. Ford through his interests in the banks." Similarly, the receiver of Guardian National, Alex Groesbeck (the former governor, who had appointed Couzens to the Senate), decided that "behind the closing of the big national banks was the attempt of the New York bankers to get Henry Ford" as part "of a great nation-wide plan to eliminate thousands of banks and establish a chain-bank system."[44]

Ford had since 1930 provided $16 million in aid to the Guardian Group and had already told the group's chairman that "he had done enough." The RFC had been so informed on February 6. Consequently, when Chapin and Ballantine asked him to put up additional capital to save Guardian Trust, he angrily refused. He told them they had been duped by his "competitors" or the "people back of them" who wanted to destroy his business. There was only one way, he said, to abort this "conspiracy" and to protect his banking interests: "If the Reconstruction Finance Corporation does not make this loan promptly and immediately," he warned, "I will have representatives at every Detroit bank the first thing Tuesday morning, when the banks open for business, and will draw my personal balances and the balances of the Ford Company from them without any further notice." He was not bluffing: during the 1914 war panic he had pulled deposits out of his own bank, and several times in the past he had debated the wisdom of using banks at all.[45]

Ford, with $65 million deposited in local banks, had the means to ruin them all. Alarmed, Chapin and Ballantine warned him that failure of the two Michigan banking groups—which he threatened— "would almost certainly bring down the whole banking structure of the country and lead . . . very likely to the failure of very many manufacturing and business institutions as well." Ford refused to yield: "All right," he replied, "let the crash come. Everything will go down the chute. But I feel young. I can build again."[46]

General Motors and Chrysler, learning of his ultimatum, immediately "bowed out altogether from their earlier offer to help." Donaldson Brown contacted Alfred Sloan, Jr., GM's president, and George Whitney, a senior Morgan partner, in New York, and they concluded that "no alternative" remained to a general banking moratorium in Michigan. Given the position taken by the automotive Big Three, Detroit's bankers had little alternative but to summon Governor William Comstock from Lansing, and early on February 14 he declared a statewide banking holiday.[47]

■ 4   It took Detroit's bankers two or three days to perceive the magnitude of the blow they had received. At first they anticipated an early reopening for all the closed institutions except the Union Guardian Trust, but by February 16 it was clear that the RFC and the Treasury Department had decided that both First National Bank–Detroit and Guardian National Bank of Commerce "would run into too much difficulty again" unless reorganized with additional capital. Together, the banks needed $25–$30 million plus a massive RFC loan. The key question then became, who would provide the money? On the answer hung the future of Detroit's banking establishment, the security of thousands of stockholders, and Detroit's pretensions as a major financial center.[48]

George W. Davison, chairman of Central Hanover Bank and Trust of New York, had one answer, which he propounded to the bankers on February 16 at the Detroit Club. They listened attentively to this man who was generally regarded as "the agent of the federal government." He had been sent by Jesse Jones of the RFC and Secretary of the Treasury Ogden Mills (a former director of the Chase National Bank, a Chrysler underwriter) to advise the local clearinghouse on a scheme for issuing scrip. Eugene Meyer, Jr., governor of the Federal Reserve Board, considered plans to use scrip "just a bunch of nonsense," yet he too recommended Davison, whom he had known on the board of the Maxwell Motor Company. Meanwhile, Maxwell had become Chrysler Corporation, with Davison still on its board and his bank the corporation's transfer agent. He therefore came to Detroit at Walter Chrysler's personal request. He had also been invited by Donaldson Brown, General Motors, and the House of Morgan, of which his brother was a partner. The closed Detroit banks, too, had wired him to come to Detroit, First National hoping he would expedite its request for an emergency loan of $20 million from its New York correspondents. With such impressive credentials and sponsorship, Davison was bound to leave his imprint on the Detroit banking crisis.[49]

He had time only to confer with Chrysler's directors and Alfred Leyburn, the national bank examiner, before addressing the assembled bankers of Detroit. With undisguised dismay the latter heard him recommend "creating either one or two banks with fresh capital" to acquire the good assets of the closed banks, paying them twenty-two cents on the dollar. He suggested that Wall Street subscribe the necessary capital and supervise the operation until Detroiters had raised the money to buy a controlling interest. The bankers listened with consternation, for Davison was the first to raise the possibility of a completely new bank. Until now they had assumed that the old banks would reopen, in some modified form, once their affairs had been put in order. But if the Guardian National and First National transferred their quick assets to the new institution proposed by Davison, their eventual bankruptcy and receivership were certain. The bankers bristled at his "ultimatum"; the entire scheme looked to them like a thinly veiled attempt by New York to "take them over" and "turn Detroit into a second Gary, Indiana."[50]

Chrysler and General Motors vigorously seconded Davison's proposals, but the bankers insisted on reorganizing the old banks "with the control and ownership [remaining] in Detroit." Davison returned to New York on February 17, his plan apparently buried. But it kept resurfacing, and a month later it formed the basis for resolving the Detroit bank crisis. Only a reorganization of the closed banks with local capital could have prevented Davison's victory, but that would have required the cooperation of Detroit's major automobile companies, which alone had the money to risk at the depth of the Depression on bank stocks that under federal law still carried double liability: that is, a potential exposure of twice the original investment. Moreover, most of the liquid capital of local businessmen was now frozen by the crash. Had Detroit's old families or even the self-made businessmen who identified with them owned or controlled one of the Big Three, the banks might have been speedily recapitalized, if only to prevent financial loss to their prominent stockholders. But Detroit's upper class had little or no say in Chrysler and General Motors, two companies controlled by eastern capital. And Ford, a locally owned company, they had systematically alienated.[51]

The directors of Detroit Bankers realized that reorganization was impossible without automotive money, and on February 17 they asked General Motors and Chrysler to freeze their deposits in First National as part of a general plan to reduce the bank's liabilities. The two auto manufacturers refused, Donaldson Brown explaining: "We had been informed that the bank was insolvent, and did not see how we could justify the subordination of our deposits, which would have meant merely a sacrifice of our equity to the extent of the capital deficiency." GM and Chrysler instead called for a new bank to assume the quick deposits of First National, its capital to be supplied by the old banks' depositors on a pro rata basis. Though the directors of First National tentatively accepted these terms on February 18, negotiations stalled when General Motors and Chrysler declined to give shareholders in Detroit Bankers an extended option to purchase stock in the new institution. The bankers protested that without such an option the "deal would be interpreted by the Detroit public as a plan to freeze out the former stockholders of the Detroit Bankers Company."[52]

But General Motors, indifferent to the fate of Detroit's banking families, regarded an option to purchase as needlessly complicating the proposed stock issue and making it less attractive to potential investors. On February 19 the directors of First National officially accepted GM's terms, but they quietly stepped up their lobbying in Washington and Lansing for legislation to permit the bank to "reopen on a partial basis, freezing [that] percentage of its deposits" that it could not immediately redeem. Such a plan would obviate the need for new capital and reduce the bankers' dependence on the automotive companies. General Motors and Chrysler, aware of the double-dealing, warned First National's president the next day that if a new bank did not soon materialize, the companies "would have to form *one of their own*."[53]

The General Motors plan came to naught: Henry Ford refused to cooperate, and the Federal Reserve Bank rejected a $35 million loan request to help the new institution reopen. The RFC, approached for a $100 million loan (its constitutional limit), dithered. Though some members of its board thought the times warranted the risk, others were unnerved by the advice of Secretary of the Treasury Ogden Mills that the loan would have to be made solely on their own responsibility. They feared as well that there would be more political heat than they could endure, since Senator James Couzens was lobbying against a loan he considered too large for the national good and as being likely only to reward those insiders who withdrew their deposits before the banks failed again.[54]

On February 24 Henry Ford made a bid for the banks. He summoned the leaders of both banking groups to his mansion and informed them that he had been "thinking the matter over" and "was now willing to take the entire capital stock" of two new banks organized to replace the closed institutions. His terms were no more palatable than those offered by Chrysler and General Motors: he demanded 100 percent ownership with no option for purchase. Furthermore, he advised the bankers that he intended to retire "most of them" and to try out his own banking ideas. Ford's proposal was awesome in its ambition: if accepted, it would give him control over $700 million worth of assets for the bargain basement price of $11 million. If the deal had gone through, as Ford critic Keith Sward later remarked, "both Wall Street and many of the local elite whom Ford had scorned for years . . . would have been crowded from the scene."[55]

Nevertheless, Detroit's bankers accepted Ford's terms on February 26. An RFC ultimatum left them little alternative, for the agency, now prepared to lend $78 million to help pay off depositors, demanded a decision that day. Given its unpopularity with Congress, the RFC said it could not guarantee that it would still have the necessary money to lend after that date. At this juncture the New York bankers intervened. Ford's rescue plan was predicated on their proceeding with an emergency $20 million loan to First National Bank–Detroit, but they now reneged on the offer, saying that their legal counsel was of the opinion that First National could not transfer to them the necessary collateral during a bank holiday. The comptroller of currency thought this excuse without merit, but it did allow the New York banks to avoid subsidizing Henry Ford's acquisition of the banks of Detroit to the inevitable detriment of their clients, General Motors and Chrysler. When Ford refused to provide the additional $20 million himself, the deal fell through.[56]

And so the Michigan moratorium continued until it was superseded by the national banking holiday declared by President Franklin D. Roosevelt on March 6. Three days later, Congress shouted through emergency legislation permitting sound financial institutions in cities like Detroit to reopen on March 14. That gave the city's bankers about four days to devise a reorganization plan acceptable to Washington, for failure to reopen the banks at the first legal opportunity would undermine whatever confidence the public retained.

On March 11, Detroit's old families took renewed heart from a plan proposed by John McKee of the RFC, who claimed to speak for new Secretary of the Treasury William Woodin. McKee advocated a new bank with capital of $25 million, one-fifth of it to be raised locally, the rest from the RFC under its newly obtained authority to subscribe to the preferred stock of financial institutions. The plan won the grudging support of the stockholders and depositors of both banks, for it envisaged a gradual and presumably profitable liquidation of the assets of Guardian National and First National. Ford alone refused to co-operate. Representatives of the two banks, already in Washington, were accordingly instructed to present the scheme to either Woodin or F. Gloyd Awalt, acting comptroller of currency; however, they lacked sufficient political influence to command an interview with either until March 13, when Awalt finally saw them. No sooner had he greeted the Detroit delegation than Woodin called him away for a meeting; when Awalt returned, he announced the appointment of conservators for both First National and Guardian National. The banks were now effectively in receivership, although the stockholders of both continued to hope and plan for their reopening, even after the courts became formally involved on March 31, 1933.[57]

Awalt somewhat disingenuously kept their hopes alive, telling the delegation "to go back to Detroit, get everyone to agree on a plan and then come back to Washington with it." The two banks now proposed the segregation of their assets into good and slow assets, with an immediate payoff to small depositors and gradual reimbursement of the rest as liquidation proceeded. If adopted, the plan would save the banks, retain control in traditional hands, and save both stockholders and depositors from the losses that failure of the two banks might entail. At a meeting on March 16 the plan was approved by all the big depositors except Chrysler and General Motors, who insisted on a variant of McKee's proposal of March 11. As a result, two delegations and two plans were sent to Washington, one to plead the bankers' cause and the other to argue for a new bank.[58]

One banker, trying to comprehend the behavior of the two automobile companies, surmised that "they were in closer touch with Washington, and knew what would be acceptable there." He was in fact correct, for even as Detroit's financial elite debated, Donaldson Brown of General Motors was huddled with Jesse Jones, the new president of RFC. On March 17 Jones informed the bankers' delegation that General Motors had decided to organize a new bank with capital of $25 million to be contributed equally by the auto company and by the RFC, the latter receiving nonvoting, preferred stock. General Motors said it had been impelled to act unilaterally because the deadlock had convinced it that "some strong organization, capable within itself of assuming that responsibility of affording the essential relief, should step forward." "It was not a problem of selection," Alfred Sloan, Jr., contended. "General Motors was the only organization that had the resources to do the job and General Motors did it." The announcement effectively ended the battle; a Chrysler lawyer later recalled, "All the other talks just seemed to blow themselves away."[59]

It took several days for Brown and Jones, aided by GM's senior counsel and a Morgan banker, to organize the National Bank of Detroit. Incorporated on March 21, it opened its doors three days later, the timetable being pushed ahead slightly by the mounting uproar in Detroit. On March 22, James K. Watkins, the socially prominent city police commissioner, took to the airwaves to tell Detroiters, "Your city is being sold from under your feet." At his urging, thousands of telegrams descended on the Department of the Treasury protesting the "Wall Street bank plan." For three days Watkins used his radio program to assail General Motors, the "cloak behind which New York bankers [were] hiding." On March 23 Abner

Larned, a clothing manufacturer, joined him on the radio. Unlike Watkins, he admitted that it was too late to restrain General Motors and the National Bank of Detroit, but he pleaded with his audience to salvage the closed banks. Detroit owed a lot to these institutions, he asserted, and should not now forget them: "As I look over the lists of names, the directors of these institutions, their faces arise before me and I remember . . . something of what they have meant to this community." They "founded the great institutions of Detroit; made possible this gigantic city." If such men were ruined, "the whole city would suffer with them," for their banks were "the warp and woof of the fabric" of Detroit.[60]

The following morning, Sloan responded with "A Statement to the People of Detroit," promising that the National Bank of Detroit would be "a Detroit institution—owned, directed, and managed by Detroit people." (In point of fact, General Motors brought in a Kansas City banker to take charge of it.) Sloan also stated that as soon as "the situation was stabilized," the motor corporation would "withdraw entirely" from the local banking scene; he offered to sell the stock of the new bank at par. General Motors did gradually keep that pledge, disposing of most of its stock in the National Bank of Detroit by 1945. Even so, the largest shareholder as of 1963 was Fisher & Co. (owned by GM's Fisher brothers); rounding out the top fourteen shareholders (who together held 21.4 percent of the bank's shares) were eleven out-of-state banks and insurance companies, Detroit Bank and Trust, and C. S. Mott, still on GM's board of directors at age eighty-eight.[61]

Henry Ford was asked by the RFC to participate in the founding of the National Bank of Detroit but, as always, insisted on total independence. In August 1933 he therefore put $5 million capital (including $2 million in subordinated deposits) into a midsized bank of his own, the Manufacturers National Bank of Detroit, to take over the deposit liabilities of institutions that had serviced his employees in Highland Park and Dearborn. Like General Motors, Ford eventually relinquished most of his bank shares, yet in 1964 his family remained second largest among Manufacturers' shareholders with approximately 4 percent of the common stock. Only an eastern bank holding company outstripped them.[62]

■ 5   By August 1933 the old families of Detroit had been routed, their defeat epitomized by shuttered banks and new signs on buildings where First National and Guardian National once reigned. Receivers were appointed for both banks in late

March, and in April the National Bank of Detroit bought their "more liquid assets" for $120 million. Thus gutted, neither Guardian National nor First National was able to reorganize or reopen. Yet the receivers of both banks later declared them solvent at the time of closing, as did a grand jury and Howard Stoddart, the founder of the Michigan National Bank. During the bank crisis he had been an RFC examiner in Detroit, and in 1934 he became assistant receiver for First National. In 1969 he told a joint committee of the Michigan legislature that the two banks "should never have been placed in receivership. With the same assistance as provided to other banks of similar size and importance, they could have been saved and not forced to close their doors."[63]

Students of banking reply that neither bank was capable of paying off its depositors in 1933 and that both were therefore technically insolvent. It took twenty-two years for the receiver to liquidate the Guardian National Bank of Commerce, and it paid back only 89.5 percent of its deposits, the $9 million loss going to the Ford interests. First National Bank–Detroit, however, had repaid its depositors in full by 1940, and two years later it threw in interest of 7.6 percent. Considering that it had not been able to engage in new banking business since February 13, 1933, and that its receiver took $15.4 million for expenses, a strong case can be made for First National's essential soundness in early 1933. Yet it was legally insolvent because its capital had been impaired and it could not meet anticipated withdrawals.[64]

But debate over the banks' solvency misses the point; it assumes that the decision to close was primarily a financial one. It is true that the two banks were technically insolvent at the prevailing values for the collateral they had accepted, yet literally thousands of other banks shared their distress in the trough of the Depression; had *their* assets been rigorously examined according to traditional standards, most of these could also have been shut down. For that reason, the national bank examiners had by 1932 decided to give banks the benefit of every doubt. In Philadelphia, for example, the Federal Reserve Bank—according to its governor, George Norris— "relaxed [its] pressure, and devoted [itself] to the task of keeping alive as many banks as could be left alive." After the national bank holiday commenced, standards became even more lenient, as President Roosevelt instructed Secretary William Woodin that "directors of the Regional Federal Reserve Banks should take a fair and equitable basis for loan values rather than a forced liquidation basis. . . . Directors should use honest, and under the circumstances, fairly liberal judgment." He was, he said, prepared to accept "some losses."[65]

In other words, the assets of Detroit's banks had no absolute, market-determined value. As Jesse Jones noted in his memoirs, "The plunge in values . . . made one man's guess as good, or bad, as another's in assessing the probable worth of many a bank portfolio." The banks were worth, in other words, what the local national bank examiner and the regional Federal Reserve Bank said they were worth. In theory, both of these could be overruled by their superiors—that is, by the comptroller of currency and the Federal Reserve Board, respectively (or for that matter, the treasury secretary)—but in bureaucratic practice, low-level decisions are difficult to reverse *unless there are powerful political incentives to do so*. Politically, First National and Guardian National had a severe disadvantage that banks in most comparable cities escaped: outside (that is, Chicago) bankers controlled the regional Federal Reserve Bank. Had Detroiters been in control, they might have been more forgiving in their evaluation of local securities and mortgages. Detroiters also had bad luck in having Alfred Leyburn as their national bank examiner. Not only was he exceptionally severe in appraising the banks' assets, but he also was quite vigorous in making his opinion known to First National's depositors (telling them their bank was a "monkey house") and to the comptroller of currency, who subsequently refused to certify the closed Detroit banks as solvent.[66]

Under normal circumstances Leyburn and the regional Federal Reserve Bank would have been difficult to overrule. But February and March 1933 were anything but normal. The national banking system was in chaos; Washington was besieged by bankers. Politics came to the fore: both the Hoover and Roosevelt administrations grasped at any excuse to save well-connected banks. Consider what happened in San Francisco: the Bank of America, judged insolvent by John Calkins, the governor of the regional Federal Reserve Bank, "contacted California's senators, Hiram Johnson and William Gibbs McAdoo, as well as a representative of the Hearst newspapers, to act as lobbyists" for its case to Washington. Their influence with Roosevelt led Secretary of the Treasury William Woodin to phone Calkins to demand "whether [he] would assume responsibility for closing the Bank of America if it later proved to be solvent." Naturally, Calkins balked, and Woodin was able to order the bank's reopening. Yet it was no more sound than Detroit's banks. As historian Susan Kennedy has observed, "The Reserve Bank then proceeded to reclassify all other banks in its jurisdiction, believing that almost every bank in its district was as sound as the Bank of America."[67]

Had Alfred Leyburn or Eugene Stevens, the Chicago banker who headed the Federal Reserve Bank in Detroit's district, received a similar phone call from the secretary of the treasury, it is likely that Detroit's banks would have been saved. But what precisely was Woodin to request in such a call? Detroiters could not agree on a single plan of action for him to implement; each time a proposal was made, some powerful group almost immediately torpedoed it.

Politically, Detroit's bankers did not count in Washington, because they lacked the financial resources to recapitalize the banks under any guise. Every one of their many plans depended on the cooperation of one or more of the automotive Big Three. That being the case, it was to be expected that both the Hoover and Roosevelt administrations would end up dealing directly with the motor companies. With the banks closed, Detroit's banking families lacked the means of their own salvation. Their delegations to Washington were accordingly shunted from one antechamber to another. It was predetermined by the mathematics of the crisis that General Motors, Chrysler, Ford, and James Couzens would decide Detroit's fate. Only the "big four" (Couzens, as a multimillionaire senator with liquid capital, counted as an independent force in Detroit's affairs) had the money to save the banks. Had they concurred on a plan, the secretary of the treasury would have had no difficulty redefining Detroit's banks as solvent—because they would have been.

But every commentary on the Detroit banking crisis has remarked on the extraordinary lack of unity in the city's ruling circles. Couzens wrote that "Detroit's banking problems could have been settled, if there had been any agreement among Detroiters." Senator Vandenberg agreed: "There was a woeful lack of leadership in Detroit." And a treasury official told a Detroit reporter that the banks had failed because there was "no leadership in Detroit's banking circles which the Government [could] hook onto and pull Detroit out of its . . . mess." The bankers, however, objected that they themselves had been united and "the only lack of unity was that right from the start the General Motors and Chrysler groups sort of played by themselves."[68]

The attitude of Chrysler and General Motors was understandable: with the spring sales season at hand, they made the restoration of banking facilities in Detroit and Michigan their first priority and therefore supported any plan that promised early reopening of the banks. Being New York concerns, however, they gave little or no thought to the issue of local ownership or control. It is doubtful, though not implausible, that they actively promoted a Wall Street takeover of Detroit's banks; rather, they simply saw no harm in it. Thus Charles S. Mott, a GM director with more ties than most to Michigan (as former mayor of Flint), stated that as a stockholder he would be "very pleased" if General Motors "could sell its stock in the new bank to Morgan, Davison or anybody else." To both General Motors and Chrysler, national corporations with a national perspective, Detroit's problems mattered less than the security of the corporations themselves and the stability of the capitalist system as a whole. Inevitably, Detroit's financial elite counted little in their calculations.[69]

Moreover, any goodwill the elite possessed going into the crisis was probably lost by their repeated suggestions that General Motors and Chrysler sink several million dollars into the city's banks without gaining any additional say in running them. Throughout the crisis the city's old families made it clear that they regarded the two corporations as stalking-horses for Wall Street, that for them a General Motors bank was no different from a Morgan or Du Pont bank. As the crisis unfolded and these attitudes became manifest, the executives of GM and Chrysler must have felt increasingly estranged from Detroit's financial elite. Surely they resented the daily charges of conspiracy against their colleagues and such former associates as William Woodin, who had represented J. P. Morgan on GM's board of directors from 1920 to 1927.[70]

As for the Ford Motor Company, it faced less open hostility, although it should be noted that the Detroit Free Press did fix the blame for the banks' collapse on Ford and Couzens. When forced to choose between General Motors and Ford, as essentially happened in late February, Detroit bankers opted for Ford on February 26. Perhaps they were looking ahead to the day when Edsel Ford, essentially one of their own, would inherit the Ford Motor Company from his difficult father, now aged seventy.

But Henry Ford had the final say in 1933, and he would not cooperate. Long estranged from the local and national economic elites, he sought above all to avoid financial entanglements that might impair his independence or threaten his control over the automobile company. He still remembered his forced departure from the Henry Ford Company (Cadillac) and the attempts made during the depression of 1921 by several New York banks to take over his company when he had become overextended. His treasurer had appeared then to collaborate with the New Yorkers, and Henry Ford now trusted no one. The fate of the city's banks took a back seat to his overriding concern for liquidity, his best defense against corporate raiders. James Couzens told the RFC that the Detroit problem "could not be solved until there was some definite leadership in Detroit in which Henry Ford had confidence," which meant in effect that the problem could not be solved.[71]

In 1933, as in 1922, the one person Ford trusted accordingly became the key actor in the entire civic drama. That was James Couzens. Like Ford, the senator was prepared to help only on his own terms. Twice he offered to invest as much as $5 million of his own money to help resolve the banking crisis. Yet he was unable throughout the crisis to work in harness with Detroit's old-family bankers. Though he argued their case in Washington and Lansing — as Michigan's senator it was difficult not to — Couzens also advised the RFC that it should not leave "the present conflicting interests" in charge of Detroit's banks but rather fund a new bank "in charge of men in whom the public would have confidence." His position was not altogether different from that of General Motors or Ford.[72]

Except that it was more vengeful: like Ford after the 1918 election, Couzens was determined to settle accounts with his enemies in the Detroit establishment. He sought, therefore, to prove that their own criminality had undone Detroit's bankers. According to Malcolm Bingay, editor of the *Detroit Free Press* (and an unsympathetic source), Couzens told him, "I'll never rest until every one of the sons of bitches are [sic] behind prison bars where I can walk up and down in front of them and laugh at them!" He rounded up the necessary evidence and presented it to a grand jury in August–September 1933 and then to his own subcommittee on currency and banking in December 1933–January 1934. According to Bingay, Couzens also pressured the Justice Department to dispatch a special assistant attorney general to investigate the Detroit fiasco.[73]

Couzens reaped a smaller though richer harvest of indictments than Ford had garnered in 1919: a federal grand jury handed down criminal indictments against twenty-eight leading Detroit bankers in June and August 1934 for violations of federal banking law. Many of them were old Detroiters — for example, James T. McMillan, William T. Barbour, T. W. P. Livingstone, and Wesson Seyburn — and all of them belonged to Detroit's financial elite in 1933. In the end, three bankers paid small fines; the rest were eventually acquitted after spending three years in court and a fortune in legal fees.[74]

This chapter has featured two trials, both starring members of Detroit's establishment. The first trial signaled the imminent political eclipse of Detroit's old families; the second, their economic eclipse. The two events are linked, for the Detroit banking crisis would probably have taken a different turn had an ally rather than an opponent of the city's banking families served on the Senate subcommittee on currency and banking. The enmity of Couzens and Ford, coupled with the indifference of Chrysler and General Motors, destroyed the last significant bastion of non-automotive wealth and power in Detroit. Control over $700 million worth of assets was at stake in February 1933, and for lack of $10 million the old families saw that control pass to General Motors and Ford.

In addition, the shareholders of Guardian National and First National lost at least $74 million; overall, the loss may well have been as high as the more than $300 million specified by a stockholder suit in 1943. That may not seem like much in these inflationary times, but then it was the equivalent of writing off the 1929 assets of Chrysler Corporation—the nation's third largest automobile company—as a total loss. Also lost was the right to future income from Guardian National and First National, and even in the depths of the Depression the latter was still earning $7.5 million a year. Recovery from these losses was difficult, especially for those preoccupied by the endless lawsuits, stretching into the 1940s, triggered by the bank failures. For Detroit's old families the 1933 bank crash was an unmitigated disaster. Fortunes were destroyed, and the ability to repair them impaired. If they had been better automotive entrepreneurs, or had not created Detroit's automotive industry in the first place, they would surely have escaped so crushing a blow.[75]

What did this all mean for Detroit? Did the average citizen have a stake in the outcome? Inasmuch as new banks soon replaced the old, did it matter that there had been a temporary suspension? What difference did it make who owned the banks? Given the inevitable circulation of elites, what difference did it make to Detroit to have had the process accelerated by the bank crash? These questions add up to one big question: does the study of an urban elite and its entrepreneurship tell us very much about urban history and development as a whole? The Conclusion tackles this question and reviews the economics, politics, and results of conspicuous production as played out in Detroit between 1899 and 1933.

Conclusion

■   "In the city of Zenith," wrote Sinclair Lewis in *Babbitt*, "a family's motor indicated its social rank as precisely as the grades of the peerage determined the rank of the English family. . . . There was no court to decide whether the second son of a Pierce-Arrow limousine should go in to dinner before the first son of a Buick roadster, but of their respective social importance there was no doubt." In Zenith in the 1920s, in America since the automobile first appeared on its roads, the automobile has been a "primary object of competitive display" that has helped to establish and define the American prestige order.[1]

So compelling was the prestige appeal of the automobile when first it appeared that not even its makers could avoid the temptation, as Thorstein Veblen would put it, to differentiate between the "noble and ignoble."[2] That is, the founders of the American automobile industry seem to have been as prone to the conspicuous production of motorcars as other Americans were to their conspicuous consumption. They apparently allowed their yearning for social status to affect and in some cases to determine their entrepreneurship.

Although this book has focused on Detroit, conspicuous production was not an exclusively local phenomenon. In the United States the big-car bug infected entrepreneurs from the start, and even before Oldsmobile, Cadillac, Chalmers, and Hupmobile had voluntarily exited the lower price-class field, bracket creep had already started in New England, the original center of the American automobile industry. The most striking example of this phenomenon was Locomobile of Bridgeport, Connecticut, the first American company to "make small, lightweight, and inexpensive cars" in quantity. Selling between 1899 and 1902 an estimated 4,700 steamers, Locomobile was the company that "demonstrated the reality of

206

a large market for small, cheap cars" in the United States. Yet when the declining popularity of steam forced it to switch to a gasoline-powered vehicle, Locomobile opted in 1902 for a four-cylinder model with a $5,000 price tag. This upward ascent, more sudden and spectacular than Detroiters ever essayed, almost bankrupted the company in 1903–1904 and forced its original backer—Amzi Barber, "the asphalt paving king"—to sell control to an outside investor. Locomobile survived to build luxury cars until 1922. Barber, who had made his fortune in an unglamorous business, may have been satisfied with this outcome even though he personally lost considerable money on the investment.[3]

Locomobile's decision to go upmarket, L. J. Villalon and J. M. Laux have remarked, was one of two key decisions (the other being the decision by Pope, a Hartford, Connecticut firm and the nation's leading bicycle manufacturer, to build electric cars) which "meant that the industry would shift westward." But midwestern manufacturers also eventually succumbed to the big-car bug, and Detroit was able to establish its primacy only through a succession of new entries into the lower-price field (many of them spinoffs from Oldsmobile) as well as the singular persistence of Henry Ford.[4]

Surely, conspicuous production played a role in the early American automotive industry. While individual cases can and have been explained away by industry historians, there were simply too many companies that priced themselves out of the mass market for prestige behavior *not* to have played a role in determining success and failure in the early American automotive industry. Also pointing in this direction are the data showing a statistical correlation between the social background of Detroit's automotive leaders and their choice of price-class. In sum, it requires considerable faith in the intrinsic rationality of American businessmen to rule out the possibility that many, maybe most, of the founders of the U.S. auto industry sought to build a car that their social peers would be honored to drive. Indeed, it would have been almost "un-American" had American entrepreneurs behaved otherwise. It was not the American style to treat motor vehicles with cold calculation; as the noted social historian Lewis Mumford has remarked, "The modern American way of life is founded on the worship of the motorcar, and the sacrifices that people are prepared to make for this worship stand outside the realm of rational criticism."[5]

What of other lands? A priori, we would assume that countries with more ascriptive status systems would be less susceptible to conspicuous production but that some auto entrepreneurs in every socially democratic country would succumb to its appeal. We would also expect that countries with social structures roughly comparable to that of the United States would be most afflicted by the big-car bug. The automotive industry of Canada, in many ways the most "American" society outside the United States, would appear to fit the American model, although Canada did lack a Henry Ford.[6]

The Canadian automotive industry was controlled by members of the preexisting socioeconomic elite who, like their counterparts in the United States, sought to build expensive cars for their social peers. It was standard practice in the early Canadian auto industry to take a low-priced American make and revamp it for the Canadian upper-class market. Thus Sam McLaughlin, an elite carriage-maker, acquired the Canadian rights to the Buick 10—an economy car in the United States—and transformed it into a luxury model by importing, as he recalled, "black material from England for the top, East African mahogany for the instrument panels, fine wood for the bodies . . . beautiful wool upholstery from England and leather and cords. Always the best." Other Canadian manufacturers similarly upgraded the Everitt, the Dort, and the Model T Ford. While the last was too plebeian ever to compete in the upper-class market, it was nevertheless built to higher, more expensive specifications in Canada; for example, the Canadian version came with four doors, the American with two.[7]

Overall, the Canadian pattern was to take a product that Canadians, their incomes appreciably lower than those of Americans, already had difficulty affording and to make it even more expensive. This self-defeating market strategy helped to ensure that Canada's motorization lagged well behind that of the United States. Canadian auto manufacturers appear, then, to have succumbed to the big-car bug as much as any Detroiter. Fittingly, the most patrician group to enter the Canadian auto industry—Toronto financiers linked to Canada's bicycle monopoly and to Massey-Harris, the country's leading maker of agricultural implements—built the Russell, Canada's most prestigious marque.[8]

As we might expect, Canadians and Americans appear to have been more prestige-oriented in their marketing strategy than Europeans, who operated within a less fluid status system and who accordingly probably felt less pressure to flaunt their good taste. British and French manufacturers were also less likely than North Americans to specialize in a single price-class. British capitalists could be found building cars of every price and specification. Even so, there is evidence that the American pattern at least occasionally replicated itself in Britain: Rolls-Royce was, predictably, financed by an aristocrat, whereas two farmers' sons founded Morris and

Austin, the quantity producers. In France, Parisian manufacturers seem to have been oblivious to status considerations, but "provincial establishments" apparently did succumb to the big-car bug. According to James Laux, they "manifested less interest and success in producing small cars than did Paris firms." Perhaps entrepreneurs operating outside the French metropolis suffered from status anxieties similar to those experienced by North American producers.[9]

Conspicuous production was not, then, an exclusively American or Detroit phenomenon. Its existence requires us to reexamine the assumption that mass production was a joint project of American capitalism, that business as a whole was somehow committed to democratizing the automobile. In fact, most automobile companies sought an elite clientele, if not with their original model (for lack of capital or the right design), then subsequently. Only a minority of manufacturers actually attempted to serve the mass market before World War I and even fewer persisted in the effort.

American businessmen responded to the automobile neither in the unitary fashion assumed by so much of the automotive literature nor in the dualistic manner assumed by those who, like Lewis Mumford, believe that there has been a basic, continuing polarity between democratic and authoritarian technologies. Rather, there were as many responses as niches in the price-class hierarchy. Since social background was so important in determining which market segment an automotive manufacturer elected to serve, the task of democratizing the American automobile ultimately fell to those who, like Henry Ford, identified with the masses.[10]

Whether this was true of other industries as well is still unknown, although it is suggestive that Andrew Carnegie, Ford's counterpart as a mass producer in the steel industry, also surrounded himself with self-made men. A study of Pittsburgh's steel elite for 1874–1901 concluded that all five of the men who were "immigrants from poor backgrounds . . . were officers in the Carnegie mills," including Carnegie himself. It is possible, then, that it was those entrepreneurs who came from the common people, identified with them, knew their needs and their potential demand, and remained estranged from the world of the rich and powerful who spearheaded the thrust toward the democratization of goods in America, and perhaps elsewhere.[11]

At least that was the situation in Detroit's automotive industry. The only company to persist in the lower-class market before 1920 was a company whose key entrepreneurs were basically antiestablishment. Auto manufacturers who did identify with the establishment typically allowed their prices to soar as they endeavored to present a car worthy of the high social status they sought or already possessed. Henry Ford's persistence in the lower price-class—attributed by scholars to either his entrepreneurial acumen or his psychological inertia—seems more likely to have been socially derived. Given the dynamic of conspicuous production, the continued loyalty of the Ford Motor Company to the lower-class market should be taken as evidence of the failure of Detroit's upper class to co-opt the two key entrepreneurs at Ford—Henry Ford and James Couzens—into their social set. Indeed, the primary identification of Ford and Couzens with the common people appears to have increased as they became wealthier, thanks to the continuing hostility of Detroit's social arbiters.

Several controversies—starting with Ford's dismissal from the Henry Ford company, then extending through his struggle with Alex Malcomson for control over model policy at the Ford Motor Company and with the Association of Licensed Automobile Manufacturers for the unfettered right to sell cars—kept Henry Ford and his company faithful to the mass market. Although Ford and Couzens still seemed anxious to win elite approval in the period from 1910 to 1913 when both served on the local Board of Commerce, by 1922, after clashes over the five-dollar day, war preparedness, banking, charities, public transit, and party politics, it had been made quite clear to them that their values were unacceptable to Detroit's upper class. Repeatedly ridiculed and rebuffed, Henry Ford and James Couzens no longer cared to join a group whose leading members, they were beginning to think, belonged in jail (at least that is where they attempted to put several scions of Detroit's old families in 1919 and 1933). Detroit's upper class failed through their own conservatism to win over the two capitalists whose help they would most need if they were to come through the Great Depression with their fortunes and power intact.

The goodwill of Couzens and Ford would have been less important to Detroit's upper class had the latter controlled either General Motors or Chrysler, but Detroit's old families had passed up several opportunities to buy into them and had treated General Motors like a penny stock, insisting on cash for Cadillac and ridding themselves as quickly as possible of the GM shares they received for Oldsmobile. Excluded from the three leading automotive producers, then, Detroit's old families—indeed its entire upper class—headed into the Great Depression with inadequate resources to protect vital economic interests. They were also politically vulnerable after Henry Ford had helped to purge Senators Newberry and Townsend in 1922 and once Couzens, his former general manager, had been installed in the "Detroit seat" in the United States Senate—which he still occupied in 1933 as Detroit's banking establishment, foundering, searched frantically for political allies.

While it is possible to blame the ensuing bank crash in Detroit on the troubles of an industrial city that had grown too rapidly and speculatively in the 1920s, it is also obvious that the banks failed for lack of unity within Detroit's ruling circles. *Business Week* remarked in April 1933 that the lineup was quite complicated: "Detroit vs. Wall Street. Detroit group vs. Detroit group. General Motors and Chrysler vs. Ford." The disunity reflected the extent to which the interests of Detroit's old families diverged from those of the Big Three auto companies. Unable to refinance the banking groups themselves, the families foiled any rescue plan that envisaged an enhanced role for the Big Three, whom they regarded as outsiders in one way or another. That same issue of *Business Week* astutely observed that the determination of "Old Detroiters" to "keep the directorates of the banks representative of Detroit's best families" impeded a speedy resolution of the crisis. It was not until the federal government, General Motors, and Ford decided simply to ignore the wishes of Detroit's old families that new banks could be opened and a semblance of normality restored.[12]

It took a long time, however, for Detroit's banks to recover from the 1933 crash. The double assessments for the stockholders of the closed banks, still in the news after World War II, made Detroiters leery of owning bank stocks, thereby ensuring that the banks remained undercapitalized for years. That made them behave conservatively, as did the local assumption that recklessness had caused the bank crash. Public opinion after 1933, therefore, compelled local banks to tighten their lending policies. Loans in 1950 accounted for only 25 percent of the investments of Detroit banks, as an obsessive desire for liquidity led them to concentrate on safer but less lucrative government securities. In 1963, three decades after the crash, a report on Detroit banks still commented on the "conservative approach to banking by management still living in the shadows of the great debacle of 1933." The failure of two expansion-minded banking groups and the substitution of smaller, more conservative institutions undoubtedly retarded Detroit's development after the crash. This would be especially true if, as many social scientists believe, banks play the dominant role in organizing the American capitalist system.[13]

Moreover, the crash struck the local elite a crippling blow, for "a large part of the wealth of Detroit was represented by bank stocks" that had been rendered valueless. It is likely that a prediction made by the *Detroit Free Press* in 1933 also came to pass: that is, that assessments imposed by the banks' receivers "compelled" local capitalists to "sell their holdings in Detroit industries . . . to outsiders." Though the old families have survived as a *rentier* class, with incomes still sufficient to finance their elite social status and their philanthropies, they have for decades not wielded decisive economic power in Detroit. They have thus paid a high price for the decision made between 1908 and 1910 not to build a low-price automobile. Loss of the motor industry, followed by loss of the banks, has probably left Detroit's local elite weaker than their counterparts in comparable cities.[14]

Since the 1930s there has been considerable research on the ownership and control of American business. Several studies have argued that a relative handful of "interest groups" form the central core of American capitalism. The methodology of the researchers has varied, some looking at corporate interlocks, others at stock ownership. Their conclusions have also differed, the number of groups identified ranging from four to thirty-two. Yet the researchers have agreed that at most a dozen cities have produced family or institutional cliques capable of playing a central role in organizing the national economy. Detroit's economic elite either rates near the bottom of such lists or is entirely absent. The core groups of Cleveland, Pittsburgh, and Chicago—to name three cities highlighted by the studies—appear more influential in a national context than Detroit's elite.[15]

Detroit does not appear, then, to have developed a local elite comparable to those found in many other major metropolises. The city's upper class today resembles less C. Wright Mills's description of the "Metropolitan 400" in the *Power Elite* than it does "local society" in the medium-sized cities where the leading families have been dwarfed by the executives of the national corporations located there. Social standing in these satellite communities, Mills wrote, "is increasingly obtained through association with the leading officials of the great absentee-owned corporations, through following their style of living, through moving to the suburbs outside the city's limits." Without the Henry Ford clan to offer some counterweight, the social dominance of the corporate managers in Detroit and the ascendancy of Bloomfield Hills, their suburb, would be by now complete.[16]

The relative weakness of Detroit's socioeconomic elite has probably hampered their efforts to revitalize the city's economy. Certainly the literature on urban renewal has emphasized the strategic role played by local business elites. Not all businessmen, however, have been equally involved. The entrepreneurs of renewal have tended to come from "place-related firms" with a direct economic stake in the outcome. In general, they have been newspapers, downtown merchants, land developers, public utilities, banks and insurance companies, and all "those that are locked into the city by investment or tradition and for whom changing locations would be very costly." These businesses depend on the continued health of the metropolitan region. Transnational corporations, on the other hand, have been less interested in urban renewal, save in communities so small (for example, Poughkeepsie, New York, and New Brunswick, New Jersey) that their decay blights the corporate image. The most spectacular projects have stemmed from the efforts of proprietary capitalists to finance the salvage of a city long identified with their families. Though Richard King Mellon of Pittsburgh is the most celebrated of these patrician entrepreneurs, Henry Ford II performed a similar role in Detroit after 1967.[17]

Urban renewal projects have varied considerably in their impact. They appear to have been most economically successful in such cities as Pittsburgh, Chicago, Boston, Philadelphia, and Minneapolis: that is, cities whose old families still have a major say in the local economy. Cities dependent on absentee-owned, transnational corporations have had more difficulty finding the funds and the will to renew themselves. In other words, Detroit might have had more success since 1949 in recharging its economy (and its hopes) had its pre-automotive elite not lost control of first the automobile industry and then the banks to absentee-owned corporations. Of course, General Motors and Chrysler are no longer quite so much the outsiders they were in 1933. As the engineer-entrepreneurs and bankers who created them faded from the scene, and as the Du Ponts were forced by an antitrust suit to divest themselves in the early 1960s of their GM shares, career managers resident in the suburbs of Detroit have come to have a much greater say in the decision-making of the two corporations. These managers identify with Detroit far more than Pierre du Pont, Alfred P. Sloan, Jr., C. S. Mott, Charles Kettering, and Walter Chrysler ever did. In that identification there is hope for Detroit's regeneration.[18]

Yet those managers will have to resist the urge to produce conspicuously. Unfortunately, status considerations still seem to be affecting decision-making in the American auto industry. For example, Brock Yates, the noted automotive journalist, has attributed the development of the Chevrolet Caprice in 1966 to a corporate edict requiring Chevrolet's senior managers to give up their Cadillacs and drive (there being no alternative) a Chevrolet Impala, "the same menial machine being wheeled into the parking lots by their foremen and junior accountants." Hence the Caprice: "It was nothing more than an Impala gussied up . . . but it was Chevrolet's executive-brand pseudo-Cadillac and it was marketed," according to Yates, "as much for the benefit of a small cadre of Detroit and Flint executives as for the general public." This may seem a trivial incident, but Chevrolet's upscale model further blurred the boundaries between General Motors divisions, thereby making it more difficult for the corporation to convince potential customers that the best way for them to satisfy their status cravings was through progression in the General Motors line. There were so many overlapping rungs on GM's "ladder of consumption" by the 1970s that consumers in pursuit of status sometimes stumbled right off it and into the seat of a BMW or Mercedes.[19]

Even more problematic for General Motors and the American auto industry was the industry's capitulation in the 1970s to the big-car bug of the earlier generation. American auto companies in the 1970s were out of touch with consumers. It may well be, as both Brock Yates and John De Lorean have suggested, that the social isolation of the industry's senior executives caused them to overestimate the extent to which Americans both desired and could afford the behemoths that Detroit was designing for them. Perhaps they thought the whole world was getting wealthier with them. Which is to say that the theme of conspicuous production may be applicable to all stages of the industry's development in America.[20]

Certainly, it has played an important part in the Motor City's development. By 1933 Detroit had already paid a steep price for the entrepreneurial blunders of its pre-automotive elite. It was by then a city with an enfeebled upper class, crippled banks, and an economy largely dominated by absentee interests. Normally, a city benefits from the circulation of elites, from the replacement of tired blood. But the transfusion occasioned by the automotive revolution seems to have weakened Detroit. Detroit became a giant city afflicted with giantism.

It is ultimately difficult to see how it could have been otherwise, given the inability of consumer and producer alike to deal objectively with the automobile. The problem, after all, was—and is— that automobiles evoke passion.

Notes

Abbreviations used throughout the notes

BCGB   House Committee on Banking and Currency, *Hearings: Branch, Chain, and Group Banking,* 71st Cong., 2d sess., 1930

BHC   Burton Historical Collection, Detroit Public Library

CC   Corporate Identity Office, Chrysler Corporation

CLP   Detroit Citizens League Papers, Burton Historical Collection, Detroit Public Library

CR   Corporate Records, Baker Library, Harvard University

FA   Ford Archives, Dearborn, Michigan

GJP   Grand Jury Proceedings, "Banking Situation in Detroit, 1933," Department of Attorney General, Michigan History Division, RG 76-105 B10 F11, Michigan State Archives

GMI   General Motors Institute Alumni Foundation's Collection of Industrial History, Flint, Michigan

HJP   Henry B. Joy Papers, Burton Historical Collection, Detroit Public Library

JCP   James Couzens Papers, Library of Congress, Washington, D.C.

JDP   Joseph M. Dodge Papers, Burton Historical Collection, Detroit Public Library

JPP   J. G. Perrin Papers, National Automotive History Collection, Detroit Public Library

LC   Library of Congress, Washington, D.C.

LP   Henry M. and Wilfred C. Leland Papers, National Automotive History Collection, Detroit Public Library

MHC   Michigan Historical Collection, Bentley Historical Library, University of Michigan, Ann Arbor

NAHC   National Automotive History Collection, Detroit Public Library

RCP   Roy D. Chapin Papers, Michigan Historical Collection, Bentley Historical Library, University of Michigan, Ann Arbor

RFCP   Reconstruction Finance Corporation Papers, RG 234, National Archives, Washington, D.C.

RTCP   Detroit Rapid Transit Commission Papers, Burton Historical Collection, Detroit Public Library

SCP   Studebaker Corporation Papers, Discovery Hall Museum, South Bend, Indiana

SEP   Senate Committee on Banking and Currency, *Hearings: Stock Exchange Practices*, 73d Cong., 1st sess., 1933

TNP   Truman H. Newberry Papers, Burton Historical Collection, Detroit Public Library

Preface

1. Beverly Duncan and Stanley Lieberson, *Metropolis and Region in Transition* (Beverly Hills, Calif., 1970), app. table A; Donald Bogue, *The Population of the United States: Historical Trends and Future Projections* (New York, 1985), 713–19. Two other metropolitan areas—San Jose and Anaheim–Santa Ana–Garden City—have also grown as rapidly as Detroit over a thirty-year period (1940–1970 and 1950–1980, respectively), but they are effectively parts of larger conurbations. Motor vehicles (excluding parts and bodies) were the nation's third largest industrial category in 1919 in value of output (behind meat-packing and iron and steel) and second in 1927 (behind meat-packing). As of 1929, motor vehicles ranked first; motor vehicle parts and bodies, a separate category, ninth. See U.S. Department of Commerce, Bureau of the Census, *Fifteenth Census of the United States: Manufactures, 1929* (Washington, D.C., 1932), vol. 1, General Summary, table 6.

2. C. B. Glasscock, *The Gasoline Age* (New York, 1937), 209–10; T. D. Schuby, "Class, Power, Kinship, and Social Cohesion: A Case Study of a Local Elite," *Sociological Focus* 8 (August 1975): 243–55; Lynda Ann Ewen, *Corporate Power and Urban Crisis in Detroit* (Princeton, N.J., 1978); Olivier Zunz, *The Changing Face of Inequality: Urbanization, Industrial Development, and Immigrants in Detroit, 1880–1920* (Chicago, 1982).

3. *Detroiter* 12 (January 22, 1921): 7; U.S. Department of Commerce, Bureau of the Census, *Fourteenth Census of the United States: Manufactures, 1920* (Washington, D.C., 1922), 9:684–85; G. Walter Woodworth, *The Detroit Money Market* (Ann Arbor, Mich., 1932), 10. The leading product accounted for 26.4 percent of New York's industrial output (clothing); 19.2 percent of Pittsburgh's (iron and steel); 16.0 percent of Chicago's (slaughtering and packing); 14.9 percent of Cleveland's (motor vehicles and parts); and 13.3 percent of Philadelphia's (textiles). Automobiles and auto parts produced in Detroit in 1927 exceeded $981 million, an amount almost equal to all of Cleveland's industry. The next largest industry in Detroit was the foundry and machine-shop sector; its manufactures in 1927 were worth $52 million.

4. Norman S. B. Gras, *An Introduction to Economic History* (New York, 1922), 293–95, 338; James E. Vance, Jr., *The Merchant's World: The Geography of Wholesaling* (Englewood Cliffs, N.J., 1970), 94.

5. Samuel P. Hays, "The Politics of Reform in Municipal Government in the Progressive Era," *Pacific Northwest Quarterly* 55 (October 1964): 157–68; James Weinstein, *The Corporate Ideal in the Liberal State : 1900–1918* (Boston, 1968), chap. 4.

Introduction

1. Walter P. Chrysler, *Life of an American Workman* (New York, 1937), 103–4.

2. Ibid., 105–7, 127; Robert S. Lynd and Helen Merrell Lynd, *Middletown: A Study in American Culture* (New York, 1929), 251–55.

3. John B. Rae, "Why Michigan?" in David L. Lewis and Laurence Goldstein, eds., *The Automobile and American Culture* (Ann Arbor, Mich., 1983), 6; Robert P. Thomas, "The Automobile Industry and Its Tycoon," *Explorations in Entrepreneurial History*, ser. 2, 6 (Winter 1969): 147; Benjamin Briscoe, "The Inside Story of General Motors," pt. 1, *Detroit Saturday Night*, January 15, 1921, p. 9.

4. Joseph A Schumpeter, *The Theory of Economic Development* (Cambridge, Mass., 1934), 93.

5. For the Ford lawsuit, see Allan Nevins and Frank Ernest Hill, *Ford: Expansion and Challenge, 1915–1933* (New York, 1957), 88–105. Historians have frequently commented on the technological perfectionism of European auto entrepreneurs; see S. B. Saul, "The Motor Industry in Britain to 1914," *Business History* 5 (December 1962): 22–44; James M. Laux, *In First Gear: The French Automobile Industry to 1914* (Montreal, 1976); James Laux et al., *The Automobile Revolution* (Chapel Hill, N.C., 1982). Less common in the United States, where few of the automotive pioneers had formal technical training (only one-eighth of Detroit's auto leaders attended an engineering school, judging from a sample of 292), it nonetheless stymied the ambitions of such well-known entrepreneurs as Alexander Winton and C. Harold Wills; see John B. Rae, *American Automobile Manufacturers* (Philadelphia, 1959), 14, 148.

6. Thomas C. Cochran, "Role and Sanction in American Entrepreneurial History," in H. G. J. Aitken, ed., *Explorations in Enterprise* (Cambridge, Mass., 1967), 95; Robert Lamb, "The Entrepreneur and the Community," in William Miller, ed., *Men in Business: Essays on the Historical Role of the Entrepreneur* (New York, 1952), 114.

7. C. Wright Mills, *The Power Elite* (New York, 1959), 50.

8. Thorstein Veblen, *The Theory of the Leisure Class* (1899; rpt. New York, 1965), 84.

9. Ibid., 74; W. Lloyd Warner et al., *Social Class in America* (New York, 1960), 21–23; Daniel W. Rossides, *The American Class System* (Boston, 1976), 293. See also S. M. Lipset and Reinhard Bendix, *Social Mobility in Industrial Society* (Berkeley, Calif., 1959), 273–75.

10. Vance Packard, *The Status Seekers* (New York, 1959), 312–18; John Brooks, *Showing Off in America: From Conspicuous Consumption to Parody Display* (Boston, 1979), 275–78. For the Automobile Club of America, see James J. Flink, *America Adopts the Automobile, 1895–1910* (Cambridge, Mass., 1970), 145–50. The ALAM is discussed in John B. Rae, "The Electric Vehicle Company: A Monopoly That Missed," *Business History Review* 29 (December 1955): 298–311; William Greenleaf, *Monopoly on Wheels: Henry Ford and the Selden Patent Suit* (Detroit, 1961).

11. Daniel Boorstin, *The Americans: The Democratic Experience* (New York, 1973), 552–54.

12. Packard, *Status Seekers*, 313; Minutes, Sales and Advertising Meeting, Hudson Motor Car Company, January 25, 1910, in Hudson Minutebooks, Bentley Historical Library, MHC; Frank Presbrey, *The History and Development of Advertising* (New York, 1968), 559; Kathleen A. Smallzried and Dorothy James Roberts, *More Than You Promise* (New York, 1942), 195; George S. May, *R. E. Olds, Auto Industry Pioneer* (Grand Rapids, Mich., 1977), 166; Curtis Publishing Company, *A Table of Leading Advertisers, 1919* (Philadelphia, 1921).

13. See Stuart Ewen, *Captains of Consciousness: Advertising and the Social Roots of the Consumer Culture* (New York, 1976); and William Leiss et al., *Social Communication in Advertising* (New York, 1986), for an interpretation contrary to the views presented here.

14. Lewis, *Henry Ford*, 63; Rudolph Anderson, *The Story of the American Automobile* (Washington, D.C., 1950), 96.

15. For J. L. Hudson, see J. C. Long, *Roy D. Chapin* (privately printed, 1945), 71–98; Paul Leake, *History of Detroit* (Chicago, 1912), 3:1186–90; *Detroit News*, July 5, 1912; and Chapter Four.

16. Lewis, *Henry Ford*, 63; *Floyd Clymer's Historical Motor Scrapbook* (Los Angeles, 1946), 3:86; Roy Chapin to Julian Street, May 21, 1914, Box 1, RCP. In similar vein, the Henderson Motor Car Company introduced its first model with the advertisement: "The Hendersons of Indianapolis build and guarantee it, and little more need be said." See *Saturday Night* (Toronto), December 28, 1912.

17. Quoted in Anne Jardim , *The First Henry Ford: A Study in Personality and Business Leadership* (Cambridge, Mass., 1970), 26.

18. W. C. Runciman, ed., *Max Weber: Selections in Translation* (Cambridge, 1978), 52–54.

19. They were snobs in the sense of Margaret Moore Goode's definition of snobbery as "the inability to think objectively about class distinctions." The word is not intended as a slur, for as the Duke of Bedford observed, "not to be snobbish means not to be human." See M. M. Goode, *Three Satirists of Snobbery* (Hamburg, 1939), 26; John, Duke of Bedford, *The Duke of Bedford's Book of Snobs* (London, 1965), 8.

20. U.S. Board of Tax Appeals, Estate of John F. Dodge et al. v. Commissioner of Internal Revenue, Transcript of Hearings, Washington, D .C., January–February 1927, 3: 1281.

21. Chris Sinsabaugh, *Who, Me? Forty Years of Automobile History* (Detroit, 1940), 89 .

22. Rae, "Why Michigan," 440. The concept of a historical paradigm is explained by Thomas Kuhn, *The Structure of Scientific Revolutions* (Chicago, 1962), and Anthony F. C. Wallace, *Rockdale* (New York, 1980), app. Many of the pertinent elite studies are cited in Donald F. Davis, "The Price of Conspicuous Production: The Detroit Elite and the Automobile Industry, 1900–1933," *Journal of Social History* 16 (November 1982): 21–46.

23. Suzanne Keller, *Beyond the Ruling Class: Strategic Elites in Modern Society* (New York, 1963), 237–41.

24. E. E. Hagan, *The Economics of Development* (Homewood, Ill., 1980), 224–25. See also Homer G. Barnett, *Innovation: The Basis of Cultural Change* (New York, 1953), 378–410; Everett M. Rogers, *The Diffusion of Innovation* (New York, 1962), 193–207; Morris Ginsberg, "Social Change," *British Journal of Sociology* 9 (September 1958): 205–29.

25. William B. Stout, *So Away I Went!* (Indianapolis, Ind., 1951), 105 (emphasis added).

Chapter One

1. James Laux et al., *The Automobile Revolution* (Chapel Hill, N.C., 1982), 112; Ralph Epstein, *The Automobile Industry* (1928; rpt. Chicago, 1968); Lawrence Seltzer, *A Financial History of the Automobile Industry* (Boston, 1928).

2. Seltzer, *Financial History*, 19–21; Epstein, *Automobile Industry*, 37–40, 224.

3. Seltzer, *Financial History*, 21; Epstein, *Automobile Industry*, 39, 258–65.

4. John B. Rae, "The Engineer-Entrepreneur in the American Automobile Industry," *Explorations in Entrepreneurial History* 8 (October 1955): 1–2; Rae, *American Automobile Manufacturers* (Philadelphia, 1959), 203; Rae, *The American Automobile Industry* (Boston, 1984), 14, 17, 28.

5. John B. Rae, "Why Michigan?" in David L. Lewis and Laurence Goldstein, eds., *The Automobile and American Culture* (Ann Arbor, Mich., 1983), 3-5; Rae, *American Automobile Industry*, 29.

6. George S. May, *A Most Unique Machine: The Michigan Origins of the American Automobile Industry* (Grand Rapids, Mich., 1975), 82, 331. See also May, *R. E. Olds, Auto Industry Pioneer* (Grand Rapids, Mich., 1977).

7. James J. Flink, *The Car Culture* (Cambridge, Mass., 1975), 42–43.

8. For petroleum economics in the 1860s, see Harold F. Williamson and Arnold F. Daum, *The American Petroleum Industry: The Age of Illumination, 1859–1899* (Evanston, Ill., 1959), 212. For important examples of the radical (typically Marxist) approach to technology, see Harry Braverman, *Labor and Monopoly Capital: The Degradation of Work in the Twentieth Century* (New York, 1974); Richard Edwards, *Contested Terrain* (New York, 1979); David F. Noble, *Forces of Production: A Social History of Industrial Automation* (New York, 1984); Dan Clawson, *Bureaucracy and the Labor Process: The Transformation of U.S. Industry, 1860–1920* (New York, 1980); Michael Burawoy, *The Politics of Production* (London, 1985). For the concept of a democratic technology, see Eugene S. Ferguson, "The American-ness of American Technology," *Technology and Culture* 20 (January 1979): 3–24; Hugo A. Meier, "Technology and Democracy, 1800–1860," *Mississippi Valley Historical Review* 43 (1957): 618–40; John A. Kouwhoven, *Made in America: The Arts in Modern Civilization* (Newton Center, Mass., 1948); John E.

Kasson, *Civilizing the Machine: Technology and Republican Values in America, 1776–1900* (New York, 1976).

9. Average capitalization was calculated from a sample comprising the following companies: Brush Engine Association, Buick, Detroit Automobile, Detroit Motor Car, E-M-F, Ford, Hudson, Hupp, King, Maxwell-Briscoe, Metzger, Olds, Owen, Packard, Regal, Reo, Suburban, Thomas-Detroit. For the attitude of bankers, see Robert P. Thomas, "Business Failures in the Automobile Industry, 1895–1910," *Papers Presented at the Annual Business History Conference* (Kent, Ohio, 1965), 11; Franklin Escher, "The Auto and the Bond Market," *Bankers' Magazine* 81 (October 1910): 580ff; "Bond Houses Now in Open Enmity," *Motor World* 24 (July 7, 1910): 26; C. B. Glasscock, *The Gasoline Age* (New York, 1937), 45–49; Anne Jardim, *The First Henry Ford: A Study in Personality and Business Leadership* (Cambridge, Mass., 1970), 9; Benjamin Briscoe, "The Inside Story of General Motors," pt. 1, *Detroit Saturday Night*, January 15, 1921; Arthur Pound, *The Turning Wheel: The Story of General Motors through Twenty-Five Years, 1908–1933* (Garden City, N.Y., 1934), chap. 8.

10. John N. Ingham, *The Iron Barons: A Social Analysis of an American Elite, 1874–1965* (Westport, Conn., 1978), 21.

11. I wish to thank David T. Drummond for creating a computer program enabling me to cross-reference fourteen variables: (1) date of birth; (2) place of birth; (3) education; (4) date of arrival in Detroit; (5) date of joining the auto industry; (6) last job held before joining the auto industry; (7) number of auto companies worked for; (8) number of years in the auto industry as of 1930; (9) highest corporate post attained as of 1930; (10) political preference; (11) religious preference; (12) career of father at the time auto leader entered the business world; (13) chief automotive concern with which auto leader was identified; (14) activity in collateral industries, such as auto parts, auto accessories, and truck manufacturing.

12. F. W. Taussig and C. S. Joslyn, *American Business Leaders: A Study in Social Origins and Social Stratification* (New York, 1932); Mabel Newcomer, *The Big Business Executive: The Factors That Made Him, 1900–1950* (New York, 1955); William E. Miller, "American Historians and the Business Elite," in William Miller, ed., *Men in Business* (Cambridge, Mass., 1952). Limiting the data to Detroit to keep them pertinent to the auto industry's role there does leave the outside possibility that auto leaders in other cities did not fit the pattern described here. Detroit's auto elite was a typical American business elite, however, and a fair approximation of the early American auto elite, inasmuch as the city dominated the industry after 1910. In 1925, eight of the twelve largest producers, including the top five, had their headquarters in Detroit; the sixth, Studebaker, did the bulk of its manufacturing there through the early 1920s and so has been included here. To offset whatever bias may have arisen in compiling the collective biography, a sample from A. N. Marquis & Co., *The Book of Detroiters* (Chicago, 1914) has also been used where feasible. The directory contains names and thumbnail biographies of approximately 3,500 local notables compiled from lists submitted to Marquis from business, professional, and civic

sources. Of the 1,369 entries selected at random for further analysis, 98 had an identifiable connection with the motor industry. See Richard Jensen, "Quantitative Collective Biography: An Application to Metropolitan Elites," in Robert Swierenga, ed., *Quantification in American History* (New York, 1970), 390–91, for a discussion of the Marquis directories.

13. U.S. Department of the Interior, Census Office, *Twelfth Census of the United States, 1900: Abstract* (Washington, D.C., 1902), 103.

14. Between 29 and 45 percent of the automotive leaders (depending on the sample) attended at least one year of college as opposed to only 18 percent of Detroit's industrial elite in 1900 (i.e., heads of manufacturing companies with 100 or more employees); see Olivier Zunz, *The Changing Face of Inequality: Urbanization, Industrial Development, and Immigrants in Detroit, 1880–1920* (Chicago, 1982), app. 6.

15. Epstein, *Automobile Industry*, 73–74.

16. Epstein arbitrarily grouped his original nine classes into three equal parts, thereby ignoring his own admonition that $100 meant far more to the purchaser of basic transportation than it did to the well-heeled buyer. His low-price category includes cars costing as much as $1,374, or four times the price of the Model T Ford. It is difficult to see any conceptual advantage in grouping such disparate makes into a single class. They were definitely, to use Epstein's own phrase, "non-competing." Table 8, in setting $675 as the boundary, puts the dividing line very close to where Allan Nevins placed it for 1914 ($625). See Epstein, *Automobile Industry*, 94; Allan Nevins, *Ford: The Times, The Man, The Company* (New York, 1954), 489.

17. Epstein, *Automobile Industry*, 336–37. Those who have read my article "The Price of Conspicuous Production: The Detroit Elite and the Automobile Industry, 1900–1933," *Journal of Social History* 16 (November 1982): 21–46 or "The Decline of the Gasoline Aristocracy: The Struggle for Supremacy in Detroit and the Automobile Industry 1896–1933" (Ph.D. diss., Harvard University, 1976), will find that I have used different criteria here for categorizing companies. Though most firms were quite consistent in their social origins, price and model policies, and social attitudes (that is, they were always lower, middle, or upper class no matter what the index), in some firms—most notably Dodge, Cadillac (before 1909), and Saxon— designation became, as readers have advised me, arbitrary. For example, Dodge was treated as a lower-class firm, even though its prices were strictly middle class; Cadillac was treated as an upper-class firm, even though its prices were at first (as in 1907) more modest. In both cases, noneconomic criteria were being used to characterize the companies. In this book the quantitative analysis is based on a single criterion—the price of the cheapest standard model—in order to reduce to a minimum any subjectivity that might have crept into earlier analyses. Hence, on the basis of their pricing policies, Saxon and Dodge have been reassigned. Cadillac has been dropped and the Olds Motor Works not included because both firms radically changed their model policies, and thus their class identities. The table is clearly not comprehensive (there were, after all, forty-three Detroit automobile companies in 1913), but most of the omissions were much too ephem-

eral to be characterized. It is worth noting that companies could rarely be judged by their first or second seasons, because they were often selling a borrowed design; their true intentions—and biases—emerged with the first models conceived after they became going concerns.

18. U.S. Department of Commerce, Bureau of the Census, *Historical Statistics of the United States, Colonial Times to 1957* (Washington, D.C., 1961), ser. D72–122.

Chapter Two

1. U.S. Department of the Interior, Census Office, *Twelfth Census of the United States, 1900: Abstract* (Washington, D.C., 1902), 100; Webb Waldron, "Where is America Going? Industrial Conditions in Detroit," *Century* 100 (May 1920): 58; Thomas J. Ticknor, "Motor City: The Impact of the Automobile Industry upon Detroit, 1900–1975" (Ph.D. diss., University of Michigan, 1978), 43–45, 99; Beverly Duncan and Stanley Lieberson, *Metropolis and Region in Transition* (Beverly Hills, Calif., 1970), 115; Judith Krass, "Detroit as a Center of Commerce, 1880–1900" (M.A. thesis, Wayne State University, 1965), 86; Melvin Holli, "The Impact of Automobile Manufacturing upon Detroit," *Detroit in Perspective* 2 (Spring 1976): 177–78. See also Melvin Holli, "Before the Car: Nineteenth-Century Detroit's Transformation from a Commercial to an Industrial City," *Michigan History* 64 (March–April 1980): 33–39; Almon E. Parkins, *The Historical Geography of Detroit* (Lansing, Mich., 1918), 170–308; Robert B. Ross and George B. Catlin, *Landmarks of Wayne County and Detroit* (Detroit, 1898), 25–442, 499–506, 560–66; C. M. Burton, *The City of Detroit, Michigan, 1701–1922* (Detroit, 1922), 1:485–529, 682–99; Silas Farmer, *The History of Detroit and Michigan* (Detroit, 1884), 735–936; Wayne E. Roock, "The Automobile Age in the Making: Industrial Detroit, 1880–1900" (M.A. thesis, Wayne State University, 1964); Bayrd Still, "Patterns of Mid-Nineteenth-Century Urbanization in the Middle West," in Paul Kramer and Frederick Holborn, eds., *The City in American Life* (New York, 1970), 152–71; James E. Vance, Jr., *The Merchant's World: The Geography of Wholesaling* (Englewood Cliffs, N.J., 92–95; Harold H. McCarty, *The Geographic Basis of American Life* (New York, 1940), 644.

2. For automotive developments before 1896, see James Laux et al., *The Automobile Revolution* (Chapel Hill, N.C., 1982), 3–13; John B. Rae, *The American Automobile: A Brief History* (Chicago, 1965), 1–36; Allan Nevins, *Ford: The Times, The Man, The Company* (New York, 1954), 59–70, 93–103, 125–57; George S. May, *A Most Unique Machine: The Michigan Origins of the American Automobile Industry* (Grand Rapids, Mich., 1975), 15–95. According to Oliver Barthel, Ford used an article from the January 9, 1896, issue of the *American Machinist* to design his original engine. See his *Reminiscences*, unpublished bound typescript, FA.

3. U.S. Department of the Interior, Census Office, *Twelfth Census of the United States, 1900: Manufactures*, (Washington, D.C., 1902), 2:427–31; 4:310–19. The urban and industrial network of the United States around

the turn of the century is discussed in Duncan and Lieberson, *Metropolis and Region*, chaps. 4–7; Mark Abrahamson and Michael A. DuBick, "Patterns of Urban Dominance: The U.S. in 1890," *American Sociological Review* 42 (October 1977): 756–68; J. R. Borchert, "American Metropolitan Evolution," *Geographical Review* 57 (1967): 301–32; Allan R. Pred, *The Spatial Dynamics of U.S. Urban-Industrial Growth, 1800–1914: Interpretive and Theoretical Essays* (Cambridge, Mass., 1966); Michael P. Conzen, "The Maturing Urban System in the United States, 1840–1910," *Annals of the Association of American Geographers* 67 (1977): 88–108.

4. *Twelfth Census: Manufactures*, 2:412–31; U.S. Department of Commerce, Bureau of the Census, *Census of Manufactures, 1904* (Washington, D.C., 1905), 24–27; Automobile Quarterly, *The American Car since 1775* (New York, 1971), 139; George Kirkham Jarvis, "The Diffusion of the Automobile in the United States: 1865–1929" (Ph.D. diss., University of Michigan, 1972), 64–71; John B. Rae, "Why Michigan?" in David L. Lewis and Laurence Goldstein, eds., *The Automobile and American Culture* (Ann Arbor, Mich., 1983), 1–9. In 1900, Michigan ranked fourth among states in the production of wagons and carriages (by value), third in steam railroad cars, eighth in bicycles.

5. Parkins, *Historical Geography* 298–300; Willis Dunbar, *Michigan: A History of the Wolverine State* (Grand Rapids, Mich., 1965), 504–5; Jarvis, "Diffusion of the Automobile," 66–73.

6. Jarvis, "Diffusion of the Automobile," 66, 71.

7. Ibid., 71–72; Robert P. Thomas, "Business Failures in the Automobile Industry, 1895–1910," in *Papers Presented at the Annual Business History Conference* (Kent, Ohio, 1965), 20.

8. For the early model history at Ford and Cadillac see Nevins, *Ford: The Times*, chaps. 11–12; Maurice D. Hendry, *Cadillac: Standard of the World* (New York, 1973).

9. *Horseless Age* 9 (January 1, 1902): 2; Thomas, "Business Failures," 20–21; Hendry, *Cadillac*, 37.

10. Jane Jacobs, *Cities and the Wealth of Nations: Principles of Economic Life* (New York, 1984), chap. 10.

11. E. D. Kennedy, *The Automobile Industry* (New York, 1941), 11–15; Nevins, *Ford: The Times*, 194–98; Robert P. Thomas, "Automobile Industry and Tycoon," 146–47; James J. Flink, *America Adopts the Automobile, 1895–1910* (Cambridge, Mass., 1970), 56–58; Association of Licensed Automobile Manufacturers (ALAM), *Handbook of Gasoline Automobiles, 1904–1906* (rpt. New York, 1969).

12. Lawrence Seltzer, *A Financial History of the Automobile Industry* (Boston, 1928), 248–52.

13. Olivier Zunz, *The Changing Face of Inequality: Urbanization, Industrial Development, and Immigrants in Detroit, 1880–1920* (Chicago, 1982), app. 6; Sidney Ratner, ed., *New Light on the History of Great American Fortunes* (New York, 1953), 99. Auto leaders on Zunz's list of 115 (in their own right): W. C. Anderson (Detroit Electric), G. H. Barbour (E-M-F), W. T. Barbour (Northern), J. Boyer (Cadillac), B. Briscoe (Buick), T. D. Buhl (Maxwell-

Briscoe), D. D. Buick (Buick), H. Carharrt (Carharrt), E. W. Clark (GM), J. S. Gray (Ford), C. H. Haberkorn (Universal Truck), F. Hecker (Detroit Auto), W. C. McMillan (Detroit Auto), W. H. Miller (Lozier), F. T. Moran (Welch), M. J. Murphy (GM), T. H. Newberry (Packard), R. E. Olds (Olds), Carl Reese (Herreshoff), G. H. Russel (Olds). Industrialists whose sons or sons-in-law invested in the industry: W. Chittenden (E-M-F), H. C. Colburn (R-C-H), G. DuCharme (Packard), C. F. Hammond (Federal Truck), H. C. Hodges (Paige), James McMillan (Packard), George Peck (Detroit Horseless Carriage), J. Scripps (Scripps-Booth), O. Scotten (Regal). Auto leaders listed in Ratner as millionaires in 1902: E. H. Butler (Chalmers), F. J. Hecker (Detroit Auto), H. B. Joy (Packard), R. P. Joy (Packard), A. E. F. White (Cadillac), (sixth, Hiram Walker was a founder of Ford of Canada but is not counted here). Millionaires whose sons or sons-in-law (or grandson in one instance) became automotive leaders: R. A. Alger, Sr. (Packard), C. H. Buhl (Maxwell-Briscoe), T. H. Eaton (Imperial), D. M. Ferry, Sr. (Packard), G. H. Hammond (Federal Truck), A. M. Henry (Lozier), J. F. Joy (Packard), T. McGraw (Commerce), J. McMillan (Packard), W. B. Moran (Welch), S. J. Murphy (Cadillac), J. S. Newberry, Sr. (Packard), Francis Palms (Wayne, E-M-F), Oren Scotten (Regal), David Whitney (Lozier).

14. *Michigan Manufacturer* 6 (June 18, 1910): 21; Zunz, *Changing Face*, 212–13. For the political and business careers of McMillan and Newberry, see also Milton R. Palmer, ed., *Detroit—the Marvel City* (Detroit, 1922), 75; Paul Leake, *History of Detroit* (Chicago, 1912), 2:458–61; George B. Catlin, *The Story of Detroit* (Detroit, 1923), 571–75; Charles Moore, "James M'Millan, United States Senator from Michigan," *Michigan Historical Collections* 39 (1915): 173–86; Marie Heyda, "Senator James McMillan and the Flowering of the Spoils System," *Michigan History* 54 (Fall 1970): 186–88; David J. Rothman, *Politics and Power: The United States Senate, 1869–1901* (Cambridge, Mass., 1966), 164–66, 210; Arthur C. Millspaugh, "Party Organization and Machinery in Michigan since 1890," *Johns Hopkins University Studies in Historical and Political Science* 25 (1917); Stephen Sarasohn and Vera Sarasohn, *Political Party Patterns in Michigan* (Detroit, 1957), 3–17.

15. John C. Lodge, *I Remember Detroit* (Detroit, 1949), 128; *Detroiter* 8 (January 15, 1917): 6; Burton, *City of Detroit*, 1:537–38; Don Lochbiler, *Detroit's Coming of Age, 1873–1973* (Detroit, 1973), chap. 26; Charles Moore, *History of Michigan* (Chicago, 1915), 3:1354, 1484–85; *Detroit News*, September 26, 1919; Leake, *History of Detroit*, 3:1008–14.

16. Charles Moore, *History of Michigan* (Chicago, 1912), 2:688–91, 1127; *Detroit Saturday Night*, May 22, 1915, p. 13; Henry Taylor & Co., *Compendium of History and Biography of the City of Detroit and Wayne County, Michigan* (Chicago, 1909), 189: Leake, *History of Detroit*, 1:274; 2:816; 3:872; "The Detroit Telephone Company," *Electrical Engineer* 29 (June 26, 1897): 838–45; Melvin Holli, *Reform in Detroit: Hazen S. Pingree and Urban Politics* (New York, 1969), 86–100; Catlin, *Story of Detroit*, 598–608; Ross and Catlin, *Landmarks*, 726–30; Burton, *City of Detroit*, 1:386–87, 599; 2:144.

17. Women's Bi-Centenary, *Souvenir, Detroit, 1701–1901* (Detroit, 1901),

143; Fred Carlisle, comp., *Chronography of Notable Events in the History of the Northwest Territory and Wayne County* (Detroit, 1890), 442; Leake, *History of Detroit*, 2:575–79.

18. Holli, *Reform in Detroit*, 53–54; Catlin, *Story of Detroit*, 622; Burton, *City of Detroit*, 4:5.

19. Ross and Catlin, *Landmarks*, 626, 640–41, 666–98, 780–81; Burton, *City of Detroit*, 1:548–49; 3:556; Farmer, *History of Detroit*, 814–17.

20. For Detroit's banks around 1900, see Walter L. Dunham, *Banking and Industry in Michigan* (Detroit, 1929), 66–108; Emory Wendell, ed., *Wendell's History of Banking and Banks and Bankers of Michigan* (Detroit, 1901); Sidney Glazer, *Detroit: A Study of Urban Development* (Detroit, 1965), 52; and Michigan Bureau of Labor and Industrial Statistics, *Annual Reports* (Lansing, 1900–1903).

21. Holli, "Before the Car," 38; Lochbiler, *Coming of Age*, 222–38; Burton, *City of Detroit*, 3:266, 274; Leake, *History of Detroit*, 3:1008–14, 1057–59; *Michigan Manufacturer* 32 (November 10, 1923): 26; Herbert V. Book, *Family Records* (Detroit, 1963). In 1917 the Palms-Book estate was appraised at $15 million by the People's State Bank. See Combined Balance Sheet, September 30, 1917, Box 308, TNP.

22. Duncan and Lieberson, *Metropolis and Region*, chap. 5.

23. Silas Farmer, *All about Detroit* (Detroit, 1899), 42; Zunz, *Changing Face*, 97–100.

24. Holli, "The Impact," 178.

25. For Olds, see George S. May, *R. E. Olds, Auto Industry Pioneer* (Grand Rapids, Mich., 1977), chaps. 3–7; Glenn Niemeyer, *The Automotive Career of Ransom E. Olds* (East Lansing, Mich., 1963), 16–43; Duane Yarnell, *Auto Pioneering* (New York, 1949).

26. May, *R. E. Olds*, 109; Burton, *City of Detroit*, 4:647; Samuel L. Smith, "Pre-Historic and Modern Copper Mines of Lake Superior," *Michigan Historical Collections* 39 (1915): 137; May, *Unique Machine*, 59–65.

27. May, *R. E. Olds*, 109; Niemeyer, *Olds*, 16–21; May, *Unique Machine*, 66–70; F. L. Smith, *Motoring Down a Quarter of a Century* (Detroit, 1928), 16, 21; Richard Crabb, *Birth of a Giant: The Men and Incidents That Gave America the Motorcar* (Philadelphia, 1969), 50; Yarnell, *Pioneering*, 65–68.

28. Niemeyer, *Olds*, 27–28; May, *Unique Machine*, 70–71; *Detroit Saturday Night*, May 22, 1915; Burton, *City of Detroit*, 5:5; Ross and Catlin, *Landmarks*, 662–63; Moore, *History of Michigan*, 2:691, 1043–44, 1127.

29. B. C. Forbes and O. D. Foster, *Automotive Giants of America* (New York, 1926), 230–31; May, *Unique Machine*, 116; Niemeyer, *Olds*, 30–31; Automobile Quarterly, *Car since 1775*, 138–39.

30. May, *R. E. Olds*, 127, 142.

31. May, *Unique Machine*, 115–39; Niemeyer, *Olds*, 34–36, 41–43; Smith, *Motoring*, 17; *Horseless Age* 8 (April 3, 1901): 20; Crabb, *Birth of a Giant*, 56; *Cycle and Automobile Trade Journal* 14 (December 1909): 124–25.

32. May, *R. E. Olds*, 212–17.

33. Ibid., 262–65, 282–83.

34. Ibid., 217, 239, 282–83; May, *Unique Machine*, 316.

35. Seltzer, *Financial History*, 154–56; May, *Unique Machine*, 316; Crabb, *Birth of a Giant*, 246.

36. Christy Borth, "Automotive Center of the World," *Inside Michigan* 4 (March 1954): 53; Smith, *Motoring*, 18; Niemeyer, *Olds*, 52; James R. Doolittle, *The Romance of the Automobile Industry* (New York, 1916), 44; Kennedy, *Automobile Industry*, 22.

37. *Lehigh Alumni Bulletin* 14 (January 1927); John Parker, "A History of the Packard Motor Car Company from 1899 to 1929" (M.A. thesis, Wayne State University, 1949), 3–9; Minutes, First Meeting of the Incorporators of Ohio Automobile Company, October 24, 1900, scp; Arthur W. Einstein, Jr., "The Advertising of the Packard Motor Car Company, 1899–1956" (M.A. thesis, Michigan State University, 1959), 17; *Horseless Age*, May 16, 1900, p. 11; Warren Packard, typed biography of James Packard, dated 1927, copy in Packard Biography File, nahc.

38. Leake, *History of Detroit*, 3:1021–25; Ross and Catlin, *Landmarks*, 504–5; Palmer, *Detroit*, 57; Stephen Gilchrist, "Henry Bourne Joy," *Detroit Saturday Night*, November 14, 1936, p. 6; Henry B. Joy, Biographical Sketches, Box 1, hjp.

39. *Detroit News*, August 1, 1910; Theodore F. MacManus and Norman Beasley, *Men, Money, and Motors* (New York, 1929), 49; "Notes from the Minute Book of the Ohio Automobile Company," typescript, Packard Company File, nahc.

40. "Notes from the Minute Book of the Ohio Automobile Company"; H. B. Joy to James Packard, January 9, 1903, and Henry Joy to Truman Newberry, July 13, 1903, in Henry B. Joy Letterbooks, mhc; Minutes, Board of Directors, Packard Motor Car Company, September 8, 1903, scp; C. B. Glasscock, *The Gasoline Age* (New York, 1937), 51–53.

41. *Cycle and Automobile Trade Journal* 14 (December 1909): 128; Einstein, "Advertising of Packard," 23; Henry Joy to Richard P. Joy, September 29, 1920, Box 376, tnp.

42. List of Large Stockholders in Packard Company, September 22, 1920, Box 376, tnp.

43. Einstein, "Advertising of Packard," 9, 63; Glasscock, *Gasoline Age*, 52–53; "Packard," *Fortune* 15 (January 1937): 58, 110; A. H. Allen, "Motors, Machines, Men—and Millions," *Steel* 124 (May 9, 1949): 4.

44. *Horseless Age* 9 (April 9, 1902): iv; also Alvan Macauley to Truman Newberry, June 22, 1922; Truman Newberry to R. P. Joy, January 10, 1918; R. P. Joy to Truman Newberry, January 29, 1919, in Boxes 375 and 378, tnp.

45. R. P. Joy to Henry Bodman, February 7, 1921, Box 377, tnp.

46. Pamphlet in Alvan Macauley Biography File, nahc.

47. May, *Unique Machine*, 96–102; Sydney Olson, *Young Henry Ford* (Detroit, 1963), 89, 103, 109–17; Nevins, *Ford: The Times*, 170–72; A. N. Marquis & Co., *The Book of Detroiters* (Chicago, 1908), 62, 278, 284; *Detroit Free Press*, February 14, 1924; Taylor, *Compendium*, 500–501; *Detroiter* 16 (September 14, 1925): 6.

48. Olson, *Young Henry Ford*, 118, 121–25; Nevins, *Ford: The Times*, 177–85, 190–91; *Detroit Journal*, November 30, 1901.

49. *Detroit Free Press*, December 1, 1901; *Detroit Journal*, November 30, 1901; Olson, *Young Henry Ford*, 125; May, *Unique Machine*, 240–43; Barthel, *Reminiscences*, 24–27, FA; Nevins, *Ford: The Times*, 206; William Simonds, *Henry Ford, A Biography* (London, 1946), 58–59.

50. May, *Unique Machine*, 243–45; Frederick Strauss, *Reminiscences*, 36, FA; Nevins, *Ford: The Times*, 211–19; Anne Jardim, *The First Henry Ford: A Study in Personality and Business Leadership* (Cambridge, Mass., 1970), 44–47.

51. Olson, *Young Henry Ford*, 111; Nevins, *Ford: The Times*, 211–19; Barthel, *Reminiscences*, 28–36, FA; Strauss, *Reminiscences*, 36, 62–64, FA; Jardim, *First Henry Ford*, 43–47.

52. Mrs. Wilfred Leland, *Master of Precision: Henry Leland* (Detroit, 1966), 66–68; Wilfred Leland, typewritten history of Cadillac, Box 3, LP; Barthel, *Reminiscences*, 38–40, FA; Niemeyer, *Olds*, 39–40; Zunz, *Changing Face*, app. 6.

53. Leland, history of Cadillac; undated list of stockholders (presumably 1905), both in LP.

54. "Cadillac," *Antique Automobile* 20 (Spring 1956): 23–24; ALAM, *Handbook, 1904–1906*; Automobile Quarterly, *Cars since 1775*, 138–39; Ed Cray, *Chrome Colossus: General Motors and Its Times* (New York, 1980), 80; Maurice D. Hendry, *Cadillac: Standard of the World* (New York, 1973), 41.

55. Bernard Weisberger, *The Dream Maker: William C. Durant, Founder of General Motors* (Boston, 1979), 134–37; Lawrence Gustin, *Billy Durant: Creator of General Motors* (Grand Rapids, Mich., 1973), 118–22; Leland, *Master of Precision*, 93–97; Seltzer, *Financial History*, 89–99. The stockholders of Cadillac at the time of the sale to General Motors were Lem Bowen with 2,840 shares; Clarence A. Black, 2,840; W. H. Murphy, 3,055; Wilfred Leland, 1,340; Henry Leland, 1,340; Albert White, 1,607; E. A. Leonard, 179; E. E. Sweet (company engineer), 107; Harry Pettee, 50; A. C. Leonard, 35; and the Union Trust (as trustee), 1,607. See Alfred P. Sloan, Jr., *My Years with General Motors* (New York, 1963), 5.

56. *Detroit News*, June 19, 1917; Leland, *Master of Precision*, 97; Cycle and Automobile Trade Journal 14 (August 1, 1909), 69.

57. *Detroit News*, June 19, 1917.

58. Leland, *Master of Precision*, 169; Henry Leland, Address to the Society of Automobile Engineers, June 24, 1914, Box 3, LP.

59. Kennedy, *Automobile Industry*, 23; Leland, *Master of Precision*, chaps. 1–3; Leake, *History of Detroit*, 3:1064–66; Maurice D. Hendry, "Henry Leland," in Ronald Barker and Anthony Harding, eds., *Automobile Design: Great Designers and Their Work* (Newton Abbot, Eng., 1970), 87–88; Leland, history of Cadillac, LP; Henry Leland to John Bourne, February 25, 1926, Box 3, LP; Q. David Bowers, ed., *Early American Car Advertisements* (New York, 1966), 30; *Cadillac Craftsman*, Silver Anniversary issue,

July 1926, p. 12; John B. Rae, *American Automobile Manufacturers* (Philadelphia, 1959), 35.

60. *Detroit News*, January 15, 1911; *Cadillac Craftsman*, July 1926, p. 7; "The Automobile Industry in Michigan," *Michigan History Magazine* 8 (July 1924): 223.

61. Leland, *Master of Precision*, 93; "Cadillac," 23; Einstein, "Advertising of Packard," 33. For Cadillac prices 1912–1920, see Joseph J. Schroeder, ed., *The Wonderful World of Automobiles, 1895–1930* (Chicago, 1971), 279–86.

Chapter Three

1. *Detroit Saturday Night*, January 22, 1910; Lawrence Seltzer, *A Financial History of the Automobile Industry* (Boston, 1928), 76. It is impossible to determine exactly how many companies entered the Detroit automobile industry before World War I: definitions vary, and some of the entrants will always remain shadowy figures. Any number, then, is—no matter how precise it appears—an approximation. My statistics in Chapters Three and Four are derived from Automobile Manufacturers Association, *Automobiles of America* (Detroit, 1968), chap. 5; and Automobile Quarterly, *The American Car since 1775* (New York, 1971), chap. 9, plus various trade journals and the local press.

2. *Cycle and Automobile Trade Journal* 14 (December 1909): 122; Oliver Barthel, *Reminiscences*, 52, FA; Frank B. Woodford, *We Never Drive Alone: The Story of the Automobile Club of Michigan* (Detroit, 1958), 15.

3. *Detroit News*, January 20, 1907; *Automobile* 17 (October 31, 1907): 646–47.

4. Although the company was put together in 1903 and took orders at auto shows that year, actual production did not begin until 1904. For a list of Wayne stockholders in 1906, see Box 1, RCP. For further information on the company's origins, see *Cycle and Automobile Trade Journal* 14 (December 1909): 123–24; John B. Rae, *American Automobile Manufacturers* (Philadelphia, 1959), 51. Max Wollering, who joined Wayne in 1908 as production manager, claimed that Barney Everitt had been one of the company's organizers, but other evidence suggests that Everitt did not join Wayne until 1907. See Max Wollering, *Reminiscences*, 33, 39–42, FA; *Automobile* 17 (September 19, 1907): 408, and 17 (October 24, 1907): 581–82; Minutes, Board of Directors, E-M-F Company, April 29, 1909, SCP; C. B. Glasscock, *The Gasoline Age* (New York, 1937), 94; Allan Nevins, *Ford: The Times, The Man, The Company* (New York, 1954), 365.

5. Minutes, Board of Directors, E-M-F Company, April 29, 1909, SCP.

6. *Horseless Age* 23 (October 7, 1908): 510; Minutes, Board of Directors, E-M-F Company, October 2, 1908, SCP. In his letter of April 29, 1909, to the board, Flanders related that the purchase of Northern had been "regarded by the E-M-F directors, as a rather poor business proposition" but that it had nonetheless been bought because of the "earnest solicitation" of William Metzger; see Minutes, E-M-F Company, April 29, 1909, SCP. Despite the directors' original misgivings, the deposition of Northern's

assets and the last-minute sales of Northern autos and parts brought E-M-F a net profit of $50,000.

7. Albert R. Erskine, *History of the Studebaker Corporation* (Chicago, 1918), 45; Minutes, Special Meeting of E-M-F Stockholders, September 17, 1908, SCP. For the origins of the agreement with Studebaker, see Minutes, Board of Directors, E-M-F, April 29, 1909, for attached letters: Walter Flanders to B. F. Everitt et al., July 29, 1908, and Walter Flanders to William Metzger, July 30, 1908. In his debate with the rest of the Board in April 1909, Flanders reminded them of the company's shaky start: "Why should the directors of the E.M.F. Company have any grounds for believing that this company—with its limited working capital, with a factory building on its hands, without any equipment, and obliged to erect practically a duplicate factory before complete cars could be manufactured—could produce as many automobiles per day . . . as the Cadillac Company could with a completely equipped factory."

8. Minutes, Board of Directors, E-M-F, March 8, 1909; Balance Sheet as of December 31, 1909, SCP.

9. F. S. Fish to Walter Flanders, April 8, 1909, letter attached to Minutes, Board of Directors, E-M-F, April 29, 1909, SCP; James J. Flink, *America Adopts the Automobile, 1895–1910* (Cambridge, Mass., 1970), 317.

10. Minutes, Board of Directors, E-M-F, December 31, 1909, SCP; Wollering, *Reminiscences*, 42, FA. Traditional accounts (e.g., Glasscock, *Gasoline Age*, 187–89) incorrectly state that Studebaker abrogated the contract.

11. Wollering, *Reminiscences*, 42, FA; *Detroit News*, March 9, 1910. Studebaker bought 63,528 shares at $60 per share, or $3.8 million.

12. Minutes, Board of Directors, E-M-F, October 12, 1909, SCP.

13. Minutes, Board of Directors, August 4, 1908, and July 13, 1909, E-M-F, SCP; Automobile Quarterly, *Car since 1775*, 139.

14. J. W. Leonard, *The Industries of Detroit* (Detroit, 1887), 198; *Motor World*, June 11, 1908, p. 343, clipping in Paige-Detroit File, NAHC; *Horseless Age* 12 (November 18, 1903): 539, and 20 (July 27, 1907): 320; *Detroit News*, November 15, 1933; *Motor Age* 6 (December 29, 1904): 15; Ed Cray, *Chrome Colossus: General Motors and Its Times* (New York, 1980), 76.

15. Bernard Weisberger, *The Dream Maker: William C. Durant, Founder of General Motors* (Boston, 1979), 73–81, 116–39; Olivier Zunz, *The Changing Face of Inequality: Urbanization, Industrial Development, and Immigrants in Detroit, 1880–1920* (Chicago, 1982), 442; Benjamin Briscoe, "The Inside Story of General Motors," pt. 2, *Detroit Saturday Night*, January 22, 1921, p. 4; Alfred Reeves, "Benjamin Briscoe, 1867–1945," *Old Timers News* 3 (July 1945): 31; Glasscock, *Gasoline Age*, 98.

16. Briscoe, "Inside Story," pt. 2, January 22, 1921, p. 4; Rae, *American Automobile Manufacturers*, 52; C. M. Burton, *The City of Detroit, Michigan, 1701–1922* (Detroit, 1922), 4:261.

17. *Detroit News*, October 3, 1909; Eugene W. Lewis, *Motor Memories* (Detroit, 1947), 125; "The Automotive Industry in Michigan," *Michigan History Magazine* 8 (July 1924): 255–56; *Horseless Age* 24 (October 6, 1909):

385; Joseph J. Schroeder, Jr., *The Wonderful World of Automobiles, 1895–1930* (Chicago, 1971), 279–86; *Motor World* (June 11, 1908): 343, clipping in Paige-Detroit File, NAHC; *Motor Age* 6 (December 29, 1904): 15.

18. *Detroit Journal*, April 20, 1916; *Detroit News*, August 24, 1907, January 17, 1908, and October 3, 1909; Charles Moore, *History of Michigan* (Chicago, 1915), 2:722, 728, 1080–81, and 3:1477–79; "Charles Beecher Warren," typescript biography in Charles B. Warren Papers, BHC; Burton, *City of Detroit*, 3:78, 322, 491, and 5:261–62; Paul Leake, *History of Detroit* (Chicago, 1912), 2:498–500, 508–10; Robert B. Ross and George B. Catlin, *Landmarks of Wayne County and Detroit* (Detroit, 1898), 726–30; *National Cyclopaedia of American Biography* (Ann Arbor, Mich., 1967), 39: 72; *New York Times*, June 16, 1933; C. M. Burton et al., *History of Wayne County and the City of Detroit, Michigan* (Detroit, 1930), 5:484–85; Henry Taylor & Co., *Compendium of History and Biography of the City of Detroit and Wayne County, Michigan* (Chicago, 1909), 194–95; *Cycle and Automobile Trade Journal* 14 (December 1909): 155.

19. "1911–1912 Reorganization," typescript, JPP; James R. Doolittle, *The Romance of the Automobile Industry* (New York, 1916), 43; *Horseless Age*, January 8, 1911, p. 155; *Automobile*, February 8, 1917, p. 311; *Automotive Industries*, April 16, 1922, p. 436 (last three are clippings in Paige-Detroit Motor Car Co. File, NAHC); *Detroit Saturday Night*, May 17, 1913; Q. David Bowers, ed., *Early American Car Advertisements* (New York, 1966), 148; *Floyd Clymer's Historical Motor Scrapbook* (Los Angeles, 1946), 3:71; Automobile Quarterly, *Car since 1775*, 141.

20. *Detroit News*, January 15, 1911. See also Schroeder, *Wonderful World*, 124.

21. Clipping from *Plattsburgh Republican*, May 30, 1908, JPP; *Detroit Free Press*, December 3, 1911; O.E.D. to McGuire, April 20, 1909, JPP; John G. Perrin to H. A. Lozier, April 20, 1909, JPP; *Detroit Journal*, January 24, 1910. For a complete list of the Lozier investors, consult *Detroit News*, January 25, 1910.

22. *Detroit Free Press*, June 6, 1911; *Horseless Age* 30 (July 31, 1912): 17; "1911–1912 Reorganization," JPP; *Automobile*, March 13, 1913, and *Motor Age*, September 29, 1914, clippings in Lozier Motor Co. File, NAHC. For the reasons behind Lozier's forced receivership, see "To the Stockholders of Lozier Motor Company," a printed broadside, September 29, 1914, JPP; *Automotive Industries*, May 8, 1923; p. 588; Automobile Quarterly, *Car since 1775*, 140.

23. Automobile Quarterly, *Car since 1775*, 138–41.

24. See Lawrence Gustin, *Billy Durant: Creator of General Motors* (Grand Rapids, Mich., 1973).

25. Ross and Catlin, *Landmarks*, 542–44, 726–30; Moore, *History of Michigan*, 2:1207–09; *Detroit News*, February 1 and October 19, 1912; Graeme O'Geran, *A History of the Detroit Street Railways* (Detroit, 1931), pts. 1–2; Harry Dahlmeier, *Public Transportation in Detroit* (Detroit, 1951); William H. Lane, *A History of Electric Service in Detroit* (Detroit, 1937); Burton, *City of Detroit*, 1:388–89.

26. "F.O.B. Detroit," *Outlook* 111 (December 22, 1915): 985; Leake, *History of Detroit*, 1:215; *Detroiter* 8 (January 15, 1917): 6.

27. U.S. Department of the Interior, Census Office, *Twelfth Census of the United States, 1900: Abstract* (Washington, D.C., 1902), 100–101.

28. Arthur Hill, "The Pine Industry in Michigan," *Publications, Michigan Political Science Association* 3 (1898): 3; Rolland Maybee, *Michigan's White Pine Era, 1840–1900* (Lansing, Mich., 1960), 11–13, 53; Maria Quinlan, "Lumbering in Michigan," *Michigan History* 62 (1978): 37–41; William B. Gates, Jr., *Michigan Copper and Boston Dollars: An Economic History of the Michigan Copper Mining Industry* (Cambridge, Mass., 1951), 203–4.

29. Walter Flanders, "Large Capital Now Needed to Embark in Automobile Business," *Detroit Saturday Night*, January 22, 1910.

30. Paul Leake noted in 1912 that Detroit's "companies are virtually closed companies in which men of means and public spirit are directors"; see Leake, *History of Detroit*, 1:215. In Chandler's terms, this paragraph is arguing that Detroit's pre-automotive elite resisted making the transition from family to managerial capitalism; see Alfred D. Chandler, Jr., *The Visible Hand: The Managerial Revolution in American Business* (Cambridge, Mass., 1977), intro.

31. *The Farmer and the Facts about His Motor Truck*, booklet published by Packard Motor Car Co., 1919, copy in Widener Library, Harvard University.

32. Max Weber quoted in E. Digby Baltzell, *The Protestant Establishment: Aristocracy and Caste in America* (New York, 1960), 19. See also Baltzell, *Philadelphia Gentlemen: The Making of a National Upper Class* (Chicago, 1958, 1971), 335–63; G. William Domhoff, *Who Rules America Now? A View for the '80s* (Englewood Cliffs, N.J., 1983), 28–32, for the role of men's clubs in the social life of the upper class, and their function in the circulation of elites.

33. The Detroit Club and the Yondotega have been named by several commentators as the most prestigious clubs in the city. See Dixon Wecter, *The Saga of American Society: A Record of Social Aspiration, 1607–1937* (New York, 1937), 147; Lucy Kavaler, *The Private World of High Society* (New York, 1960), 252; *Detroit Free Press*, April 19, 1970, and January 25, 1973. The officers of both clubs for 1900–1920 are listed in *Dau's Blue Book* for Detroit, the local social register. For the officers of the Detroit Club from its founding in 1882, see *The Detroit Club: Articles of Association, Rules and By-Laws, Officers and Members* (Detroit, 1911), copy in BHC.

34. For General Motors, see the list of stockholders in file D74-2.48, William C. Durant Papers, GMI, which is consistent with a list of preferred and debenture stockholders prepared November 28, 1919, by J. Raskob for Durant (same folder) and an incomplete list for 1916 in folder D74-2.86. In two stages in 1919 and 1926 GM bought Fisher Body from the two controlling families, the Mendelssohns and Fishers; the latter were the most important Detroit stockholders in GM in the 1920s and 1930s. Studebaker's ownership is discussed in Donald F. Davis, "Studebaker Stumbles into Detroit," *Detroit in Perspective* 4 (Fall 1979): 16–35. Less is known about Chrysler's stockholders, but for the principal investors as of

1937, see U.S. Federal Trade Commission, *Report on Motor Vehicle Industry* (Washington, D.C., 1939), 552.

Chapter Four

1. In Table 20 the entries include reorganizations (e.g., Cadillac in 1902, E-M-F in 1908) and arrivals from other cities (e.g., Studebaker in 1910). The exits include takeovers (e.g., Cadillac in 1909, E-M-F in 1910) and departures for other cities (e.g., Studebaker in 1926). The table starts in 1897 because although Olds initiated quantity production in Detroit, the Detroit Horseless Carriage Company (1897) and Pioneer (1898) preceded it—at least in terms of announced ambition. Little is known about these two companies, even whether they truly existed, but they and others equally obscure have been included for the sake of completeness—in no case, however, without having received either a "complete entry" in Automobile Quarterly's *The American Car since 1775* (New York, 1971) or third-party comment in the Detroit press. The entry and exit dates for many companies are arbitrary, since they took a long time being birthed and a long time dying.

2. George S. May, *A Most Unique Machine: The Michigan Origins of the American Automobile Industry* (Grand Rapids, Mich., 1975), 165; John B. Rae, *American Automobile Manufacturers* (Philadelphia, 1959).

3. Lawrence Seltzer, *A Financial History of the Automobile Industry* (Boston, 1928), 19–21; Ralph Epstein, *The Automobile Industry* (1928; rpt. Chicago, 1968), 136–37; Eugene W. Lewis, *Motor Memories* (Detroit, 1947), 187–88.

4. Four-fifths of the companies listed in Table 8 for 1915–1918 (see Chapter One) were concentrating on the middle price-class even though by then it accounted for less than half of the industry's sales volume. See Ralph C. Epstein, "The Rise and Fall of Firms in the Automobile Industry," *Harvard Business Review* 5 (January 1927): 157–74.

5. J. C. Long, *Roy D. Chapin* (privately printed, 1945), 39–48, 54–55. Brady came from the poorest background, being the son of a horticulturalist. He had become a newsboy at age seven, paying for his education out of his savings. See C. M. Burton, *The City of Detroit, Michigan, 1701–1922* (Detroit, 1922), 3:419. The son of a farmer, Coffin attended the University of Michigan, but his father's death forced him to drop out before graduation. His mother ran a boardinghouse for university students; it was there that Roscoe B. Jackson (see below), Chapin, and Coffin struck up their lifelong friendship. See Paul Leake, *History of Detroit* (Chicago, 1912), 3:1216–18; Long, *Chapin*, 23; *Detroit Free Press*, June 17, 1917. Less is known about Bezner; his education was limited to business college, and he began his business career at age nineteen as a stenographer for Goodrich Tire. See *Detroit Saturday Night, Notable Men of Detroit* (Detroit, 1911), 29; A. N. Marquis & Co., *The Book of Detroiters* (Chicago, 1908), 59; Articles of Association, E. R. Thomas Detroit Company, May 8, 1906, RCP; Long, *Chapin*,

52–54. E. R. Thomas received 10,000 shares; Chapin and Coffin, 1,500 each; Bezner and Brady, 1,000 each.

6. Long, *Chapin*, 62–63.

7. Samuel Crowther, *John H. Patterson, Pioneer in Industrial Welfare* (New York, 1922, 1926), 233; *Automobile Topics*, June 21, 1937, p. 292; B. C. Forbes and O. D. Foster, *Automotive Giants of America* (New York, 1926), 22–23; *Automobile* 17 (November 28, 1907): 830; A. W. Shaw, "Scientific Management in Business," *Review of Reviews* 43 (March 1911); *Horseless Age* 38 (August 15, 1916): 138; James R. Doolittle, *The Romance of the Automobile Industry* (New York, 1916), 160; C. B. Glasscock, *The Gasoline Age* (New York, 1937), 91–93; *Detroit News*, January 25, 1955; "Hugh Chalmers, a Man of Action," *Detroit Saturday Night*, January 1, 1910; Long, *Chapin*, 65–66; Rae, *American Automobile Manufacturers*, 56.

8. Chandler Bros. and Company, Special Letter re Chalmers Motor Company, October 15, 1915, CR; Long, *Chapin*, 69–91; Christy Borth, "The Saga of a Supersalesman: Hugh Chalmers," *D.A.C. News* 50 (January 1965): 35–38. The eight individuals holding these posts before 1917 (the year Chalmers lost its autonomy) were Hugh Chalmers, E. C. Morse, Lee Counselman, C. C. Hildebrand, C. A. Pfeffer, Lee Olwell, W. P. Kiser, Harry W. Ford. The latter's story was typical: originally the sports editor for a Chicago newspaper, he joined the advertising department of NCR in 1905. In 1908 he became advertising manager of Chalmers-Detroit; in 1910, corporate secretary; in 1912, assistant general manager. In 1913 he was picked to head Saxon and directed its affairs until his death in 1918. See Leake, *History of Detroit*, 3:1171–72; *Detroit Saturday Night*, March 23, 1912; Milton R. Palmer, ed., *Detroit—The Marvel City* (Detroit, 1922), 133.

9. *Floyd Clymer's Historical Motor Scrapbook* (Los Angeles, 1946), 1:94; Walter O. MacIlwain, "Chalmers-Detroit," *Bulb Horn* 28 (September–October, 1967): 4; Glasscock, *Gasoline Age*, 93; Chalmers Motor Company to J. S. Bache & Co., November 4, 1916 (printed letter), CR.

10. Automobile Quarterly, *Car since 1775*, 138–39; Annual Report, Chalmers Motor Company, June 30, 1917, CR; John Holmes, "History of Maxwell Organization" (Statistical Department, Chrysler Corporation, 1936), 18–19, copy in NAHC; J. T. Keena to Truman Newberry, August 22, 1917, Box 388, TNP; E. J. McIntyre et al., "A History of Events Leading Up to the Formation of the Chrysler Corporation" (1954), typescript, copy in Corporate Identity Office, CC; Lewis, *Motor Memories*, 71.

11. Long, *Chapin*, 69–70.

12. Harry LeDuc, "What Made J. L. Hudson Go into Auto Business in 1908," *Detroit News*, January 7, 1955; *Detroit News*, February 27, 1909; Leake, *History of Detroit*, 3:1186–90; A. N. Marquis & Co., *Who Was Who in America, 1897–1942* (Chicago, 1942), 1:624; Long, *Chapin*, 71–73, 87–91, 98.

13. Long, *Chapin*, 92, 99–101; Roy Chapin to R. B. Jackson et al., May 10, 1911, Box 1, RCP; Robert Dunn, *Labor and Automobiles* (New York, 1929), 41; Robert Cuff, *The War Industries Board* (Baltimore, Md., 1973), 17–28.

14. *Hudson Triangle* 4 (January 30, 1915); 2 (August 24, 1912); 1 (November 18, 1911); Q. David Bowers, ed., *Early American Car Advertisements* (New York, 1966), 66–68. A list of Hudson "firsts" is located in the Hudson Motor Car Co. File, NAHC.

15. R. B. Jackson to Roy Chapin, March 1, 1918, Box 5, RCP; *Automobile Quarterly, Car since 1775*, 138–41.

16. Theodore F. MacManus and Norman Beasley, *Men, Money, and Motors* (New York, 1929), 82–84; Forbes and Foster, *Automotive Giants*, 115–16; Burton, *City of Detroit*, 3:708, 758; *Detroit Saturday Night*, September 16, 1911; *Detroit Free Press*, December 8, 1931.

17. Marquis, *The Book of Detroiters* (1908), 149; *Detroit News*, November 28, 1941; C. M. Burton et al., *History of Wayne County and the City of Detroit, Michigan* (Detroit, 1930), 3:371–72.

18. Charles Moore, *History of Michigan* (Chicago, 1915), 2:1033–34; Leake, *History of Detroit*, 3:1257–58; *Detroit News*, September 7, 1910; *Detroit Free Press*, March 12, 1949; *Pipp's Weekly* 1 (May 8, 1920): 7; J. J. Kennedy to Edwin Denby, February 6, 1923, Box 1, Edwin Denby Papers, MHC.

19. Joseph J. Schroeder, Jr., *The Wonderful World of Automobiles, 1895–1930* (Chicago, 1971), 279–86; *Commercial and Financial Chronicle* 101 (November 6, 1915): 1555, and 101 (November 27, 1915): 1810.

20. *Motor World*, October 26, 1911; *Horseless Age*, August 30, 1911, p. 316; *Automobile*, September 4, 1913; *Automotive Industries*, December 12, 1931, clippings in R.C.H. Corp. File, NAHC.

21. *Commerical and Financial Chronicle* 101 (November 6, 1915): 1555; 101 (November 27, 1915): 1810; 105 (September 29, 1917): 1313; also R. P. Joy to Truman Newberry, January 24, 1921, Box 377, TNP; *Automobile Quarterly, Car since 1775*, 138–40; Annual Report, Hupp Motor Corporation, June 30, 1918, NAHC; "The Automobile Industry in Michigan," *Michigan History Magazine* 8 (July 1924): 249. Hupp's principal bankers after 1915 were A. G. Becker & Co. of Chicago and Ladenburg, Thalman & Co. of New York.

22. Burton, *City of Detroit*, 3:250; Glasscock, *Gasoline Age*, 195–99; *Automotive Industries* 43 (December 16, 1920): 1237; Allan Nevins, *Ford: The Times, The Man, The Company* (New York, 1954), 230–31.

23. Nevins, *Ford: The Times*, 231; May, *Unique Machine*, 273; Dodge Bros. v. Ford Motor Company, Michigan Supreme Court, Court Record, 1917, 507–9. The contract stipulated that the Dodges could seize the unsold machinery if Malcomson and Ford failed to meet their obligations, but this would have been small solace. All the advertising had been done in the Ford name, and it is doubtful that the Dodges had sufficient funds at the time to acquaint the public with a "Dodge" car.

24. C. H. Bennett, *Reminiscences*, 35–36, FA, George Holley, *Reminiscences*, 111, FA; Cameron Currie to Truman Newberry, February 13, 1918, Box 1, TNP; Norman Beasley and George W. Stark, *Made in Detroit* (Detroit, 1957), 226–28.

25. *Detroit News*, June 15 and 19, 1920; Glasscock, *Gasoline Age*, 208–9;

Leake, *History of Detroit*, 3:1193–95. Although Glasscock perpetuates the local legend that the Country Club of Detroit blackballed John Dodge, the story actually involved the Detroit Club, according to his widow, Mrs. Alfred G. Wilson; see her letter to Frank W. Wylie, May 7, 1964, cc. See also Malcolm Bingay, *Detroit Is My Home Town* (Indianapolis, Ind., 1946), 42–43; Horace Dodge to James Couzens, May 28, 1917, Box 5, General Correspondence, jcp. Ernst Liebold, the Ford secretary, was also black-balled from the Detroit Club, according to his *Reminiscences* in fa; he believed Truman Newberry was behind the move, presumably in revenge for Ford's political harassment of Newberry after the 1918 election. It is interesting to note that the only two known blackballings involved Ford executives.

26. "Chrysler," *Fortune* 12 (August 1935): 36; *Dodge Brothers International Review* 1 (August 1917): 8; Niran D. Pope, *Dodge Brothers Works* (1919), 3 (pamphlet in Dodge Bros. File, nahc); Richard Crabb, *Birth of a Giant: The Men and Incidents That Gave America the Motorcar* (Philadelphia, 1969), 349–53; *Fortune* 10 (December 1933); 128; Dodge Biography File, David Beecroft Papers, nahc; D. C. Smith, "How John and Horace Dodge Made Good: The Untold Story of the Dodge Boys," *Detroit Free Press*, April 17, 1966. As of July 1914 there were only three stockholders: the two brothers and A. L. McMeans, who held the minimum shares to qualify for the board of directors.

27. Forbes and Foster, *Automotive Giants*, 137; F. J. Haynes, "The Sound Progress of Dodge Brothers Business," August 1924, Dodge Brothers File, cr; *Fortune* 12 (August 1935): 36; Dave Chambers, "Dodge Brothers First 50 Years," *Antique Automobile* 28 (November–December 1964); Crabb, *Birth of a Giant*, 354; Chrysler Corporation, *A History of Dodge, 1914–1964* (1972), 7; Lawrence Seltzer, *A Financial History of the Automobile Industry* (Boston, 1928), 240; "The Automobile Industry in Michigan," 225.

28. Prices for twenty-five different makes (including Dodge) for 1913–1921 can be found in Leonard P. Ayres, *The Automobile Industry and Its Future*, 28 (pamphlet published by Cleveland Trust Co., 1921, copy in Widener Library, Harvard University).

29. *Fortune* 12 (August 1935): 36; *Detroit News*, August 5, 1928; Rae, *American Automobile Manufacturers*, 163–64; E. D. Kennedy, *The Automobile Industry* (New York, 1941), 193.

30. Ralph Epstein, *The Automobile Industry* (1928; rpt. Chicago, 1968), 336–37.

31. *Horseless Age*, November 15, 1917, p. 18; *Automotive Industries* 46 (February 16, 1922): 326.

32. Glasscock, *Gasoline Age*, 95–96; William Davies, "The Saxon Story from A to B," *Bulb Horn* 18 (October 1957): 10–14; *Automotive Industries* 67 (December 31, 1922): 1251; Schroeder, *Wonderful World*, 156; Automobile Quarterly, *Car since 1775*, 138–39; Rae, *American Automobile Manufacturers*, 114–15; *Detroit Saturday Night*, December 6, 1913, and September 29, 1917; L. R. Scaife to H. S. Maynard, August 16, 1952, Box 1, H. S. Maynard Papers, bhc.

33. *Automobile*, February 3, 1916, p. 249; February 17, 1916, p. 335; January 11, 1923, p. 95; also *Motor World*, July 25, 1916, 21; *Automobile Trade Journal* 21 (November 1, 1916): 194.

34. For the Metzger company, see *Cycle and Automobile Trade Journal* 14 (November 1909): 82; *Horseless Age* 24 (September 22, 1909): 321; *Automobile*, May 16, 1912, 1145; *Motor World*, September 12, 1912, p. 10. Organized in September 1909, Metzger Motor Car underwent two name changes in 1912, becoming first Everitt Motor Car Co. and then the Flanders Motor Co. For an overview of William Metzger's career, see *Automotive Industries* 68 (April 16, 1933): 473–77. For the Rickenbacker Car Co., see Walter O. MacIlwain, "Rickenbacker," *Bulb Horn* 20 (Summer 1959): 11–14; Edward V. Rickenbacker, *Rickenbacker* (Englewood Cliffs, N.J., 1967), chap. 7; Hans Christian Adamson, *Eddie Rickenbacker* (New York, 1946), 233–36. For Flanders's career, see *Horseless Age*, December 15, 1916, clipping in Walter Flanders File, NAHC.

35. E. Digby Baltzell, *Puritan Boston and Quaker Philadelphia: Two Protestant Ethics and the Spirit of Class Authority and Leadership* (New York, 1979), 25.

36. William Domhoff, *Who Really Rules? New Haven and Community Power Reexamined* (Santa Monica, Calif., 1978), chap. 2; John N. Ingham, *The Iron Barons: A Social Analysis of an American Elite, 1874–1965* (Westport, Conn., 1978), 98–100.

37. Frederic Cople Jaher, *The Urban Establishment* (Urbana, Ill., 1982), 5–13. See also Jaher, "Nineteenth Century Elites in Boston and New York," *Journal of Social History* 6 (Fall 1972): 32–77.

38. Burton, *City of Detroit*, 1:570–81; *Detroit News*, May 22, 1910; Long, *Chapin*, 97–105; *Detroiter* 4 (November 1913).

39. Clem Studebaker, Jr. to Board of Directors, E-M-F Company, September 21, 1910, SCP; Mrs. Wilfred Leland, *Master of Precision: Henry Leland* (Detroit, 1966), 89–104; MacManus and Beasley, *Men, Money, and Motors*, 89–90; Bingay, *Home Town*, 119.

40. *Detroit Saturday Night*, September 22, 1917; Leake, *History of Detroit*, 1:275.

41. Dodge v. Ford Motor Company, Henry Ford, et al., 204, Michigan Supreme Court Records and Briefs, January 1919, 331; Liebold, *Reminiscences*, FA; *Detroit Free Press*, August 16, 1924.

42. *Annual Report*, [Michigan] Commissioner of Banking, 1911–1913, BHC.

43. *Detroiter* 1 (February 1911): 9–13; 2 (January 1913): 24; 9 (November 19, 1917): 1; also *Detroit News*, March 6, 1911, and January 25, 1955; editorial, *Detroit Saturday Night*, November 20, 1915.

44. Nevins, *Ford: The Times*, 376–80, 513–23; Chester M. Culver, *Reminiscences*, 6–10; FA; *Detroit Saturday Night*, July 1, 1916.

45. Henry Leland to George H. Barbour, October 11, 1912, Box 1, CLP; William P. Lovett, *Detroit Rules Itself* (Detroit, 1930), 77–79; *Civic Searchlight* 3 (November 1916): 2, and 1 (October 1913): 1–4. Further information on the League and municipal reform in Detroit can be found in Jack D.

Elenbaas, "Detroit and the Progressive Era: A Study of Urban Reform, 1900–1914" (Ph.D. diss., Wayne State University, 1968); Elenbaas, "The Boss of the Better Class: Henry Leland and the Detroit Citizens' League, 1912–1924," *Michigan History* 58 (Summer 1974): 131–50; Raymond R. Fragnoli, "Progressive Coalitions and Municipal Reform: Charter Revision in Detroit, 1912–1918," *Detroit in Perspective* 4 (Spring 1980): 119–42; Fragnoli, *The Transformation of Reform: Progressivism in Detroit—and After, 1912–1933* (New York, 1982); Merle Jacob, "Efficiency and Local Reform: A Study of the Businessmen's Role in the Detroit Reform Movements of the Progressive Era, 1900–1916" (honors essay, University of Michigan, 1968), copy in MHC; Donald F. Davis, "The City Remodelled: The Limits of Automotive Industry Leadership in Detroit, 1910–1929," *Histoire sociale— Social History* 26 (November 1980): 451–86.

46. A list of the contributors to the Detroit Civic Uplift League (the original name of the Citizens League) for September–December 1912 can be found in Box 1, Additional Papers, CLP. Almost half of the listed subscribers manufactured motorcars or parts. They included Joseph Boyer, E. W. Clark, M. J. Murphy, and Thomas Neal (GM), Henry and Wilfred Leland (Cadillac); A. F. Demory and E. W. Lewis (Timken-Detroit Axle); W. H. DuCharme (Kelsey Wheel); F. O. Bezner, Roy Chapin, and R. H. Webber (Hudson); Hugh Chalmers (Chalmers); W. T. Barbour, A. H. Buhl, and G. H. Barbour (Lozier); D. M. Ferry, Jr., Henry and Richard Joy (Packard); C. A. Grinnell (Grinnell); Milton McRae (McRae and Roberts); W. R. Kales (Detroit Gear & Machine); J. T. Whitehead (Michigan Copper & Brass). For a definition of structural reform in the sense used here, see Melvin Holli, *Reform in Detroit: Hazen S. Pingree and Urban Politics* (New York, 1969), chap. 8.

47. Pliny W. Marsh, "Detroit Becomes a Home Rule City," Oral Reminiscences, BHC; Lovett, *Detroit Rules*, 90–98; Fragnoli, *Transformation of Reform*, 134–67. The Citizens' Charter Committee raised $15,657, almost all of which came from John and Horace Dodge (Dodge Brothers); Louis Mendelssohn (Fisher Body); Edsel Ford, C. Harold Wills, and Horace H. Rackham (Ford); Oscar Webber (Hudson); A. H. Buhl (Lozier); Henry Joy (Packard); Henry Leland (Cadillac); Joseph Boyer (ex-Packard, ex-GM); W. H. Murphy (Lincoln, ex-Cadillac); and four downtown businessmen.

48. Chapter Seven discusses the 1918 election. For the disintegration of the reform coalition after 1918, see Fragnoli, *Transformation of Reform*, chap. 6; Davis, "City Remodelled," 462–86.

49. *Horseless Age* 22 (December 2, 1908): 814; Tariff Brief of Motor Vehicle Manufacturers, 1913, HJP; *Detroit Saturday Night*, April 3, 1920; *Time* 14 (July 22, 1929): 41–42.

50. Nathan B. Scott to James Couzens, October 23, 1916, and James Couzens to Charles B. Warren, October 10, 1916, Box 4, General Correspondence, JCP; Charles A. Hughes to Roy Chapin, September 22, 1916, and Hugh Chalmers et al. to Roy Chapin, November 25, 1916, Box 3, RCP.

51. G. M. Kaye to A. A. Schantz, September 15, 1916, James McMillan Papers, BHC; *Detroit News*, October 3, 1920; George B. Catlin, *The Story*

of Detroit (Detroit, 1923), chap. 114. Among other prominent contributors to the symphony were Abner Larned, Julius H. Haass, Sidney T. Miller, Ralph Dyar, F. M. Alger, and Henry B. Joy.

52. *Detroit News*, January 21, 1909, and April 14, 1912; Milton McRae, *Forty Years in Newspaperdom* (New York, 1924), 372; William Greenleaf, *From These Beginnings: The Early Philanthropies of Henry and Edsel Ford, 1911–1936* (Detroit, 1964), 32–34.

53. *The Detroiter* 9 (February 25, 1918): 1–2; Pierce Williams and Frederick E. Coxton, *Corporation Contributions to Organized Community Welfare Services* (New York, 1930), 13–32, 82–88.

54. Burton, *City of Detroit*, 3:973; Bingay, *Home Town*, 23; Norman Beasley and George W. Stark, *Made in Detroit* (Detroit, 1957), 13–14. A complete list of the Detroit Club's officers and directors to 1930 can be found in its Articles of Association and By-Laws for 1930, copy in BHC.

55. Alfred P. Sloan, Jr., *Adventures of a White-Collar Man* (New York, 1941), 79–80.

56. George W. Stark, *In Old Detroit* (Detroit, 1939), 13; William B. Stout, *So Away I Went!* (Indianapolis, Ind., 1951), 258; Glasscock, *Gasoline Age*, 192–94.

57. Burton, *City of Detroit*, 4:803–4; Charles A. Hughes, "The Story of the Organization," *Detroit Saturday Night*, April 17, 1915; W. E. Metzger, "Brief History of the Detroit Athletic Club," *DAC News* 6 (May 1921): 21. The 104 charter members of the DAC included the following auto men: J. W. Anderson, David Gray, Norval Hawkins (Ford); H. H. Emmons (Regal); W. E. Metzger (Metzger); H. E. Bodman, J. G. Vincent, Sidney Waldon, G. M. Black, Alvan Macauley, F. F. Beall (Packard); M. P. Rumney (Detroit Steel Products); E. H. and H. M. Jewett (Paige); E. W. Lewis (Timken-Detroit Axle); J. F. Hartz (R.C.H.); W. H. DuCharme, John Kelsey (K. H. Wheel); Hugh Chalmers (Chalmers); R. H. Webber, R. D. Chapin (Hudson); Joseph Boyer, E. W. Clark (GM); F. W. Eddy (Morgan & Wright, tire manufacturer); B. S. Warren, W. H. Miller (Lozier); Milton McRae (McRae & Roberts); C. B. Warren (Paige, Hupp); C. M. Hall (C. M. Hall, auto accessories); C. D. and Frank Widman (Autoparts Mfg.); Neil W. Snow (Detroit Gear & Machine). Many of the rest were "fellow travelers" of the auto industry: e.g., John Ballantyne, Oscar Marx, George B. Fowler, and Frank Navin were close friends and political allies of John Dodge; K. B. Alexander handled automobile accounts for his ad agency; R. B. Tannahill was connected to Hudson through the department store; and F. H. Holt was one of Henry Ford's few personal friends among the local business elite. A complete list of the charter members can be found in Box 1, RCP.

58. *Automobile Topics* 34 (May 16, 1914): 32.

59. Metzger, "Brief History," 21; Bingay, *Home Town*, 26; C. A. DuCharme to John Kelsey, March 12, 1918, and W. Howie Muir to Truman Newberry, March 5, 1918, Box 1, TNP.

60. U.S. Department of Commerce, Bureau of the Census, *Census of Manufactures, 1914* (Washington, D.C., 1918) 1:699; School of Public Affairs

and Social Work of Wayne University, report no. 10, *Accumulated Social and Economic Statistics for Detroit* (Detroit, 1937), 3.

61. Vilfredo Pareto, *A Treatise on General Sociology* (New York, 1963), 1426–30, 1796–97; Harold D. Laswell and Daniel Lerner, eds., *World Revolutionary Elites* (Cambridge, Mass., 1965), 27.

62. Stout, *So Away I Went!*, 105.

Chapter Five

1. Henry Ford, *My Life and Work* (1922; Garden City, N.Y., 1923), 36, 40, 176 (emphasis added).

2. For the Anderson material, see his testimony, U.S. Board of Tax Appeals, Estate of John F. Dodge et al. v. Commissioner of Internal Revenue, Transcript of Hearings, Washington, D.C., January–February 1927, 3:1279; see also *Detroit Saturday Night*, June 5, 1915; *Detroit Journal*, October 27, 1902.

3. *National Cyclopaedia of American Biography* (Ann Arbor, Mich., 1967), 22: 190–91; George S. May, *A Most Unique Machine: The Michigan Origins of the American Automobile Industry* (Grand Rapids, Mich., 1975), 256–57; Allan Nevins, *Ford: The Times, The Man, The Company* (New York, 1954), 225; Henry Barnard, *Independent Man: The Life of Senator James Couzens* (New York, 1958), 35–36; John Wandersee, *Reminiscences*, 6, FA.

4. Nevins, *Ford: The Times*, 234-38.

5. C. M. Burton, *The City of Detroit, Michigan, 1701–1922* (Detroit, 1922), 3:108–10; Theodore F. MacManus and Norman Beasley, *Men, Money, and Motors* (New York, 1929), 31–34; C. H. Bennett, *Reminiscences*, 21, FA.

6. *Detroit News*, July 11, 1918; Richard Crabb, *Birth of a Giant: The Men and Incidents That Gave America the Motorcar* (Philadelphia, 1969), 206; William Simonds, *Henry Ford: A Biography* (London, 1946), 64, 105–6.

7. Milo M. Quaife, *The Life of John Wendell Anderson* (Detroit, 1950), 45–68, 89; Charles Moore, *History of Michigan* (Chicago, 1915), 4:1928; Robert B. Ross and George B. Catlin, *Landmarks of Wayne County and Detroit* (Detroit, 1898), 3:197; C. M. Burton et al., *History of Wayne County and the City of Detroit, Michigan* (Detroit, 1930), 3:628; May, *Unique Machine*, 270; Sydney Olson, *Young Henry Ford* (Detroit, 1963), 178–79.

8. Burton, *City of Detroit*, 4:843; Barnard, *Independent Man*, chaps. 1–6.

9. Nevins, *Ford: The Times*, 240–41. In 1903, 66.4 percent of new cars sold sported only one cylinder. See Ralph Epstein, *The Automobile Industry* (1928; rpt. Chicago, 1968), 90, 339.

10. Nevins, *Ford: The Times*, chap. 12 (quotation from p. 277).

11. Ibid., 274–83, 644–46; Epstein, *Automobile Industry*, 76–77; Roger Burlingame, *Henry Ford: A Great Life in Brief* (New York, 1955), 51.

12. Keith Sward, *The Legend of Henry Ford* (New York, 1948), 21–22; Nevins, *Ford: The Times*, 279–81, 329–32.

13. Bennett, *Reminiscences*, 25, FA; Oliver Barthel, *Reminiscences*, 45, FA; *Detroit Free Press*, December 5, 1905; Minutes, Board of Directors,

Ford Motor Company, December 15, 1905, Accession 85, FA; Henry Ford to James Couzens, August 1, 1907, Box 8, Additional Correspondence, JCP; *Detroit News*, August 5, 1907.

14. *Automobile* 14 (January 11, 1906): 107–19; James J. Flink, *America Adopts the Automobile, 1895–1910* (Cambridge, Mass., 1970), 272; *Automobile Quarterly, The American Car since 1775* (New York, 1971), 138–40.

15. Anne Jardim, *The First Henry Ford: A Study in Personality and Business Leadership* (Cambridge, Mass.), 63; Crabb, *Birth of a Giant*, 254; Norman Beasley, *Knudsen: A Biography* (New York, 1947), 59. In 1908 the Model T provided twenty horsepower; as of 1915 the most powerful car selling for less than $1,000 was the 25.6-hp Willys-Overland "81" touring car. Only Saxon tried to compete with Ford on price in 1915, but its engine produced only 12.1 hp. See Association of Licensed Automobile Manufacturers (ALAM), *Handbook of Automobiles, 1915–1916* (rpt. New York, 1970).

16. *Detroit News*, November 4, 1916, and May 14, 1917; John F. Dodge and Horace E. Dodge v. Ford Motor Company, Henry Ford, et al., 204 Michigan Supreme Court Records and Briefs, January 1919, 614–18; Federal Trade Commission, *Report on Motor Vehicle Industry* (Washington, D.C., 1939), 632–33; E. D. Kennedy, *The Automobile Industry* (New York, 1941), 159; Allan Nevins and Frank Ernest Hill, *Ford: Expansion and Challenge, 1915–1933* (New York, 1957), 267. The price of the Model A in 1928 was placed well below cost, since neither development nor retooling costs were factored into it. See Harold Katz, *The Decline of Competition in the Automobile Industry, 1920–1940* (New York, 1977), 131–32.

17. John B. Rae, "Why Michigan?" in David L. Lewis and Laurence Goldstein, eds. *The Automobile and American Culture* (Ann Arbor, Mich., 1983), 7.

18. Charles Sorensen, *My Forty Years with Ford* (New York, 1956), 6; S. S. Marquis, *Henry Ford: An Interpretation* (Boston, 1923), 160, 164–65; Nevins, *Ford: The Times*, 581.

19. Mrs. Wilfred Leland, *Master of Precision: Henry Leland* (Detroit, 1966), 174, 177; May, *Unique Machine*, 258; Bernard Weisberger, *The Dream Maker: William C. Durant, Founder of General Motors* (Boston, 1979), 222; Transcript of Wilfred Leland's testimony to the U.S. Department of Justice, June 12, 1918 (Hughes Committee Hearings), copy in LP; Burton, *City of Detroit*, 3:74; Milton R. Palmer, ed., *Detroit—the Marvel City* (Detroit, 1922), 73. For a list of Lincoln stockholders, see Lincoln Motor Co., Annual Report for 1917, copy in LP. Of the 8,401 shares the Lelands held 4,600, Boyer 500, William Murphy 1,000, Dayton Metal Products 1,000. For the last, see Stuart W. Leslie, *Boss Kettering: Wizard of General Motors* (New York 1983), 77–82; T. A. Boyd, *Professional Amateur: The Biography of Charles Franklin Kettering* (New York, 1957).

20. A statement of the Lelands' assets in 1917 and 1922 is found in LP. For the reference to a "super Cadillac," see Maurice D. Hendry, "Henry Leland," in Ronald Barker and Anthony Harding, eds., *Automobile Design: Great Designers and Their Work* (Newton Abbot, Eng., 1970), 105.

21. Leland, *Master of Precision*, 198–204, 213; *Wall Street Journal*, November 10, 1921; *Detroit Saturday Night*, March 6, 1920; *Detroiter* 11 (December

15, 1919): 22, and 13 (July 31, 1922): 9, 17; W. C. Leland, "Summary of Lincoln Memories" (1924), typescript, LP.

22. *Detroit News*, January 11, 1922.

23. Ibid.; *Pipp's Weekly*, February 3, 1923.

24. Sward, *Legend*, 169; Nevins and Hill, *Ford: Expansion and Challenge*, 192. Nevins and Hill whitewash Ford in one of the most unconvincing chapters of their book; it considers only the relationship between Leland and Ford as industrialists, totally overlooking their community roles and the Lelands' involvement in a political campaign that bitterly wounded both Henry and Edsel Ford.

25. Nevins and Hill, *Ford: Expansion and Challenge*, 172; Sward, *Legend*, 169; *Detroit Journal*, February 4, 1922; Ernest Liebold, *Reminiscences*, FA; Sorensen, *Forty Years*, 307–8; John B. Rae, *The American Automobile Industry* (Boston, 1984), 56.

26. Leland, *Master of Precision*, 258. Edsel married Eleanor Clay, daughter of William Clay and niece of J. L. Hudson.

27. William B. Stout, *So Away I Went!* (Indianapolis, Ind., 1951), 105.

28. Burlingame, *Henry Ford*, 56.

29. Allan L. Benson, *The New Henry Ford* (New York, 1923), 213; Nevins and Hill, *Ford: Expansion and Challenge*, 323.

30. For Kanzler, see George Holley, *Reminiscences* (2d interview), 51, FA; for Nash, see John B. Rae, *American Automobile Manufacturers* (Philadelphia, 1959), 90–92.

31. Jardim, *First Henry Ford*, chap. 5.

32. Lucian Cary, "Henry Ford," *Collier's* 62 (November 2, 1918): 27; Benson, *New Henry Ford*, 193. See also *Dearborn Independent*, October 8, 1915; Dodge v. Ford Motor Company, 207; Ford, *My Life and Work*, 254; Sward, *Legend*, 69.

33. Reynold M. Wik, *Henry Ford and Grass-Roots America* (Ann Arbor, Mich., 1972), 10, 163; Benson, *New Henry Ford*, 211; Garet Garrett, *The Wild Wheel* (New York, 1952), 163.

34. Charles Beard, "Written History as an Act of Faith," *American History Review* 39 (January 1934): 219–29.

35. E. G. Pipp, *Henry Ford, Both Sides of Him* (Detroit, 1926), 54–55; *Detroit News*, June 8, 1915; Benson, *New Henry Ford*, 304; Harry Bennett, *We Never Called Him Henry* (New York, 1951), 42, 65–70; Jardim, *First Henry Ford*, 123; "Henry Ford at Bay," *Forum*, August 1919, 141; Malcolm Bingay, *Detroit Is My Home Town* (Indianapolis, Ind., 1946), 95–96; W. J. Cameron, *Reminiscences*, 24, FA; James J. Flink, *The Car Culture* (Cambridge, Mass., 1975), 109.

36. For the Selden patent see Nevins, *Ford: The Times*, chap. 13; William Greenleaf, *Monopoly on Wheels: Henry Ford and the Selden Patent Suit* (Detroit, 1961); John B. Rae, "The Electric Vehicle Company: A Monopoly That Missed," *Business History Review* 29 (December 1955); Henry B. Joy to J. W. Packard, January 4, 1903, and Joy to George H. Day, January 5, 1903, Joy Letterbooks, MHC.

37. Greenleaf, *Monopoly on Wheels*, 101, 173–74.

38. House Temporary National Economic Committee, *Hearings: Investigation of Concentration of Economic Power*, pt. 2, *Patents*, 75th Cong., 3d sess., 1939, 268; MacManus and Beasley, *Men, Money, and Motors*, 56; Frederic L. Smith, "Motoring Down a Quarter Century," *Detroit Saturday Night*, October 2, 1928; Quaife, *Anderson*, 116.

39. Nevins, *Ford: The Times*, chaps. 13, 17.

40. *Automobile* 9 (November 21, 1903): 550, and 24 (January 19, 1911): 232; Greenleaf, *Monopoly on Wheels*, 239–40; *Detroit Journal*, January 11, 1911; Nevins, *Ford: The Times*, 434–37.

41. Seward Prosser to James Couzens, October 13, 1915, Box 1, General Correspondence, JCP; Jardim, *First Henry Ford*, 106.

42. Sorensen, *Forty Years*, 167–68; Nevins and Hill, *Ford: Expansion and Challenge*, 159–66; Liebold, *Reminiscences*, FA; Ford, *My Life and Work*, 173.

43. Automobile Quarterly, *Car since 1775*, 138–39.

44. *Automobile* 24 (January 19, 1911): 232.

45. *Detroiter* 1 (September 1910): 8; *Detroit News*, January 21, 1909, and April 14, 1912; William Greenleaf, *From These Beginnings: The Early Philanthropies of Henry and Edsel Ford, 1911–1936* (Detroit, 1964), 32–34.

46. Greenleaf, *From These Beginnings*, 33–40, 69; Pipp, *Henry Ford*, 31–32; Frank P. Stockbridge, "Henry Ford, Amateur," *World's Work* 36 (September 1918): 510; *New York Times*, June 5, 1914.

47. Barnard, *Independent Man*, 70–71; Liebold, *Reminiscences*, FA.

48. Liebold, *Reminiscences*, FA; *Detroit News*, December 19, 1913; Barnard, *Independent Man*, 71.

49. *Detroit Journal*, January 9, 1914; *Detroit News*, January 6, 1914. On the five-dollar day, see also Beasley, *Knudsen*, 64; Edward A. Rumely, "Mr. Ford's Plan to Share Profits," *World's Work* 27 (April 1914): 665; Ford, *My Life and Work*, 522–40; Henry Faigin, "The Industrial Workers of the World in Detroit and Michigan" (M.A. thesis, Wayne State University, 1937); James Couzens, "American Industry and the Social Good," *Printer's Ink Monthly* 23 (July 1931): 29; *Detroit Saturday Night*, January 30, 1915; *Detroit News*, October 18, 1915; MacManus and Beasley, *Men, Money, and Motors*, 155–57; Barnard, *Independent Man*, chap. 13; Simonds, *Henry Ford*, chap. 12; Sorensen, *Forty Years*, 137–40; Liebold, Cameron, Joseph Galamb, and Charles Sorensen, *Reminiscences*, FA.

50. Sorensen, *Forty Years*, 141; Minutes, Board of Directors, Studebaker Corporation, January 19, 1914, SCP; Max Wollering, *Reminiscences*, 35, FA; *Detroit News*, November 29, 1916; Barnard, *Independent Man*, 95–96.

51. Sward, *Legend*, 54–58; Garet Garrett, "A World That Was," *Saturday Evening Post*, June 8, 1940.

52. *Michigan Manufacturer and Financial Record*, January 10, 1914; Charles Culver, *Reminiscences*, 25, FA.

53. *Detroit News*, October 18, 1915; Barnard, *Independent Man*, 96–97; *Detroit Saturday Night*, January 30, 1915.

54. James Couzens to S. S. Kresge, December 10, 1915, Box 9, Additional

Papers, JCP; *Pittsburgh Press*, August 18, 1924, clipping in Box 29, General Correspondence, JCP.

55. *Detroit Saturday Night*, August 7, 1915, and January 15, March 25, 1916; Roy Chapin to Theodore Roosevelt, January 11, 1916, Box 1, RCP.

56. Henry B. Joy to Alvan T. Fuller, February 28, 1916, Box 1, HJP; G. D. Pope to Mrs. Edwin Denby, May 9, 1917, Box 1, Edwin Denby Papers, MHC; *New York Herald*, January 7, 1916.

57. *Detroit Free Press*, August 22, September 5, 1915, and April 9, 1916; *Detroit News*, November 15, 1915; Sward, *Legend*, 83–84; *New York Times*, April 11, 1915; *Detroit Saturday Night*, September 11, 1915.

58. *Detroit Free Press*, August 22, 1915; John Parker, "A History of the Packard Motor Car Company from 1899 to 1929" (M.A. thesis, Wayne State University, 1949), 93; *Detroit News*, July 16, 1919.

59. For the Peace Ship affair, see David E. Nye, *Henry Ford: "Ignorant Idealist"* (Port Washington, N.Y., 1979); Nevins and Hill, *Ford: Expansion and Challenge*, chap. 2; Louis P. Lochner, *Henry Ford—America's Don Quixote* (New York, 1925); Sward, *Legend*, chap. 6.

60. *Detroit Free Press*, October 7 and November 2, 1916; *Detroit News*, October 14, 1916, and February 5, October 16, 1917; Ford, *My Life and Work*, 245.

61. James Couzens to Robert M. Thompson, December 6, 1915, and Couzens to R. W. Austin, March 19, 1917, Boxes 1 and 6, General Correspondence, JCP; *Detroiter* 7 (February 21, 1916): 1–2.

62. *Detroit News*, October 2, 1916.

63. *Detroit News*, November 6, 1924; Barnard, *Independent Man*, 107–8.

64. Barnard, *Independent Man*, 108–12.

65. Charles W. Wood, "He Had Millions, but Wanted a Job," *Collier's* 70 (August 5, 1922): 10.

66. Bingay, *Home Town*, 116–17; F. R. Kent, "Couzens of Michigan," *American Mercury* 11 (May 1927): 48–55; B. C. Forbes and O. D. Foster, *Automotive Giants of America* (New York, 1926), 108–9; James Couzens to Ralph Stone, August 23, 1918, Box 6, Special Correspondence, JCP.

67. Couzens quoted in B. C. Forbes to James Couzens, December 7, 1922, Box 16, General Correspondence, JCP; Ford quoted in Wik, *Henry Ford*, 10.

68. Marquis, *Henry Ford*, 75–76; Julian Street, "Detroit the Dynamic," *Collier's Weekly* 53 (July 4, 1914): 27; Simonds, *Henry Ford*, 90; Liebold, *Reminiscences*, FA; Sorensen, *Forty Years*, 16–19; Paul Hale Bruske to James Couzens, July 19, 1918, Box 5, Special Correspondence, JCP; John Mangum to Truman Newberry, September 21, 1918, Box 6, TNP; Bingay, *Home Town*, 117.

69. Heinz Eulau, "Elite Analysis and Democratic Theory: The Contribution of Harold D. Lasswell," in Eulau and Moshe M. Czudnowski, eds., *Elite Recruitment in Democratic Polities* (New York, 1976), 24–25. This paragraph is not arguing in favor of technological determinism. Mass production was not an "inevitable" technology but rather a social construct with a system of social values built into it. See Michael J. Piore and Charles F. Sabel,

The Second Industrial Divide: Possibilities for Prosperity (New York, 1984), chap. 2.

70. *Detroit News*, February 4, 1917; *Hudson Triangle* 6 (April 7, 1917): 814.

71. *Automotive Industries* 38 (June 13, 1918): 1116, and 37 (November 8, 1917): 814; Franklin H. Martin, *Digest of the Proceedings of the Council of National Defense during the World War*, U.S. Cong., S. Doc. 193, 73d Cong., 2d sess. (Washington, D.C., 1934), 364–81, 411–12; Alvan Macauley to R. P. Joy, December 11, 1922, Joy Letterbooks, MHC; Minutes, Board of Directors, November 14, 1918, Packard Motor Car Co., SCP; Minutes, Annual Meeting, Studebaker Corporation, April 1, 1919, SCP; Kennedy, *Automobile Industry*, 102–3; Alfred D. Chandler, Jr., *Strategy and Structure: Chapters in the History of the Industrial Enterprise* (Cambridge, Mass., 1962), 124; R. B. Jackson to Roy Chapin, February 1, 1918, Box 5, RCP; Nevins, *Ford: The Times*, app. 6; Rae, *American Automobile Industry*, 180.

72. R. B. Jackson to E. A. Deeds, May 29, 1917, Box 4, RCP; Packard Motor Co., *The Saga of Packard* (Detroit, 1949), 80–82; Isaac Marcosson, *Colonel Deeds, Industrial Builder* (New York, 1947), chap. 11; transcript of Wilfred Leland's testimony to the Department of Justice, June 12, 1918, pp. 25–40, LP; Martin, *Digest of Proceedings*, 463–70; Cadillac Motor Car Company, *Cadillac Participation in the World War* (Detroit, 1919), 39; Lincoln Motor Co., *A Pledge Made Good by Deeds* (Detroit, 1919); House Select Committee of Inquiry into Operations of the United States Air Services, *Hearings*, pt. 2, 68th Cong., 2d sess. (Washington, D.C., 1925), 1275–76; Sward, *Legend*, 96.

73. Weisberger, *Dream Maker*, 222; J. L. Pratt to Ernest Dale, June 30, 1962, File P76-5.38, John Lee Pratt Papers, GMI; Lawrence Gustin, *Billy Durant: Creator of General Motors* (Grand Rapids, Mich., 1973), 196.

74. Greenleaf, *From These Beginnings*, 7–8.

75. Weisberger, *Dream Maker*, 184.

Chapter Six

1. Alfred P. Sloan, Jr., *My Years with General Motors* (New York, 1963), 67–69.

2. E. D. Kennedy, *The Automobile Industry* (New York, 1941), 189; Arthur Pound, *The Turning Wheel: The Story of General Motors through Twenty-five Years, 1908–1933* (Garden City, N.Y., 1934), 338; Federal Trade Commission, *Report on Motor Vehicle Industry* (Washington, D.C., 1939), 419.

3. Lawrence Gustin, *Billy Durant: Creator of General Motors* (Grand Rapids, Mich., 1973), 17–25, 55–62; Bernard Weisberger, *The Dream Maker: William C. Durant, Founder of General Motors* (Boston, 1979), chaps. 1–2; John B. Rae, "The Fabulous Billy Durant," *Business History Review* 32 (Autumn 1958); Carl Crow, *The City of Flint Grows Up* (New York, 1945), 29–37; George S. May, *A Most Unique Machine: The Michigan Origins of the American Automobile Industry* (Grand Rapids, Mich., 1975), 179–99.

4. C. B. Glasscock, *The Gasoline Age* (New York, 1937), 125; Gustin, *Billy Durant*, chap. 3; Weisberger, *Dream Maker*, chap. 4.

5. Hardy cited in Lawrence Seltzer, *A Financial History of the Automobile Industry* (Boston, 1928), 157; J. L. Pratt to Alfred P. Sloan, Jr., November 22, 1957, File D76-5.34, J. L. Pratt Papers, GMI.

6. Arthur Pound, "General Motors Old Home Town," *Michigan History* 40 (March 1956): 88; Crow, *Flint Grows Up*, 57; Weisberger, *Dream Maker*, chap. 5. For a negative assessment of Durant's acquisitions, see Cray, *Chrome Colossus: General Motors and Its Times* (New York, 1980), 88–89.

7. May, *Unique Machine*, 317–28; Seltzer, *Financial History*, 154–59; Pound, *Turning Wheel*, chap. 8; John B. Rae, *American Automobile Manufacturers* (Philadelphia, 1959), 87–88.

8. *Cycle and Automobile Trade Journal* 14 (August 1, 1909): 69; Ernest Dale, *The Great Organizers* (New York, 1960), 82–83; Dale, "Contributions to Administration by Alfred P. Sloan, Jr., and GM," *Administrative Science Quarterly* 1 (June 1956): 32–34.

9. Weisberger, *Dream Maker*, 147–52; Pound, *Turning Wheel*, 125–26; Mrs. Wilfred Leland, *Master of Precision: Henry Leland* (Detroit, 1966), 104–6.

10. Pound, *Turning Wheel*, 125, 131–32; Minutes, Annual Meeting, E-M-F Company, November 25, 1910, SCP; *Detroit Free Press*, July 31, 1939; Alfred D. Chandler, Jr., and Stephen Salsbury, *Pierre S. du Pont and the Making of the Modern Corporation* (New York, 1971), 438; H. G. Pearson, *Son of New England: James J. Storrow* (Boston, 1932), 123–40. Detroit lost its representative in the presidency in November 1912, though Neal continued on GM's board until 1916.

11. Seltzer, *Financial History*, 166–72; Gustin, *Billy Durant*, 165.

12. Gustin, *Billy Durant*, chap. 8; Pound, *Turning Wheel*, 143–54; Automobile Quarterly, *The American Car since 1775* (New York, 1971), 138.

13. *New York Times*, March 11, 1942, obituary (Louis Kaufman); Chandler and Salsbury, *Pierre du Pont*, 434–36, 450–55, 587; Theodore F. MacManus and Norman Beasley, *Men, Money, and Motors* (New York, 1929), 185–90; *United States Supreme Court Records*, vol. 353, *Records and Briefs*, United States v. E. I. du Pont de Nemours and Co. et al., October 1956, 795–808; Gustin, *Billy Durant*, 173–76; Annual Report, General Motors Corporation, 1917, CR; *Horseless Age*, December 1, 1917, p. 52; *Detroiter* 13 (August 7, 1922): 7; Crow, *Flint Grows Up*, 57–60; U.S. v. Du Pont, Gov't. Exhibit 124: Memorandum from J. J. Raskob to Finance Committee of E. I. du Pont de Nemours & Co., December 19, 1917; Sloan, *My Years*, 12–14.

14. U.S. v. Du Pont de Nemours & Co., Raskob memorandum; also pp. 687, 830–37.

15. U.S. v. Du Pont, 665–66; Chandler and Salsbury, *Pierre du Pont*, 458; Alfred D. Chandler, Jr., *Strategy and Structure: Chapters in the History of the Industrial Enterprise* (Cambridge, Mass., 1962), 127; Sloan, *My Years*, 14.

16. Margery Durant, *My Father* (New York, 1929), 253; Donaldson Brown, *Some Reminiscences of an Industrialist* (privately printed, 1957), 41.

17. Sloan, *My Years*, 27–39; Arthur Pound and S. T. Moore, eds., *They Told Barron* (New York, 1930), 102–8.

18. Annual Report, General Motors Corporation, 1921, CR; Chandler and Salsbury, *Pierre du Pont*, 476–79, 508; B. C. Forbes and O. D. Foster,

Automotive Giants of America (New York, 1926), 3–12; House Temporary National Economic Committee, *Monograph 29* (Washington, D.C., 1940), 436–37. In 1939 the three directors with the greatest holdings of GM stock were A. P. Sloan, Jr., with 0.82 percent of GM's common shares; C. S. Mott with 1.4 percent; and C. F. Kettering with 0.87 percent. According to U.S. v. Du Pont, 373–80, the Fishers held 2.1 million shares in the late 1920s but apparently sold most of them after 1930.

19. Pound, *Turning Wheel*, 195–96.

20. Alfred P. Sloan, Jr., "Modern Ideals of Big Business," *World's Work* 52 (September 1926): 698; Sloan, *My Years*, 55.

21. Sloan, "Modern Ideals," 699; Sloan, *My Years*, 130–31; Chandler, *Strategy and Structure*, 157–60; Brown, *Some Reminiscences*, 48–51; C. S. Mott, "Organizing a Great Industrial," *Management and Administration*, May 1924.

22. Brown, *Some Reminiscences*, 26–48; Sloan, *My Years*, xxiii, 139–43; Sloan, "Modern Ideals," 699.

23. *Detroit News*, April 4, 1919; Sloan, *My Years*, 104; see *Michigan Manufacturer and Financial Record* 23 (April 26, 1919): 39.

24. *Detroiter*, 14 (May 14, 1923): 9, 15.

25. Ibid., 13 (June 19, 1922): 7, 13; 13 (October 2, 1922): 5–10; 14 (May 14, 1923): 9, 15.

26. *Detroit News*, November 3–16, 1926, and October 31–November 10, 1927. See Michael Aitken and Paul E. Mott, eds., *The Structure of Community Power* (New York, 1970), esp. two articles on GM's activities in Michigan by D. A. Clelland and W. H. Form, and R. O. Schulze and L. U. Blumberg; also Norton Long, "The Corporation, Its Satellites, and the Local Community," in Edward S. Mason, ed., *The Corporation in Modern Society* (New York, 1966), 202–17. For Mott's civic activities in Flint, see C. A. Young and W. A. Quinn, *Foundation for Living* (New York, 1963), chaps. 4–8; for Kettering's in Dayton, see T. A. Boyd, *Professional Amateur: The Biography of Charles Franklin Kettering* (New York, 1957), 128–29.

27. Benjamin Briscoe, "Inside Story of General Motors," pt. 2, *Detroit Saturday Night*, January 22, 1921; E. J. McIntyre et al., "A History of Events Leading Up to the Formation of the Chrysler Corporation" (1954), 2, typescript, CC; Alfred Reeves, "Benjamin Briscoe, 1867–1945," *Old Timers News* 3 (July 1945): 31; John Holmes, "Maxwell Organization" (Statistical Dept., Chrysler Corp., 1936), 1–2, typescript, NAHC.

28. Reeves, "Benjamin Briscoe," 32; Glasscock, *Gasoline Age*, 99.

29. Benjamin Briscoe, "Inside Story of General Motors," *Detroit Saturday Night*, January 29, 1921; Holmes, "Maxwell Organization," 6; *Directory of Directors in the City of New York, 1913–14* (New York, 1913), 67–68; Merlo J. Pusey, *Eugene Meyer* (New York, 1974), 89.

30. Benjamin Briscoe, "Inside Story of General Motors," *Detroit Saturday Night*, February 5, 1921; Seltzer, *Financial History*, 37–38; Holmes, "Maxwell Organization," 11–13; *Automobile Trade Journal* 17 (December 1912): 80. The reorganization committee in 1912–1913 included George W.

Davison, chairman (president, Central Union Trust); Eugene Meyer, Jr. (partner, Eugene Meyer & Co.); Charles H. Sabin (chairman, Guaranty Trust); Benjamin Strong, Jr. (president, Bankers Trust); James C. Brady (vice-president, Brooklyn Edison Co.; trustee, Central Union Trust); A. H. Wiggins (chairman, Chase National Bank); Elisha S. Williams (president, U.S. Tire); Neal Rantoul (partner, F. S. Moseley & Co., Boston).

31. *Automobile*, February 28, 1915, pp. 316–17; February 6, 1913, p. 405; and December 1916, clippings in Maxwell Corporation File, NAHC; also Rae, *American Automobile Manufacturers*, 96–97; James J. Flink, *America Adopts the Automobile, 1895–1910* (Cambridge, Mass., 1970), 316–17; Annual Report, Maxwell Motor Company, September 1, 1916, CR; Seltzer, *Financial History*, 39; *Detroit Saturday Night*, December 6, 1913; *Automobile Topics*, December 15, 1917, clipping in NAHC; Pusey, *Meyer*, 91–92, 94–95.

32. Automobile Quarterly, *Car since 1775*, 138–39; Imbrie & Co., Bankers, "Report on Maxwell Motor Company," April 20, 1920, CR; *Automobile*, February 6, 1913, p. 405; Nicholas Kelley, "Reminiscences," 189–94, Oral History Research Office, Columbia University.

33. Walter P. Chrysler, *Life of an American Workman* (New York, 1937), 11–163; *Motor Age*, August 19, 1920, 26.

34. Chrysler, *American Workman*, 165; Rae, *American Automobile Manufacturers*, 140–43; *Directory of Directors in the City of New York, 1921–1922* (New York, 1921), 340.

35. *Automotive Industries* 43 (August 12, 1920): 343; Chrysler, *American Workman*, 176–77; *Automobile Topics*, August 21, 1920, clipping in Maxwell Corporate File, NAHC; McIntyre, "Chrysler Corporation," 15–16; Kelley, "Reminiscences," 199–200.

36. Chrysler, *American Workman*, 170–71; Federal Trade Commission, *Report on Motor Vehicle Industry*, 549; Automobile Quarterly, *Car since 1775*, 140–41.

37. Mark Howell, "The Chrysler Six—America's First Modern Automobile," *Antique Automobile* 36 (March–April 1972): 18–20; Chrysler, *American Workman*, 182–89; Federal Trade Commission, *Report on Motor Vehicle Industry*, 552.

38. Annual Report, Chrysler Corporation, December 31, 1925, CR; Charles Moore, *History of Michigan* (Chicago, 1915), 2:1119; 4:1924–25. Maxwell's board in 1921 included three Detroiters: Fred T. Murphy, Allen Edwards, and C. C. Jenks, president of Security Trust. All three belonged to the Detroit upper class, with Jenks—president of Jenks & Muir Manufacturing and formerly chief executive of American Radiator—especially counting among the city's leading citizens.

39. Chrysler Corporation, *The Growth of Chrysler* (Detroit, 1928), 20–21; Federal Trade Commission, *Report on Motor Vehicle Industry*, 610.

40. John B. Kennedy, "You Can't Afford to Walk: An Interview with Walter P. Chrysler," *Collier's* 80 (July 26, 1927): 46; Chrysler, *American Workman*, 161–62; *Fortune* 12 (August 1935): 31–32.

41. Arthur G. Abrom, "Chrysler, Reverence for Engineering," *Vintage Vehicles* 1 (September–October 1968); Howell, "The Chrysler Six," 16–20; Kennedy, "You Can't Afford to Walk," 17.

42. Automotive Quarterly, *Car since 1775*, 140–41; *Automotive Industries* 60 (February 23, 1929): 294–95, and 50 (January 10, 1924): 381.

43. *Detroit News*, November 11, 1926. Nothing was reported in the *News* from Chrysler during the 1927 fund drive.

44. Quoted in Henry Barnard, *Independent Man: The Life of Senator James Couzens* (New York, 1958), 100.

Chapter Seven

1. Bradford Snell, "American Ground Transport: A Proposal for Restructuring the Automobile, Bus, and Rail Industries, February, 1974," in Senate Committee of the Judiciary, Subcommittee on Antitrust and Monopoly, *Hearing on Bill 1167*, 93d Cong., 2d sess., 1974, A1–3, 21–27.

2. David J. St. Clair, *The Motorization of American Cities* (New York, 1986). Other authors who have cited or used Snell's thesis include Glenn Yago, *The Decline of Transit: Urban Transportation in German and US Cities, 1900–1970* (New York, 1984), chap. 4; Kenneth Jackson, *The Crabgrass Frontier: The Suburbanization of the United States* (New York, 1985), 170–71; J. Allen Whitt, *Urban Elites and Mass Transportation: The Dialectics of Power* (Princeton, N.J., 1982), 46–48; K. H. Schaeffer and Elliott Sclar, *Access for All: Transportation and Urban Growth* (Middlesex, Eng., 1975), 45–46; Jonathan Kwitney, "The Great Transportation Conspiracy," *Harpers* 262 (February 1981): 15; J. Allen Whitt and Glenn Yago, "Corporate Strategies and the Decline of Transit in U.S. Cities," *Urban Affairs Quarterly* 21 (September 1985): 37–65. For an overview of the controversy, see Timothy P. O'Hanlon, "General Motors, Nazis, and the Demise of Urban Rail Transit," *Government Publications Review* 11 (1984): 211–32.

3. See Donald N. Dewees, "The Decline of the American Street Railways," *Traffic Quarterly* 24 (October 1970): 563–81; Stanley Mallach, "The Origins of the Decline of Urban Mass Transportation in the United States, 1890–1930," *Urbanism Past and Present*, no. 8 (Summer 1979): 1–17; Mark S. Foster, *From Streetcar to Superhighway: American City Planners and Urban Transportation, 1900–1940* (Philadelphia, 1981), chaps. 2–4; Foster, "City Planners and Urban Transportation: The American Response, 1900–1940," *Journal of Urban History* 5 (May 1979): 365–96; Paul Barrett, *The Automobile and Urban Transit: The Formation of Public Policy in Chicago, 1900–1930* (Philadelphia, 1983), chaps. 1, 6; Barrett, "Public Policy and Private Choice: Mass Transit and the Automobile in Chicago between the Wars," *Business Historical Review* 49 (Winter 1975): 473–97; Glenn E. Holt, "The Changing Perception of Urban Pathology: An Essay on the Development of Mass Transit in the United States," in Kenneth T. Jackson and Stanley K. Schultz, eds., *Cities in American History* (New York, 1972), 324–43; David Owen Wise and Marguerite Dupree, "The Choice of the Automobile for Urban Passenger Transportation: Baltimore in the 1920s," *South Atlantic*

Urban Studies 2 (1978): 153–79. Not all of these address Snell's thesis directly. For the most succinct rejoinders, see Foster, *Streetcar to Superhighway*, 219; Larry Sawers, "American Ground Transportation Reconsidered," *Review of Radical Political Economics* 11 (Fall 1979): 66–69; Ed Cray, *Chrome Colossus: General Motors and Its Times* (New York, 1980), 576.

4. Lang and Soberman are quoted in John B. Rae, *The Road and Car in American Life* (Cambridge, Mass., 1971), 276. See also Barrett, *Automobile and Urban Transit*, 128–29; Mallach, "The Decline of Urban Mass Transportation," 1–17; Carlos A. Schwantes, "The West Adapts the Automobile: Technology, Unemployment, and the Jitney Phenomenon of 1914–1917," *Western Historical Quarterly* 16 (1985): 307–13; Christopher Armstrong and H. V. Nelles, *Monopoly's Moment: The Organization and Regulation of Canadian Utilities, 1830–1930* (Philadelphia, 1986), chap. 2. It is useful to read the Canadian and American stories together, since the former puts into perspective some of the more specifically American explanations for universal phenomena, especially those involving a General Motors "conspiracy." See also Donald F. Davis, "Mass Transit and Private Ownership: An Alternative Perspective on the Case of Toronto," *Urban History Review*, no. 3–78 (February 1979): 60–98; Michael Doucet, "Politics, Space, and Trolleys: Mass Transit in Early Twentieth Century Toronto," in Gilbert A. Stelter and Alan F. J. Artibise, eds., *Shaping the Urban Landscape: Aspects of the Canadian City-Building Process* (Ottawa, 1982). Motor vehicles also seemed more ideologically correct than steam railroads in America in this era; see Warren Belasco, "Cars versus Trains: 1980 and 1910," in George H. Daniels and Mark Rose, eds., *Energy and Transport: Historical Perspectives on Policy Issues* (Beverly Hills, Calif., 1982), 39–53.

5. *Detroit Saturday Night*, November 12, 1912; *Detroit News*, November 2, 1914. The best sources for Detroit's transit politics between 1890 and 1922 are Melvin Holli, *Reform in Detroit: Hazen Pingree and Urban Politics* (New York, 1969), chaps. 3, 5–6; Graeme O'Geran, *A History of the Detroit Street Railways* (Detroit, 1931); Henry Barnard, *Independent Man: The Life of Senator James Couzens* (New York, 1958), 101–33; George B. Catlin, *The Story of Detroit* (Detroit, 1923), 621–40; Paul Leake, *History of Detroit* (Chicago, 1912), 1:171–95; Jere C. Hutchins, *A Personal Story* (Detroit, 1938); Ashod Apprahamian, "The Mayoral Politics of Detroit, 1897–1912" (Ph.D. diss., New York University, 1968); John M. T. Chavis, "James Couzens: Mayor of Detroit, 1919–1922" (Ph.D. diss., Michigan State University, 1970); Delos F. Wilcox, "The Street Railway Crisis in Detroit," *Economic World*, 96 (October 23, 1915): 526–29. See also Donald F. Davis, "The City Remodelled: The Limits of Automotive Industry Leadership in Detroit, 1910–1929," *Histoire Sociale—Social History* 26 (November 1980): 451–86, for an extended discussion of the themes in this chapter.

6. *Detroit Times*, March 12, 1929; *Detroit News*, February 9, 1929; Allan Nevins and Frank Ernest Hill, *Ford: Expansion and Challenge, 1915–1933* (New York, 1957), 279, 687; and Memorandum of Conference with E. G. Liebold, November 14, 1924, Box 9, RTCP.

7. Leonard S. Wilson, "Functional Areas of Detroit, 1890–1933," *Papers of

the Michigan Academy of Science, Arts, and Letters 22 (1936): 401–3; Jerome G. Thomas, "The City of Detroit: A Study in Urban Geography" (Ph.D. diss., University of Michigan, 1929), 57; Daniel Nelson, *Managers and Workers: Origins of the New Factory System in the United States, 1880–1920* (Madison, Wis., 1975), 9–16.

8. Thomas, "City of Detroit," 58; Wilson, "Functional Areas," 403–6; Thomas J. Ticknor, "Motor City: The Impact of the Automobile Industry upon Detroit, 1900–1975" (Ph.D. diss., University of Michigan, 1978), 59, 193. Also the construction of mass transit systems to serve their outlying plants would allow them to socialize many of the costs of production, in effect lowering their land costs by transferring them to the transit company.

9. Donald R. Deskins, *Residential Mobility of Negroes in Detroit, 1837–1965* (Ann Arbor, Mich., 1972), 79; City Plan Commission, *The People of Detroit* (Detroit, 1946), 28; Wilson, "Functional Areas," 403.

10. *Detroit News,* July 15, 1914; Malcolm Bingay, introduction to Hutchins, *Personal Story.*

11. Apprahamian, "Mayoral Politics," 285–86, 341–42; O'Geran, *Detroit Street Railways,* 249–69, 281–82; *Detroit News,* July 15, 29, 1910, and January 7, 10, 24, 1912; *Detroit Times,* September 30, 1915.

12. Barnard, *Independent Man,* 84; O'Geran, *Detroit Street Railways,* 275; *Detroit News,* August 6, 1913. Mahon resigned in April 1914 (apparently feeling that his fellow commissioners were insufficiently zealous for municipal ownership). Dodge then obtained the appointment of James Wilkie, chief mechanical engineer of Parke-Davis, the pharmaceutical company. See *Detroit News,* April 21, 23, 1914, and October 19, 1915.

13. Hutchins, *Personal Story,* 244–49; O'Geran, *Detroit Street Railways,* 275–77.

14. Jay G. Hayden to Couzens, August 4, 1915, Box 1, General Correspondence, JCP; O'Geran, *Detroit Street Railways,* 274–89; *Detroit Journal,* September 28 and October 30, 1915; *Detroit News,* October 23, 1915; Henry B. Joy, "Placing the Blame for Our Street Car Troubles," *Detroit Saturday Night,* October 23, 1915.

15. *Detroit News,* October 13, 14, 1915.

16. *Detroit News,* August 24, October 13, 14, 20, 26–28, November 3, 1915. Journalist William Lutz has attributed the defeat to the refusal of Dodge and Couzens to distribute $5,000 to saloonkeepers, then the core of the city's political machine; see Lutz, *The News of Detroit* (Boston, 1973), 46.

17. Richard Barry, "Newberry's Successor: A Study of Senator Couzens," *Outlook* 132 (December 20, 1922): 697.

18. *Detroit Free Press,* October 23, 1936; Barry, "Newberry's Successor," 697.

19. Circular from F. R. Randall, dated August 21, 1918, JCP; Couzens to J. W. Anderson, September 13, 1918, Box 6, General Correspondence, JCP; *Detroit News,* August 24 and July 16, 1918; *Detroit Times,* July 26, 1918.

20. *Detroit Times,* July 13 and August 22, 1918; *Detroit News,* August 24, 1918.

21. Couzens to Otto Kirchner, July 23, 1918; Ralph Stone to Couzens, August 5, 1918; C. B. Van Dusen to W. J. Kennedy, August 12, 1918; and Couzens to O. P. Holloway, August 19, 1918, all in Box 6, Special Correspondence, JCP; also Henry Leland to "Patriotic Voters," August 24, 1918; S. S. Kresge to "My Friends," [August 1918]; and Pliny Marsh to George E. Miller, August 6, 1918, all in Box 4, CLP; *Detroit News*, July 23 and August 24, 1918; *Detroit Times*, July 26, 1918.

22. *Detroit News*, July 27 and August 3, 1918; *Detroit Journal*, July 11 and August 3, 1918.

23. *Detroit News*, July 27 and August 8–11, 1918; Barnard, *Independent Man*, 115–16.

24. Leland to Philip H. Reid [editor, *Detroit Free Press*], August 12, 1918, Box 4, CLP; *Detroit Saturday Night*, August 10, 1918; *Detroit News*, August 13, 1918.

25. Couzens to Walter C. Piper, September 4, 1918; Judson Bradway to Couzens, October 30, 1918; and John V. Moran to Frank Randall, August 24, 1918, all in Boxes 6 and 7, Special Correspondence, JCP; *Detroit Times*, August 28, 29, 1918; *Detroit News*, August 28, 1918. Mayor Marx, Gillespie, and Duffield waited only one-day before declaring for Couzens; see *Detroit News*, August 29, 1918.

26. Barnard, *Independent Man*, 126; *Detroit News*, March 20, 1919; O'Geran, *Detroit Street Railways*, 290–98.

27. Barnard, *Independent Man*, 127–28; *Detroit News*, April 6, 1919. Ford's opposition may be explained by his quarrel with his minority stockholders, Couzens among them. Once Couzens had come to terms, Ford became more cooperative on municipal ownership.

28. *Detroit News*, April 8, 1919; O'Geran, *Detroit Street Railways*, 302–8; Hutchins, *Personal Story*, 274.

29. *Detroit News*, November 6, 12, 1919.

30. *Detroit News*, October 24, 30 and November 18, 19, 1919; January 28, 1920. With respect to the auto industry's role in the 1920 referendum campaign, see Henry B. Joy, "Rides-at-Cost-Plan for Street Railway Service in Detroit" (unpublished), February 20, 1920, BHC, and *Detroit Saturday Night*, March 20, 1920, which give the membership of the Citizens' Committee on Street Railway Service, a business lobby against Couzens's M.O. plan. Its members included H. M. Leland, Joseph Boyer, W. Rex Johnston (Lincoln), Sidney Waldon (ex-Packard, ex-Cadillac), E. W. Clark (ex-GM), F. W. Hodges (Detroit Lubricator Co.), C. D. Hastings (Hupmobile), Henry Joy (Packard), S. Wells Utley (auto parts), and D. M. Ireland (Hayes Manufacturing Co.). The Detroit Board of Commerce voted 1,275 to 82 in favor of the Tayler Plan; see *Detroiter* 11 (November 17, 1919): 16.

31. Hayden quoted in Barnard, *Independent Man*, 130; Chavis, "James Couzens," 128; *Detroit News*, April 16, 1922.

32. Barnard, *Independent Man*, 130; O'Geran, *Detroit Street Railways*, 347–72; Frederick R. Barkley, "The People Win in Detroit," *Nation* 110 (May 18, 1920): 617–18.

33. *Detroit News*, April 18, 1922; O'Geran, *Detroit Street Railways*, 358–67.

34. *Detroit News*, October 24, 30, 1919.

35. *Automotive Industries* 41 (December 25, 1919): 1288; *Detroit News*, November 4, 1919, and March 16, April 4, 1920; *Detroiter* 10 (June 16, 1919): 8; *Detroit Saturday Night*, March 13, 1920. Detroit Motor Bus was organized in November 1919 at a meeting called by Henry Leland. He said buses would help until a subway could be built. By 1925 the company was carrying 36 million passengers in twenty-four buses. It was strongest in the northwest suburbs, where it competed directly with the DUR. The municipal Department of Street Railways started using buses in 1924; it had eight bus lines, sixty-four buses, and fifty-two miles of routes by the following year. The DSR buses charged a ten-cent fare for express service to outlying districts. In 1927 the board of Detroit Motor Bus boasted several members of the automotive community, including W. B. Mayo (Ford), A. B. C. Hardy (ex-GM), H. H. Emmons (ex-Regal); W. E. Metzger (ex-E-M-F, Rickenbacker), S. D. Waldon (ex-Packard, Cadillac). See *Detroit Times*, September 1, 1925; *Detroit News*, August 3, 1924, and March 14, 1926.

36. *Detroit News*, November 4, 1919; March 16, 31, and April 4, 1920; also *Automotive Industries* 41 (December 25, 1919): 1288; *Detroiter* 10 (June 16, 1919), and 14 (September 3, 1923): 9; *Detroit Saturday Night*, March 13, 1920.

37. The organization of the RTC can be followed in the correspondence between Couzens and the Rapid Transit Committee, Detroit Section, American Society of Civil Engineers, July-November 1922, Box 4, Detroit Mayor's Papers, 1922, BHC. See also *Detroit News*, December 30, 1922; *Detroiter* 17 (August 30, 1926): 11.

38. Clipping from *Motor News* dated March 1945, Sidney D. Waldon File, NAHC; *Detroit Saturday Night*, May 30, 1931; *Detroit News*, January 21, 1945. At the time of his appointment Waldon headed both the Detroit Automobile Club and the Detroit Aviation Society.

39. Waldon to Colonel Robert McCormick, July 25, 1924, Box 1, RTCP; Waldon to T. S. Seeley, September 19, 1923, Box 2, Sidney D. Waldon Papers, BHC; *Detroit News*, March 14, 1926.

40. Minutes, Rapid Transit Commission, April 10, 1924, RTCP; "Commission's Report to the Mayor for the Month of March," April 3, 1923, Box 9, RTCP; *Detroit News*, February 9 and March 28, 1929.

41. "Report on Proposed Ten Year Program for Street Widening," March 22, 1929, Box 4, RTCP; C. E. Rightor, "The Progress of Rapid Transit in Detroit," *National Municipal Review*, March 1927, pp. 310–13.

42. *Detroit News*, August 14, 1924, and February 14, 1925; *Detroiter* 17 (August 30, 1926): 11; C. E. Rightor, *The Progress of Rapid Transit in Detroit* (1926), pamphlet, Box 4, Waldon Papers, NAHC. The RTC was told by the mayor that its plan must not increase taxes or require the municipal government to issue new bonds. The delay was also explained by the need to amend the State Home Rule Act to permit construction of a subway system and to amend the city charter. These two legal hurdles were not cleared until November 1925.

43. *Detroit News*, September 8, 1924, August 17, 1926, and March 24,

1929; RTC minutes, November 29, 1926, RTCP; memorandum of conference with Mr. Frick, November 9, 1926, Box 10, RTCP. The commission hoped to have a referendum in the spring of 1925, but the Michigan Manufacturers' Association bottled up the necessary enabling legislation, preventing a vote. The automobile industry's control of the association can be inferred from the delegation it sent to the RTC to discuss subways: Arthur T. Waterfall, vice-president of Dodge Brothers; Milton Tibbets, Packard counsel; Earl W. Webb of General Motors; Hal H. Smith, president of Hayes Manufacturing (wheels); J. Mallery, president of the association; and John Lovett, its executive director. See *Detroit News*, February 15, 1925, for an account of this meeting.

44. Davis, "City Remodelled," 469–72.

45. Report, J. P. Hallihan to Mayor John C. Lodge, January 8, 1929, Box 3, 1929, Detroit Mayor's Papers, BHC; *Detroit News*, January 11, 1929; *Detroit Times*, January 10, 1929; *Detroit Free Press*, February 2, 1929.

46. Memoranda of meetings with the Business Property Association, December 26, 1928, and February 7, 1929, RTCP; *Detroit News*, January 27, February 9, and March 24, 1929; *Detroit Free Press*, February 9, 1929; Ticknor, "Motor City," 186. For comparison, see accounts of mass transit politics in Los Angeles and Chicago in the 1920s by Robert Fogelson, *The Fragmented Metropolis: Los Angeles, 1850–1930* (Cambridge, Mass., 1967), 175–82; Barrett, *Automobile and Urban Transit*, chaps. 2–3, 6; Foster, *Streetcar to Superhighway*, chap. 4; Mark S. Foster, "The Model-T, the Hard Sell, and Los Angeles's Urban Growth: The Decentralization of Los Angeles during the 1920s," *Pacific Historical Review* 44 (November 1975): 459–84.

47. *Detroit News*, February 9, 22, and March 10, 24, 27, 1929; minutes of joint meeting of the Rapid Transit Commission and Department of Street Railways, February 8, 1929, Box 12, RTCP; memoranda of meetings of Citizens' Better Transportation Committee, February 25 and March 4, 1929, Box 16, RTCP; *Detroit News*, March 14, 1926.

48. *Detroit Times*, March 12, 1929; Nevins and Hill, *Ford: Expansion and Challenge*, 279, 524, 687; *Detroit News*, February 9 and March 17, 24, 1929; minutes of joint meeting of RTC and Department of Street Railways, February 8, 1929, Box 12, RTCP.

49. *Detroit News*, March 23 and April 2, 1929; *Detroit Free Press*, April 2, 1929.

50. Minutes of joint meeting of RTC and Department of Street Railways, April 5, 1929, Box 12, RTCP; R. D. McKenzie, *The Metropolitan Community* (New York, 1933), 8.

51. Waldon to Couzens, April 4, 1929, Box 3, RTCP. Only eight precincts beyond Grand Boulevard gave 60 percent support to the subway.

52. *Detroit News*, February 4, 9, March 9, and April 2, 1929; *Detroit Labor News*, March 29, 1929; *Detroit Times*, February 12, 14, 1929; *Detroit Free Press*, March 25, 1928; memorandum of conference with Downtown Property Owners Association, February 7, 1929, RTCP; minutes, joint meeting of RTC and Department of Street Railways, April 5, 1929, Box 12, RTCP; Howard P. Jones, "Barber Shop Opinion and Rapid Transit in Detroit," *National*

Municipal Review (June 1929): 359–63; Foster, *Streetcar to Superhighway*, 80–86; Barrett, *Automobile and Urban Transit*, 184. For a more extended discussion of the opposition to rapid transit in Detroit, see Davis, "City Remodelled," 474–85; Maurice Ramsey, "Some Aspects of Non-Partisan Government in Detroit, 1918–1940" (Ph.D. diss., University of Michigan, 1944), 183–201; Raymond R. Fragnoli, *The Transformation of Reform: Progressivism in Detroit—and After, 1912–1933* (New York, 1982), chap. 7.

53. Foster, *Streetcar to Superhighway*, 86.

54. There is little consensus among transportation experts on the merits of fixed-rail rapid transit; even so, there is evidence of a correlation between transit well-being and the early existence of either subways or municipal ownership (or preferably both). See, e.g., Yago, *Decline of Transit*, 25, 62, 182; McKenzie, *Metropolitan Community*, chap. 20; Lewis M. Schneider, *Marketing Urban Mass Transit* (Boston, 1965), chap. 2; Fogelson, *Fragmented Metropolis*, 171–75.

55. These comments are limited to the period before 1930. There is evidence that the automotive industry had by 1934 adopted the same negativism toward rail transit in Detroit as it apparently had nationwide. John P. Hallihan of the RTC wrote a Ford official in April 1934: "The forces that are preventing [the federal Public Works Administration from considering Detroit's latest subway proposal] are the Manufacturers Association, the N.A.C.C. [National Automobile Chamber of Commerce, the auto manufacturers' trade association] and Senator James Couzens"; see Hallihan to Ernest Liebold, April 16, 1934, Box 5, RTCP.

56. See Holli, *Reform in Detroit*, chap. 6.

Chapter Eight

1. For an extended account of the Newberry-Ford contest, consult Spencer Ervin, *Henry Ford vs. Truman H. Newberry* (New York, 1935); Allan Nevins and Frank Ernest Hill, *Ford: Expansion and Challenge, 1915–1933* (New York, 1957), 116–24; Donald F. Davis, "The Decline of the Gasoline Aristocracy: The Struggle for Supremacy in Detroit and the Automobile Industry, 1896–1933," (Ph.D. diss., Harvard University, 1976), 416–39. For Newberry's biography, see Ervin, *Ford vs. Newberry*, 7–8; Thomas Phillips, "Truman Newberry, Citizen and Patriot," *Detroit Saturday Night*, October 26, 1918.

2. Josephus Daniels, *The Wilson Era: Years of War and After, 1917–1923* (Chapel Hill, N.C., 1946), 293–98; Seward Livermore, *Politics Is Adjourned: Woodrow Wilson and the War Congress, 1916–1918* (Middleton, Conn., 1966), 158–60; Ray S. Baker, *Life and Letters of Woodrow Wilson* (New York, 1939), 8:209; *Detroit News*, June 12 and 15, 1918; *New York Times*, June 23, 1918; *Detroit Journal*, June 14, 1918.

3. According to the *New York Times*, September 18, 1918, Truman Newberry received 48 percent of the Republican primary vote, Henry Ford 30 percent. In the Democratic primary Ford led with 79 percent, James Helme following with 21 percent. For the role of the Newberry campaign in

Helme's candidacy (to deter Ford Democrats from cross-voting in the Republican primary), see Ervin, *Ford vs. Newberry*, 265–71; the James Helme Papers and a typescript by Beatrice Ecker titled "The Famous Senatorial Election of 1918," both in MHC; Senate Subcommittee on Privileges and Elections, *Hearings: Senator from Michigan*, 67th Cong., 1st sess., 1920, 446–49, also containing *Bill of Exceptions* presented to Supreme Court in Truman Newberry et al., Plaintiffs in Error v. the United States of America, 675–77, 904–5.

4. *Detroit News*, November 6, 7, 1918; *New York Times*, November 7, 27, 1918, and February 3, 1921. The final count was 217,085 to 212,751. John Dodge, chairman of the State GOP's finance committee, attributed Ford's strong showing to a backlash from the German community: a Newberry advertisement had castigated Ford for being a "Hun-lover" when he refused to fire 250 German aliens then in his employ. See J. D. Mangum to Truman Newberry, November 26, 1918, Box 9, TNP.

5. *Congressional Record* 62, pt. 1 (January 9, 1922), 962; *New York Times*, August 23, September 27, 1918, and November 2, 1922; Ervin, *Ford vs. Newberry*, 18–21, 298–308. The Michigan Corrupt Practices Act of 1913 limited campaign spending to one-quarter of the first year's salary of the office being sought; for a United States Senator that meant $3,750. The Federal Corrupt Practices Act of 1910 set a limit of $10,000 (for both nomination and election) or the state limit, whichever was lower.

6. *Bill of Exceptions*, 280; *New York Times*, August 24, November 21, 1918, November 29, 1919, and February 6, 1920; Henry B. Joy to C. S. Osborn, April 17, 1919, Chase Osborn Papers, MHC.

7. *Hearings: Senator from Michigan*, 893, 947; also Truman Newberry to H. B. Joy, September 20, 1918; Newberry to Alvan Macauley, June 25, 1921; Newberry to H. E. Bodman, September 16, 1918; and Harry M. Jewett to Newberry, June 24, 1918, all in Boxes 1, 6, 377, TNP.

8. Russell Alger to Truman Newberry, October 7, 1918, Box 7, TNP.

9. Ervin, *Ford vs. Newberry*, 12; *Hearings: Senator from Michigan*, 715–20; S. T. Miller to Truman Newberry, September 1, 1918, Box 6, TNP, *Bill of Exceptions*, 824, 830.

10. The scope of the auto industry's support for Newberry can be divined from an advertisement in the *Detroit Times* of November 2, 1918, which carried endorsements from (among others) Alvan Macauley and R. Alger, Jr. (Packard), John and Burt Lambert (ex-Regal; Lambert & Clayton, auto parts), H. P. Carrow (Hayes Manufacturing), R. D. Chapin (Hudson), Horace and John Dodge (Dodge Brothers), H. M. Jewett and Gilbert W. Lee (Paige), Garvin Denby (Denby Truck), Percy Owen (Liberty), W. E. Flanders (Maxwell), A. R. Demory (Timken-Detroit Axle), A. H. Zimmerman (Continental Motors), C. D. Hastings (Hupp), Joseph Boyer and Henry Leland (Lincoln), R. H. Collins and W. C. Durant (GM). The Newberry Papers also contain several dozen letters of support from auto industry investors and executives. For William Durant's contribution, see *New York Times*, June 14, 1921, and *Automotive Industries* 44 (June 16, 1921), 1354; he was accused of having Buick executives impose overtime on Ford's supporters to keep them

from voting. For Roscoe Jackson's position, see Roy Chapin to Inez Chapin, October 27, 1918, RCP.

11. *Detroit Times*, October 14 and November 25, 1918; Keith Sward, *The Legend of Henry Ford* (New York, 1948), 119; Allan Nevins, *Ford: The Times, The Man, The Company* (New York, 1954), 399; Nevins and Hill, *Ford: Expansion and Challenge*, 120, 149; *Detroit News*, June 14, July 7, 1918; E. G. Liebold and George M. Holley, Sr., *Reminiscences*, FA; Harvey Firestone, *Men and Rubber* (Garden City, N.Y., 1926), 1–10, cf. 77.

12. James O. Murfin to Truman Newberry, August 1, 1918, Box 1, TNP; *Detroit Saturday Night*, October 26, 1918; Sward, *Legend*, 95; Nevins and Hill, *Ford: Expansion and Challenge*, 119; *Detroit News*, August 29, 1918.

13. *New York Times*, November 16, 21, 1918; Ervin, *Ford vs. Newberry*, 30–31; Liebold, *Reminiscences*, FA; Sward, *Legend*, 120–21.

14. Nevins and Hill, *Ford: Expansion and Challenge*, 122–23; Liebold, *Reminiscences*, FA; Sward, *Legend*, 120–21; E. G. Pipp, *Henry Ford, Both Sides of Him* (Detroit, 1926), 31. The grand jury mentioned here was the second to examine the Newberry affair. The first was convened in New York City in October 1918; its inquiry collapsed when Newberry and his political lieutenants cited its lack of jurisdiction and refused to testify.

15. Ervin, *Ford vs. Newberry*, 40–56; *New York Times*, November 30, 1919, March 22, 1920, and May 3, 1921.

16. *Congressional Record* 62, pt. 1 (January 9, 11, 12, 1922), 963, 1053, 1099; *New York Times*, January 13, 1922.

17. *New York Times*, January 14, 1922.

18. *Detroit News*, July 15, September 11 and 22, 1922; *New York Times*, March 9, June 11, and July 22, 1922; *Pipp's Weekly*, June 24, 1922; Chapin to Albert D. Lasker, July 31, 1922, Box 11, RCP. Newberry himself contributed $1,000 to Townsend's campaign. He also subsidized *Pipp's Weekly*, whose only journalistic purpose seems to have been Henry Ford's comeuppance. See Newberry to E. G. Pipp, April 21, 1922, Box 32, TNP; Sward, *Legend*, 118; *Detroit News*, November 22, 1922.

19. *New York Times*, August 27, 1922; *Detroit News*, July 8, September 11, 13, 30, and November 3, 1922.

20. *Congressional Record* 62, pt. 1 (January 7, 1922), 935; *Detroit News*, August 6 and November 2, 6, 8, 1922.

21. *Detroit News*, November 8, 1922; *New York Times*, November 9, 15, 20, 1922.

22. *Congressional Record* 62, pts. 1, 2 (January 7, 27, 1922), 935, 1811.

23. Truman Newberry to George Moses, November 28, 1922, and Newberry to Charles Townsend, November 29, 1922, Box 34, TNP.

24. *New York Times*, November 30, 1922; Henry Barnard, *Independent Man: The Life of Senator James Couzens* (New York, 1958), 137–38; Frank B. Woodford, *Alex J. Groesbeck: Portrait of a Public Man* (Detroit, 1962), 187–90.

25. Mrs. Wilfred Leland, *Master of Precision: Henry Leland* (Detroit, 1966), 259, 253; J. Walter Drake to Edwin Denby, December 23, 1925, and James Inglis to Denby, February 4, 1926, Box 1, Edwin Denby Papers, MHC;

Detroit Times, December 13, 1925; C. M. Burton, *The City of Detroit, Michigan, 1701–1922* (Detroit, 1922), 4:423; *Detroit News*, March 2, 1924.

26. "Charles B. Warren," typescript biography in C. B. Warren Papers, BHC; Burton, *City of Detroit*, 2:498–500; William Allen White, *A Puritan in Babylon: The Story of Calvin Coolidge* (New York, 1938), 320–23; Donald R. McCoy, *Calvin Coolidge: The Quiet President* (New York, 1967), 278–80; *Detroit News*, March 11, 1925; *Congressional Record* 67, pt. 1 (March 10, 11, 16, 1925), 100, 101, 254; *Detroit Free Press*, March 11, 1925.

27. Orla B. Taylor, "The Plot to Give the Cream of the Banking Profits of the Entire Country to the Customers of the New York Investment Bankers," typescript, Box 1, Orla B. Taylor Papers, MHC; Walter L. Dunham, *Banking and Industry in Michigan* (Detroit, 1929), 145–46.

28. BCGB, 2 (pt. 9): 1039–41. SEP, 4210, 4543; John Joseph Holland, Jr., "The Detroit Banking Collapse of 1933" (Ph.D. diss., New York University, 1972), 210–11; *Detroit News*, February 8, 1927, and May 19, 1964; *Detroit Times*, June 7, 1958; Ferdinand Pecora, *Wall Street under Oath: The Story of Our Modern Money Changers* (New York, 1939), 235; Susan Kennedy, "The Michigan Banking Crisis of 1933," *Michigan History* 57 (1973), 239–41; Nevins and Hill, *Ford: Expansion and Challenge*, 465; Liebold, *Reminiscences*, FA; Woodford, *Alex Groesbeck*, 275. The founders of the Guardian Detroit Bank were R. H. Booth (*Detroit News*), Ernest Kanzler (ex-Ford), Edsel Ford, W. Ledyard Mitchell (Chrysler), Henry Bodman and Alvan Macauley (Packard), William R. Wilson (ex-Maxwell), Fred T. Murphy (ex-Lincoln), Roy Chapin, Roscoe Jackson and Howard E. Coffin (Hudson), J. E. J. Keane (investment broker), W. O. Briggs (Briggs Manufacturing), James Murray (Murray Body), Fred J. Fisher and C. S. Mott (GM), George R. Fink (Michigan Steel), Albert Kahn (architect), Alger Shelden (capitalist). Edsel Ford originally owned 1.5 percent of the Guardian Group's shares; by 1933 this was up to 3.5 percent.

29. SEP, 4203–17; Pecora, *Wall Street*, 235; Guardian Detroit Union Group, Inc., *Semi-Annual Report*, June 30, 1931, Box 11, James Couzens Papers, LC. The decision to create a group rather than a unit bank is explained by the need for a holding company to acquire the suburban Ford banks. Michigan law then restricted branching to a single municipality, in this case Detroit proper; see BCGB, 2 (pt. 9): 1041.

30. *Detroit News*, January 24, 1934; SEP, 4208, 5077–80; G. Walter Woodworth, *The Detroit Money Market* (Ann Arbor, Mich., 1932), 2. Of the banks going into Detroit Bankers, only one was a product of the automotive revolution: the Bank of Michigan was the progeny of a merger between Dime Savings and Merchants National, the latter having been launched by the Dodge brothers in 1914. See Arthur M. Woodford, *Detroit and Its Banks: The Story of Detroit Bank & Trust* (Detroit, 1974), 158–61. The Mendelssohns, who bankrolled Fisher Body, constituted a partial exception. They made the money for this venture at Modern Match Company before 1909. See E. G. Pipp, *Men Who Have Made Michigan* (Detroit, 1927), 32.

31. SEP, 4211, 4217, 4548, 4789; Woodworth, *Money Market*, 18–19; *Group News* [Guardian Detroit Union Group] 1 (April 1930): 5, and 2 (July

1931): 6, in BHC; BCGB, 2 (pt. 9): 1048, 1162–63. New York City residents owned 2.13 percent of the shares of the Guardian Group in December 1929 (there were 8,090 stockholders in all).

32. *Detroit Free Press*, December 29, 1927; Pecora, *Wall Street*, 236; SEP, 5077–80; Ruth D. Roth, "Nightmare in February" (M.A. thesis, Wayne State University, 1956), 13; Woodworth, *Money Market*, 2; "Brief History of First National Bank–Detroit," Box 1, JDP. The fear of external takeover was widespread in midwestern banking circles in the late 1920s, although a smaller city like Milwaukee was often as afraid of such regional centers as Minneapolis–Saint Paul as it was of Wall Street. For the defensive character of banking mergers in the 1920s and early 1930s, see BCGB, 1 (pt. 4): 1796 and 1 (pt. 8): 792–877; George S. Eccles, *The Politics of Banking* (Salt Lake City, Utah, 1982), 68; Gaines Thomson Cartinhour, *Branch, Group, and Chain Banking* (New York, 1931), 127–31; *American Banker*, February 20, 1930, p. 2.

33. SEP, 5058–68, 5474–76, 5743–44; Allan Nevins and Frank Ernest Hill, *Ford: Decline and Rebirth, 1933–1962* (New York, 1962), 5–8. Ninety percent of First National's deposits came from its 9,000 shareholders. Old-family entrepreneurs with significant holdings (more than 20,000 shares) in the Guardian Group included Henry B. Joy, the heirs of Simon Murphy, the heirs of Martin Smith (Senator Alger's lumber partner), and the Alger, McMillan, and Newberry families. See *Detroit News*, April 10, 1934.

34. School of Public Affairs and Social Work, Wayne University, report no. 10, *Accumulated Social and Economic Statistics for Detroit* (Detroit, 1937), 3, 5, 17; Automobile Quarterly, *The American Car since 1775* (New York, 1971), 140–41; Woodworth, *Money Market*, 3–4; SEP, 5488; *Detroit Free Press*, March 20, 1933. First National's deposits peaked in June 30, 1931, at $566.2 million but had fallen to $398.1 million by February 11, 1933, a drop of almost 30 percent. See "Brief History of First National Bank–Detroit," JDP.

35. SEP, 4218, 4626, 4663, 4677–85; Barnard, *Independent Man*, 219; *Detroit Free Press*, February 15, 1933; *Detroit News*, June 16, 1933.

36. SEP, 4554–63, 4723–28, 4740–42; Barnard, *Independent Man*, 219; *Detroit News*, June 16, 1933.

37. For the uproar over the Dawes loan, see Bascom Timmins, *Portrait of an American: Charles G. Dawes* (New York, 1953), 316–20; Jesse Jones, *Fifty Billion Dollars: My Thirteen Years with RFC* (New York, 1951), 72–81; F. Cyril James, *The Growth of Chicago Banks* (New York, 1938), 2:1032–93.

38. Herbert Hoover, *Memoirs* (New York, 1952), 3:206–7.

39. "Draft of Statement on Bank Closings by Couzens for Senator's Committee, 1936," Box 140, JCP; Barnard, *Independent Man*, 224; Jones, *Fifty Billion Dollars*, 61.

40. Barnard, *Independent Man*, 224–26; *Detroit News*, June 20, August 17 and 25, 1933; Hoover, *Memoirs*, 3:206; C. David Tompkins, *Senator Arthur Vandenberg: The Evolution of a Modern Republican, 1884–1945* (East Lansing, Mich., 1970), 76–77; SEP, 5793; Arthur A. Ballantine, "When All the Banks Closed," *Harvard Business Review* 26 (March 1948): 135–36.

41. Donaldson Brown, *Some Reminiscences of an Industrialist* (privately printed, 1957), 74–75; Alfred P. Sloan, Jr., *Adventures of a White-Collar Man* (New York, 1941), 172; SEP, 4732; GJP, 199; "Chronology of Banking Holiday" for February 12, 1933, typescript, JDP.

42. Brown, *Some Reminiscences*, 75–77; Ballantine, "When All the Banks Closed," 136; SEP, 4736–37, 5795–98; Barnard, *Independent Man*, 230; *Detroit News*, July 17, 1933; RFC Board Minutes, vol. 13, pt. 1, February 11, 1933, 750, RFCP.

43. *Detroit News*, February 11, 1934; Jones, *Fifty Billion Dollars*, 62; A. N. Marquis & Co., *Who Was Who in America* (Chicago, 1968), 4:53; Ballantine, "When All the Banks Closed," 142. For Chapin, see J. C. Long, *Roy D. Chapin* (privately printed, 1945).

44. GJP, 102, 135. See also W. E. Scripps, publisher *Detroit News*, to James Couzens, April 12, 1933, Box 140, JCP.

45. Susan Kennedy, *The Banking Crisis of 1933* (Lexington, Ky., 1973), 91; Ballantine, "When All the Banks Closed," 137; Barnard, *Independent Man*, 81; Sward, *Legend*, 250–51; GJP, 239; RFC Minutes, vol. 13, pt. 1, February 6, 1933, p. 417, RFCP; Francis G. Awalt, "Recollections of the Banking Crisis in 1933," *Business History Review* 43 (Autumn 1969): 353–54.

46. Barnard, *Independent Man*, 229–30; Jones, *Fifty Billion Dollars*, 62–63; Raymond Moley, *The First New Deal* (New York, 1966), 137–38; Ballantine, "When All the Banks Closed," 136; SEP, 5511, 5797; Kennedy, *Banking Crisis*, 91; RFC Minutes, vol. 13, pt. 2, February 13, 1933, p. 812, RFCP.

47. Barnard, *Independent Man*, 231; Brown, *Some Reminiscences*, 78; Kennedy, *Banking Crisis*, 91–92; Awalt, "Recollections," 356. First National Bank–Detroit opposed the moratorium but closed upon the instructions of F. Gloyd Awalt, acting comptroller of currency, who said that otherwise they would get no help from the RFC. See "Chronology of Banking Holiday" for February 13, 1933, JDP. The RFC, though kept informed of events in Detroit on an hourly basis by Ballantine and Melvin Traylor, president of the First National Bank of Chicago, was a largely helpless observer. Its board minutes show that the moratorium decision was made in Detroit. See RFC Minutes, vol. 13, pt. 2, February 13, 1933, pp. 811–24, RFCP.

48. SEP, 5803; Kennedy, *Banking Crisis*, 98–99.

49. Brown, *Some Reminiscences*, 80–81; *Detroit Free Press*, February 17, 1933; *Detroit News*, June 21 and August 16, 1933; *Detroit Times*, August 16, 1933; Taylor, "The Plot," 16; Merlo J. Pusey, *Eugene Meyer* (New York, 1974), 89–95; Barnard, *Independent Man*, 243; *New York Times*, June 17, 1953; GJP, 161; "Chronology of Banking Holiday" for February 12, 1933, JDP; "Draft of Statement, 1936," JCP; Ogden Mills to W. G. Zeamer, June 26, 1933, and George W. Davison to W. G. Zeamer, June 23, 1933, Box 42, Ogden L. Mills Papers, LC.

50. GJP, 57, 160; Brown, *Some Reminiscences*, 80; *Detroit News*, June 21, August 17, and September 8, 1933; *Detroit Times*, February 21, 1933; *Detroit Free Press*, June 14, 1933. In a telegram to the *Detroit Times*, Davison

denied the charge: "There was never any suggestion or offer that New York or any one I represented would underwrite or participate in any way in the formation of the new bank." Yet he did admit suggesting that the bank be controlled "by the depositors of the old banks," which, given the numbers, meant the Big Three motor companies, two of whom had asked him to come to Detroit. His omission of Walter Chrysler and Donaldson Brown of General Motors from the list of people who suggested he go to Detroit makes his account less plausible than that of the bankers' sworn testimony at various hearings. The variance between his recollections and those of Detroit's bankers may come from the fact that he did not consider General Motors and Chrysler to constitute "New York" interests, while they did. See Davison to Zeamer, June 23, 1933, Ogden Mills Papers, LC.

51. Brown, *Some Reminiscences*, 80–81; *Detroit News*, August 17, 1933, and September 8, 1933; "Chronology of Banking Holiday" for February 17, 1933, JDP.

52. Brown, *Some Reminiscences*, 80–83. Ford was asked by Detroit Bankers on February 22 to contribute to their recapitalization, but he refused because the plan did nothing to salvage the Guardian National Bank of Commerce. See "Chronology of Banking Holiday" for February 22, 1933, JDP.

53. Brown, *Some Reminiscences*, 83; *Detroit News*, August 17, 1933; Kennedy, *Banking Crisis*, 99 (emphasis added).

54. *Detroit News*, August 17, 1933; SEP, 4748–51, 5806, 5816–19; "Chronology of Banking Holiday" for February 24, 1933, JDP; RFC Minutes, vol. 13, pt. 3, February 25, 1933, p. 1702, RFCP; "Draft of Statement, 1936," JCP.

55. *Detroit News*, February 27 and August 17, 1933; *New York Times*, February 27, 1933; *Detroit Times*, February 27, 1933; Tompkins, *Vandenberg*, 80; Sward, *Legend*, 253.

56. *Detroit News*, August 17, 1933; Barnard, *Independent Man*, 241–43; SEP, 4752–54, 5770; Tompkins, *Vandenberg*, 81; "Chronology of Banking Holiday" for February 13 and 28, 1933, JDP; "Draft of Statement, 1936," JCP; RFC Minutes, vol. 13, pt. 3, February 26, 1933, pp. 1785–86, RFCP; Nicholas Kelley, Reminiscences, 273, Oral History Research Office, Columbia University.

57. GJP, 129, 190; William Alfred Lucking and Margaret Holmes Davis v. Preston Delano, Comptroller of the Currency, and Reconstruction Finance Corporation, District Court for District of Columbia, Civil Cause 19333, filed April 13, 1943, p. 19, copy in JDP; *Detroit Free Press*, August 26, 1933; *Detroit Times*, July 7, 1933; James Couzens to W. E. Scripps, April 14, 1933, Box 140, JCP.

58. Lucking and Davis v. Delano, 22; GJP, 160–66, 498; D. Valley to Ernest C. Kanzler, June 29, 1933, Box 1, JDP.

59. GJP, 160–72; Lucking and Davis v. Delano, 25; *Detroit News*, June 15, 1933; SEP, 5473–75; Sloan, *White-Collar Man*, 174; Jones, *Fifty Billion Dollars*, 67; Kelley, Reminiscences, 273. It was only with the Banking

Act of March 9, 1933, that the RFC received the power to hold nonassessable, preferred stock issued by national banks. Under Michigan law the agency could not make a loan to a bank "known by the lender to be insolvent"; thus it could not use the preferred stock plan to reopen the two closed banks. See J. F. T. O'Connor, *The Banking Crisis and Recovery under the Roosevelt Administration* (Chicago, 1938), 56–58; "Memorandum to Mr. Bennett," May 3, 1933, RG 234, Entry 12, Box 8, RFCP. The decision to create the new bank was apparently made on March 16, or the day after the RFC's Detroit task force recommended that a new bank be formed by purchase of assets (through a "Spokane sale") of Guardian National and First National. See Richard D. Poll, *Howard J. Stoddard, Founder, Michigan National Bank* (East Lansing, Mich., 1980), 65.

60. *Detroit News*, March 23 and 25, 1933; *Detroit Free Press*, March 23 and 24, 1933; Richard D. Lunt, *The High Ministry of Government: The Political Career of Frank Murphy* (Detroit, 1965), 39.

61. Alfred P. Sloan, Jr., "A Statement to The People of Detroit," March 24, 1933, copy in BHC; Arthur Pound, *The Turning Wheel: The Story of General Motors through Twenty-Five Years, 1908–1933* (Garden City, N.Y., 1934), 423–24; *Business Week*, April 5, 1933, p. 6; Brown, *Some Reminiscences*, 86; Jones, *Fifty Billion Dollars*, 69; House Committee on Banking and Currency, Subcommittee on Domestic Finance, *Twenty Largest Stockholders of Record in Member Banks of the Federal Reserve System*, 88th Cong., 2d sess., October 15, 1964, 845. As of 1964 Fisher & Co. owned 4.2 percent of the shares. The second largest stockholder, First Pennsylvania Bank and Trust, held 2.5 percent. Mott owned 0.91 percent. The Chrysler Corporation, owner of 5 percent of National Bank of Detroit in 1933, was not among the top twenty stockholders in 1964. General Motors owned 90 percent of the bank as of 1934. The relationship between the bank and GM remained close even in 1976; that year the bank was "the largest stockvoter in General Motors," and its holding company placed two directors on GM's board of directors; see Senate Committee on Governmental Affairs, Subcommittee on Reports, Accounting and Management, *Interlocking Directorates among the Major U.S. Corporations*, 95th Cong., 2d sess., 1978, S. Doc. 95–107, 79.

62. *Detroit News*, August 10, 13, 1933; Jones, *Fifty Billion Dollars*, 69; Bascom Timmons, *Jesse H. Jones: The Man and the Statesman* (New York, 1956), 192; Patricia O'Donnell Mackenzie, "Some Aspects of the Detroit Bank Crisis" (Ph.D. diss., Wayne State University, 1963), 203; Manufacturers National Bank of Detroit, *"For the General Good": The First Ten Years of The Manufacturers National Bank of Detroit* (Detroit, 1943), 3–5; *Twenty Largest Stockholders*, 786. Note also that Edsel Ford blocked a merger of Manufacturers National with the Michigan National Bank during World War II because the new institution would not be under Ford financial control; see Poll, *Stoddard*, 168.

63. Jones, *Fifty Billion Dollars*, 68; SEP, 5481–82; *Detroit News*, September 17, 1933; Woodford, *Alex Groesbeck*, 278; Poll, *Stoddard*, 46, 59–63, 239.

64. Mackenzie, "Detroit Bank Crisis," 191–93, 212–13; Roth, "Nightmare in February," 60–61; *Detroit Free Press*, September 3, 1942, and May 12, 1949; *Detroit News*, October 4, 1945.

65. Confidential Minutes of Federal Reserve Agents, Washington Conference, November 1932; Carl P. Dennett to Eugene Meyer, June 23, 1932; Franklin D. Roosevelt to William Woodin, March 11, 1933, Boxes 17, 44, 118, all in Eugene Meyer Papers, LC; George W. Norris, *Ended Episodes* (Chicago, 1937), 215–16. The argument here owes much to Holland, "Banking Collapse," 156–58, 185–87.

66. Jones, *Fifty Billion Dollars*, 21; James Couzens to A. R. Treanor, May 29, 1933, Box 140, JCP; SEP, 5488, 5656, 5769–77, 5802–40; Kennedy, *Banking Crisis*, 98–99; Holland, "Banking Collapse," 158. Leyburn considered mortgage loans (of which First National Bank–Detroit had $150 million worth, thanks to the savings banks it had absorbed) "unsound" by definition for a commercial bank.

67. Thomas M. Storke, *California Editor* (Los Angeles, 1958), 344–45; Kennedy, *Banking Crisis*, 186–87. See also Marquis James and Bessie Rowland James, *Biography of a Bank: The Story of the Bank of America N.T. and S.A.* (New York, 1954), 368–74.

68. *Detroit Times*, March 14 and 15, 1933; *Detroit News*, July 17, 1933; GJP, 160, 167–72; James Couzens to Ernest Kern, March 22, 1933, Box 140, JCP; RFC Minutes, vol. 13, pt. 3, February 25, 1933, p. 1174, RFCP.

69. GJP, 190–92; Brown, *Some Reminiscences*, 83. Mott did not, it would appear, help to determine GM's response to the 1933 bank crisis. Judging from the memoirs of Donaldson Brown and Alfred Sloan (and the public record), at no time were the *Michigan* directors of either Chrysler or General Motors consulted. The New York offices of both corporations dictated their response, inasmuch as the affair was handled by their financial offices and bankers.

70. Pound, *Turning Wheel*, 450. Acting Comptroller of Currency F. G. Awalt was often identified as Wall Street's secret agent, even though he was a Baltimore lawyer until he joined the Treasury Department in 1920; he subsequently set up practice in Washington (see his obituary, *New York Times*, December 31, 1966). If there was a "conspiracy"—though I am inclined to agree with the *Wall Street Journal* (July 24, 1933) that Detroit's "Wall Street" plots were "childish tales" that appealed to "credulous natures or overstrained nerves"—then Couzens would seem closest to the mark in identifying William Woodin as the head of it. For Couzens's suspicions and evidence, see Barnard, *Independent Man*, 251–52. See also *Detroit News*, March 14 and August 23, 1933; Taylor, "The Plot," 13–25; Raymond Moley, *After Seven Years* (New York, 1939), 142; *New York Times*, May 4, 1934. This chapter argues that New Yorkers looked to their own self-interest, with minimal concern for the effect of their policies on Detroit's financial elite or the city's economic independence. It was a matter of indifference rather than conspiracy.

71. RFC Minutes, vol. 13, pt. 3, February 26, 1933, p. 1798, RFCP.

For the 1921 crisis, see Nevins and Hill, *Ford: Expansion and Challenge*, 163–68; Charles Sorensen, *My Forty Years with Ford* (New York, 1956), 167–68; and Harry Bennett, *We Never Called Him Henry* (New York, 1951), 28.

72. RFC Minutes, vol. 13, pt. 3, February 26, 1933, p. 1798–99, RFCP; *Detroit News*, June 16, August 17, and September 15, 1933; Arthur J. Lacy, *Reminiscences*, 45, MHC; Barnard, *Independent Man*, 232; "Draft of Statement, 1936," JCP.

73. Barnard, *Independent Man*, 286; *Detroit Free Press*, September 18, 1933; Malcolm Bingay, *Detroit Is My Home Town* (Indianapolis, Ind., 1946), 130–31. See also Couzens's testimony to the Keidan grand jury (which investigated the bank closures), reported in *Detroit News*, August 18, 1933.

74. *Detroit News*, August 1, 1934, and June 9, 1937; *New York Times*, June 30, 1934, and April 7, 1935.

75. The estimate of the loss on the two banks includes $67.3 million in capital, surplus, and undivided profits (as of February 11, 1933) and $6.9 million in assessments from the receiver, but it excludes any interest forgone on money subsequently returned by the receiver or dividends that would have accrued to the shareholders had these banks remained open. It is, accordingly, a rock-bottom figure. The original assessment levied in 1934 was $35 million, of which $24 million was actually collected by 1944. In 1946–1949, $16.9 million was returned to the shareholders of First National. See *Detroit Free Press*, March 29, 1933, June 5, 1943, and May 12, 1949; Mackenzie, "Detroit Bank Crisis," 193; Cyril B. Upham and Edwin Lamke, *Closed and Distressed Banks: A Study in Public Administration* (Washington, D.C., 1934), 99–100.

Conclusion

1. Lewis is cited in Horace Sutton, "Way Back When: Frisky, Risky Birth of the Auto Age," *Smithsonian* 11 (September 1980), 145. See also John Brooks, *Showing Off in America: From Conspicuous Consumption to Parody Display* (Boston, 1979), 275.

2. Thorstein Veblen, *The Theory of the Leisure Class* (1899; New York, 1965), 74.

3. L. J. Andrew Villalon and James M. Laux, "Steaming through New England with Locomobile," *Journal of Transport History*, n.s. 5 (September 1979), 67–82. The authors point out that the Stanley brothers (of Stanley Steamer renown) left Locomobile in 1899 at least in part because of "the company's redesign of their car [the original Locomobile] that was going to make it heavier." Although Villalon and Laux attribute Locomobile's leap into the upper price-class to the zeal for "technical excellence" among the engineering staff, who were coming increasingly to the fore, they also observe that "most of its . . . models betrayed a tendency toward more substantial and higher priced cars" even before Locomobile moved toward internal combustion. See also John B. Rae, *American Automobile Manufacturers* (Philadelphia, 1959), 26–28, 63, 71, 148–49, 167–68.

4. Villalon and Laux, "Steaming," 80.

5. Mumford is quoted in Automobile Quarterly, *General Motors: The First 75 Years* (New York, 1983), 6.

6. See Donald F. Davis, "Dependent Motorization: Canada and the Automobile to the 1930s," *Journal of Canadian Studies* 21 (Autumn 1986): 106–32.

7. Hugh Durnford and Glenn Baechler, *Cars of Canada* (Toronto, 1973), 113, 123, 130, 158, 229, 240. For the early Canadian auto industry, other useful sources include O. J. McDiarmid, "Some Aspects of the Canadian Automobile Industry," *Canadian Journal of Economics and Political Science* 6 (1940): 258–74; Howard Aikman, *The Automobile Industry of Canada*, McGill University Economic Studies No. 8 (Montreal, 1926); Robert Ankli and Fred Frederiksen, "The Influence of American Manufacturers on the Canadian Automobile Industry," *Business and Economic History*, 2d series 9 (1981): 101–13; Tom Traves, *The State and Enterprise: Canadian Manufacturers and the Federal Government, 1917–1931* (Toronto, 1979), chap. 6; Herman L. Smith, "The Neighboring Industry: Growth of the Motorcar in Canada," in Automobile Quarterly, *The American Car since 1775* (New York, 1971), 94–111.

8. The history of the Russell Motor Car Company can be found in Merrill Denison, *C.C.M., The Story of the First Fifty Years* (Toronto, 1946); Michael Bliss, *A Canadian Millionaire: The Life and Business Times of Sir Joseph Flavelle, Bart., 1858–1939* (Toronto, 1978).

9. James M. Laux, *In First Gear: The French Automobile Industry to 1914* (Montreal, 1976), 162. The conclusions for France are based on this book and Laux, "Some Notes on Entrepreneurship in the Early French Automobile Industry," *French Historical Studies* 3 (1963): 124–39; Patrick Fridenson, "Un industrie nouvelle: L'automobile en France jusqu'en 1914," *Revue d'Histoire Moderne et Contemporaine* 19 (1972): 557–78; Jacques Wolff, "Entrepreneurs et firmes: Ford et Renault de leur débuts à 1914," *Revue Économique* 9 (1957): 297–323; and a special issue on the automobile in *Mouvement Social* 81 (1972). For England, see R. J. Overy, *William Morris, Viscount Nuffield* (London, 1976); Roy Church, *Herbert Austin: The British Motor Car Industry to 1941* (London, 1979); Church and Michael Miller, "The Big Three: Competition, Management, and Marketing in the British Motor Industry, 1922–1939," in Barry Supple, ed., *Essays in British Business History* (Oxford, 1977), 163–86; and S. B. Saul, "The Motor Industry in Britain to 1914," *Business History* 5 (December 1962): 22–24; R. J. Irving, "New Industries for Old? Some Investment Decisions of Sir W. G. Armstrong, Whitworth and Co. Ltd., 1900–1914," *Business History* 17 (1975): 150–69; H. B. Castle, *Britain's Motor Industry* (London, 1950). European historians do not in general agree with the analysis offered here, although they have noted the behavioral pattern it seeks to explain. Typical of the European consensus is the comment in James Laux et al., *The Automobile Revolution* (Chapel Hill, N.C., 1982), 22: "Most of the European and many of the American makers during this period preferred . . . to aim at the wealthy with a limited output. . . . This attitude, however, should not be

considered as solely the result of snobbishness or feeble entrepreneurship. Most of the early producers of cars were technicians or engineers. They aimed to make high-quality products to satisfy their own standards and those of their peers. Reflecting their training and experience, their interests focused on elegant design and technical innovation. Yet such attitudes made their cars expensive. Few of them recognized a challenge or potential profits in factory management or marketing, for these were 'less noble' matters."

10. See Lewis Mumford, *The Myth of the Machine: The Pentagon of Power* (New York, 1970). An excellent discussion of dualistic thinking can be found in Joel Novek, "Alternative Technology: The Machine in the Garden Revisited," *Canadian Review of American Studies* 13 (Winter 1982): 291–308.

11. John N. Ingham, *The Iron Barons: A Social Analysis of an American Elite, 1874–1965* (Westport, Conn., 1978), 32. There is a growing literature that identifies mass production with the military ethos and sees it as an outgrowth of armory practice. The analysis here does not dispute that literature but does note that mass production technology simultaneously evolved out of the nation's wooden clock industry; as more civilian industries developed sufficient volume, they would probably have moved toward mass production techniques even without the example of the New England armories. This is not to deny that, having made the decision for mass production, they did not find it useful to hire someone with an armory background to teach them how to implement it. See Brooke Hindle and Steven Lubar, *Engines of Change: The American Industrial Revolution, 1790–1860* (Washington, D.C., 1986), esp. chap. 13; David Hounshell, *From the American System to Mass Production, 1800–1932* (Baltimore, Md., 1984); John Joseph Murphy, "Entrepreneurship in the Establishment of the American Clock Industry," *Journal of Economic History* 26 (1966): 169–85; Otto Mayr and Robert C. Post, eds., *Yankee Enterprise: The Rise of the American System of Manufactures* (Washington, D.C., 1981); Merritt Roe Smith, *Harpers Ferry Armory and the New Technology* (Ithaca, N.Y., 1977).

12. *Business Week*, April 5, 1933, p. 5.

13. John Joseph Holland, Jr., "The Detroit Banking Collapse of 1933" (Ph.D. diss., New York University, 1972), 251–52, 276; Patricia O'Donnell Mackenzie, "Some Aspects of the Detroit Bank Crisis" (Ph.D. diss., Wayne State University, 1963), 205–6. The "bank control" or "hegemony" thesis is argued by Anna Rochester, *Rulers of America: A Study of Finance Capital* (New York, 1936); Victor Perlo, *The Empire of High Finance* (New York, 1957); Sergei Menshikov, *Millionaires and Managers* (Moscow, 1969); Robert Fitch and Mary Oppenheimer, "Who Rules the Corporations?" *Socialist Revolution* 1 (July–August 1970): 73–103; Peter Mariolis, "Interlocking Directorates and Control of Corporations: The Theory of Bank Control," *Social Science Quarterly* 56 (1975): 425–39; Michael Patrick Allen, "Economic Interest Groups and the Corporate Elite Structure," *Social Science Quarterly* 58 (March 1978): 597–615; Davita Silfen Glasberg and Michael Schwartz, "Ownership and Control of Corporations," *Annual Review of Sociology* 9 (1983): 311–32; Beth Mintz and Michael Schwartz, "Financial

Interest Groups and Interlocking Directorates," *Social Science History* 7 (Spring 1983): 183–204; David M. Kotz, *Bank Control of Large Corporations in the United States* (Berkeley, Calif., 1978); Mark Mizruchi, "Relations among Large American Corporations, 1904–1974," *Social Science History* 7 (Spring 1983): 165–82; James Bearden and Beth Mintz, "Regionality and Integration in the American Network," in Frans N. Stokman et al., *Networks of Corporate Power* (Oxford, 1985), 234–49.

14. SEP, 5497; *Detroit Free Press*, June 27, 1933; Mackenzie, "Detroit Bank Crisis," 205–6. See also the comments of Alex Groesbeck in GJP, 116. The conclusion in this paragraph conflicts with the findings of Detroit sociologist Lynda Ann Ewen in her *Corporate Power and Urban Crisis in Detroit* (Princeton, N.J., 1978). Ewen stresses continuity, the inertial force of class relationships. She argues that the local "ruling class" has not only endured the upheavals of this century but has grown stronger through intermarriage, and her kinship charts do demonstrate remarkable endogamy among the descendants of Detroit's pre-automotive elites. Ewen is less successful, however, in showing that these interlocked families still wield power over Detroit's economy; she too readily assumes that a seat on a corporate board denotes or confers control, whereas patrician directors of companies long controlled by outside capital may simply have been chosen as a public relations gesture. They undoubtedly have less influence than representatives of interlocked banks and corporations of national stature. Ewen endeavors to support her thesis that Detroit's traditional ruling class has survived with its economic power intact by providing information on stock ownership, where known, for the major corporations with headquarters in the Detroit area. She has found data for eleven of the twelve Detroit-based companies ranked among the 500 largest industrials by *Fortune* magazine in 1979; she identifies seven as being owned and controlled by local money at the time of her study. Of these, however, only Ford ranks among the top five industrials in Detroit, and none of the seven is owned by the city's old families unless the Fords be so regarded. The two firms that conform best to Ewen's thesis are Wydandotte Chemicals and Parke-Davis, both independent and locally controlled in 1969, the year for which she collected ownership data. Yet neither firm was listed among the *Fortune* 500 in 1979 because they had in the interim become wholly owned subsidiaries of non-Michigan companies; they went the way of J. L. Hudson department stores—another old family business mentioned by Ewen—which was sold to a Minneapolis firm in 1969.

15. See Rochester, *Rulers of America*; Temporary National Economic Committee, *The Distribution of Ownership in the 200 Largest Nonfinancial Corporations*, Monograph 29 (Washington, D.C., 1940); Paul Sweezy, *The Present as History* (New York, 1953); Perlo, *Empire of High Finance*; William Goodwin, "The Management Center in the United States," *Geographical Review* 55 (1965): 1–16; J. D. Stephens and B. P. Holly, "City System Behavior and Corporate Influence: The Headquarters Location of US Industrial Firms, 1955–1975," *Urban Studies* 18 (1981): 285–300; Menshikov,

Millionaires and Managers; Peter C. Dooley, "The Interlocking Directorate," *American Economic Review* 59 (1969): 314–23; Jean-Marie Chevalier, *La structure financière de l'industrie américaine* (Paris, 1970); Mariolis, "Interlocking Directorates"; John A. Sonquist and Thomas Koenig, "Interlocking Directorates in the Top U.S. Corporations: A Group Theory Approach," *Insurgent Sociologist* 5 (1975): 196–227; Allen, "Economic Interest Groups"; Kotz, *Bank Control*; Mark Mizruchi, *The American Corporate Network, 1904–1974* (Beverly Hills, Calif., 1982); Mintz and Schwartz, "Financial Interest Groups"; Beth Mintz and Michael Schwartz, *The Power Structure of American Business* (Chicago, 1985). An exception that emphasizes the power of Detroit's elite is *Who Rules the U.S.?* published in 1973 (location unknown) by the Progressive Labor Party. Another paper has identified General Motors, though not necessarily Detroit capitalists, as one of the twelve "star nuclei" of the American "interlock network." See Bearden and Mintz, "Regionality and Integration." The "interest group" thesis has its critics as well as the proponents cited above. For an introduction to the debate, see Maurice Zeitlin, "Corporate Ownership and Control: The Large Corporation and the Capitalist Class," *American Journal of Sociology* 79 (March 1974): 1073–1119; Glasberg and Schwartz, "Ownership and Control."

16. C. Wright Mills, *The Power Elite* (New York, 1959), 44. Mills adds that "Society" in Detroit is "who you are in the auto industry" (p. 78). See also David Rogers and Melvin Zimet, "The Corporation and the Community: Perspectives and Recent Developments," *Business of America* (New York, 1968), 52–53.

17. For the business leadership role in urban renewal, see Nancy Kleniewski, "Local Business Leaders and Urban Policy: A Case Study," *Insurgent Sociologist* 14 (Winter 1987): 33–56; Timothy Barnekov and Daniel Rich, "Privatism and Urban Development: An Analysis of the Organized Influence of Local Business Elites," *Urban Affairs Quarterly* 12 (June 1977): 431–59; Robert A. Beauregard and Briavel Holcomb, "Dominant Enterprises and Acquiescent Communities: The Private Sector and Urban Revitalization," *Urbanism Past and Present*, no. 8 (Summer 1979): 18–31; R. Friedland and D. Palmer, "Park Place and Main Street: Business and the Urban Power Structure," *Annual Review of Sociology* 10 (1984): 393–416; William Domhoff, *Who Really Rules? New Haven and Community Power Reexamined* (Santa Monica, Calif., 1978); Chester Hartman, *The Transformation of San Francisco* (Totowa, N.J., 1984). Detroit's urban renewal efforts before the 1967 riot are discussed by Leo Adde, *Nine Cities: The Anatomy of Downtown Renewal* (Washington, D.C., 1969), chap. 10; Robert Conot, *American Odyssey* (New York, 1975); Robert J. Mowitz and Deil S. Wright, *Profile of a Metropolis* (Detroit, 1962). For Henry Ford II and post-riot urban renewal, see Richard Child Hill, "Crisis in the Motor City: The Politics of Economic Development in Detroit," in Susan Fainstein et al., *Restructuring the City: The Political Economy of Urban Redevelopment* (New York, 1983), 80–125; Helen Graves, "New Detroit Committee/New Detroit, Incorporated: A Case Study of an Urban Coalition, 1967–1972" (Ph.D. diss.,

Wayne State University, 1975); Ewen, *Corporate Power*, chaps. 8–9; Katherin Warner et al., "Detroit's Renaissance Includes Factories," *Urban Land* 41 (June 1982): 3–14.

18. For the current relationship between the motor executives and Detroit, see Brock Yates, *The Decline and Fall of the North American Automobile Industry* (New York, 1984). The remarks here should not be interpreted as blanket approval for urban renewal as practiced in the 1945–1974 period. There was simply too much low-income housing razed, too many viable neighborhoods destroyed, and too much racial bias in the planning to permit urban renewal to escape criticism. Still, historically speaking, it was the only alternative to inactivity, and in some places it did help improve a city's self-image, morale, and ability to retain and to attract major corporations. See Heywood T. Saunders, "Urban Renewal and the Revitalized City: A Reconsideration of Recent History," in Donald B. Rosenthal, ed., *Urban Revitalization* (Beverly Hills, Calif., 1980), 103–26; Anthony Penna, "Changing Images of Twentieth-Century Pittsburgh," *Pennsylvania History* 43 (January 1976): 49–63.

19. Yates, *Decline and Fall*, 61, 191.

20. Ibid., 80–109, 122, 136; J. Patrick Wright, *On a Clear Day You Can See General Motors: John Z. De Lorean's Look Inside the Automotive Giant* (New York, 1979).

Index

Abbott Motor Co., 33, 87
Adams, Robert, 152
Advertising. *See* Automobile industry, U.S.
Aerocar Co., 121
Age, of business elites, 20, 27
Alden, Herbert W., 114, 170
Alger, Frederick (son of Russell), 102; and banks, 187; and charities, 113–15; and Packard, 58, 60; and politics, 105, 182
Alger, Russell, 48, 49, 82, 105, 177
Alger, Russell, Jr. (son of Russell), 105, 113–15; and banks, 187; and Packard, 58, 60; and politics, 179, 255n; and urban mass transit, 163
American Blower Co., 113
American Car & Foundry Co., 47, 51, 76, 79, 115
American Injector Co., 123
American Motors Corp., 90
American Radiator Co., 48, 74, 76
American Shipbuilding Co., 115
American Twist Drill Co., 74
Anderson, John W.: and charities, 115; and Ford, 9, 117, 119; and Selden patent, 129–30
Anderson, Rudolph, 7
Armstrong, Christopher, 160
Associated Charities of Detroit. *See* Charities, Detroit
Association of Licensed Automobile Manufacturers, 5, 129–31, 210
Austin (automobile), 209
Autocar (automobile), 55
Auto Trimming (company), 98

Automobile industry, Detroit: and absentee-ownership, 21–22, 213; and Detroit upper class, 16–17, 45–51, 53, 128–30; and early backwardness of, 43–44; and entries into, 67, 84, 86; and exits from, 84, 86; and founding of, ix, 41, 61, 232n; and impact of Great Depression on, 188; and location of, 161; and market segments in, 21, 24, 209; and mass urban transit, 161–76; and reasons for growth of, 16–17, 41–45, 53, 57, 79, 207; and role in local economy, ix–x; and size of, 67, 84, 86, 101. *See also* Automotive elite, Detroit; Banking and finance, Detroit; Detroit; Old families, Detroit; Upper class, Detroit
Automobile industry, U.S., ix; and advantages of multimodel policy in, 144, 151, 156; and advertising by, 6–8, 218n; and "Big Three" in, 110–11; and capital requirements of, 14–19, 79, 85; and concentration of, in Detroit and Michigan, 41–44, 53, 207; and early practices of, 7, 15–16; and economic importance of, ix, 216n; and failure rate in, to 1910, 2; and managerial revolution in, 80; and price-classes in, 21, 97; and production by state (1904), 43; and total production, 67; and urban mass transit, 159; and war, 141–42
Automobile parts industry, 15, 85, 107. *See also names of companies*
Automobile races, 41, 62
Automobiles: arrival of, in Detroit, 40;

Automobiles (*continued*)
    attitudes toward, 1, 207, 214; and
    design features of, 43–44, 85; and
    prices, 21, 44; and social status in U.S.,
    3–8, 206, 214. *See also names of
    Individuals, makes, and companies*
Automotive elite, Detroit: arrival in
    Detroit, 22–23, 39; and banks, 16,
    101–2, 109, 131–33, 185–205; and
    buses, 161, 170; and charities, 106,
    113–15; and community life, 101–16,
    158; composition of, 20, 26, 34, 45;
    marriages of, 58, 74, 90, 93, 100, 109;
    and mass urban transit, 161–71, 173,
    175–76, 254n; and 1918 mayoralty
    election, 165–66; and political contri-
    butions of, 104–5, 112; and representa-
    tiveness of, 220n; and Senate politics,
    176–85; and social origins of, 17,
    19–32, 36–37. *See also* Automobile
    industry, Detroit; Banking and
    finance, Detroit; Conspicuous produc-
    tion; Old families, Detroit; Upper
    class, Detroit; *and names of individuals
    and companies*
Automotive industry. *See* Automobile
    industry, Detroit; Automobile indus-
    try, U.S.
Awalt, F. Gloyd, 197–98, 262n

Bachle, Andrew, 73
Backus, Standish, 102, 115, 147, 187
Baker, John E., 92
Ballantine, Arthur A., 191–93
Ballantyne, John, 189
Baltzell, E. Digby, 100
Bank of America (San Francisco), 201–2
Bankers Trust (N.Y.C.), 130, 154, 191
Banking and finance, Detroit, x, 40, 55;
    and auto industry, 16, 102, 109,
    131–33, 185–205; and concentration
    in, 13, 185–86; and financial elite,
    45–51, 53, 57, 61, 63, 67, 74, 76, 79–82,
    84, 204; and impact of Great Depres-
    sion on, 188, 190; and old families,
    185–205. *See also* Detroit bank crisis
    (1933)
Banking crisis of 1933. *See* Detroit bank
    crisis (1933)
Barber, Amzi, 207
Barbour, George H., 68; and banks, 46,

50, 187; and community life, 49–50,
    82, 104, 113–14; and mass urban
    transit, 163; and politics, 180
Barbour, William T., 113–14; and banks,
    187, 189, 204; and E-M-F, 68–69, 71;
    and municipal reform, 104
Barney, Charles D., & Co. (N.Y.C.), 156
Barrett, Paul, 160, 174
Barthel, Oliver, 62, 222n
Barton, Bruce, 152
Bayerline, J. G., 99
Beall, F. F., 103
Beard, Charles, 127
Bennett, Charles H., 118, 121
Bezner, Fred O., 109, 114, 232n; and auto
    industry, 88–89, 91
Bi-Car (automobile), 84
Big businessmen, definition of, 20
Bingay, Malcolm, 107, 204
Black, Clarence A., 61–62, 64
Blair, Frank W., 179, 181
Board of Street Railway Commissioners.
    See Detroit, City of
Bodde, J. R., 189
Bodman, Henry, 257n
Bollinger, T. A., 99
Book, James B., 46, 50, 68–71
Boorstin, Daniel, 5
Booth, George G., 115, 132, 184
Booth, R. H., 115
Borth, Christy, 57
Boston, 22, 213
Bowen, C. C., 48
Bowen, Lem W., 61–64
Bowers, Joseph, 131
Bowery Savings Bank (N.Y.C.), 192
Boyer, Joseph: and auto industry, 58,
    123, 147; and charities, 113–15
Brady, Anthony N., 153–54
Brady, James Cox (son of Anthony N.),
    154–56
Brady, James J., 88, 91, 232n
Breer, Carl, 155
Briggs, W. O., 102, 114
Briggs-Detroiter Co., 33
Briggs Mfg., 102, 114, 173
Briscoe, Benjamin, 2, 73; and Briscoe
    Motor Corp., 33; and Buick, 72; and
    Maxwell-Briscoe, 72, 153–54
Briscoe Manufacturing Co., 153
Bronner, Harry C., 156
Brown, Donaldson, 191–95, 198

Browning, McPherson, 189
Brush Runabout Co., 33, 87, 153
Bryant, Milton, 62
Buhl, Arthur H. (son of Theodore D.), 74–75; and charities, 113–15; and municipal reform, 104
Buhl, Theodore D., 73–74
Buhl, Willis (son of Theodore D.), 74–75; and community life, 104, 113, 115
Buhl Malleable Co., 73
Buhl Stamping Co., 73
Buick Motor Co., 72, 208; and Durant, 72, 142, 145–46; and product policy, 33, 147; and sales, 145–46
Burlingame, Roger, 125
Burroughs Adding Machine Co., 115, 123, 147
Buses: and auto industry, 161, 170, 252n; and public preference for, 159–60. *See also* Mass transit, Detroit; Street railways, Detroit
Butzel, Fred M., 113–14
Butzel, J. L., 155

Cadillac Automobile Co., 63
Cadillac Motor Car Co., 46, 51; and early history, 60–66, 87, 102, 147; and GM, 64–65, 76, 82, 146–47; and prices, 64, 66; and product policy, 33, 43, 45, 64–66, 221n; and sales, 41, 59, 64, 77; and standardization, 65–66
Cady, William B., 73–74
Calkins, John, 201
Cameron Currie & Co., 62
Campbell, Henry M., 54
Canada: and auto industry, 208; and mass transit, 160
Carhartt Automobile Corp., 87
Carnegie, Andrew, 209
Carriage industry, 145
Carter, Mrs. F. E., 113
Carter (automobile), 33
Carton, John J., 146
Central Hanover Bank & Trust (N.Y.C.): as Central Trust, 146; as Central Union Trust, 154–55; and Detroit bank crisis (1933), 191–92, 194
Central Republic Bank (Chicago), 190
Chalmers, Hugh: and auto industry, 9, 89–91, 98, 155–56, 233n; and banks, 102; and community life, 101, 103–10,

114; and Ford, 133; and NCR, 89; and politics, 105; and war, 135, 141
Chalmers-Detroit Motor Co. (Chalmers Motor Co.), 104, 155–56; and failure, 9, 88; and history, 87–90; and prices, 90; and product policy, 9, 33, 90; and Saxon, 98
Chapin, Roy: and auto industry, 88–91; and banks, 102; and community life, 107–9, 114–15; and Detroit bank crisis (1933), 191–93; on Henry Ford, 182; and politics, 101, 105, 185; and Senate elections, 180, 182; and war, 135
Charities, Detroit, 106, 113–15, 152, 157
Chase National Bank (N.Y.C.), 154–55, 191, 194
Chatham-Phenix Bank (N.Y.C.), 148
Cheboygan Paper Co., 74
"Chemical" Fords, 113–15, 187
Chevrolet Motor Co.: and Detroit, 151; and founding, 148; and GM, 149; and product policy, 33, 57, 213–14
Chicago: banks in, 190–91; economic elite of, 212; industry in, x, 41, 216n; population growth of, ix; urban renewal in, 213
Chicago bankers: and Detroit auto industry, 234n; and Detroit bank crisis, 191, 201–2
Chittenden, H. L., 189
Chrysler, Walter: and Chrysler Corp., 155–56; and Detroit bank crisis, 191–92, 194–95; and early career, 1, 154; and Locomobile car, 1, and Maxwell, 154–55
Chrysler Corp., 84, 87; and absentee-ownership, 21, 195, 202, 213; capitalization of, 188; and charities, 157; and Detroit, 12, 156–57, 213; and Detroit banks, 185, 190–98, 202–3, 205, 211; founding of, 153–56; and National Bank of Detroit, 262n; organization of, 156; and prices, 156; and product policy, 22, 33, 110, 143–45, 156–57; and stockholders, 155–56; and subways, 173
Citizens' Better Transportation Committee, 173
Citizens' Charter Committee, 104, 237n
Citizens' Street Railway Company, 48
Clark, Emory W.: and banks, 189; and

Clark, Emory W. (*continued*)
GM, 147; and mass urban transit,
167; and social clubs, 108
Clark, Myron H., 189
Clement-Bayard (automobile), 44
Cleveland: economic elite in, 212; indus-
tries in, x, 41, 216n
Clifton, Charles, 131
Cochran, Thomas, 3
Coffin, Howard E., 101, 109, 232n; and
auto industry, 88–91; and charities,
114–15; and war, 142
Cole, R. E., 99
Colt, S. Sloane, 191–92
Columbia Motor Car Co., 33, 87, 99
Columbia Motor Car Co. (Hartford,
Conn.), 153
Commuting (Detroit), 161–62
Comstock, William, 193
Connally, William, 165–66, 178
Conspicuous consumption, as concept,
4–6
Conspicuous production: and absentee-
ownership, 22, 151; and Cadillac, 66,
81, 151; and Canada, 208; and
Chalmers, 9, 88, 90–91; and Chrysler,
143–45, 156–57; as concept, xi, 4,
7–11, 23–25, 44–45, 88, 128, 206–14;
and Detroit's social order, 11–13, 157,
176; and diffusion of autos, 18; and
Dodge, 88, 94–97; and E-M-F, 71–72,
81; and Ford, 11–12, 111, 117, 120–43,
209–10; and France, 209; and GM,
143–47, 150–51, 156–57, 213–14; and
Great Britain, 208–9; and Hudson, 6,
88, 91–92; and Hupmobile, 88, 93; and
Lincoln, 123–25; and Locomobile,
206–7; and Lozier, 74–75; and
Maxwell, 154; and middle-class entrepreneurs, 85, 88, 94, 97–110, 145, 157,
209–10; in the 1960s, 213–14; and
Northern, 68; and old families, 145,
157, 209–10; and Olds, 55–57, 81, 88;
and Packard, 59, 66, 81; and Paige,
74–75, 81; and retreat of financial
elite, 81–82; and Saxon, 88, 98; and
Selden patent, 129–30
Continental and Commercial National
Bank (Chicago), 155
Continental Motors, 85
Copper mining, and auto industry, 50, 53
Corporations, as social institution, x–xi

Counselman, Lee, 89
Country Club of Detroit, 106, 116
Couzens, James: and banks to 1933, 102,
132–33; and community life, 103, 115,
210–11; and Detroit bank crisis, 191,
196, 202–5; early career of, 120; and
Ford, 119–21; and Henry Ford, 168,
180; mayoralty campaign of, 165–66,
176; and municipal ownership of
streetcars, 163–70, 175–76, 183; as
police commissioner, 137–38,
164–65; and politics, 137; as populist,
175; and Republican party, 105; and
Selden patent, 131; in Senate, to 1933,
183–85, 211; as social outsider, 11–12,
129, 132–35, 137–43, 157, 165–69,
175–76, 184–85, 210; and subways,
170; and war, 180
Currie, Cameron, 82

Daly, W. L., 99
Darracq (automobile), 44
Davidson, James E., 187
Davison, George W.: and auto industry,
155, 194; and Detroit bank crisis,
194–95, 203
Dawes, Charles G., 190–91
Dayton Metal Products Co., 123
Delano, Safford S., 61
De Lorean, John Z., 214
Demory, A. R., 102, 115, 237, 255
Denby, Edwin, 103, 135–36; and Hupmobile, 92–93; and politics, 105, 184
Dennis, F. W., 167–68
Depew, Sherman, 74–75
Depression. *See* Great Depression
Detroit: and absentee-ownership, 214;
and Chrysler Corp., 156–57; economic
elite in, 45–51; economic independence of, 150, 212–14; economic structure of, x, 40–41, 48, 50–53, 79, 216n;
first motorcars in, 40; and GM,
151–53, 157; impact of Great Depression on, 188, 190; implications of bank
crash for, 205, 211–14; importance of
auto industry to economy of, ix–x,
109, 216n; mass urban transit in,
158–76; municipal reform in, 103–4;
population growth of, ix, 109; public
mood in, 175; residential districts in,

162, 173, 174; urban renewal in, 213; and U.S. urban hierarchy, 40, 79. *See also* Automobile industry, Detroit; Automotive elite, Detroit; Banking and finance, Detroit; Detroit bank crisis; Detroit, City of; Mass transit, Detroit; Municipal ownership of mass transit; Old families, Detroit; Politics, Detroit; Subways; Upper class, Detroit

Detroit, City of: Board of Street Railway Commissioners (1913), 163, 167–70; Department of Street Railways, 168, 174, 252n; Rapid Transit Commission (1922), 170–73

Detroit Athletic Club, 95, 101, 107–9, 116, 140

Detroit Automobile Co., 46, 61–62, 116

Detroit Bank and Trust, 199

Detroit bank crisis (1933), xi, 190–205; conspiracy interpretation of, 192–93, 203, 262n; impact of, 13, 176, 199–200, 204–5, 211–12; and reasons for bank failures, 211; and Reconstruction Finance Corp., 190–94, 196–99, 204; solvency of banks during, 190–91, 194–95, 200–202

Detroit Bankers Co.: and auto elite, 188–89; and Detroit bank crisis, 191–205; and fear of N.Y.C., 188, 194–95, 203; and old families, 185–89; origins of, 185–86, 188; resources of, 186, 188; stockholders of, 186–87

Detroit Board of Commerce: and auto industry, 101–3, 131, 134, 152, 210; and mass urban transit, 168, 172; and 1918 elections, 165, 179

Detroit Boat Club, 116

Detroit Citizens League: and GM, 152; and municipal reform, 103–4; and 1918 elections, 165, 180; and rapid transit, 172

Detroit City Gas, 113

Detroit Clearing House Association, 133

Detroit Club, 82, 95, 106–7, 116, 134, 180, 194, 235n

Detroit Common Council, 138; and mass urban transit, 163, 166, 168, 171, 174

Detroit Drydock, 61

Detroit Edison Co., 76, 115

Detroit Electric (automobile), 87

Detroit Engineering Society, 172

Detroiter, 152

Detroit Free Press, 166, 173, 203, 204, 212

Detroit Golf Club, 116

Detroit Horseless Carriage Co., 232n

Detroit Institute of Art, 124

Detroit Lubricator Co., 74

Detroit National Bank, 74

Detroit News, 56, 115, 182; on Cadillac, 65; and Couzens, 183–84; and Henry Ford, 132, 180, 184; on mass urban transit, 163–64

Detroit Real Estate Board, 168, 172

Detroit Saturday Night, 160, 166

Detroit Seed Co., 49

Detroit Shipbuilding, 61

Detroit Steam Radiator, 48

Detroit Stove Works, 49

Detroit Symphony Orchestra, 95, 105

Detroit Terminal Railway, 161

Detroit United Railway (DUR), 76, 160–61, 163–69

Detroit Yacht Club, 116

Dillon, Read (N.Y.C.), 96

Dime Savings Bank (Detroit), 102

Doble (automobile), 87

Dodge, Horace E., 102; and auto industry, 94–96, 118; and charities, 113, 115; and Detroit Symphony Orchestra, 95, 105; and upper class, 94–95, 109

Dodge, John F.: and auto industry, 94–96, 118; and banks, 102; and charities, 113, 115; and municipal ownership of streetcars, 163–64, 168; and politics, 95, 105, 165, 255n; and subways, 170; and upper class, 94–95; and war, 135

Dodge Brothers, Inc., 60, 87, 152; under bank control, 96–97; and charities, 115; and Dodge car, 95–97; and Ford, 94–95, 133; and prices, 96; and product policy, 33, 96, 156, 221n; and sale to Chrysler, 88, 97

Dort (automobile), 33, 108

Douglas, D. D., 189

Douglas, S. T., 189

Drake, J. Walter, 92–93, 113, 182, 184

Drake, Joseph R., 92

DuCharme, Charles A., 49–50, 108; and Packard, 46, 58; and urban mass transit, 163

Duffield, Divie B., 165–66

Duncan, Beverly, 40, 51

Du Pont, Pierre S., 149–50

Du Pont de Nemours Company, 148, 203, 213
Du Pont family, 148
Durant, William C., 123, 145; and Buick, 72, 142, 145–46; and Cadillac, 64–65; and Chevrolet, 148; and Detroit, 156, 168; and GM, 145–50, 154; and politics, 180, 255n; and product policy, 145; and war, 142
Durant-Dort (company), 145
Durant Motors, Inc., 33
Dwyer, James, 49
Dwyer, Jeremiah, 49

Eddy, Frank W., 61
Edison Illuminating Co., 61
Education, of elites, 20, 23–24, 29, 38, 217–18
Edwards, Allen F., 156, 187
Einstein, Arthur, 59
Electric Vehicle Co., 129
Elites: circulation of, 101, 109–11, 128, 139–40, 143, 162, 176, 205, 210, 214; comparisons of, 19–39, 209, 212; decline of, 11, 157, 204–5; definitions of, 45, 100–101. See also Banking and finance, Detroit; Old families, Detroit; Upper class, Detroit
Elliott, W. H., 46, 49
E-M-F Co., 46, 50, 82; history of, 68–71, 87, 228–29n; and product policy, 71; and sales, 67, 71, 77
Employers Association of Detroit, 101, 103, 134; and rapid transit, 172
Entrepreneurship, x–xi, 2–3, 11, 15–16
Epstein, Ralph C., 14–17, 20–21
Erskine, Albert, 133
Erskine (automobile), 22
Essex Motors. See Hudson Motor Car Co.
Eulau, Heinz, 140
Everitt, Byron (Barney) F., 68–71, 155, 228n
Everitt (automobile), 99, 208
Ewen, Lynda Ann, ix, 266n
Expressways. See Superhighways, and Detroit

Farmer, Silas, 50, 51
Farrand, J. S., Jr., 113
Ferris, Woodbridge, 182–84

Ferry, Dexter M., 187; and business, 46, 48–49, 55; and charities, 113; and politics, 48–49
Ferry, Dexter M., Jr.: and banks, 187; and charities, 114–15; and municipal reform, 104; and Packard, 58; and politics, 105, 182
Financial elite. See Banking and finance, Detroit; Elites; Old families, Detroit; Upper class, Detroit
Firestone, Harvey S., 180, 181
First National Bank–Detroit, 188, 191; and Detroit bank crisis, 194–205; and First and Old National, 155; as First National and Peoples Wayne County Bank, 186; as First National Bank of Detroit, 102, 147; incorporation of, 186
Fish, Frederick S., 70
Fisher, C. T., 115, 199
Fisher, Fred J., 114–15; and banking, 185, 189, 199, 257; and GM, 149, 185
Fisher & Co., 199
Fisher Body Co., 85, 153; and charities, 115, 152; and GM, 151
Five-dollar wage. See Ford Motor Co.
Flanders, Walter E.: and auto industry, 69–71, 99, 154; and politics, 180
Flink, James J., 17
Flinn, E. H., 46, 50
Ford, Clara (wife of Henry), 124
Ford, Edsel (son of Henry), 100; and banks to 1933, 102, 185; and community life, 104, 115, 124; and conspicuous production, 124–25; and Detroit bank crisis, 190, 192, 203; and Detroit upper class, 124–25, 203; and Lincoln, 123–25; and politics, 12; and subways, 173; and war, 128, 180
Ford, Emory L., 113–15
Ford, Harry W., 89, 98, 233n
Ford, Henry: and banks to 1933, 102, 130–33, 193, 203; career to 1903, 40–41, 61–63, 222n; and charities, 106, 113, 115; and community life, 103, 109, 131–32, 210; and conspicuous production, 11–12, 111, 117, 120–28; and Couzens, 168, 184, 204; and Detroit bank crisis, 190, 192–97, 199–200, 202–5; as entrepreneur, 2, 12; and financial elite, 63; and five-dollar wage, 133–34, 142–43; and

Lincoln, 122–25; and municipal ownership of streetcars, 163–64, 167–68; and politics, 105, 136, 176–84; and Selden patent, 5, 129; as social outsider, 11–12, 118, 125–43, 164, 168–69, 176–95, 209–11; and subways, 172; and war, 135–37, 141–42

Ford, Henry, II (son of Edsel), 212–13

Ford, John B., 189. *See also* "Chemical Fords"

Ford Manufacturing Co., 120

Ford Motor Co., 53, 60, 84, 85, 87; capitalization of, 14, 118, 188; and charities, 115; and Detroit banks, 132–33, 185, 202, 205, 211; early history of, 117–22; and Employers' Association, 103; and five-dollar wage, 133–34, 142–43; leadership of, 22; and Lincoln, 122–25; and mass urban transit, 161, 164, 167, 169, 173; and Model T, 121, 137, 208; and 1921 crisis, 130–31; and plant location, 161; and prices, 96, 120–22; and product policy, 33, 43, 57, 96, 111, 120–22, 126, 156; and sales, 41, 121, 131; and Selden patent, 129–31; and war, 142. *See also* Ford, Henry

Foster, Mark S., 174

France: and auto styling, 43–44; and conspicuous production, 209

Freer, Charles, 48, 82

Fry, Vernon C., 119–21

Garford (automobile), 69–70

Gasoline aristocracy, defined, ix, 3

General Motors building (Detroit), 149, 151, 153

General Motors Corp., 84, 87; and absentee-ownership, 21, 151–53, 195, 202, 213; and Cadillac, 64, 146; capitalization of, 188; and Chevrolet, 149; and community life, 104, 115, 152; and Detroit, 12, 151–53, 173, 213; and Detroit banks, 185, 190–99, 202–5, 211; and Du Pont, 148–50; early history of, 145–49; and 1918 Senate election, 180; and Oldsmobile, 57; organizational structure of, 64, 143, 146, 148–51; and product policy, 22, 110, 143–47, 151, 157, 213–14; and profits, 144; and sales, 147, 149; and

Sloan, 150–51; and stockholders, 57, 64, 82, 146–49; and trucks, 72; and urban mass transit, 159, 173; and war, 141–42

General Motors of Canada, 149

German-American Bank (Detroit), 118–19

Gillespie, John, 165–66

Ginsburg, Bernard, 113

Glasscock, C. B., ix

Goldman, Sachs Co. (N.Y.C.), 186

Good Roads movement, 101

Gotfredson, Benjamin, 98

Grabowsky Power Wagon Co., 113

Graham-Paige. *See* Paige-Detroit Motor Car Co.

Grand Boulevard (Detroit), 149, 151–53

Grand Rapids (Mich.), 177

Grant (automobile), 87

Gras, Norman S. B., x

Gray, David (son of John S.), 102, 115

Gray, John S., 114, 118–21

Gray, Paul (son of John S.), 102, 105, 115, 132

Gray Motor Co., 153

Great Britain, and auto industry, 208–9

Great Depression, impact of, on Detroit economy, 188, 190

Great Lakes Engineering Co., 115

Green, Andrew H., Jr., 147, 167, 170, 180

Greenleaf, William, 132

Grinnell Electric Automobile Co., 87

Griswold Street (Detroit), 131

Groesbeek, Governor Alex J., 183–84, 193

Guaranty Trust (N.Y.C.), 154, 191

Guardian Detroit Bank, 185, 186

Guardian Detroit Union Group, Inc.: and automotive elite, 185; and Detroit bank crisis, 190–205; and fear of N.Y.C., 186, 194–95, 203; and old families, 188; and origins, 185–86; and stockholders, 186. *See also* Detroit bank crisis (1933)

Guardian National Bank of Commerce, 186, 194–205. *See also* Detroit bank crisis (1933)

Guardian Trust Co., 185

Gunderson, G. Bert, 68–69

Haass, Julius, 189–90

Hagan, E. E., 11

Hallgarten & Co. (N.Y.C.), 156
Hamilton, W. L., 153
Hammond, George, 74
Harbeck, Jervis R., 155
Hardy, A. B. C., 145, 146
Harper Hospital, 106
Hastings, Charles D., 92, 97
Hawkins, Norval, 113
Hayden, Jay, 168
Hayes Mfg., 107
Hays, Samuel P., xi
Heaslet, James G., 71, 109
Hecker, Frank J.: and auto industry, 46,
    61, 63; business interests of, 46, 48;
    and charities, 113–14; on Henry Ford,
    179
Hendrie, George, 46, 49, 82
Henkel, Peter, 189
Henry Ford Co., 61–62
Henry Ford Hospital, 132
Herreshoff Motor Company, 8
Highland Park State Bank (Mich.),
    132–33, 185
Highways. See Good Roads movement;
    Superhighways, and Detroit
Hill, Arthur, 79
Hill, Frank E., 124
Hodges, Charles H., 48, 74–75, 105
Hodges, Henry C., 48
Holden, James S., 113
Holley, George, 180
Holli, Melvin, 40, 50, 51, 53
Hoover, Herbert, 190–92
Hopkins, Mark, 61–62
Hornblower & Weeks, 130
Howell, Mark, 156
Hubbell, Clarence W., 170
Hudson, Joseph L.: and auto industry, 7,
    90–91; and community life, 100, 109,
    113; and mass urban transit, 163
Hudson Motor Car Co., 84, 87, 88; and
    banks, 185; capitalization of, 14; and
    community life, 104, 115; and Essex,
    33, 88, 92; origins of, 89–91; and
    politics, 180; and prices, 91–92; and
    product policy, 6, 33, 88, 91–92; and
    sales, 92; and subways, 173; and war,
    141
Hughes, Charles A., 107
Hupmobile. See Hupp Motor Car Co.
Hupp, Robert C., 92–93
Hupp Motor Car Co., 84, 88; history of,
    87, 92–93; and politics, 180; and

prices, 93; and product policy, 21, 33,
    93

Industrial National Bank (N.Y.C.), 155
Ingham, John, 18, 100
Inglis, James, 113

Jackson, Roscoe B., 100, 180; and auto
    industry, 89–91; and charities, 114–15
Jacobs, Jane, 44
Jaher, Frederic C., 100
James Flower & Brothers Machine Shop,
    61
Jardim, Anne, 126
Jarvis, G. K., 41–43
Jenks, C. C., 247n
Jewett, Edward, 74–75
Jewett, Harry M., 109, 135; and auto
    industry, 74–75, 97; and mass urban
    transit, 167
Jewett (automobile). See Paige-Detroit
    Motor Car Co.
Johnson, Hiram, 201
Jones, Jesse, 194, 198, 201
Joslyn, C. S., 19–20
Journey to work (Detroit), 161–62
Joy, Henry B. (son of James): and
    community life, 104–9, 113–15;
    family of, 57–58; and mass urban
    transit, 162–63, 167–69, 251; and
    Packard, 57–59, 61; and politics, 179;
    and Selden patent, 129–30; and war,
    135–36, 179
Joy, James F., 57–58, 224
Joy, Richard P. (son of James F.), 131,
    224; and banking, 102; and community
    life, 104, 109, 113–15; and Packard,
    58–60
Joy Realty Co., 168
J. P. Morgan & Co., 76, 130–31; and auto
    industry, 146, 149, 153, 202; and
    Detroit bank crisis, 191–94; 198, 203
J. S. Bache (company), 90

Kanzler, Ernest C., 100, 126
Kaufman, Louis G., 148
Keeton Motor Co., 21, 33
Keller, Suzanne, 10
Kelley, Patrick, 182
Kelly, William, 68

Kelsey, John, 105
Kelsey Wheel, 85, 105, 113
Kennedy, Susan, 201
Kettering, Charles F., 149, 152
King, Charles B., 40, 68
King Motor Car Co., 33, 46, 87, 99
Kresge, S. S., 135
Krit Motor Car Co., 33, 87

Labor unions, in Detroit, x
La Follette, Robert, 183
Lamb, Robert, 3
Lang, A. S., 160
Larned, Abner, 108, 163, 199
Lasswell, Harold, 110
Laux, James M., 207, 209
Ledyard, Henry B., 46, 49, 54, 187
Lee, Gilbert W., 73, 75
Lee, Higginson & Co. (Boston), 146
Leland, Henry M.: and buses, 252n; and
    Cadillac, 63–64; and charities,
    113–14; and community life, 103, 110,
    151; and conspicuous production,
    65–66, 123, 125; and Couzens, 165–66,
    170, 180; on Durant and GM, 142,
    146; and early career, 65; and Lincoln,
    123–25; and municipal ownership of
    streetcars, 162, 166–67, 169–70, 251;
    and municipal reform, 103–4; and
    Newberry, 255; and subways, 170
Leland, Wilfred (son of Henry M.), 114;
    and Cadillac, 63–64, 147; on Durant,
    142; and Lincoln, 123–25
Leland & Faulconer Co., 63–64
Lewis, Eugene W., 90, 102, 115
Lewis, Sinclair, 206
Leyburn, Alfred, 194, 201–2
Liberty aircraft engines, 142
Liberty Motor Car Co., 33, 87, 99
Liberty National Bank (N.Y.C.), 131
Lieberson, Stanley, 40, 51
Lincoln Motor Co., 33, 123–25, 142, 169
Livingstone, T. W. P. (son of William),
    187, 204
Livingstone, William, 102, 180, 187
Locomobile Co. of America, 1, 55, 206–7
Lodge, John C., 167
Long, Thomas G., 188
Los Angeles, population growth, ix
Lovett, John, 173
Lovett, William P., 103, 165
Lozier Motor Co., 46; history of, 74–75;

and prices, 74; and product policy, 18,
    33, 74; and stockholders, 67
Lucking, Alfred, 163–64, 181
Lumber industry (Mich.), 48, 50, 53, 62,
    79
Lynd, Robert and Helen, 1

McAdoo, William G., 201
McAneeny, William J., 91
McCord Manufacturing Co., 113
McGregor, James C., 187
McGregor, Tracy W., 114–15
McKee, John, 197–98
McLaughlin, R. Samuel, 149, 208
McMeans, A. L., 103
McMillan, Hugh (brother of James),
    46–47, 55, 82
McMillan, James, 74, 106, 187; and
    business, 46–49, 55; and politics,
    47–48, 105, 177
McMillan, James Thayer (grandson of
    James), 187, 204
McMillan, Philip H. (son of James), 47;
    and charities, 113–15; and Packard,
    46, 58, 60; and war, 135
McMillan, William C. (son of James), 47,
    55, 76; and auto industry, 46, 61
McMillan alliance, 48–49, 53, 56, 58,
    60–61, 66, 76, 82, 85, 100, 105, 123,
    130, 156, 176, 177
McPherson, Alex, 74
McPherson, William, 189
Macauley, Alvan, 102, 133; and mass
    urban transit, 162, 167–68; and
    Packard, 59; and politics, 182
Mahon, William D., 163
Malcomson, Alexander Y., 118–21, 210
Malcomson Fuel Co., 119
Manufacturers National Bank of Detroit,
    199
Marquis, S. S., 122, 139
Marriages. See Automotive elite, Detroit
Marx, Oscar, 95, 137, 163, 165
Massey-Harris Co. (Canada), 208
Mass transit, Detroit, 160–64, 166–76;
    and auto elite, 158–64, 166–76; and
    possibilities for, 175–76. See also
    Buses; Rapid Transit; Subways
Maxwell, Jonathan D., 68, 72–73
Maxwell Motor Co. (Maxwell Motor
    Corp.), 87, 185, 194; and absentee-
    ownership, 21; and Chalmers, 90;

Maxwell Motor Co. (*continued*)
history of, 154–55; and politics, 180;
and product policy, 22, 33, 154; and
sales, 154; and Walter Chrysler,
154–55
Maxwell-Briscoe Motor Co., 53, 67;
history of, 72–73, 153–54; and
product policy, 33
May, George S., 16, 17, 85; on Olds, 53,
54, 56, 57
Maybee, Rolland, 79
Maybury, William C., 61
Mayo, William B., 168
Meat-packing industry, 74
Mellon, Richard King, 213
Mendelssohn, Aaron, 115, 187
Mendelssohn, Louis, 115, 187
Merchants' National Bank, 102, 109
Metzger, William E., 108; and auto
industry, 64, 68–70, 99
Metzger Motor Car Co., 99, 236n
Meyer, Eugene, Jr., 153–54, 194
Meyer, Eugene, & Co., 153
Michigan Anti-Saloon League, 165
Michigan bank crash. *See* Detroit bank
crisis (1933)
Michigan Car Co., 47
Michigan Carbon Works, 113
Michigan Central Railroad, 48, 49, 57,
120
Michigan Manufacturer, 47, 134
Michigan Manufacturers' Association,
173, 253n
Michigan National Bank, 200
Michigan Radiator Co., 48
Michigan State Telephone Co., 48
Michigan Stove Co., 49, 68
Michigan Sugar Co., 73
Middle West, and automobiles, 20, 207
Miller, Harry, 174
Miller, Sidney D., 46, 49
Miller, Sidney T. (son of Sidney D.), 72,
180
Miller, William, 19
Miller-Schorn system, 174
Mills, C. Wright, 3, 212
Mills, Merrill I., 50
Mills, Ogden, 194, 196
Mining industry, 79. *See also* Copper
mining, and auto industry
Mitchell, W. Ledyard, 167
Moran, Fred T., 163

Moran, John Bell, 124
Morgan, J. P., 127, 153, 198
Morris (automobile), 208
Morse, E. C., 89
Motor vehicles. *See* Automobiles
Mott, Charles S., 149, 152; and Detroit
banks, 199, 203
Mulkey, J. M., 72
Mumford, Lewis, 207, 209
Municipal Ownership League, 163, 167
Municipal ownership of mass transit
(Detroit), 160–64, 166–70; as barrier
to subways, 175–76. *See also* Detroit,
City of; Rapid Transit
Murphy, Michael J., 113, 147, 187
Murphy, Simon J., 62, 187
Murphy, William H. (son of Simon J.),
105, 115; and auto industry, 62–64,
123

Nash, Charles W., 126
Nash Motors Co., 33
National Automobile Chamber of
Commerce, 141
National Bank of Commerce, 102, 109,
185–86
National Bank of Detroit, 198–200
National Cash Register Co., 89
National Municipal League, 104
National origins. *See* Place of birth
Naumberg Co., E., 91
Neal, Thomas, 147
Nelles, H. V., 160
Nevins, Allan, 94, 120, 122, 124
Newberry, Helen (daughter of John S.),
58
Newberry, John S., 47–49, 177, 187
Newberry, John S., Jr. (son of John), 102,
113–15; and banks, 187; and Packard,
58, 60
Newberry, Truman H. (son of John),
113–15, 224; and banks, 187; and
clubs, 82; on Couzens, 183; on Henry
Ford, 179; and "Newberryism,"
182–83; and Packard, 46, 58–60; and
politics, 177–84, 210
New Center, 152–53, 173
New England, and auto industry, 206–7
New York City, x, 216
New York financial community: and
Detroit auto industry, 22, 93, 141, 234;

and Detroit bank crisis, 191–98,
202–3, 211, 260n; and Dodge, 96; and
Ford, 130–31, 203; and GM,
146–48, 152–53; and Maxwell-
Chrysler, 73, 155–57
New York Life Co., 193
New York Trust, 193
Newcomb, Endicott Co., 113–14
Newcomber, Mabel, 19
Nobel Co. (U.K.), 149
Norris, George, 200
North American Co., 76
Northern Manufacturing Co., 68
Northern Motor Car Co., 50; history of,
68–69, 87; and prices, 68; product
policy, 33, 68; and sales, 77

Oakland (automobile), 33, 147
O'Connor, Hugh, 72
Ohio Automobile Co., 57
Old families, Detroit: attitude of, toward
wealth, 3; and auto industry, 10, 23,
67–84, 128; and Chrysler Corp.,
156–57, 210; and Couzens, 131–35,
137–43, 157; and Detroit bank crisis,
185–205; economic weakness of, 195,
204–5, 210–14; and family capitalism,
79–81, 231; and GM, 147, 149, 157,
210; and Guardian Group, 186; and
Henry Ford, 128–37, 139–43, 176–80;
and merger movement, 76, 79; political weakness of, 179–85, 204–5,
210–11; and share of auto industry,
75–78; and social clubs, 81–82; and
war, 135, 179. *See also* Automotive
elite, Detroit; Elites; Upper class,
Detroit
Olds, Ransom E., 53–56, 129
Oldsmobile. *See* Olds Motor Works
Olds Motor Vehicle Co., 54
Olds Motor Works, 46, 51, 87; and advertising, 6; and Briscoe, 72; and founding
of Detroit auto industry, ix, 55, 207;
and GM purchase, 57, 82; and
Leland, 63; origins of, 53–54; and
product policy, 33, 43, 45, 55–57, 88;
and profits, 53; and sales, 41, 55, 77
Olson, Sidney, 61, 62
Osborne, Frederick S., 62
Oscar II, 136
Outer Belt Line (Detroit), 73–74
Owen, Percy, 99

Packard, James W., 57–59
Packard, Vance, 5
Packard, William (brother of James W.),
59
Packard Motor Car Co., 82, 84, 87; and
banks, 102, 185; and charities, 115,
152; and concern for reputation, 60,
81; management of, 80; and mass
urban transit, 169, 173; origins of,
57–58, 61; and politics, 180; and
prices, 59; and product policy, 10, 18,
33, 59–60; and sales, 77; and Selden
patent, 130; and stockholders, 46,
58–59; and war, 141–42
Paige, Fred O., 72–75
Paige-Detroit Motor Car Co., 46, 67,
81–82; and Graham-Paige, 84; history
of, 73–75, 87; and politics, 180; prices
of, 73; and product policy, 33, 73–75;
and sales, 74–75, 77
Palms, Charles L. (grandson of Francis),
46, 50, 68–69, 71
Palms, Francis, 50
Panhard-Levassor (automobile), 44
Paradigm for auto history, 9, 14–20, 24,
53
Pareto, Vilfredo, 110
Parke-Davis Co., 73
Parker, Mrs. W. R., 114
Parlin, C. C., 8
Pelletier, LeRoy, 107
Peninsular Car Co., 47–48
Peninsular Electric Light, 74
Philadelphia, x, 200, 213, 216n
Pierce-Arrow Motor Car Co., 23, 59, 206
Pingree, Hazen, 160, 166, 176
Pingree & Smith, 74
Pioneer (automobile), 232n
Pipp, E. G., 93
Pittsburgh: business elite in, 18, 209,
212; industries in, x, 41, 216; urban
renewal in, 213
Place of birth: of American businessmen,
28; of Detroit auto elite, 20, 22–23, 28,
35; of Detroit industrialists, 20, 28
Plymouth (automobile), 22, 57, 143, 157
Politics, Detroit: and 1918 mayoralty
election, 165–66; and 1918 Senate
election, 177–84; and 1922 Senate
election, 182–83. *See also* Politics,
Michigan; *and names of individuals*
Politics, Michigan: and Democratic

Politics, Michigan (*continued*)
  party, 105, 112, 165–66, 178, 180–82;
  and Republican party, 49, 95, 101,
  104–5, 112, 136–37, 166, 178, 181–84.
  See also Politics, Detroit; *and names of
  individuals*
Ponchartrain Hotel, and auto industry,
  107
Pontiac (automobile), 147
Pope, Willard D., 114, 170
Pope Mfg. Co., 207
Post, Hoyt, 74
Pratt, John Lee, 142, 145, 148
Price-classes: concept of, 21, 221n; by
  make, 33
Property Holders' Protective Association,
  174
Prosser, Seward, 130
Public utilities, Detroit, 47–48
Pungs-Finch Co., 85, 87

Rackham, Horace H., 104, 114, 115, 119
Radiator industry, steam, 48, 76
Rae, John B., 2, 9, 15–17, 85, 122
Railroad-car manufacturing, in Detroit,
  47, 51, 61, 82
Railroads, steam, 40, 47, 48, 57. *See also
  names of railroads*
Rainier (automobile), 151
Rapid Transit: business support for,
  172–74; in Chicago, 174; in Detroit,
  161, 169–76; financing of, in Detroit,
  171–72; in Los Angeles, 174. *See also*
  Automotive elite, Detroit; Subways, in
  Detroit; Superhighways, and Detroit
Rapid Transit Commission. *See* Detroit,
  City of
Raskob, John J., 148
R.C.H. Corp., 33, 87, 93
Recession: of 1907, 80; of 1920–21, 131,
  154–55
Reconstruction Finance Corporation
  (RFC): and Chicago banks, 190–91;
  and Detroit bank crisis, 190–94,
  196–99, 204
Referendums: of 1915, on municipal
  ownership of street railways, 163–64;
  of 1919, on municipal ownership of
  street railways, 167; of 1920, on
  municipal ownership of street
  railways, 168; of 1921, on municipal
  ownership of street railways, 168; of

1922, on municipal ownership of street
  railways, 169; of 1924, on RTC
  financial plan, 172; of 1925, on super-
  highways, 171; of 1929, on rapid
  transit, 172–75
Reliance Motor Car Co., 46, 67, 72
Remick, Jerome, 105
Renault (automobile), 44
Reo Motor Car Co., 33, 56
Regal Motor Car Co., 33, 87
Richard Irvin & Co. (N.Y.C.), 153
Rickenbacker Motor Co., 33, 99
Robinson, Bernard, 181
Rockefeller family, 148
Rolls-Royce (automobile), 208
Roosevelt, Franklin D., 197, 200–201
Roosevelt, Theodore, 177
Runabout (automobile type), 73; decline
  of, 44, 64, 74; and E-M-F, 71; and
  Northern, 68; and Olds Motor Works,
  55–56; and rise of Detroit auto indus-
  try, 43–44
Russel, George, 156; and auto industry,
  54; and business, 48–49, 187; and
  clubs, 82
Russel, Henry (brother of George), 156;
  and auto industry, 46, 54, 56; and
  business, 46, 48–49, 187
Russel Wheel and Foundry Co., 48
Russell Motor Car Co. (Canada), 208

St. Clair, David J., 159
Sanderson, Henry, 156
Saxon Motor Co., 87, 88; history of,
  97–99; and product policy, 33, 98, 221;
  and sales, 98
Schorn, Nicholas J., 174
Schuby, T. D., ix
Schumpeter, Joseph, 2
Scripps, W. E., 115
Scripps-Booth Motor Corp., 33, 115, 149
Selden, George B., 129
Selden patent, 129–31
Seligman, J. and N., Co. (N.Y.C.), 146
Seltzer, Lawrence, 14–17
Seyburn, Stephen Y., 46, 50
Seyburn, Wesson (son of Stephen Y.),
  187, 204
Shaw, James T., 147
Shaw, John T., 102
Shelden family (heirs of Henry D.
  Shelden), 187

Sherer, Hugo, 187
Sheridan Motor Car Co., 149
Shipping and shipbuilding, in Detroit, 47
Siegel, Benjamin, 113
Skae, Edward A., 68
Skelton, Owen, 155
Sloan, Alfred P., Jr., 107, 149–50, 156; and Detroit bank crisis, 193, 198–99; on Leland, 65
S&M (automobile), 84
Smith, Angus (son of Samuel L.), 54
Smith, Frederic L. (son of Samuel L.): and Olds Motor Works, 54–57, 88, 120; and Selden patent, 129–30
Smith, Hal H., 107
Smith, Samuel L., 53–54
Smith, William Alden, 177
Snell, Bradford, 159–60
Soberman, R. M., 160
Social networks, x, 93
Social origins: of Detroit auto elite, 20–32, 36–37; of Pittsburgh business elite, 18–19; of U.S. auto elite, 17; of U.S. business elite, 9, 31; of U.S. males in 1900, 24. See also Age, of business elites; Automotive elite, Detroit; Detroit; Education, of elites; Place of birth
Social snobbery, 9, 218n
Society of Automobile Engineers, 65
Solvay Process Co., 115, 147
Sorensen, Charles, 122, 167
Sparrow, Edward, 54
Special assessments. See Taxation, in Detroit
Stair, E. D., 73, 75
Standish, James D., 46, 74, 187
Stark, George W., 107
Starret, Howard, 174
State Savings Bank, 48
Stevens, Eugene, 202
Stevenson, Elliott G., 133
Stoddart, Howard, 200
Stoepel, Edith Seyburn, 187
Stone, Ralph, 187
Stout, William, 11, 111, 125
Stove industry, in Detroit, 49–50, 67
Strauss, Fred, 62
Streetcar companies. See Detroit United Railway (DUR)
Street Railway Commission. See Detroit, City of
Street railways, Detroit, 48, 49, 82; and auto industry, 161–70; and Detroit politics, 160; municipal ownership of, 160–70, 175–76; and problems of, 159–60, 163
Strelow, Albert, 119, 121
Studebaker Brothers Mfg. Co., 33, 102; and E-M-F, 69–71
Studebaker Corp., 87, 133, 155, 220; and absentee-ownership, 21; and charities, 115; and product policy, 22, 33; and stockholders, 82; and war, 141
Subways, in Detroit, 170–75, 254. See also Rapid Transit
Sullivan, Roger J., 68
Superhighways, and Detroit, 171
Sward, Keith, 181, 196

Tariffs on autos, 105
Taussig, Frank, 19–20
Taxation, in Detroit, 171–72
Tayler Plan, 167–69
Technology: and advantage of backwardness, 43–44; and democracy, 17–18, 209; and determinism, 4, 243n; and five-dollar wage, 142–43; and mass production, 265n; and perfectionism, 2–3, 8, 217n; and sources of innovation, 17–18; and war, 141–42
Tefft, William, 189
Templeton, Allan, 103, 179, 181
Thomas, Erwin R., 7, 88–89
Thomas-Detroit Co., E. R., 33, 88–89, 99
Thurber, Marion, 93
Timken-Detroit Axle Co., 85, 102, 114–15, 170, 173
Tinker, E. R., 155
Tobacco industry, in Detroit, 52, 53
Tom Thumb (automobile), 84
Touring car (automobile type), 43
Townsend, Charles, 182–83, 210
Transit. See Mass transit, Detroit
Trix, John, 123
Trolleys (electric). See Street railways, Detroit
Tyro (automobile), 84

Union Depot (Detroit), 58
Union Guardian Trust, 190–94. See also Detroit bank crisis (1933)
Union Trust, 54, 156, 179; and Guardian Group, 185–86

U.S. Chamber of Commerce, 137
U.S. government: comptroller of
    currency, 197, 201; federal reserve
    system, 194, 196, 200–202; Justice
    Department, 181, 204; Reconstruction
    Finance Corp., 190–94, 196–99, 204;
    Treasury Department, 194, 196–98,
    200–202
U.S. Senate. *See* Politics, Detroit;
    Politics, Michigan
USS Yosemite, 92
United States Motor Co., 22, 153–54
Universal Credit Corp., 185
Upper class, Detroit: and Chrysler Corp.,
    156–57, 202–3, 205; and Couzens,
    131–35, 137–41, 143, 176, 184–85,
    204; definition of, 100–101; and Detroit
    bank crisis, 185–99, 202–5; economic
    weakness of, 195, 202, 204–5, 210, 212;
    and Ford, 128–41, 143, 203, 211; and
    General Motors, 147, 151, 157, 195–96,
    198–99, 202–5, 211; and mass urban
    transit, 162–63; and mayoralty
    election in 1918, 165; and middle-class
    entrepreneurs, 88, 101–11; political
    weakness of, 179–85, 204–5, 210–11;
    and social clubs, 81–82, 106–9, 116
Urban renewal, 213, 268n

Vandenberg, Arthur, 191, 202
Van Vechten, Ralph, 154–55
Veblen, Thorstein, 4–6, 8, 88, 206
Verdier Act (Mich.), 163
Villalon, L. J., 207

Walburn, Thomas, 69
Waldon, Sidney D.: and auto industry,
    170; on automobiles, 171, 173; and
    municipal ownership of street
    railways, 169; and rapid transit,
    170–71, 173; and Senate politics, 182.
    See also Rapid Transit
Walker, Hiram, 113
Wall Street. *See* New York financial
    community
War Industries Board, 141
Warren, Charles B., 103, 113; and auto

industry, 73, 75; and business, 73–74,
    102; and politics, 105, 184
Warren, Homer, 67, 103
Warren-Detroit Motor Car Co., 87, 103
Watkins, James K., 198–99
Wayne Automobile Co., 46, 50; history of,
    68–69, 228; and prices, 68, 69; and
    product policy, 33, 68–69; and sales,
    77
Weber, Max, 8, 81
Weinstein, James, xi
Weisberger, Bernard, 143, 147
Welch-Detroit Car Co., 163
Wenger, E. P., 113
Wesson, W. B., 187
Westinghouse Electric, 61
Wetherbee, George, 72
Wetmore, Helen, 74
Whitcomb, Anna Scripps, 115
White, Albert E. F.: and business, 46, 48;
    and Cadillac, 61–62, 64
White, Christina A., 187
White, H. Kirke, 46, 48
Whitney, D. C., 115
Whitney, George, 193
Whitney family, 113–15
Whitney Realty, 114–15
Wiffler (automobile), 84
Wik, Reynold, 127
Wills, C. Harold, 104, 113, 115
Willys, John N., 7
Willys-Overland Co., 7, 33; as Willys
    Corp., 155
Wilson, Woodrow, 136–37, 178
Winton, Alexander, 62
Wirth, H. M., 99
Wollering, Max, 69, 70, 228n
Wolverine Club, 109
Woodall, C. J., 119–21
Woodin, William, 197, 200–203, 262n

Yates, Brock, 213–14
Yondotega Club, 81–82, 108, 116, 165
Younker, Henry S., 8

Zeder, Fred, 155
Zunz, Olivier, ix, 45, 47, 51